TORAH FOR LIVING

Daily Prayers, Wisdom, and Guidance

Mark Lanier

1845BOOKS

Cover design by *the*BookDesigners
Cover image: © Shutterstock/ittipon

The Library of Congress has cataloged this book under the ISBN
978-1-4813-0981-3.

Printed in the United States of America on acid-free paper with a minimum of 30 percent post-consumer waste recycled content.

This book is dedicated to my family—
the prior generation (Mom),
my generation (my sweet wife, Becky,
our children—Will and his wife, Nora;
Gracie and her husband, J. T.; Rachel; Bettah; and Sarah),
and the next generation (our granddaughter Ebba)

INTRODUCTION

In 2016, Baylor graciously published a daily devotional book I wrote for my adult children, using the Psalms each day. In the back of my brain, I kept thinking that I wanted to write a book on the Jewish law, or Torah, that would be useful for Jew and Christian alike.

In Christian circles, we call these books collectively "the books of Moses," or "the Pentateuch." They are Genesis, Exodus, Leviticus, Numbers, and Deuteronomy. In Judaism, the books are grouped together and called the *Torah*, the Hebrew word for "law" or "instruction." It always seemed appropriate to me that as a lawyer, I would write a devotional book on the law.

As I decided to write it, the obvious question was which passages to use on which days. I opted to follow a Jewish reading program (in Hebrew, a *parashah*). These programs provide a method for practicing Jews to read through the Torah in a year.

I write these devotions as a Christian but with an eye toward their benefit for the Jewish faithful, whether they see Yeshua (Jesus) as Messiah or not. The Torah is important to Jew and Christian alike. Both see it as God's word to his people. In the early days of Christianity, when it was seen by many as a sect of Judaism, an early Jewish rabbi named Shaul (in Hebrew; his Latin name was Paul) became a believer that Yeshua was Messiah. He wrote to his young protégé about the importance of reading and studying the Jewish scriptures, explaining they are "inspired by God and profitable for training in righteousness" (2 Tim. 3:16). They are no less so for the follower of Jesus today.

Similarly, the Psalms often speak of the importance of meditating on the Torah (usually translated "law"). For thousands of years, it has served as an integral part of life.

The version I have used, save for the rare occasion where I do some of the translation myself, is the English Standard Version. Thank you to the great people at Crossway for allowing me to use it. The prayers I add to each day are "in the name of God." I do that because of my belief that we do not approach God on our own merit or by our own strength. We speak to him on his terms and through his strength. As Christians we often pray more specifically in the name of Jesus/Yeshua, but as I see him to be God, I simply pray in God's name.

I had a lot of help with proofreading. My special thanks to my sweet wife, Becky; Mark Wilke; Dean Ron Phillips; Lorraine Hibbert; Dale

Hearn; Sue Jones; Renee Kennedy; and Charles Mickey. Special thanks for checking my theology, history, and Hebrew goes to Tremper Longman III. I also thank the class I teach at Champion Forest Baptist Church for letting me try out many of these devotions on them.

May God use these to his glory in bringing people into a closer walk with him.

Blessings,
Mark Lanier

JANUARY 1

In the beginning, God created the heavens and the earth. The earth was without form and void, and darkness was over the face of the deep. And the Spirit of God was hovering over the face of the waters. (Gen. 1:1–2)

The Bible places God at the beginning, and rightfully so. God is at the start of everything. He is at the start of our new year. He is present when we make decisions about life. Nothing we do and nothing we are predates the Lord. Our parents did not predate him, nor did their parents, their parents' parents, and so on. Nothing predates God.

Not only is God present in each moment, but he is also active. His Spirit is "hovering." God is at work. He has plans and the means to see those plans to fruition. In this first passage in the Bible, we sense that something is coming. We are told that the earth was formless and empty, yet God was there.

Over the next verses of this poem, we read that God first gave form to the formless, and then he filled the emptiness. First, God formed light and darkness, calling them "day" and "night" (day one). He then formed an expanse in heaven, separating the waters on earth from the heavens (day two). Finally, God formed the dry land in the midst of the seas on earth so that the land gave forth vegetation (day three). God filled these empty forms over the next three days. He filled the day with the sun and the night with the moon and stars on day four. On day five, he filled the waters with fish and the heavens with birds. On the sixth day, he filled the earth with animals and humans, giving humanity dominion over the animals.

There is so much to appreciate in these first verses of Genesis. They speak to me on New Year's Day especially, as I commence a new year. I know that I don't begin this year alone or in isolation. The Spirit of God is hovering. He is present. He is in this beginning, and most importantly, he isn't here simply to watch. He is ready to take this formless and empty year and give it shape and content. He can take my days and nights and infuse them with meaning. He can give me purpose as he assigns works for me to do. I am not merely existing to eat, work, sleep, and keep my mind numb to anything greater. I am here with a chance to sense the work of God's Spirit and align myself with him. That excites me. It fills me with joy and expectancy. I can't wait to see what God has in store for me and through me as he forms and fills me this year!

Creator God, create and form in me one who is attentive to you, one who seeks you, one who serves you. Form me and my year around you, and fill my life with meaning for your sake. Amen.

JANUARY 2

Then God said, "Let us make man in our image, after our likeness. And let them have dominion over the fish of the sea and over the birds of the heavens and over the livestock and over all the earth and over every creeping thing that creeps on the earth." So God created man in his own image, in the image of God he created him; male and female he created them. (Gen. 1:26–27)

This passage is written in the same chapter that explains God creating the world. God not only created light, but he called it "light." The same is true for "darkness," the "heavens," and the "earth." Repeatedly, we read of God creating and naming his creation. Then God makes people.

Both men and women are created in God's image. This is not some tale to teach that God has a nose, two arms, two legs, and a beating heart. People are not made to look like God, but we are made to be *creative* like the *creative* God. We have an artistic ability and an ingenuity unlike any other animal. Our creative thoughts set us apart from other beings. In creating we reflect the creative God. But with this empowerment also comes responsibility.

God started naming creation, but after making people in his image, God instructed us to name the animals. God gave responsibility and authority to people. God tells Adam to name the animals, and the animals become whatever Adam calls them. People mirror what God did. God also instructed Adam to exercise dominion and care over the earth and its inhabitants. He was called to a responsible stewardship.

Ability and authority do not come without responsibility. With the aspects of earth under our dominion, we should be careful and responsible. For example, if we have pets, we should treat them responsibly. But our responsibility does not end there. We have a creative ability that we should bring into every area of this world and life. Problems are opportunities to find responsible answers. If someone is sick, we should try to find a cure. If someone is hurting, we should bring comfort. If someone is lost, we should help that person find his or her way.

All of us are a part of something much bigger than ourselves. The world was never set up to revolve around you or me. In this great creation of God's, we have been assigned the ability, the authority, and the responsibility to act. We are in God's image, and we should show it!

Lord, thank you for who I am. Let me see how to live today in ways that reflect you. In your name, amen.

JANUARY 3

The LORD God took the man and put him in the Garden of Eden to work it and keep it. And the LORD God commanded the man, saying, "You may surely eat of every tree of the garden, but of the tree of the knowledge of good and evil you shall not eat, for in the day that you eat of it you shall surely die." (Gen. 2:15–17)

These are seminal verses for the entire Bible. This passage is found near the beginning of the story of Adam's creation. Adam is placed in the garden of Eden to "work it and keep it." God tells him which plants to eat and which ones to avoid. God also explains the implications of Adam's choices.

We live in a world where we make a difference. Our actions are not those of a puppet, with God as the puppeteer. Our actions shape and mold the world around us. When we plant crops, we can harvest food. When we plant a tree, the tree can take root and grow, establishing shade where otherwise it would be sunny. When we mow the grass, the lawn is shorter than it was, and its appearance is altered. This principle applies in gardening, but it goes far beyond that. It goes into our interactions with each other and into our interactions in the world, whether garden-related or not.

In personal matters, how I eat will affect my health. Whether I exercise will affect my body's stamina. The influence of alcohol will affect one's judgment and reaction time, and choosing to drive under the influence of alcohol can cause fatal accidents. This isn't God's fault, and it isn't God being "mean" when this happens. It is a fact of creation. My actions have real effects.

Similarly, in relational matters, when I show my family sacrificial love, they will grow and prosper differently than when I lash out in anger or when I live a selfish life. When I model godly behavior for my children, they will learn and grow up quite differently than when I model ungodliness. I will have true friends when I am a true friend to others. When I can be relied upon, responsibility will find its way to my doorstep.

This is the way of life. What I do makes a difference. I can choose to be active in positive, building ways, or I can choose otherwise. That doesn't mean God plays no role in human events. He made us; he instilled in us abilities; he gives us opportunities; he enlightens us; he empowers us—but still, we make choices. I want to make good choices. I want to be a good gardener in this world and eat from the right trees.

Lord, thank you for the abilities you have given me. Open my eyes to see what I can do today to be responsible. Help me make good choices. In you I pray, amen.

JANUARY 4

Then the LORD God said, "It is not good that the man should be alone; I will make him a helper fit for him." (Gen. 2:18)

We are social beings. We function best when we are in relationships with others. That doesn't mean different people don't need different amounts and times of solitude, but we also need to be with others. The ancients said, "One man is no man," while John Donne in the Renaissance phrased it, "No man is an island."

In the Genesis story, Adam looked through all the created beings to find a suitable companion. He found no one. I have always thought that those other created beings likely included many we would today term "hominids." These were very human in appearance and genetics, but they weren't the spiritual being Adam was. Adam had that special breath of God and was made in God's image in a unique way. So without finding a sufficient mate among the other beings, Adam fell asleep. He then awoke to find one made from his own substance. Eve, as she is named, is like Adam, made in God's image, filled with God's breath, and suitable for Adam.

Because we don't function best alone, we spend time trying to find our crowd. Whether deliberately or unconsciously, we seek out companionship and fellowship. We find people to befriend, and we become friends to others.

I find a principle at work in this passage, relevant to the friends we make and friends we become. For people who are following God, true friends who are helpers, especially those who will become spouses and mates, need also to be plugged into a relationship with God. Believing and faithful friends and spouses are always going to provide help and direction in life that will not be found among those who live outside of step with God.

This informs not only whom I seek out as my closest confidants, but it also instructs me in who I need to be for others. I am thankful my wife has an intimate relationship with God. Our whole family is better because of it. Heaven forbid I should ever fail to be the same. I want to be in an intimate fellowship with God to be the best kind of father, husband, and friend that I can be. Nothing else is suitable!

Lord, thank you for the godly people in my life. Thank you for the godly ones in my family and among my friends and associates. Help me to be a godly influence in their lives as well. To your glory and in your name, amen!

JANUARY 5

And the man and his wife were both naked and were not ashamed. Now the serpent was more crafty than any other beast of the field that the LORD God had made. (Gen. 2:25–3:1)

At first blush, these two verses do not seem to go together, yet they do. The storyline has Adam and Eve blissfully happy in a lush garden. God gave them tasks to do and great liberty to do the chores and enjoy freedom in the garden. The only limitation God set on them was to abstain from eating of one certain tree.

Now enter the serpent. The serpent tempts the woman, using half-truths in the form of questions to lure and seduce her into sin. Eve, and then Adam, defy God and the one small limitation God placed on them. Afterward, Adam and Eve are changed. We read that after sinning, "the eyes of both were opened, and they knew that they were naked. And they sewed fig leaves together and made themselves loincloths" (Gen. 3:7).

There is a subtle wordplay going on in the Hebrew text that gives us a deeper understanding of the message. The word for "naked" (*'arom*) sounds much the same as the word translated "crafty" or "shrewd" (*'arum*). Adam and Eve are naked without shame, meaning they were oblivious to it. Along comes the most shrewd and crafty serpent. He seduces the woman with the promise that she might become like God in her knowledge and experience. So, with an eye toward becoming something they aren't, Adam and Eve sin. They do not accomplish their goal of becoming wise. They remain naked (not shrewd) but now with shame. Their eyes are opened and they realize they are naked.

There is a value and bliss in being who God made us to be and doing what he instructed us to do. The allure of something more, when it is tied to disobedience, is as satisfying as a mirage. There is nothing in it to sate our thirsts or appetites. We do not become something better by stepping outside of God's will and plans. It only leads to shame, disappointment, and dissatisfaction.

I want to learn and understand God's instructions for me. I want satisfaction in who he made me to be. I do not want to lose who I am through the seduction of empty promises.

Lord, teach me your ways. Give me the joy and peace that comes from following you alone. May I find satisfaction in being who you made me to be. In your name, amen.

JANUARY 6

But the serpent said to the woman, "You will not surely die. For God knows that when you eat of it your eyes will be opened, and you will be like God, knowing good and evil." (Gen. 3:4–5)

BEWARE! This passage reproduces a profound temptation that overcame Adam and Eve's sensibilities and convictions. It can do the same for us.

God gave great freedom to Adam and Eve. They had nearly unlimited options for eating and working in the garden. The only restriction was to avoid eating from the tree of knowledge of good and evil. The tempter entered their world, and that restriction was the one thing the serpent beguiled them into doing. What was his appeal? What was the line that hooked them? How did he convince them to disobey the God who made them and loved them? The serpent convinced them that they could be gods themselves. Maybe they wouldn't be the big-G God, but they could be like him. They could be little-G gods.

Now you and I might say, "Oh, we know better. We would never seek to be gods," but I'm not so sure! I see them looking to be little-G gods, and it seems very similar to something we do! Adam and Eve weren't persuaded that they would have godlike powers. They didn't think they would become omnipresent, existing everywhere. They weren't even seeking to become self-sufficient. In some ways, I think they thought it would be business as usual, with one major exception. Adam and Eve thought they would become godlike in their knowledge of right and wrong, or good and evil. They wouldn't need to rely on God for such things. They would get to decide what was good on their own. What they were blinded to was that such a choice on their part was in and of itself wrong. It was rebellion against God and God's instructions.

Here is our trap. This is a key way we can be beguiled and tempted even today. We are all prone to the suggestion that we know better than God. We can see or read from Scripture about who God is and what he instructs for his people, but we are often dismissive *unless it is consistent with what we already want!* As long as what we read in the Bible follows our own desires, we can be quite obedient. But once we decide we know better, once we take actions that are motivated by our own selfishness, we walk into our own version of rebellion against God. We are setting ourselves up as God, the decider of good and evil. This is something we must guard against. We should study God's word, seek to understand his will, and determine to follow it.

Lord, we confess our own guilt in seeking our ways instead of yours. Please forgive our transgressions, humble us in our conceit, and lead us in your truth. In your name, amen.

JANUARY 7

And they heard the sound of the LORD *God walking in the garden in the cool of the day, and the man and his wife hid themselves from the presence of the* LORD *God among the trees of the garden. But the* LORD *God called to the man and said to him, "Where are you?"* (Gen. 3:8–9)

Here we read of the aftermath of Adam and Eve's rebellion against God. They succumbed to the temptation of sin, ate the forbidden fruit, and suffered the effects. Those consequences are manifested first in their reaction to God. They tried to hide themselves from God. (Yes, there is a certain gallows humor here. They thought that by eating the fruit, they would gain knowledge. Yet in the aftermath, they were so stupid as to think they could hide themselves from God.)

Sin comes with consequences. To quote Bruce Springsteen, "You want it; you take it; you pay the price" (from "Prove It All Night"). Our consequences are often not too different from Adam and Eve's. Immediately after our sin, we often try to flee from God's presence. We seek to hide ourselves from interacting with him. We divert our gaze from his. We know that we have done wrong and don't want to confront the reality of our sin.

Our attempts to hide can take different forms. We may get indignant with God and blame him for our poor choices. Sometimes, we decide God himself is hidden or he doesn't exist. Other times our temptation might be simply to wallow in guilt and defeat.

Even as we attempt to hide, however, we are still dealing with a God who made us for a relationship with himself. He doesn't let us hide without pursuing us. As we read in the story, he calls out to us: "Where are you?" This is not the cry of a God so limited that he doesn't know where we are. It is the cry of a pursuing God seeking our response. God calls out to us when we are rebellious sinners, and we have a choice. We can turn to him in repentance or we can ignore him in continued rebellion. One option restores a relationship. In choosing the other, we persist in sin and alienation.

I do wrong. I do sin before a holy God. I know the temptation to run and hide. I also know the forgiveness and restoration from repentance. I want to get better about this whole thing.

Lord, thank you for your pursuit of me, even when I defy you. Please forgive my sins for your sake and in your graciousness. Amen.

JANUARY 8

To the woman he said, "I will surely multiply your pain in childbearing; in pain you shall bring forth children. Your desire shall be contrary to your husband, but he shall rule over you." (Gen. 3:16)

Sin is not a good thing. It doesn't produce good fruit. The fruit may *look* good. The fruit might appeal to one's senses. But the fruit of sin is painful and can have lifelong consequences.

Today's passage comes in the judgment section of the story of Adam and Eve's sin. Adam and Eve ate fruit from a certain tree, directly contrary to God's instructions. As a result of that sin, God pronounced consequences that would flow to each of the participants.

Eve's consequences are tied directly to the sin in some ways that are not obvious unless we are reading this passage in its original Hebrew. Hebrew has several words for "pain," and the one chosen here is not the normal one for the pain of childbirth. The word here is *'tzv* (עצב—pronounced *etzev*). It is a pun from the Hebrew word for "tree," pronounced *etz* and spelled with the same first two letters. The writer tells the reader that Eve's pain—and the pain is mentioned multiple times to emphasize it—is directly rooted to her rebellion at the tree.

I was not at the tree, and I haven't even visited the garden of Eden. But I have made choices just as wrong as Eve's. There have been more times than I care to remember when I have reached out my hand, picked the fruit of sin, and tasted it. It can look attractive, and it can taste sweet, but make no doubt about it, it is rotten to the core. What it does to us is not good but bad.

It took me a while to figure out that God doesn't arbitrarily designate certain things as sinful. What is sinful is what is inherently destructive; the pain stems from the tree. God's designation of sin is a warning to us. God teaches us what is good, healthy, and conducive to happiness. He also teaches us what is harmful, destructive, and leading to pain and despair. That is the nastiness of sin.

Knowing this, the logical question becomes, Why do we keep going back to that bad tree? When will we grow up and get enough sense to make better choices?

Lord, I have made wrong choices. Left to myself, I will undoubtedly do so again soon. Please forgive my sin, and lead me in a righteous path. In your name, amen.

JANUARY 9

And the Lord regretted that he had made man on the earth, and it grieved him to his heart. So the Lord said, "I will blot out man whom I have created from the face of the land, man and animals and creeping things and birds of the heavens, for I am sorry that I have made them." But Noah found favor in the eyes of the Lord. (Gen. 6:6–8)

The flood story is well known to most everyone. Mankind was evil except for Noah and his family. God decided to destroy creation and start anew, but he gave instructions to Noah to save his family and enough animals for a fresh start. It rained and rained, flooding the earth, killing everything and everyone outside of the ark. But the rain stopped, the waters subsided, and by sending a succession of birds, Noah finally determined it safe to disembark. Life on earth began again with the rainbow promise that no more floods would wipe out everything.

Aside from the well-known narrative, there are a number of subtleties in the Noah story that likely escape our attention unless we are carefully studying the Hebrew text. One of my favorites is built into the name of Noah. We find it set out in today's passage where "Noah found favor in the eyes of the Lord."

The Hebrew shows a deliberate turn on Noah's name. "Noah" is only two letters in the Hebrew, *nun* (an "n" sound) and *chayt* (a "ch" sound). The Hebrew pronunciation of "Noah" is more of a "No-ach." "Favor" (which is what Noah found in the Lord's eyes) is the same two letters, but backward: *chayt* ("ch") plus *nun* ("n"). This passage is placed on the heels of the statement that God was sorry he had made man. Noah found favor with God in a way that turned things around!

God doesn't always see things as we do. I think in this instant, it may be God who saw things aright, and the world that saw them backward. God straightens things out in the end, however!

I like this subtlety. It speaks to me. God can take those who follow him, turn them and their names around, and use them to change the world. God can and will do that with you and me. We need to conscientiously pray to put ourselves into his hands. I want to be more concerned about living for him than about anything else my life.

Lord, please straighten out my life and role in this world. I have a tendency to make things crooked, and too often I need you to fix my messes. Thank you for your faithful willingness to do so over and over. In your name, with gratitude, I pray, amen.

JANUARY 10

Noah found favor in the eyes of the LORD. These are the generations of Noah. Noah was a righteous man, blameless with his generation. Noah walked with God. (Gen. 6:8–9)

Noah is introduced to us in the Torah account with three statements. These three are important aspects that will shape Noah's future. Noah was "righteous," he was "blameless" before others, and he "walked with God."

The Hebrew word for "righteous" is an important word in Scripture. It is the word *tzaddiq*. The word was used for someone who was fair and just, who did right and treated people as they should be treated. The righteous did right because it was "who they were." It was intrinsic to their character. A *tzaddiq* did right whether one was looking or not. It wasn't a question of appearances or getting caught; it was simply a matter of doing right because it was right to do so. This was Noah.

Noah was also "blameless with his generation." Noah's goodness wasn't hidden from others. He stood out from others because he was righteous. His time was a dark and perverse time. Those around him were intensely evil. Yet not Noah. He stood out as a beacon in the night. Those around him were without excuse. They could see goodness and righteousness, but they chose instead darkness.

The third comment on Noah was that he "walked with God." This is almost a summation of what had already been said. There really is no righteousness, no blamelessness before the world, unless one is in a right relationship with God. God is the source and definition of righteousness and blamelessness. When we "walk" with God, we are in daily contact with him. We are seeking to go the same direction he goes. He is a key part of our every step in every day. We don't walk with God by going in the opposite direction from him. We go the way he goes and become people who reflect his goodness to the world.

This is the key to our being righteous: walk with God. This is the key to our shining into the dark world: walk with God. The world may join us, or it may not. People may change, or they may not. But like Noah, we will "find favor in the eyes of the Lord," and God can use us to accomplish his mighty purposes. That is a good thing!

Lord, please give me insight and desire to walk with you. Change my life, and use me to change others! In your holy name, amen.

JANUARY 11

Now the earth was corrupt in God's sight, and the earth was filled with violence. And God saw the earth, and behold, it was corrupt, for all flesh had corrupted their way on the earth. And God said to Noah, "I have determined to make an end of all flesh, for the earth is filled with violence through them. Behold, I will destroy them with the earth." (Gen. 6:11-13)

We people are funny creatures. We tend to sit in judgment of others quite readily. We even sit in judgment of God! Many of us are guilty of reading these verses, and others like them, and thinking, "Ugh! I don't like that image of God!" We read them quickly because dwelling on them seems to make it even worse. "What kind of good God wipes out humanity simply because he doesn't like what they are doing?" These questions cause me to study these verses more carefully.

I have a friend who has horses. One of his horses became sick—very sick. The horse had no hope of being cured and was in misery. Each day got worse, and the horse would die eventually, but it would be weeks and maybe a month of agony first. My friend had the horse put down. It was hard for my friend, but the mercy killing was the best thing to do. It saved the horse from prolonged misery.

I think of that with today's passage. People were corrupted—not a little but a lot. They were violent, full of hate, destructive toward each other, and beyond hope. They had passed a point of no return where there was no changing who they were and what they would do. They were broken beyond repair. God saw that, understood that, and determined the mercy killing was the best and only real solution.

We might say, "But if God is God, then can't he change anyone?" Yes, but only if they want to be changed. God didn't make us puppets, pulling our strings to make us behave. We are people who get to choose what we do and who we are. God didn't end these people's existence until they had made their choices. They made them irrevocably. They needed to be put down. We might see this as a harsh act of God, but somewhere, can we see it as an act of mercy? Is it better to go on living in destruction, violence, and worse? Isn't it OK to end the life of an Adolf Hitler? This is not a passage to skip over. It is one to chew on in an effort to learn more of God and life.

Lord, I confess that I don't understand all of your ways. I know your compassion and mercy and rely on it daily. Help me understand the ways you have rescued me from destruction, and help me to live in your holiness. In your name I pray, amen!

JANUARY 12

Noah did this; he did all that God commanded him. . . . They went into the ark with Noah, two and two of all flesh in which there was the breath of life. And those that entered, male and female of all flesh, went in as God had commanded him. And the LORD shut him in. (Gen. 6:22, 7:15-16)

There is a nice order to this passage. It has a flow that is instructive for me. It begins with God telling Noah what he should do. Then Noah does all—not some—that God commanded him. After Noah followed the instructions, going into the ark with the assembled animals and family, God shut the ark's door. This story started with God, and it will end with God.

God was on a mission. His mission was to clean up the mess that the earth had become. In the process, he was determined to save the remnant of Noah and his family, resupplying them and the earth with what they would need for the future. God instructed Noah about how he should prepare for God's coming judgment. Noah wisely proceeded exactly as God instructed him. Then as God shut the ark, God went to work, and God set about finishing his plans.

I want God to work in my life. I want him to use me for something greater than me. I want to be a part of his grand designs for humanity and this planet. I want to have a front row seat and see him in all his power and wisdom. How do I get this chance? It's simple, actually. Not always easy, but simple!

I need to do as God commands me. If God tells me to be nice, I need to be nice. If God tells me to be patient, I need to be patient. If God tells me to show love, I need to show love. If God tells me to share about him, I need to share about him. If God tells me to tell the truth, I need to tell the truth. If God tells me to have pure thoughts, I need to have pure thoughts. If God tells me not to gossip, I need to shut my mouth. If God tells me to be gentle, I need to be gentle. This list can go on and on, for if God tells me to learn his ways, I need to learn his ways.

When and if I do these things, when and if I follow his instructions and get where I am supposed to be, God will shut me in, roll up his sleeves, and get to work! I will get to observe and be a part of something far greater than me. God is amazing that way.

Lord, I don't always know what to do. Please teach me. I don't always have the discipline and drive to do right. Please strengthen and motivate me. Let me be a part of what you are doing to your glory and in your name! Amen!

JANUARY 13

The waters prevailed on the earth 150 days. But God remembered Noah and all the beasts and all the livestock that were with him in the ark. And God made a wind blow over the earth, and the waters subsided. (Gen. 7:24–8:1)

I can be absentminded. I lose keys, forget my billfold, and if I didn't write them down, would miss more appointments than I'd make. As a result, I can read a passage like this and wonder, "What kind of God would we have if he had forgotten Noah?" Heavens, if he can forget Noah in the midst of a cataclysmic flood, what chance do I have with my little problems among the eight billion people on earth today?

This thinking is not fair to God, to the biblical account of Noah, or to you and me! While we might think that the passage effectively says that God had forgotten Noah, as if Noah's plight had slipped his mind, it doesn't read that way in the original Hebrew.

The Hebrew word translated "remember" is the verb *zakhar.* It conveys something a bit different from simply, "Something I had forgotten suddenly occurred to me." It is an *action* verb. It signals that God took an action because of something of which he was aware. The emphasis is not that something forgotten was suddenly remembered. It is that God chose to take an action because of something he knew. God knew Noah, knew his plight, knew the flood, and knew the time was right. So God took action. He made a wind blow over the earth, and the waters subsided. He finished his job of saving Noah and cleaning the earth of evil.

The same word is used in Exodus 2:24 and 6:5, where it describes God taking action on behalf of the enslaved Israelites in Egypt because God "remembered" his covenant with Abraham, Isaac, and Jacob. God had not forgotten, but because of that covenant, with that in his mind (to use a human term for a divine God), God took action.

God is an action God, not a forgetful God. He doesn't forget you or me. He doesn't forget his plans or the works of his hands. He doesn't forget his promises. He remembers, and he acts. There was an Old Testament prophet who wrote a book we call "Zechariah." The "-iah" part of his name is an abbreviation for the LORD ("Yah," short for the letters *YHWH*). The "Zechar" part of the name is the same word translated "remember." Zechariah had it right in his prophecy, and his name declares it. God is an action God, not a forgetful one. I want to watch him act today!

Lord, act in my life. True to your nature and character, take care of my needs, and bring me into greater awareness of you. In your name I pray, amen!

JANUARY 14

Now the whole earth had one language and the same words. . . . And they said to one another ". . . Come, let us build ourselves a city and a tower with its top in the heavens, and let us make a name for ourselves, lest we be dispersed over the face of the whole earth." And the LORD came down to see the city and the tower, which the children of man had built. And the LORD said, ". . . Come, let us go down and there confuse their language, so that they may not understand one another's speech." So the LORD dispersed them from there over the face of all the earth, and they left off building the city. Therefore its name was called Babel, because there the LORD confused the language of all the earth. (Gen. 11:1–8)

The tower story takes place in the plain of Shinar, an area most scholars reckon to be near Babylon in southern Mesopotamia (think modern Iraq near Baghdad). Using burned bricks for stone and bitumen for mortar, the people decide to "build ourselves a city and a tower with its top in the heavens" (Gen. 11:4). In this way, the people planned on making "a name" for themselves.

The tower in question was what is now called a *ziggurat*. These buildings were part of a temple complex that, in Mesopotamian literature, was described as having its "head touch heaven." These ziggurats were not built for the people to go up to heaven and access God. Rather they were built as staircases for the gods to descend. At the top of the ziggurats were gates/rest stops which were to "entice" the gods down to earth.

This ploy to manipulate God didn't work.

The Lord's response was to "go down" but not to be at the beck and call of the people. He went down to disperse the people and confuse their language. From that time on, the area was named "Babel." God judged the people, for it was not their place to command or coax God into their midst to get the desires of their hearts. Instead, God descends with his own plans.

I should never think for a minute that I can control God. I can't entice him with my projects. My charm doesn't work on him. Flattery will get me nowhere. Not even my goodness is adequate to buy me his favor. No. God meets you and me at the place of his choosing. He has plans, and my opportunity in life is to plug into his, not vice versa.

Lord, forgive me for trying to make you my personal genie, granting my wishes and agenda. Help me to see your plans, and use me to further those. In your name, amen.

JANUARY 15

Now the LORD said to Abram, "Go from your country and your kindred and your father's house to the land that I will show you. And I will make of you a great nation, and I will bless you and make your name great, so that you will be a blessing. I will bless those who bless you, and him who dishonors you I will curse, and in you all the families of the earth shall be blessed." So Abram went, as the LORD had told him. (Gen. 12:1–4)

This was a bold move by Abram (whose name was later changed to Abraham). God instructed him to leave his family and strike out in faith that God would settle him somewhere new, blessing him and his family for his obedience. That takes a lot of faith today, but it took even more in Abram's time.

Unlike today, people didn't just up and move for no reason at all. There was no common currency that Abram could use to find a place to rent. No easy chain of hotels along the way. No realtor waiting at the other end to find the perfect home. Traveling was not safe. There were no locked cars he could use for transportation, no moving vans that were insured. Bandits awaited the unwary on the highway, knowing they traveled with valuables. After all, no one was able to wire transfer their assets or overnight them through a delivery service. In an emergency, there were no cell phones to use for calling. No police force was around to help in time of need. Of course, all of these difficulties just added to the problems associated with leaving family behind.

But God told Abram to do it, and he did it. It doesn't seem he questioned God. It doesn't seem he worried God wasn't up to the task. Abram heard from God and followed him, and history would never be the same.

It is amazing what can happen when we hear God with faith and choose to trust him. This is not simply a "Gee, I guess I will trust you. After all, the downside is slight" but a genuine trust that can have a major downside if things fall apart. That is serious faith!

Yet that is what God calls us to. God calls us to hear his direction and move as he directs. God calls us to step out in faith, trusting that he will secure our future and our path. Proverbs assures us that a wholehearted trust in God, one in which we commit our ways to him, will result in God ensuring our paths are straight. God gives all of us directions in life. Our choice is whether we believe him enough to walk in his ways.

Lord, thank you for direction in life. Give me greater faith and trust to follow you in the bold ways and the small ways. In your name, amen.

JANUARY 16

Then Abram said to Lot, "Let there be no strife between you and me, and between your herdsmen and my herdsmen, for we are kinsmen. Is not the whole land before you? Separate yourself from me. If you take the left hand, then I will go to the right, or if you take the right hand, then I will go to the left." (Gen. 13:8–9)

I like to look at the qualities of Abram and see what I can learn from them. He wasn't a perfect man. His treatment of his wife Sarai was not the best. But he had outstanding qualities of trust in God, and that trust manifested itself in actions like we see in today's passage.

Abram and his nephew Lot both had significant flocks, with a number of hired hands who worked for them. The large numbers were causing friction, and Abram determined to eliminate the problems. Abram had options. He could have chosen the land he wanted and sent his nephew packing. But instead Abram gave his nephew the choice. Abram said, Here are two options that are both fair and good. You decide which one you would prefer, and I will take the other one.

When I was growing up, I experienced this wise approach from my mother. There was a really good pie in the fridge and only enough left for two pieces. My sister and I both wanted some, so Mom said we could finish it. I wanted to know who was going to cut it, wanting to keep my eye out for which piece might be bigger. Mom told us, "One of you cuts it, and the other chooses which piece to eat." I quickly realized the fairness of that. If I cut, I was going to make sure it was as even as possible, lest I get the short end of the deal. Likewise, my sister Kathryn would be careful.

There may be something about this that speaks to fairness, but on a much more basic level, it speaks to me of peacemaking. Abram was a peacemaker. He was intent on removing the strife that existed, and the best way to do it was to divide things equally and let his nephew choose his path. Lot couldn't complain, because he got his choice. If one part of the land seemed better than the other, Lot was free to choose it.

Wisdom and blessing are closely tied to being a peacemaker. As we confront strife, problems, discord, and frustrations among people, we should prayerfully seek wise solutions and try to implement them. Peace will move people forward. Strife is destructive. I want to pursue peace.

Lord, give me wisdom to sow peace in this world. Even though some will refuse it, may I always seek to be a peacemaker, bringing peace to those in pain. In your name, amen.

JANUARY 17

When Abram heard that his kinsman had been taken captive, he led forth his trained men . . . and went in pursuit . . . And he divided his forces against them by night, he and his servants, and defeated them . . . Then he brought back all the possessions, and also brought back his kinsman Lot with his possessions, and the women and the people. (Gen. 14:14–16)

Family is powerful and family is worth fighting to preserve. Not everyone has a family, and not every family is close, but sometimes we need to broaden the definition of family.

In today's passage, Abram learned some bad news about his nephew Lot. Two different sets of rulers had been fighting over several different towns. The rulers that included the "king" of Lot's town lost, and Lot was captured along with all his possessions. When Abram found out, he assembled all of his own shepherds, hands, and workers, and set out to rescue Lot. Abram came upon the enemies, fought, and defeated them, freeing Lot and regaining all of Lot's possessions. The passage also makes it clear that a reason for Abram's victory was the military strategy he employed, dividing his forces and attacking in the night.

One time when I was young, before I learned this story of Abram, someone asked my mother what traits my father had that she respected. Though she wasn't speaking to me, I was paying careful attention. I was young, but I was old enough to be curious what trait she would pick. One of the first things she said was that Dad always put his family first. He put great effort into taking care of his family. I loved Dad and determined then that I wanted to grow up and be such a person.

Now that I am older, I see the commitment to family by Abram, whose name means "exalted father." Abram's commitment to his family was worth his risking his own possessions and even his own life. Abram went on this rescue mission personally. He didn't just send his people.

While some don't have immediate family, and some are not in families that are close, everyone who follows God is part of a larger family—God's family. It is a family where God as Father is committed to the good of his family, even at his own personal expense. We should share that commitment in the ways we treat and care for each other.

Father God, please instill in us the commitment to our families, both those that are directly ours as well as your larger family of which we're a part. In your name, amen.

JANUARY 18

The king of Sodom said to Abram, "Give me the persons, but take the goods for yourself." But Abram said to the king of Sodom, "I have lifted my hand to the LORD, God Most High, Possessor of heaven and earth, that I would not take a thread or a sandal strap or anything that is yours, lest you should say, 'I have made Abram rich.'" . . . After these things the word of the LORD came to Abram in a vision: "Fear not, Abram, I am your shield; your reward shall be very great." (Gen. 14:21–15:1)

God is worthy of our trust. He will meet our needs. He might use others, but we should never fear that God is unable to see and fashion in our lives whatever is necessary to bring his will to fruition.

In today's passage, we continue a storyline where Abram successfully rescued his nephew Lot. In the process, Abram also freed the king of Sodom and others who had been captured when Lot was captured. The king of Sodom asked for his retinue and servants back, but he offered Abram the booty that had been taken as a reward. Abram refused the booty.

Why? Abram had promised God that no reward would be taken. Abram had not dared the rescue because he wanted the king's goodies. Abram rescued his nephew, and the king of Sodom was a collateral benefit. The rescue should never be understood as Abram seeking something of the king's. Abram sought what God had entrusted to him, and he then trusted God to see the task to completion. God got this credit, not Abram, and certainly not the king of Sodom.

When we are about God's work, we always need to remember to make it about God. It is easy to get caught up in rewards and earthly benefits from our actions. Sometimes it is actual money; other times it might be praise and glory. Regardless of what the earthly benefits are, we should remember we choose to act because of a higher purpose and calling. We choose to act because we are pursuing God's agenda. God's rewards are the ones we seek, not those of earthly rulers.

We should look to God for direction and purpose. We should trust God for the wisdom and strength to achieve what is before us. We should be motivated by doing right before God rather than the rewards of people, and we should give God the credit for the successes we enjoy.

Lord, in humility may I serve you today and every day. May I be satisfied finding your purposes fulfilled in my life and trust you with whatever may come. In your name, amen.

JANUARY 19

Now Sarai, Abram's wife, had borne him no children. She had a female Egyptian servant whose name was Hagar. And Sarai said to Abram, "Behold now, the LORD has prevented me from bearing children. Go in to my servant; it may be that I shall obtain children by her." And Abram listened to the voice of Sarai. (Gen. 16:1–2)

How often do we try to do God's will our way rather than his? It is always admirable to want to do God's will, but it is important we try to do it *his* way rather than our own!

In today's passage, we find Sarai in a predicament. God has told Abram that he will father many nations. At this point, Abram is married to Sarai, and they are childless. Abram, whose name means "father," is a father in name only! He has no child, much less children, because Sarai is barren. Sarai must have felt it was "her fault," in a sense, and it must have weighed on her. If Abram was to be the father his name conveys, the father that God had promised, had Abram perhaps married the wrong woman? Sarai decided God needed her help in getting his will done.

So Sarai tells Abram to have sexual relations with her servant, figuring that the child would then be "Sarai's" in the sense that the servant was Sarai's. Abram does as his wife bids him (not always a good thing to do!), and the servant conceives and bears a child.

The story doesn't end there. Sarai and the mother no longer get along. Sarai has contempt for the child and the whole process has left a strong distaste in her mouth. Sarai ultimately runs the child and mother off, and only later does she find out that God never needed her help to figure out his plans. God was able to do what needed to be done. The barren Sarai, too old to have a child, conceived anyway, and gave birth to Isaac. Abram had his heir through whom nations and countless heirs would come.

Bob Dylan sings, "God don't make promises that he don't keep." Yet I have found that I am guilty of the Sarai syndrome. I have been guilty of trying to "help God" through my own schemes and devices. It has taken a good bit of life for me to realize that my goal should be simple: walk with open eyes and listening ears, try to do the things God would have me do, and trust him with the consequences. God has his plans, and I can trust him to succeed with those. All I need to do are the things he instructs me. He will take care of the rest, and all will be well with the world. Or at least, all will be as it should be!

Lord, teach me to walk in your ways. Let me do your will in my life and trust you to see to your plans and keep your promises. In your name, amen.

JANUARY 20

The angel of the LORD found her by a spring of water in the wilderness, the spring on the way to Shur. And he said, "Hagar, servant of Sarai, where have you come from and where are you going?" She said, "I am fleeing from my mistress Sarai." The angel of the LORD said to her, "Return to your mistress and submit to her." The angel of the LORD also said to her, "I will surely multiply your offspring so that they cannot be numbered for multitude." And the angel of the LORD said to her, "Behold, you are pregnant and shall bear a son. You shall call his name Ishmael, because the LORD has listened to your affliction. He shall be a wild donkey of a man, his hand against everyone and everyone's hand against him, and he shall dwell over against all his kinsmen." So she called the name of the LORD who spoke to her, "You are a God of seeing," for she said, "Truly here I have seen him who looks after me." (Gen. 16:7–13)

God sees those in need, even those discounted by the world. That includes you and me.

In today's passage, we find that Hagar, the servant of Sarai, has been chased out of the security and provision of Abram's household by the severity and raw treatment by Sarai. At Sarai's insistence, Hagar has become pregnant with the child of Abram. Hagar was not happy about it, and her attitude turned Sarai bitter. Sarai's harsh treatment became more than Hagar could endure, and she put her life and that of her unborn child at risk by running away. Sarai seems to have been at peace with the departure, not trying to stop Hagar or sending anyone to find or retrieve her. Sarai was glad for the pregnant Hagar to leave and to die in the wilderness.

But God wasn't like Sarai. God wouldn't abandon Hagar. God pursued her. He sent an angel to Hagar's aid, having the angel ask Hagar what was happening. Once Hagar explained the situation, the angel instructed Hagar to return. In the process, the angel assured Hagar that God had an interest in her and her unborn child. God knew the child would be a son, and God told Hagar to name him Ishmael. Ishmael can be translated into English as "God hears." Hagar notes that not only does God "hear" but he also "sees," and she returns.

I have found that God does see and hear. He has found me in times of great distress, times when my world has seemed to be coming apart at the seams, and God has reached down with a word and promise, giving me instructions on how to put one foot in front of the other and walk. Like Hagar, I can affirm that "God looks after me." So can you!

Lord, give me a trusting heart to hear you and follow you. Be my rescue and give me direction with strength to walk in your ways. In your name, amen.

JANUARY 21

"No longer shall your name be called Abram, but your name shall be Abraham, for I have made you the father of a multitude of nations. I will make you exceedingly fruitful, and I will make you into nations, and kings shall come from you. And I will establish my covenant between me and you and your offspring after you throughout their generations for an everlasting covenant, to be God to you and to your offspring after you." (Gen. 17:5–7)

God's plans are not our plans. I have a great imagination, and I can come up with some pretty outlandish plans. But I have consistently found that God is able to do exceedingly more than I can imagine. And his plans are real, not some of my harebrained ones.

Today's passage marks a subtle but important change in the life of Abram. God changed Abram's name! "Abram" in Hebrew conveys the idea of a marvelous father, but "Abraham" is a father of *many*! This passage has extra punch when read in Hebrew. In the Hebrew, many of the words in the passage are near puns on Abraham's name. They are words that sound a lot like his name. One would pronounce "Abraham" in Hebrew with a "v" sound, like "avraham." Among the words that are plays on his name are those translated "father of a multitude" (*av hamon*), "covenant" (*vareet*), and "fruitful" (*hifreti*).

God took the father with no legitimate children, and God made him a father of many. This was part of God's plans to make Abraham exceedingly fruitful. This was God keeping his covenant with Abraham. It wasn't a short-term thing; it was God's plan with repercussions that would last forever. This is God being God.

When I was a young man, I wanted to be a preacher or a lawyer. I studied for both, preparing myself to walk either path. Never in my wildest dreams did I think that God could combine the two. I never thought I might be able to practice law and open doors of ministry that would otherwise be closed. Practicing law gave me contacts; gave me the opportunity to research, teach, and write; and gave me insights that allowed me to do more than I ever could have if I had gone straight into ministry.

Everyone who wishes for a marvelous life should take his or her hopes, dreams, ambitions, talents, and opportunities and set them before God. Let God take those and find that he and his plans will exceed anything we would devise on our own. God is that big!

God, help me to give you all that I am and all that I have. Use me in ways that bring your plans into fruition. In you I trust and in your name I pray, amen.

JANUARY 22

And the Lord appeared to him by the oaks of Mamre, as he sat at the door of his tent in the heat of the day. He lifted up his eyes and looked, and behold, three men were standing in front of him. When he saw them, he ran from the tent door to meet them and bowed himself to the earth and said, "O Lord, if I have found favor in your sight, do not pass by your servant." (Gen. 18:1–3)

Can you imagine a chance to visit with God? Would you let that pass by?

In today's passage, the nomad Abraham is sitting out in the midday heat in the door of his tent, no doubt praying for a breeze. When he looks up, he sees the Lord coming into his day in the form of three men. Ignoring the heat, which in days of no air-conditioning in the arid climate of the Middle East dictated people move slowly, if at all, Abraham runs to meet the three. Abraham urges the three to return with him to his encampment for a fuller visit. The men do so, and as tomorrow's passage will indicate, the meeting is pregnant with significance for Abraham.

There are days in my life when, I confess, I move from one thing to the next, everything seems to be running fine, and once the evening comes, I register being one day older but otherwise have little more to note. But there are other days when things aren't so smooth. Some of these days are filled with difficulty, where I find it hard to do all I need to do. Others are filled with strife, where relationships need work or where my job is not as easy as I might wish. People everywhere know the stress of economic pressure and health scares. There are also days of uncertainty when we fear what may come. We wonder if we are going the direction that is best. We try to figure out questions without the crystal ball to tell us answers with greater definiteness.

As a practical matter, I would like to find God in every day. I would like to find him when things are humdrum, things are difficult, things are in flux, and even when things are going great. I need and want God to come and spend time with me.

This passage has me on full alert! I am going to watch for chances to spend time with God. I am going to run to him and seek him out. These devotions are great chances to do that very thing. I want to see God, and I don't want him to pass by.

Lord, please open my eyes to see you. Quicken my heart to want you and watch for you. Please do not pass me by, but commune with me in your love and mercy. In your name, amen.

JANUARY 23

They said to him, "Where is Sarah your wife?" And he said, "She is in the tent." The LORD said, "I will surely return to you about this time next year, and Sarah your wife shall have a son." And Sarah was listening at the tent door behind him. Now Abraham and Sarah were old, advanced in years. The way of women had ceased to be with Sarah. So Sarah laughed to herself, saying, "After I am worn out, and my lord is old, shall I have pleasure?" The Lord said to Abraham, "Why did Sarah laugh and say, 'Shall I indeed bear a child, now that I am old?' Is anything too hard for the Lord?" (Gen. 18:9–14)

Have you found anything in your life too hard for God? Have you decided that God's promises have passed you by? Today's passage should give us greater faith.

For decades, Sarah and Abraham had been trying to have children. They lived before modern fertility clinics, and they didn't know why she couldn't get pregnant. They just knew that their efforts weren't working. Over the years, God had promised them a child, but even that promise must have rung hollow as months turned into years, into decades, and nothing happened. I suspect they had many thoughts about why. Perhaps they weren't good enough for God. Perhaps they had messed up in some way. Maybe they hadn't heard God as clearly as they thought. I'm sure many reasons popped into their minds as they faced reality.

But reality is not always what it seems. Reality is not only what we see with our eyes or experience in our lives. Reality includes a God who sits on high, and this God is interested in you and me. He cares. He has plans, and his plans will not be thwarted.

I have seen some of God's promises manifested in my life in ways that only a crude, shortsighted person would think were anything less than miraculous. Some of God's promises have not yet been fulfilled, and I steadfastly await them, with prayers regularly coming from my heart. I know that I will need to trust him. He will be true to his word, which means that he will either fulfill his promises or he will teach me that I didn't understand them properly. This is no cop-out for when things turn out differently than I wish. This is no laughing matter. This is reality. This is the life of faith and trust in an Almighty God.

God's promises are real. Hold on to them. Nothing is too hard for the Lord!

Lord, thank you for your faithfulness. Thank you for touching my life in so many ways, bringing forth incredible blessings and opportunities. May I hold firm to my trust in you. In your name, amen.

JANUARY 24

As morning dawned, the angels urged Lot, saying, "Up! Take your wife and your two daughters who are here, lest you be swept away in the punishment of the city. . . . Escape for your life. Do not look back or stop anywhere in the valley. Escape to the hills, lest you be swept away." Then the LORD rained on Sodom and Gomorrah sulfur and fire from the LORD out of heaven. And he overthrew those cities, and all the valley, and all the inhabitants of the cities, and what grew on the ground. But Lot's wife, behind him, looked back, and she became a pillar of salt. (Gen. 19:15–26)

I should be a pillar of salt. I've looked back too many times.

Today's passage is a story of missed redemption. Sodom and Gomorrah had become infested, diseased towns of hatred, abuse, and rebellion. God was going to eradicate the disease, a type of radiation treatment for the cancerous infestation.

In his mercy, God was pulling out those who would listen to him. Any who had a chance of becoming something better than they were, God was intent to rescue. To continue the medical analogy, God didn't want to cut out healthy tissue with the dead tissue. God gave clear instructions and warnings: "Flee, don't stop, and don't look back! Destruction is coming, and this is your chance to escape." Lot's wife chose to look back and was destroyed.

Life is interesting. There is a stickiness to sin that makes it very difficult to flee. Those plagued by the disease of gossip, even knowing it is wrong, find it hard to stop. I love to eat. Gluttony is a sin I know much too well. How many people are unable to flee sexual temptation or the trap of alcoholism? Yes, we know some things are wrong, yet we do them anyway.

Thankfully there is a growing process that God has for us. In many ways, change comes little by little, day by day. It's like weight loss (or gain). It comes from persistent living, not a one-day diet or feast. Yet even with that, there are sometimes defining moments where events have an immediate, irrevocable repercussion. I have seen this firsthand, having represented too many people seriously injured or even killed because someone decided to drive while drunk. We need to be alert, and the real answer is simple. With God's help, do right, every time and every way we can. Flee immoral choices, and putting our hands to the plow, don't look back!

Lord, thank you for forgiveness of my past. Let me be yours today. Each choice, each step, help me make them for you! In your name, amen.

JANUARY 25

The Lord visited Sarah as he had said, and the Lord did to Sarah as he had promised.
(Gen. 21:1)

Sometimes it is hard to keep one's promises. We all make assurances, affirm plans, give representations, and yet fall short of seeing them through as promised. Fortunately, God has no such problem! God is faithful to his word, and he always keeps his commitments.

Today's passage demonstrates this character trait of God. Sarah had been barren her entire life. Try as they might, Sarah and Abraham had never been able to have a child. Late in life, long after her childbearing years, God visited Abraham and told him that by the very next year Sarah would have a child. That meant conception within three months. Something she'd been unable to do for over three decades! Sarah overheard God's promise to Abraham and laughed at the mere suggestion, thinking it preposterous. Then God visited Sarah! Not in the same way that the three men sat with Abraham, but God visited Sarah unseen, opening her womb and bringing a baby into her world. God kept his promises.

When we look at life and our world four thousand years later, it is easy to get caught up in business. We see all we need to do and we understand that our world is relatively complex, compared to that of a nomadic sheik's family in the arid Middle East four thousand years ago. We might even think that our modern world justifies deception, lying, broken promises, and the like.

I handled a case once where a company had breached its agreement to sell oil fields to my client. Trying to enforce the deal in court, I cross-examined the president of the company. With a straight face and conviction in his voice, he proudly proclaimed his instructions to his underlings: "If they can make more money for this company by going back on an agreement, then I insist they breach the deal." That is a sad state of affairs.

We have a model from God of one who keeps promises. We have mantras that hold up this importance. Our word should be our bond. People should be able to rely on what we say. We should keep our word, even when it hurts to do it, even when it is to our apparent detriment. We follow a trustworthy and reliable God, and he calls us to be like him.

God visited Sarah and kept his word. I need to visit with God and make sure I keep mine!

Lord, please help me learn to speak and commit carefully. And when I do so, please embolden me to keep what I've committed to. In your name, amen.

JANUARY 26

When the water in the skin was gone, she put the child under one of the bushes. Then she went and sat down opposite him a good way off, about the distance of a bowshot, for she said, "Let me not look on the death of the child." And as she sat opposite him, she lifted up her voice and wept. And God heard the voice of the boy, and the angel of God called to Hagar from heaven and said to her, "What troubles you, Hagar? Fear not, for God has heard the voice of the boy where he is . . ." Then God opened her eyes, and she saw a well of water. (Gen. 21:15–19)

God hears the cries of the desperate and opens their eyes to see his ways.

Today's passage follows Hagar, Sarah's handmaid who was given to Abraham in Sarah's efforts to produce a child and fulfill God's promise that Abraham would have an heir. Hagar's union with Abraham produced a son, Ishmael, but he wasn't the heir of the promise. After Sarah gave birth to Isaac, Hagar was run out from the nomadic camp, left to fend for herself and Ishmael. It wasn't long before their water supply ran out, and death was knocking on the door. Hagar knew the young boy would die first, and she couldn't bear to see it. She laid him under a bush and went half a football field away so she wouldn't have to watch his final moments. She looked up to God and wept. God heard Hagar and the cries of Ishmael. Interrupting the misery, God told Hagar not to fear. God was listening, and he was coming to their rescue. God opened Hagar's eyes, and she suddenly saw a water well. God saved the day.

I have seen desperation. I have been desperate myself. Most in the Western world have never been truly dying of thirst for water, but most have thirsted for many things to the point of despair. People wonder how to make their bills. They wonder why they are unloved by the people they love. They wonder why their needs never seem to be met. They seem to have no control over their own thoughts and actions.

Here is where the story of Hagar should speak to us. We learn that God hears our cries of desperation. He hears and rescues. He opens our eyes to see his deliverance. He reaches into our world and meets our needs. Our role is simple. We are to cry out to God. We are to look to him, seeking to hear his voice and directing our attention to what he points out. As we do so, we find our God speaking into our desperation and we have our answers. The well didn't make life Easy Street for Hagar, but she lived, her son lived, and he became a nation of many. So will God take care of us.

Lord, in times of desperation, may I cry to you. Hear my cries and come to my rescue. Be my provision, and may I give you the glory. In your name, amen.

JANUARY 27

Abraham planted a tamarisk tree in Beersheba and called there on the name of the LORD, the Everlasting God. (Gen. 21:33)

Take a moment and pause. Proclaim the greatness of God. Say something out loud that God has done. He is an "Everlasting" God.

Today's passage naturally falls into three related thoughts. It comes in the context of the tent-dwelling Abraham being gifted a well in the area by the ruler Abimelek. In this way, the king acknowledged the right of Abraham to live there as long as he chose. This brought Abraham to a decision to "plant a tamarisk tree in Beersheba." Abraham planting a tree is not something done for that one day. It was a proclamation of faith. Abraham believed that he would be there for some time. The tree would grow and provide shade. It would also provide a measure of food for livestock. Abraham didn't act in this faith praising Abimelek. Abraham praised God. He knew the goodness of the king's gift was really one from the hand of God.

This brings in the second related thought. Abraham "called there on the name of the LORD." This is not a simple reference to saying God's name. In Abraham's day, one's "name" was a reference to one's character, one's reputation, and one's track record. To call on God's name meant to proclaim something of who God is. It is an out-loud proclamation of God's powerful deeds. It means that Abraham spoke of God's actions and reliability. He spoke of God's faithfulness and loyalty. Abraham took the moment to pause; to plant a tree, trusting in the future; and to proclaim God as his reason. This leads to the third related thought.

God is an "Everlasting God." The tree could be planted in confidence that Abraham's tomorrows were in the hands of a faithful God. God isn't temporary. His power, love, and compassion aren't here today but gone tomorrow. Abraham could plant trees, praise God, and trust that God would be there each and every day.

We have the same God today that Abraham had four thousand years ago. He is a faithful, loving, all-knowing, all-seeing God who cares about us and will be here tomorrow. We can plant trees and trust that God will put them to use, for us, or for those who follow us in his ways. What can I do today for God? I want to do it, proclaiming him the Everlasting God.

Lord, you are God and King. You have been faithful for the ages, and I am eager to work for you and see your faithfulness in my tomorrows. In your name, amen.

So Abraham called the name of that place, "The LORD will provide"; as it is said to this day, "On the mount of the LORD it shall be provided." (Gen. 22:14)

Some days in life challenge us to our core. We find ourselves at wit's end and see no way out. In those days, we need to have faith. Our God provides.

Abraham had many challenges in his life. Many times he was called to trust God through unusually difficult circumstances. He had family relationship issues when God called him, instructing him to lose all contact with his home and move to a foreign and strange land. He had social challenges when the kings and rulers of foreign lands were threats or impediments to his survival. He had marital problems over his wife's infertility and her attempts to manufacture solutions to that problem. In all of these challenges, Abraham walked faithfully, trusting God to secure the solutions and help him navigate the problems. In his old age, however, Abraham faced the greatest challenge of his life. God told Abraham to take his son of promise, Isaac, to a certain mountain to be offered as a sacrifice.

This was a family challenge, a marital challenge, and a social challenge (dare he be known as a child killer?), all rolled into one. It would shake any caring parent to her or his core. Abraham chose obedience and took Isaac to the mountain. Rabbis later believed that Abraham was trusting God would resurrect Isaac, keeping his promise to give Abraham future generations through this son. The Genesis account doesn't reveal Abraham's thoughts, but there is no doubt that Abraham sacrificed Isaac in his heart, willingly taking him to the place and beginning the ritual. Isaac was a smart lad. He saw everything necessary for the sacrifice except one thing—the sacrificial animal. When Isaac asked his father about it, Abraham spoke in faith, "The LORD will provide." God stopped Abraham from following through with the sacrifice. God provided a ram in the exact designated spot of the sacrifice. Abraham had sacrificed his son in his heart, and God did indeed deliver the son back. God provided.

In all my years on earth, every time I have followed God in faith, he has provided. Sometimes it is difficult and emotional in the process, but God provides. Even down to the days of Moses, over seven hundred years after Abraham, the saying was still known, "On the mount of the LORD it shall be provided." Now over another three thousand years have passed, but the saying is still true. God will provide.

Lord, thank you for your provision. Please grow my faith. In your name, amen.

JANUARY 29

Sarah died at Kiriath-arba (that is, Hebron) in the land of Canaan, and Abraham went in to mourn for Sarah and to weep for her. (Gen. 23:2)

Everyone faces death. This is a harsh reality. My first memory of death is of a pet goldfish I had as a very young boy. The funeral was in the bathroom where we ceremoniously flushed the dead fish down the commode. As I aged, others around me died. Usually they were several generations removed, but as I got older, the age gap diminished. Some died in fear; others died in faith.

In today's passage, we read of the death of Sarah, the wife of Abraham's youth and mother of his beloved son Isaac. As a man of faith, Abraham surely had a measure of confidence in God being present in death. Yet that didn't stop Abraham from mourning. Death is a loss, even as it is a gain to those who pass on to eternity in God's care.

I have had the occasion to preach at a number of funerals. In funerals, I try to achieve two things. I try to remember the life of the deceased in ways that provide a full expression of emotions, for emotions run deep at those times. People need to laugh, cry, celebrate, mourn, and experience the time of remembrance in ways that help them come to grips with the passing.

But there is something else that needs to be done at a funeral. It is a time to reflect on the faith of those who follow God. The Everlasting God does not close the door on his faithful children. Death is an open door into God's provision for eternity. Faith is conviction and trust that God's mercy will extend over the imperfections of those who seek his mercy. This means something to those who attend the funerals of those who die in faith. Sharing that faith is a confident expectation that God will reunite the faithful again after this life is over.

There will come a day we face death, all of us. I want to face that day in faith, trusting God for my journey and life after death. It causes me to seek his face today while I have health and breath. I want to know him better. I want to understand his mercy. I want to pass and have those who know me mourn, but not as those who have no hope. I want them to miss me but celebrate how God has used my life and remember that I didn't die alone. God was with me. God reunited me with my family that had passed before, and one day my loved ones in faith will join us as well.

Lord, thank you for life, in this world and in what lies beyond the grave. May I learn more of you and live trusting in your grace and mercy. In your name, amen.

JANUARY 30

Now Ephron was sitting among the Hittites, and Ephron the Hittite answered Abraham in the hearing of the Hittites, of all who went in at the gate of his city, "No, my lord, hear me: I give you the field, and I give you the cave that is in it. In the sight of the sons of my people I give it to you. Bury your dead." Then Abraham bowed down before the people of the land. And he said to Ephron in the hearing of the people of the land, "But if you will, hear me: I give the price of the field. Accept it from me, that I may bury my dead there." Ephron answered Abraham, "My lord, listen to me: a piece of land worth four hundred shekels of silver, what is that between you and me? Bury your dead." Abraham listened to Ephron, and Abraham weighed out for Ephron the silver that he had named in the hearing of the Hittites, four hundred shekels of silver, according to the weights current among the merchants. (Gen. 23:10–16)

We live in an interactive society. We deal with people on a regular basis. Whether shopping for groceries, buying a car, or hiring a plumber, most everyone has some level of daily transactions. We always have a choice in how we interact with others, and today's passage teaches a simple message: deal with people fairly.

In today's passage, Abraham needs to bury his wife Sarah. He is grieving and coming to grips with the horrors of making funeral decisions. Without the ease of a modern funeral home, Abraham sought a cave and field where he could entomb his beloved. Ephron has the field, and Abraham needs to buy it. The negotiations seem odd to us today, but we should read this and understand—these were negotiations.

Ephron offered to give the field to Abraham. Had Abraham accepted, it would have been terribly offensive and unfair to Ephron. Instead, Abraham says he will pay full value. Only then does Ephron set the price, 400 shekels of silver. Ephron again offers to give him the field or at least take a reduced price. Abraham heard the price and paid it. Abraham dealt fairly with Ephron, even as Abraham was grieving.

This speaks to Abraham's character. It doesn't mean one shouldn't negotiate a car purchase. Nor does it mean one shouldn't shop for the best prices. But it does mean one shouldn't gouge another or take advantage of others. There is a difference between being fair and discerning and taking advantage. We should deal fairly. What we are and what we do, how we treat others, especially when money is at stake, is a reflection of our God. Let us reflect him honorably.

Lord, give me discernment and courage to treat people as I would like them to treat me. Help me to be fair to them in all my dealings. In your name, amen.

JANUARY 31

Now Abraham was old, well advanced in years. And the LORD *had blessed Abraham in all things. And Abraham said to his servant, the oldest of his household, who had charge of all that he had, "Put your hand under my thigh, that I may make you swear by the* LORD, *the God of heaven and God of the earth, that you will not take a wife for my son from the daughters of the Canaanites, among whom I dwell, but will go to my country and to my kindred, and take a wife for my son Isaac." (Gen. 24:1–4)*

I get asked a lot of questions as a lawyer. One that comes up regularly is "I don't have a will. Can you help me?" I confess my answer is "Not without committing malpractice!" I don't know much beyond the basics of writing wills. It's not my thing. Still, I know it is important that we live responsibly for today and tomorrow, especially where our families are concerned.

In today's passage, Abraham is elderly and recently became a single parent to Isaac. Abraham's wife has died, and Isaac is getting close to marrying age. Four thousand years ago in the bedouin world of the Middle East, getting a wife was no simple matter. It wasn't the modern Western civilization where men and women find each other; date around, getting exposed to different possible companions; then finally make a decision and choose to get married. The bedouin father was responsible for finding spouses for those under his care. With his son Isaac, Abraham wanted to ensure that the spouse would be from his own family.

Abraham was too old to make the journey, and he did not entrust this job to just anyone. With great care, and buttressed with a solemn oath, Abraham chose his oldest servant to travel and find a wife for Isaac. Abraham knew that one of his final responsibilities in his life was to make sure that the next generation was best positioned to live for God's plans.

I never picked out the spouses for my children. I didn't send anyone else to do it, either. But that doesn't mean that I was uninvolved. I have prayed for my children and their future spouses since conception. I tried to teach my children the value of faith in a spouse. Becky and I tried to model in our home love, kindness, faithfulness, and the other virtues that would make our children fruitful in life whether they married or not. Wills are important legal instruments, but I think these values are more important than writing a will.

Lord, bless my children. Give them wisdom and understanding for a full life walked faithfully before you. In your name, amen.

FEBRUARY 1

"Blessed be the LORD, the God of my master Abraham, who has not forsaken his steadfast love and his faithfulness toward my master. As for me, the LORD has led me in the way to the house of my master's kinsmen." (Gen. 24:27)

If one were asked to list the traits of God explained in the Bible, two related traits would surely appear near the top: steadfast love and faithfulness. We see them from the earliest pages of Scripture to the last. We also can see them today.

In today's passage, Abraham's oldest and most reliable servant has been sent to find a wife for Abraham's son Isaac from among Abraham's relatives. Being the oldest servant, for decades the man had seen firsthand how God made promises to Abraham and kept those promises. The servant was no Johnny-come-lately. He knew God and had enjoyed a front-row seat to some of history's most amazing interactions between God and humanity. Before his task, the servant prayed to God for success, and God answered his prayers. The answers were strong and direct affirmations that God was behind the trip, and that the servant was walking in God's blessings. Abraham may have sent his servant to find a wife, but God had already picked out that wife and prepared the way for the servant. The servant was merely God's tool for fulfilling God's plans for Abraham and the world.

This story, old as it is, speaks to my experiences in life and to how I want to live my life today and in the days to come. I have seen that God's hand is alive and working in small daily ways. I was accepted at three law schools but turned them all down, wanting instead another career path (preaching). Yet through the counsel of a dear friend, just days before law school started, I was told to be a lawyer and use the career as a chance to continue teaching and preaching as a passion rather than a necessity. Then I was able to get reinstated for law school only days before it began, at the one school where I would make the contacts and have the opportunities that steered my legal career in a very special direction. Was that all chance? Would that have happened without God's hand? Some might say yes, but faith emphatically says no! This is one of countless ways God has worked for his will in my life.

If we commit our ways to him, if we give him our lives, if we seek his will daily in big and small things, he doesn't disappoint. He is faithful in steadfast love, and we will experience and see his hand. That's just who he is!

Lord, thank you for your faithfulness and steadfast love. I give you my life for your will, and I am eager to see you move through me. In your name, amen.

FEBRUARY 2

Then the young woman ran and told her mother's household about these things. (Gen. 24:28)

How do we react to God's work? When we see God moving or experience his touch in our lives, what do we do? Do we flee from it? Does it thrill us? Do we sit and soak it in? Do we *run* and tell people about what God is doing in our lives?

Today's passage tells about Rebekah, the daughter of Bethuel and granddaughter of Nahor, Abraham's brother. Put in modern vernacular, Abraham was the great-uncle of Rebekah. Abraham's son, Isaac, was her first cousin, once removed. Rebekah was an attractive young lady who had no warning of what God had in store for her one particular day. She was headed out for her daily chores of watering the animals. A stranger was at the well, and he had prayed that God would help him in his mission, finding a wife for Isaac from Abraham's kinfolk. The stranger saw Rebekah approaching, saw her to be an attractive young woman, and *ran* to her to see if she might be a proper wife. Rebekah, from her vantage point, knew nothing of the mission. She just saw some stranger run up to her and ask for water. In kindness she offered some and graciously offered to help with his animals. This was the sign Abraham's servant had secretly asked for from God. He was elated and began giving her expensive gifts. To confirm his belief, the stranger (who was actually Abraham's servant) asked Rebekah who she was. Confirming she was kin to Abraham, the servant began praising God for leading him to Rebekah. God was afoot! Rebekah saw it, and she in turn *ran* to tell her mother all about it!

I like both times the verb *run* is used in this story. I like the idea of running to what I think God is doing, like Abraham's servant. I also like the idea of running to tell people what God is doing. Running is a reaction of excitement and anticipation. We run fueled by the energy of the moment. The servant was excited to see God's hand and was eager to play his role. When I see God at work, when I see things that are godly and needing to be done, I hope I get excited enough to run toward those opportunities. Similarly, when I see things that God has done, when I get to play a role in his unfolding history, I hope one of my reactions is to run and tell others. I want to run, not walk. I want the preciousness of the moment to infuse me with joy and energy. God is afoot in our world and in my life. I want my feet to show it!

Lord, thank you for moving in the world and my life. Help me identify your work and run to be a part. Give my feet speed to run and tell others of your marvelous deeds. In your name, amen.

FEBRUARY 3

They blessed Rebekah and said to her, "Our sister, may you become thousands of ten thousands, and may your offspring possess the gate of those who hate him!" (Gen. 24:60)

Sometimes things don't go the way we want or plan. There are days where the unexpected happens. It might not strike us as a good thing at the time, but we need to remember that there is a God at work who has vision beyond our own.

Today's passage is in the flow of the story where Rebekah is selected to be the wife of Isaac, Abraham's son. Abraham's servant made the selection after prayer and a fortuitous encounter/interaction at a well. Having decided that Rebekah was God's choice, the servant needed to persuade her family to let her leave them and return with the servant to Abraham's caravan. Having heard about the circumstances surrounding the encounter, Rebekah's family realized her marriage to Isaac was "from the Lord," and they had little they could say beyond that. They simply had to live with it (Gen. 24:50). The family wished that Rebekah could wait to go, but recognizing the servant's urgency, they allowed her to leave the next morning.

Our culture and time are different. We may expect most children to grow up and marry but not for them to leave us with twenty-four hours' notice and to have little or no contact with their family in the future. Even in Rebekah's age, this must have been a shocking development. It would break my heart to wake up one day and find out my child would be leaving the next day with little to no more contact in the future. Yet this was the story for Rebekah and her family.

Still, the family saw that God was at work. God's plans are not always what we would choose, but God has a grander purpose. Rebekah was a key part in God's plans to bring a nation out of Abraham's seed and from that nation a blessing for the entire world. The plan needed Rebekah. The family made the right choice. They let Rebekah follow the plan of God and sent her with their blessings.

When God's hand moves in my life, when things beyond my control occur, altering my well-laid plans, I need to do the same. I need to prayerfully examine whether the alterations are from God. If they are, I need to seek to bless and further the different plans. If they aren't, I need to work to stop them. If I am uncertain, I need to get counsel from those I trust and continue to pray and seek truth.

Lord, please make me aware of your plans such that I can bless and support them, even when they are not my first choice! In your name, amen.

FEBRUARY 4

Then Isaac brought her into the tent of Sarah his mother and took Rebekah, and she became his wife, and he loved her. So Isaac was comforted after his mother's death. (Gen. 24:67)

There is pain in this world. Some of it we bring on ourselves, but some of it comes regardless of what we do. Some of the greatest pain can come from loneliness, especially after the death of a close loved one. In those times, we can experience the balm of a comforting God.

Today's story reports the events of Isaac's marriage as they related to the death of his mother, Sarah. Sarah was an older parent, to put it mildly. She died before she got the joys of being a grandmother to Isaac's children. That loss was substantial to Abraham and Isaac, and their mourning was great. They maintained her tent even after her death. When Abraham's servant returned from his journey to find a wife for Isaac, he brought Rebekah with him. Rebekah and Isaac joined in marriage and moved into Sarah's tent. This brought Isaac comfort in the midst of his mourning.

We humans are emotional beings. Life can bring us thrills and highs, and it can deal us blows that leave us low. Some of us find that emotions can even dictate our reactions to others and events. I would love to think I am cerebral. It would be nice to think that my head governs my heart. Maybe it does sometimes, but I know that I am not a Vulcan. I know emotion only too well.

God is aware of this. He is our creator, and he knows we are feeling people as well as thinking people. His Scriptures teach that there is a time to weep and a time to dance. It is good to know that God doesn't recoil from our emotions. He walks with us through them. When we mourn, he brings comfort. When we suffer, he provides a salve. He also uses what we are going through—pain, suffering, hurt, and the like—to teach us important life lessons that make us better people.

Sarah's tent must have been a constant reminder of her absence and death. Isaac would have seen it each day. Yet by God's grace, that painful memory became comforting as the same tent became the tent of marriage for Isaac. By God's grace, Isaac saw the wheel of time turning, with the passing of his mother and coming of his wife. Such is our God as we move through the wheel of emotive life. He is a God of comfort in our times of sorrow.

Lord, please comfort the hurting. Use me to minister your love. In your name, amen.

FEBRUARY 5

Isaac prayed to the LORD for his wife, because she was barren. And the LORD granted his prayer, and Rebekah his wife conceived. (Gen. 25:21)

What do you do when things aren't going the way they should? Today's passage teaches that one should pray to God.

God made a promise that through Isaac, Abraham's seed would flourish, ultimately producing innumerable offspring. Isaac had a chosen wife; God's hand was evident in her selection. One would think things would naturally flow from there. Yet they didn't. Rebekah was barren, unable to have children. I don't know what kind of folk remedies might have been available, but I know that Isaac did not choose what his mother did when she had trouble conceiving. Sarah had offered up her handmaid Hagar to Abraham, thinking the substitute child would work. Not Isaac. In contrast, he prayed to God. God granted his prayer, and Rebekah conceived twins!

This passage doesn't teach that God is a cosmic genie, answering prayers like wishes. The passage is clear that the Lord "granted" his prayer, but not out of obligation. God might have chosen to say no. Yet in this instance, God said yes, but the "yes" was twenty years later! The promise came at age forty; the "yes" was realized at age sixty!

I like these stories. I know what it is like to have a need that is compelling, one where I have nowhere else to turn. In those times it is a comfort to pray to God, but even more, it is a joy to see the prayer answered affirmatively. It beats the times I have prayed and prayed, only to have the prayers seem to bounce off the ceiling right back onto me.

When my prayers seem unanswered, does this mean that I am missing some secret formula to prayer? Does this mean I am not worthy of God's attention? Does this mean God doesn't care? As a corollary, does this mean that when my prayers *are* answered, it is just coincidence? I think each of these questions must be answered "no."

God sits on high. He desires to hear our prayers. More than that, he instructs us to pray. But we are to pray for his will, not for our own. We are to use prayer as a means of discerning his will, then expressing it with a desire to see it become reality. When we do so, there is an assurance that he will answer that prayer—not because of a formula or because we are good enough but because it is how we learn his will and how we see it done.

Lord, please work your will in my life. Give me wisdom and discernment to pray your will and the life to live it. In your name, amen.

FEBRUARY 6

Once when Jacob was cooking stew, Esau came in from the field, and he was exhausted. And Esau said to Jacob, "Let me eat some of that red stew, for I am exhausted!" (Therefore his name was called Edom.) Jacob said, "Sell me your birthright now." Esau said, "I am about to die; of what use is a birthright to me?" Jacob said, "Swear to me now." So he swore to him and sold his birthright to Jacob. Then Jacob gave Esau bread and lentil stew, and he ate and drank and rose and went his way. Thus Esau despised his birthright. (Gen. 25:29–34)

BEWARE: Don't let short-term pleasure trump long-term gain. A related warning: Don't put self-indulgence before long-term spiritual gain.

Today's passage concerns the twins Jacob and Esau. Esau was the older and clearly a favorite of their father. Jacob was the younger and clearly the favorite of their mother. The saga of these brothers pits not only the two children but also the parents against each other. The story is one of a manipulative mother and a rather dim father. Before the parents become too involved in the story, the brothers' rivalry takes center stage.

Esau, the outdoors type, returned to the home exhausted. Jacob had been at home cooking stew, and Esau wanted some. A good brother would have been glad to share the stew, but not Jacob. He charged Esau, and the cost was high. Jacob wanted Esau's birthright. The birthright as firstborn entitled one to an esteemed position and privileges as well as a double portion of inheritance. Esau was cavalier about his rights, not treasuring them as he should. He was more concerned about satisfying his immediate hunger and thirst.

It is easy for one to sit and judge Esau. After all, what dummy would give up long-term gain for short-term pleasure? In truth, just about everyone! I know there have been times when the moment seemed a lot more important to me. My brain hasn't always thought through long-term consequences when faced with something I really want. I can also attest that the indulgence (which is what choosing short-term pleasure really is) was never worth the cost.

This story may not seem to be trumpeting something new or unknown. But it is trumpeting something I need to be reminded of regularly.

Lord, give me the wherewithal to think through implications of decisions, especially when they give me what I want now. I want to live wisely. In your name, amen.

FEBRUARY 7

The LORD appeared to [Isaac] and said, "Do not go down to Egypt; dwell in the land of which I shall tell you. Sojourn in this land, and I will be with you and will bless you, for to you and to your offspring I will give all these lands, and I will establish the oath that I swore to Abraham your father." (Gen. 26:2–3)

Everyone has a chance to know and relate to God one-on-one. God doesn't have grandchildren; he only has children.

Abraham walked with God. God gave Abraham directions and instructions, and more times than not, Abraham followed those. Abraham had a son, Isaac, and that son was destined to be God's conduit for fulfilling God's promises to Abraham. One main question was how Isaac would handle his role. The story unfolds with God visiting Isaac, much as God visited Abraham. God gave Isaac instructions and directions, almost the exact opposite of those given to his father. God had told Abraham to pull up his roots and move to an unknown land. God told Isaac *not* to pull up his roots and move to Egypt but instead to stay in the land God had indicated. The directions differed, but the source of instruction was the same—God.

Isaac chose to follow God, as evidenced by his obedience. This transferred to Isaac the promise made to Abraham. Isaac was no longer the tool for God fulfilling promises to Abraham; Isaac was an actual recipient of God's promises himself.

I grew up in a family of faith. My mother and father both believed God and gave their lives to him in service. Of course, they weren't perfect, but they were faithful. I knew that growing up. I also knew that my relationship with God would need to be personal. I didn't want to know God only through my parents; I wanted to know him on my own. As a result, my relationship with him has been a rich field that has borne fruits I would have never known otherwise.

My hope and prayer for my five children, their spouses, and my grandchild is that they will each know God personally and that they will seek his will and follow his directions. I know that by doing so, they will experience the fullest joys this life offers. They will have solace in the midst of loss and strength when times are tough. They will be able to face the world with courage and confidence. They will know life as children of the living God.

Lord, thank you for seeking a relationship with me. May I hear your knock and answer the call. May I walk with you daily. In your name, amen.

FEBRUARY 8

And the LORD appeared to [Isaac] the same night and said, "I am the God of Abraham your father. Fear not, for I am with you and will bless you and multiply your offspring for my servant Abraham's sake." (Gen. 26:24)

Everyone likes security. No one likes uncertainty. It can gnaw at you, especially when it concerns something with serious consequences. It is reassuring when that unsettled feeling arises to know there is a God who has you in his sights and is intent on protecting and caring for you.

Today's passage finds Isaac in turmoil and worry. His father has died, and Isaac is in charge of his caravan. They were traveling from spot to spot, feeding and watering their flocks. In our modern age, we lose track of the security issues in his day. There was no police force. There were few specific boundaries with land ownership and fences. Might and custom ruled the day. Isaac tried dwelling in the coastal lands, but the tribes there envied his prosperity. They filled his water wells and ordered him to leave their area. Isaac then moved to a nearby valley, redigging wells for his animals and people. But herdsmen in that area chased him out as well. Place after place Isaac was unable to find any peace. Finally, Isaac arrived in Beersheba, where God appeared to him and told him not to fear. God was with Isaac, and God was going to bless him.

I suspect the problems most people in the West face today are not those of a refugee, seeking a place to safely set down roots. There are other ways to feel unsettled, however. Many people have uncertainty in relationships. Jobs are precarious at times. We worry about our children. We await phone calls from our doctors to inform us about our health. It may not be our physical presence wandering all over the map, but there are a lot of ways to feel unsettled and worried. In the midst of them all, we need this visit from God.

God's word to his followers is sure. "Fear not! For I am with you and will bless you!" That consolation should melt away the insecurities and bring courage to face whatever may come. The world can present huge problems, but no problem is greater than the God who is our companion. For those who trust in God, the unsettled heart cries out and moves forward.

Lord, you have been faithful to get me to this point in my life. I thank you for that, and I pray for your continued protection and blessing. In your name, amen.

FEBRUARY 9

When Esau was forty years old, he took Judith the daughter of Beeri the Hittite to be his wife, and Basemath the daughter of Elon the Hittite, and they made life bitter for Isaac and Rebekah. (Gen. 26:34–35)

Blessed be family harmony! Regrettably, however, it doesn't exist all the time. We might try to find peace and joy in family, but sometimes there is one or more family members who make it near impossible. In those times, what should we do?

Today's passage explains what happened in the family of Isaac and Rebekah when their son Esau married outside the family and tribe. Esau married a Hittite. And then he married a second one. This was not a good thing for the family for two reasons. First, the fact that the women were Hittite indicates they were of a different faith than the family. Isaac and Rebekah worshipped the Lord, the God of Abraham. Hittites worshipped a number of ancient Middle Eastern deities. Second, there is a subtle implication in the Hebrew that Esau's polygamy was also inappropriate. Other Israelites would engage in polygamy, but it really never worked well. As Genesis set out in the beginning, it was one man to one woman. "The two" become "one flesh," not the "three or more." (The Torah later regulated the culturally accepted polygamy but never taught it as the ideal.)

The story should point us in two directions on the issue of family harmony. First, we should see in Esau's actions that what we do and who we are impacts those we love. When we honor and respect our families, that honor and respect builds a foundation of love and fulfillment. When we dishonor and show our families disrespect, it brings bitterness and sadness. Second, when someone in the family chooses a course that brings bitterness and sadness into the family, there isn't always a lot we can do about it. We surely cannot force people to live contrary to their own choices. But we can choose how we respond.

Our response in difficult family affairs speaks to who we are and how God is working in our lives. If we show love, kindness, and gentleness, and if we seek to accept those who might prove difficult, we best ensure our chances of maximizing family harmony. In the process, we should remember the importance of keeping healthy boundaries. Limits to what is "acceptable behavior" and treatment are important to keep. But within the healthy framework, love is the operative word for our behavior, even when it is not returned.

Lord, bless my family. Help us to honor others. Give us peace, patience, and kindness in dealing with difficult people. In your name, amen.

FEBRUARY 10

"Your brother came deceitfully, and he has taken away your blessing." Esau said, "Is he not rightly named Jacob? For he has cheated me these two times." (Gen. 27:35–36)

We all mess up. Fear, selfishness, envy, greed, a lack of trust, and many other sins pervade our decision-making more times than we'd like to admit. Fortunately, God's mercy trumps humanity's fallibility.

Today's reading is one passage in a longer story that illustrates the point. Jacob, whose name comes from the Hebrew for "heel," was born grasping the heel of his twin brother, Esau. The Hebrew "heel" was also used for one who snuck up and attacked another from behind. Esau, in conversation with his father, Isaac, learns that Jacob has deceitfully taken advantage of their blind father and secured the firstborn blessing by pretending to be Esau. Esau is furious, having already traded his birthright to Jacob for food. Why would Jacob do such things?

Interestingly, Jacob was God's choice to receive the promises made to Abraham and Isaac. It was through Jacob that God was going to raise up a nation and ultimately bring the Messiah to bless Israel and the nations. Why did Jacob feel compelled to work deceitfully? Couldn't God be trusted to bring his plans to fruition without Jacob forcing it? One might even think that God might change his plans once the character of Jacob was shown. But no, God's plans were not so easily thwarted. Instead, God went to work on Jacob. God let Jacob experience deceit from his future father-in-law. That would cost Jacob fourteen years of his life. God let Jacob experience the fear of Esau's wrath. God sent an angel to wrestle with Jacob and bring him to his senses. God didn't give up on Jacob. God shaped Jacob into who Jacob needed to be.

I'm glad God doesn't give up too easily. All of us who follow God have a calling from him. I want to be the man God has called me to be. I know that part of that means I need to live the life he's called me to live. Yet over and over again I find myself falling short. I don't measure up to my own standards, much less his.

His mercies are long, as is his patience. In steadfast love, he continues to mold and shape me, in spite of my own proclivities to sin. I am thankful for his mercies and want to do better.

Lord, thank you for your kindness and mercy. Mold me and make me after your will so I might serve you better. In your name, amen.

FEBRUARY 11

Now Esau hated Jacob because of the blessing with which his father had blessed him, and Esau said to himself, "The days of mourning for my father are approaching; then I will kill my brother Jacob." (Gen. 27:41)

There are certain things I hate (liver and onions). There are also people I don't like, but I try not to hate them! Somewhere there is a line, and in the life of a follower of God, there is no room for hatred of a person.

Esau hated his younger twin, Jacob. Some would say deservedly so. In all their interactions we read about, Jacob was never kind to Esau. He tricked him out of something very valuable; he deceived his father to gain another advantage; he conspired with his mother to Esau's detriment; and he was by and large despicable to Esau. Esau's hatred ran deep. He was bent on vengeance on his twin, but love for his father was staying that revenge until after his father's death.

If we read the story to the conclusion, we would see that almost fifteen years passed before Esau got the chance for revenge. In that time, God turned the tables on Jacob. Jacob was deceived by his father-in-law, Jacob was put through a great deal of family turmoil, and Jacob was deprived of his family support system for much of that. Jacob also encountered God and began a relationship with him. When Jacob next saw Esau, Jacob was filled with fear. Jacob sent gift upon gift ahead of his encounter, hoping to appease his brother. Jacob took precautions with his family, in case his brother's hatred burned hot enough for murder. But as the events unfolded, it became apparent that God was not only working in Jacob's life but had been at work in Esau's heart as well. Esau didn't kill his brother. There wasn't even a fight. Esau showed love and compassion and figured out a way the two could live in harmony.

Live long enough, and most everyone will have people in their lives who deserve being hated. Yet that is not the goal. We need the work of God in two directions. We need God to work in the lives of those who deserve the worst, turning them into something better. We also need God to work in our hearts, melting the hardness of hatred into understanding and even compassion. After all, I suspect if we could remove our filters, we would see that we have all done things worthy of being hated. We should have the same mercy on others that we need for ourselves.

Lord, forgive me for the ways I have mistreated others, and help me to show others that same forgiveness. In your name, amen.

FEBRUARY 12

Jacob came to a certain place and stayed there that night, because the sun had set. Taking one of the stones of the place, he put it under his head and lay down in that place to sleep. And he dreamed, and behold, there was a ladder set up on the earth, and the top of it reached to heaven. And behold, the angels of God were ascending and descending on it! And behold, the LORD *stood above it and said, "I am the* LORD, *the God of Abraham your father and the God of Isaac. . . . Behold, I am with you and will keep you wherever you go, and will bring you back to this land. For I will not leave you until I have done what I have promised you." Then Jacob awoke from his sleep and said, "Surely the* LORD *is in this place, and I did not know it." (Gen.* 28:11–16)

If you were to take a sheet of paper and pen, and make a list of things you need right now, what would be on it? Maybe it would be financial help, a car, a job, or the like. Maybe it would be better health. Maybe at the top of your list would be conquering some destructive lifestyle. Perhaps it would be mending torn relationships or a broken heart. Whatever our needs are and however we list them, this passage should give each of us a jolt. We need a better vision of God. We need him front and center in our lives.

Jacob was on the run from his brother. He had done his brother wrong, over and over, and his brother had reached a breaking point where he was planning on killing Jacob. While he was on the run, Jacob slept out under the stars and had an encounter with God. God spoke to Jacob in a dream. God told Jacob that he had plans for him and that he would not depart from him until those plans were successfully completed.

That changed things for Jacob. It should change things for all of us. God wishes to meet with everyone, albeit not always in a dream! In God's mercy, not based on our deserving character or actions, God has sought to establish a relationship where we can commune with him, seek his plans, and work with him to see them to fruition.

This was personal for Jacob. It was a private encounter he had with the living God. It wasn't a theological discussion. It wasn't an intellectual deliberation. It was a real encounter with a real God. I want that. It goes to the top of my "need list." Encountering God will change everything else on that list. I will have his hand in my life to conquer sin, to teach me love, to shift my priorities, and to teach me discipline necessary for financial health. He will strengthen me for any physical ordeal. I need God now.

Lord, please come into my life and give me direction, strength, love, and peace. Lead me into a real and daily walk with you. In your name, amen.

FEBRUARY 13

Then Jacob made a vow, saying, "If God will be with me and will keep me in this way that I go, and will give me bread to eat and clothing to wear, so that I come again to my father's house in peace, then the LORD shall be my God." (Gen. 28:20-21)

This passage of Scripture has always bothered me. Now that might not be a good thing to say, but give me a chance to explain. I am not a fan of people making deals with God. "God, you give me this and that, and I will follow you." Or, "God, you heal my loved one, and I will do what you want." I think that as we grow in our relationship with God, we move to a place of "God, I will follow you regardless."

This passage is instructive not because it affirms the "deal-making" approach in relating to God but rather because it offers insight into why and how we move into a more mature walk with God. At the time of this passage, Jacob has lived a life that seems woefully short of personal encounters with the divine. Jacob's reputation was not that of a godly man but of a swindler, conspirator, and deceiver. Whether swindling his brother out of an inheritance or conspiring with his mother to deceive his father, Jacob has not modeled righteousness in any sense. Then came his first detailed encounter with God. In a dream, he saw the God of heaven relating to him on earth. In his dream, God's messengers came down from heaven right where he was, returning from him to the Lord. This was true relationship, back and forth communication between God and Jacob.

God offered his promises to Jacob, but they were never conditioned on one thing or another. God simply declared that he would bless Jacob and work through Jacob to establish his plans. Jacob awoke, realized it was God, and then pitched his deal. This was Jacob in an early stage of faith and relationship, not a mature Jacob who had walked for years with God.

Over time, however, Jacob's relationship with God changed. Jacob was never the perfect man—husband or father—but almost two decades later, when Jacob is returning to his homeland, we see a different Jacob. Jacob is scared to return to his brother who had vowed to kill him. Jacob goes nonetheless because God has told him to. Jacob in his fear tells God he knows he is unworthy of God's love and faithfulness but seeks God's help anyway. This maturity is a touching departure from his young, brash, "let's make a deal" days. That is what comes from a mature walk with God.

Today's passage doesn't teach me to make a deal with God. It teaches me to grow closer to him, maturing in my walk.

Lord, may I learn more about you and grow in my walk with you. In your name, amen.

FEBRUARY 14

Jacob loved Rachel. And he said, "I will serve you seven years for your younger daughter Rachel." Laban said, "It is better that I give her to you than that I should give her to any other man; stay with me." So Jacob served seven years for Rachel, and they seemed to him but a few days because of the love he had for her. (Gen. 29:18–20)

Have you noticed how time flies when you are doing something you love or something that brings great joy? There is a pleasure even in work when the work is done in love.

In today's passage, Jacob has found Rachel to be the love of his life. He wants to marry her, but in his culture, he had to pay a price for her. The price he negotiates is seven years of service to his future father-in-law. Seven years is a long time for an engagement! But to Jacob, the time flew by. He was working for the girl of his dreams. The years seemed only a few days.

The Jewish rabbi and Christian apostle Paul wrote to a church about their "labor produced by love" (1 Thess. 1:3). His idea was rooted in the recognition that our best work before God is work we do out of love, not obligation.

My Greek professor Dr. Harvey Floyd fondly spoke of this passage, telling of a time when he and his wife visited ex-students in Japan. After a visit in one town, they were headed to the train station, and the ex-student insisted on not only taking them to the station but riding the train to their next destination to make sure they got off at the right stop. As Dr. Floyd declined the offer, the student said, "I must go. It is my duty!" Later, the Floyds visited another student. The second student also accompanied the Floyds to the train station, boarded the train, and rode to deliver them to their next destination. As Dr. Floyd tried to stop the second student, the student explained, "Dr. Floyd, this is my *pleasure*." Dr. Floyd told us how different that felt to him. Should anyone ever doubt the difference, he explained we would learn it if we told our spouses we were kind out of "duty" rather than "pleasure."

There is something strong about love that stirs up our best. We can serve and work in love with time flying by. It is our pleasure, not our duty. That centers me today on my life before God. Do I live right before him out of duty or love? Do I find his love for me so overwhelming that I respond in love? If not, I need to learn more of his love!

Lord, you have loved me and blessed me in ways I can't begin to fathom. I want to serve you in joy and love, blessing you with my life today. In your name, amen.

FEBRUARY 15

And Jacob told Rachel that he was her father's kinsman, and that he was Rebekah's son, and she ran and told her father. As soon as Laban heard the news about Jacob, his sister's son, he ran to meet him and embraced him and kissed him and brought him to his house. Jacob told Laban all these things, and Laban said to him, "Surely you are my bone and my flesh!" And he stayed with him a month. (Gen. 29:12–14)

What do you do with really good news? Have you ever had news so great, so exciting, that you burn with desire to share it?

Look carefully at today's passage. It zips along with a great Hebrew word, *rutz*. *Rutz* is Hebrew for "run." Sometimes people run in fear, but not in this passage. This is running with good news—news so exciting, so great, that people run to share it! Rachel is going about her ordinary day, doing her ordinary chores, when totally out of the blue, she finds this good-looking young fellow who is coming back with family news. Rachel doesn't wait until the end of the day to share the news back home. She doesn't walk back home. She runs home and tells her father, Laban. Upon hearing the news, Laban is excited. Laban doesn't send a messenger asking Jacob to come join the family for a meal. He doesn't send his daughter back with the invitation. Laban goes himself, and he *runs*.

Some things are worth running for. In a sense, even God runs on occasion! Two thousand years after these events, Jesus, a great-great (keep adding greats) grandson of Jacob, told a story about a man with two sons. One son asked his father for his inheritance early and, taking it, left home and squandered it living for the moment. After running through all his money, the now destitute son was living in squalor, a wasted life. The son decides to return to his father, knowing his father's workers have better living conditions than he does. With a humble speech in hand, the son sets out to apologize, explain his unworthiness for anything, and seek to work in his father's house. Seeing his son from a distance, the father *runs* to embrace, forgive, and restore his son. The father explains to his older son, "My son who was lost has come home!"

This parable of Jesus was describing God's reaction to his children who turn their hearts and lives away from rebellion and back to God. This is a time of great news and rejoicing. This is news so great that in the story, God runs to embrace the lost. I like this kind of running! I want to run and share great news. I want to run to God, and I want to run to others to speak of God. Today I run!

Lord, thank you for your compelling and capturing love. Give me feet to run and tell others. In your name, amen.

FEBRUARY 16

In the morning, behold, it was Leah! And Jacob said to Laban, "What is this you have done to me? Did I not serve with you for Rachel? Why then have you deceived me?" (Gen. 29:25)

I remember in the halls of Coronado High School when my best friend, Kevin Parker, introduced me to the phrase, "What goes around comes around." I found this humorous and true then, and I often find it no less true today. It was akin to what a lawyer friend of mine, John Gilbert, told me later in reference to how lawyers treat each other: "It is a short road that doesn't have a turn in it!"

Today's passage is inserted into the story of Jacob's interesting life. Jacob was a trickster and deceiver. He had tricked his brother Esau out of his birthright, trading the famished Esau a bowl of stew for his inheritance rights. Jacob had gone so far as manipulating and deceiving his father into giving him Esau's blessing. Jacob did this by wearing goat skins so his blind, old father would think he was Esau, the outdoor hunter. This latter deception was done with the oversight of Jacob's mother, who acted as his accomplice.

In a real instance of Kevin's Coronado Karma, what went around for Jacob came around to Jacob. Jacob got tricked and deceived by his own family member! Jacob had worked seven years for Rachel, the daughter of Laban. Finally, the wedding came. We don't know how much Jacob had to drink at the wedding, but in the darkness of night, in the tent of consummation, Jacob was given Leah, Rachel's older sister, rather than Rachel. Jacob awoke the next morning to find himself the victim of deception.

This story sets out a real principle often found in life. To put it another way, "You reap what you sow." It happens in the garden, and it happens in life. If one sows seed of dissension and anger, one will find anger in life. If one sows seeds of joy and love, one will find a harvest of joy and love. The implications of this are profound. Identify what you want in your life, and sow the seeds to produce that crop.

This is my choice today. I want to focus on it. I want to make choices where I treat others the way I'd like to be treated. I want to exhibit traits that will bear good fruit. Will it always happen immediately? Of course not. It might take time. But I should not be deceived, because what goes around comes around.

Lord, help me be attentive to what I say and do. Give me wisdom to see the fruit that will flow from my actions. Let me sow seeds of your love and kindness in my day. In your name, amen.

FEBRUARY 17

"For you had little before I came, and it has increased abundantly, and the LORD has blessed you wherever I turned." (Gen. 30:30)

There is a strong temptation in our world to place oneself in the center. I might not say, "It's all about me," but my life often betrays a different truth. A small verse like today's serves as a powerful reminder that we don't belong there.

Today's passage is selected from the Jacob and Laban story. Jacob served his father-in-law, Laban, for fourteen years, seven for each daughter he had married, Leah and Rachel. That doesn't mean the years were to be wage free, but the principal reward was the right to marry. Those were fruitful years for Laban. As Jacob served him, Laban saw great wealth grow from little investment. Under Jacob's care, the flocks multiplied, and with that came food, trade, and many other blessings.

There came a time when Jacob was ready to return home with his wife and belongings. Laban didn't want Jacob to leave. Laban knew what had happened under Jacob's oversight and didn't want to lose it. Laban had a good thing going with Jacob under his thumb, but Jacob insisted. The only thing to be negotiated was the price. How much would Laban assign to the work Jacob had given? Laban placed the negotiations into Jacob's lap, telling Jacob to set the price. Jacob responded that God was the one behind the blessings, and Jacob would let the Lord set the price. The drama of the story unfolds with Laban trying to manipulate things to keep the price low, but ultimately the God who had blessed Laban through Jacob also blessed Jacob in spite of Laban.

God can use you and me to bless others. They may not always be deserving, but if we put everyone under a microscope, we will likely find no one is deserving. There is power in seeing that God has placed us where we are today, empowering us with the gifts and skills we have, so that he can bless others through us.

This is what we are to be about. This world doesn't revolve around us. It revolves as God set it in orbit. Our lives should center not on us but on God and his plans. As we work, as we move the chess pieces in life, we need to see that God blesses us so that we can be a blessing to others. Success is not ours. It is His. And it should be put to work for His purposes.

Lord, please use me today to bless others. Make me your instrument of blessing. Then, Lord, may I readily give you the credit for the blessings! In your name, amen.

FEBRUARY 18

"Your father has cheated me and changed my wages ten times. But God did not permit him to harm me." (Gen. 31:7)

RED ALERT: We live in a world where many people—MANY PEOPLE—are driven and controlled by an obsession with money. It will drive them to do things they shouldn't, to treat people in ways that are wrong, and to see things from a skewed perspective. It can mess up our own thoughts and actions as well as those of others. The only one immune to the magnetic pull of money is God. God has no need for money. For him, it is abundant and a tool for usage, nothing more.

Today's passage may center on events four thousand years ago, but the same story happens daily today. Just change the names. Jacob worked for Laban. Laban figured out ways to use his position and power to be unfair economically to Jacob. I'm sure Laban had excuses. I suspect Laban saw it as "fair." The mind can come up with all sorts of reasons to cheat another.

I have seen this. In the legal business, I have seen it in cases that walked through my door where one person or one business has felt cheated by another. I have also experienced it firsthand when others have changed agreements with me, figuring out ways to alter the deal or pay less than owed. I knew a man who once had a walk with the Lord. He was active in his local church congregation and taught his family to be as well. Yet he entered into a business deal with a well-regarded member of the church and believed he was cheated. He never went back to church. There were multiple levels of tragedy from this business deal gone bad. How we react in faith when cheated is as important as how we treat others in business arrangements.

There are two sides of this coin. I have seen that God reigns above. His eyes watch and he sees what happens. He doesn't promise to ensure no one is cheated. He doesn't work as the heavenly arbiter and enforcer of amounts due and owing. But he does ensure that even when someone cheats his children, his children are still able to walk in God's will. God knows what we need to do the things he calls us to do, and no one will be able to cheat us of the resources we need to achieve those good works.

So, watch! You will see people cheat. But you will also see God protect his children. The question for us is, How do we treat others and honor God when we are cheated?

Lord, help me treat people fairly and honestly. Please protect me from others so I may do your will in my life. In your name, amen.

FEBRUARY 19

Then Jacob was greatly afraid and distressed. He divided the people who were with him, and the flocks and herds and camels, into two camps, thinking, "If Esau comes to the one camp and attacks it, then the camp that is left will escape." And Jacob said, "O God . . . Please deliver me from the hand of my brother, from the hand of Esau, for I fear him, that he may come and attack me, the mothers with the children." (Gen. 32:7-11)

When I was young, our preacher, Joe Barnett, delivered a sermon where he taught us to live as if our actions determined the outcome but pray as if our actions had nothing to do with the outcome. It was based on the idea that a ship's rudder only works if the ship is moving. God will come to our rescue, and God will be our strength and protection, but God does so in conjunction with our actions. We are not inanimate puppets whose strings God pulls.

We see this in today's passage. Jacob is petrified over what is going to happen when his brother Esau sees him. There is every chance that Esau will kill Jacob and take all of Jacob's possessions. After all, Jacob had his start taking from Esau what was rightfully Esau's. Jacob's plan is twofold. First, he implements the safest and best strategy he can. Second, he prays to God for deliverance. This is what I was taught when I was younger.

We face many different difficulties in our lives. Some are simple, others complex, but we often find ourselves struggling to figure out how to live and what to do. In those times, I find the twofold approach appropriate. I am constantly seeking God in prayer and wanting his guidance, his strength, his wisdom, and his protection. But in conjunction with those prayers, I am trying to determine the best course of action.

I know that course needs to be in conjunction with my prayers. God won't send me in directions of unholiness. He will want me to follow his direction and instructions. But within that framework, I need to trust that God will answer my prayers and I need to make my best decisions confident that he is guiding me. Proverbs offers the assurance that if we trust God and acknowledge him in all our ways, he will *make* our paths straight (Prov. 3:5-6).

We can trust that he is at work leading us and guiding us, not pulling our strings. So when faced with trouble and turmoil, make holy decisions as you act the best you can, but pray as if there's nothing you can do. Then watch God work!

Lord, thank you for caring and being interested in my life. May I live it for you. In your name, amen.

FEBRUARY 20

"O Lord . . . I am not worthy of the least of all the deeds of steadfast love and all the faithfulness that you have shown to your servant, for with only my staff I crossed this Jordan, and now I have become two camps." (Gen. 32:9–10)

Prayer is a lot of things, but one aspect of prayer is how it serves as a mirror. When we pray in earnest, truly baring our souls to God, we reflect our attitudes in life. Are we self-centered or other-centered? Are we proud or contrite? Does God reign as Lord of our lives, or do we see him more as our servant?

Today's passage comes from the story of Jacob and Esau. The twins have been separated for about two decades. When they had last been together, Esau was breathing death threats against his brother because Jacob had robbed Esau through multiple deceptions. Over the two decades, Jacob had found God, grown through his faith, and become a new and better person. Jacob had no idea what had happened to Esau. Had the killing anger smoldered over the years? Was it more intense or less? Jacob didn't know but was about to find out. Jacob was returning to Esau's neighborhood and was petrified. Jacob planned how to return, dividing his camp and possessions into two in hopes of saving one. Jacob also fell before the Lord in prayer.

Jacob's prayer reflected a contrite spirit and a recognition of his own sinfulness and inadequacies. It is a touching prayer that all of us can and should pray. "I am not worthy of the least" of all the good deeds God has given to me. It reminds me of the answer to "How are you doing?"—"Better than I deserve!"

Jacob saw the great blessings of God as he went from having nothing to having the resources he had split into two camps. God had been more than faithful to Jacob in spite of Jacob's unworthiness. Jacob's humble, contrite, and appreciative heart was reflected in his prayers.

I want that heart. I want those prayers. I want to see that my blessings have come from God and his faithfulness. I want to be able to pray thanks and to seek his protection in dark times. I want the assurance that the God who has been faithful to me, even when I didn't deserve it, will continue to be faithful to me today, though I still don't deserve it. Such is our amazing God!

Lord, I am unworthy of the care and blessings you show me. Please accept the gratitude of my heart, and help my feeble efforts to show you my love. In your name, amen.

FEBRUARY 21

So he stayed there that night, and from what he had with him he took a present for his brother Esau . . . For he thought, "I may appease him with the present that goes ahead of me, and afterward I shall see his face. Perhaps he will accept me." (Gen. 32:13, 20)

I have friends in my life who are amazing gift givers. Their minds are bent that way. You might say gift-giving is their love language. They express and receive love by giving gifts. Sometimes the motivation for giving may be more selfish than others, but there is an immense power in giving gifts, especially when the motives are pure!

Today's passage isn't built around the idea of giving, but it is an integral part of the story. Jacob is reuniting with his twin, Esau, after twenty years of separation. They separated with Esau furious and vowing to kill Jacob. In a real sense, Jacob had stolen blessings and more from his older twin, and desiring revenge fueled Esau's anger. At the point where their reuniting was imminent, Jacob decided to send a gift to Esau. We are not sure whether the gift was to be seen as a replacement for what Jacob stole or whether Jacob was trying to show that his brother was the superior and Jacob the servant. Either way, it was a gift seeking to soften Esau's wrath.

There is a subtlety in the Hebrew original that our translations miss. The word used for "gift" is not the ordinary word. It is *minchah*, a word used in the sacrifices of Israel for the cereal offering. The gift that Jacob was offering Esau was a sacrifice seeking to restore a relationship that was broken. (This is not to say that the text implies that Jacob sacrificed as one would sacrifice to God. This is a nonreligious usage of the idea of sacrifice!)

Gifts work wonders in the heart of the giver and the one receiving. When we give gifts, we show people we are thinking of them. We show fondness. We demonstrate the importance of the recipients to us, especially when the gift is sacrificial.

I want to be a giver of gifts. I want others to know that I think of them, care for them, and have their best interests at heart. Our God is a gift-giving God. He models the absolute best in gift giving. The New Testament writer James affirmed that every good gift comes from God (Jas. 1:17). The Christian sees in the incarnation of Jesus, and in his role as Messiah, that we have the greatest gift of all, given with the purest motives. God seeks to pay the penalty for humanity's sin through the atoning sacrifice of Jesus Messiah who brings us into peace with God.

I am inspired. To whom can I give a gift today?

Lord, thank you for all the many blessings and love I have from you. In your name, amen.

FEBRUARY 22

The same night Jacob arose and took his two wives, his two female servants, and his eleven children, and crossed the ford of the Jabbok. He took them and sent them across the stream, and everything else that he had. And Jacob was left alone. And a man wrestled with him until the breaking of the day. When the man saw that he did not prevail against Jacob, he touched his hip socket, and Jacob's hip was put out of joint as he wrestled with him. Then he said, "Let me go, for the day has broken." But Jacob said, "I will not let you go unless you bless me." And he said to him, "What is your name?" And he said, "Jacob." Then he said, "Your name shall no longer be called Jacob, but Israel, for you have striven with God and with men, and have prevailed." Then Jacob asked him, "Please tell me your name." But he said, "Why is it that you ask my name?" And there he blessed him. So Jacob called the name of the place Peniel, saying, "For I have seen God face to face, and yet my life has been delivered." The sun rose upon him as he passed Peniel, limping because of his hip. (Gen. 32:22–31)

I have put this whole story into today's devotion because it reads chock-full of mystery. Jacob is alone at night, a dark time of unseen and unknown things in the era before modern lighting. Jacob's mind is not expecting this encounter. Jacob's fear is his coming encounter with Esau. That was one of life or death. In the midst of his huge concern, Jacob goes off by himself and encounters the unexpected. A man comes to "wrestle" (more literally, "to kick up the dust"!) with Jacob. The Hebrew word for "wrestle" sounds a lot like the word for the stream (Jabbok) and also puns on Jacob's name. The place, the struggle, and Jacob are all intertwined in the narrative.

The "man" does not exactly defeat Jacob. They wrestle until dawn, and Jacob seems to hold his own. Then, in a bizarre twist, the man touches Jacob's hip, and the hip fails. It is apparent the man could have done this all along but was wrestling for Jacob's sake, not out of an inability to win. The man tells Jacob to let him go, but Jacob has fought all night and wants a blessing before releasing the man. The man gives a blessing, and as Jacob limps away, he realizes that he has struggled with God and found deliverance.

This mysterious story speaks to our encounters with God. At times, they have an otherworldly element to them that is mysterious and hard to explain. Yet from them, we learn that God is in control, and whatever we face, we face with him. Even our limps and inadequacies are part of the package deal of being in God's hands. This was a mysterious encounter with God that gave Jacob what he needed. It's hard to explain, but that is often the way with our God.

Lord, please touch me and make me who I need to be to serve you. In your name, amen.

FEBRUARY 23

And he said to him, "What is your name?" And he said, "Jacob." Then he said, "Your name shall no longer be called Jacob, but Israel, for you have striven with God and with men, and have prevailed." Then Jacob asked him, "Please tell me your name." But he said, "Why is it that you ask my name?" And there he blessed him. (Gen. 32:27–29)

How often have you called God to account? Have you ever challenged him and demanded an explanation for his actions? In this section of Jacob's encounter with God at the wrestling match of the Jabbok (see yesterday's devotion), we find a simple truth: we answer to God; he doesn't answer to us.

Jacob has spent the lonely, dark night wrestling with a man, but his real struggle has been with God. With the night over, the struggle is finished. The man tells Jacob that through his struggle with God, Jacob has found the victory he needs in his life. The man asks Jacob his name, and Jacob replies. Jacob's name spoke to his character. His name's meaning and his life in his younger days were one and the same. Jacob was a deceiver. Jacob was wily and deceptive, supplanting his older brother in the family order. The man tells Jacob that his name is to be changed. No longer is Jacob a deceiver. He is now "Israel," referencing his struggle with God. "Israel" derives from the idea of God (*El*) fighting (*ysra*). God took Jacob the deceiver and turned him into one who not only would struggle with God, but one for whom God would fight.

Then we read the reciprocal request. Just as the man had asked Jacob his name, having answered, Jacob asked for the name of the man. The man, who the story makes clear is God's messenger or angel, doesn't reply. We answer to God. God doesn't answer to us. What God does instead is take control of our destiny. God takes our name, our character, and changes it. We struggle in the change, but we find at the end that we are precisely what God needs us to be for his fight.

The fight is not ours; it is God's. He doesn't owe us an account for his actions. He is God. But we can rest assured in faith that while he may not justify himself to us, he will have his will done and will fight for us, even when we fight against him. Our God is a God of personal attention to us, but he is no less God. We must never forget that.

Lord, I do struggle at times with life. I wonder why you have allowed things to be as they are. I struggle with why bad things happen. In the midst of all of life's ups and downs, may I never forget that you are God, and may I walk in your fight with your victory. In your name, amen.

FEBRUARY 24

And Jacob lifted up his eyes and looked, and behold, Esau was coming, and four hundred men with him. . . . He himself went on before them, bowing himself to the ground seven times, until he came near to his brother. (Gen. 33:1, 3)

Today's passage continues the saga of Jacob reuniting with his twin, Esau. Twenty years earlier, before Jacob fled from Esau's murderous rage, Jacob had stolen Esau's blessing from their blind, ailing father, Isaac. By pretending to be Esau, Jacob got Isaac to bless him instead. The blessing included, "Be lord over your brothers, and may your mother's sons bow down to you" (Gen. 27:29). Through deceit and trickery, Jacob had gotten his father's prayers that Esau would bow down to him! Instead, we are seeing the exact opposite.

We can get a good glimpse into the custom of bowing down in Jacob's day through reading the Amarna letters. Written on clay tablets in the mid-fourteenth century BC, these letters repeatedly speak of the submissive bowing before the overlord seven times. Found over fifty times in the letters, the sevenfold bowing was an act of humility and submission.

When Jacob came back to his brother, he didn't come in power to lord his position and destiny over Esau. Jacob came in humility. There is power in humility. I am not speaking of being a doormat for people to abuse but rather of recognizing the inherent value of others. If we see others as important, we no longer act out of conceit or selfish ambition. We then look not only to our own interests but to those of others.

The Bible speaks over and over about the importance of humility. In passages in the Hebrew Bible as well as the New Testament Scriptures, we read of the importance of humbling ourselves before God, with the assurance he will lift us up (1 Pet. 5:6). Proverbs repeatedly speaks of humility as coming before honor, whereas destruction visits the haughty or arrogant (e.g., Prov. 18:12). The prophets urge the people to seek righteousness and humility (Zeph. 2:3). God "opposes the proud but gives grace to the humble" (1 Pet. 5:5). The psalmist declares of God, "You save a humble people, but the haughty eyes you bring down" (Ps. 18:27).

At its core, a humble heart climbs out of the self-centered narcissism of the age and sees value in others. As I more truly see God and the world, I come into a better personal perspective. It isn't all about me.

Lord, give me a humble spirit and contrite heart. In your name, amen.

FEBRUARY 25

"I have seen your face, which is like seeing the face of God." (Gen. 33:10)

When you think of God, what comes to mind? A harsh and judgmental God? A kind and loving God? A laid-back, nonchalant God? A God focused and attentive to detail? A forgiving God? A "gotcha!" God? A God who has better things on his plate than being tuned in to your life? A God who revolves himself around you? An amorphous God that we can't know or understand but who likely exists? Today's passage speaks to God's divine love and forgiveness.

The passage comes from Jacob's expression of his fear about reuniting with his twin brother, Esau. Esau had every legitimate reason to hate Jacob. Jacob stole and swindled his way into many of Esau's valuable rights and possessions, and Esau knew it. They had been separated for twenty years while Esau's anger could have smoldered and grown. As their reuniting was about to occur, Jacob sent gifts ahead to mollify Esau. The Hebrew word chosen in the narrative for "gifts" is a word used in sacrificial offerings. The writer doesn't want us to lose the recognition that Jacob was giving those gifts hoping that Esau would forgive him (as a brother; not offering a divine forgiveness). These were gifts that could be seen as a repayment to cover Jacob's earlier wrongful taking. At first, Esau rejected the gifts. The story doesn't tell us why. It might be the culture to say "no" several times to see if the giver is insistent and genuine in the gift. It might be that Esau had no need for the gifts and wanted to show his own resources. Regardless, the story does make clear that Esau was forgiving Jacob of his past. Esau held a grudge no longer. The righteous anger that Esau had was gone, and forgiveness and restoration were there for the two estranged brothers.

In this sense, Jacob says that seeing his brother and his reaction was like seeing the face of God. Jacob had wrestled with God. He had lived a life estranged from God, in direct rebellion from what God expected, and over time he had come to rely on God. Jacob had experienced first-hand God's forgiveness, guidance, protection, and provision. He knew it was never deserved but was critical to life. Jacob's journey spiritually was as long as his two-decade journey physically. Jacob was a changed man.

This is how God's divine love works. God watches. God is involved in our lives. He knows what we do and the motives in our hearts. He is a just God who pays attention. But he is also a God of forgiveness. He wants to restore our estranged relationship with him. This is the significance of the Christian understanding of Christ's sacrifice. A just God paid the just price to set our sin aside and move past estrangement into a loving relationship. That is our God!

Lord, thank you for your divine love and forgiveness. In your name, amen.

FEBRUARY 26

Now Israel loved Joseph more than any other of his sons, because he was the son of his old age. And he made him a robe of many colors. But when his brothers saw that their father loved him more than all his brothers, they hated him and could not speak peacefully to him. Now Joseph had a dream, and when he told it to his brothers they hated him even more. (Gen. 37:3-5)

Life can be hard. People don't always make wise choices, and people don't always treat others as they should. Jealousy and favoritism can both sow seeds of discord and trouble. There is a reassurance, however, that regardless of how others choose to treat us, as long as we walk in God's will, God will work out his plans and callings in our lives. No one can thwart God and his plans.

In this part of the Joseph story, Joseph's father ("Israel") is shown playing favorites among his twelve sons, loving Joseph more than the others. Jacob/Israel showed the world his favoritism through the gifts he gave Joseph, notably a special robe. It was a visible sign of special treatment everyone would recognize whenever Joseph chose to wear it.

The favoritism of the father incited hatred among Joseph's brothers. As the story unfolds, the brothers' hatred grew as Joseph told them about one of his dreams. Joseph dreamed that all the brothers were in a field binding up sheaves of grain. Joseph's sheaves stood upright, and the sheaves of all his brothers bowed down paying homage to Joseph's sheaves. The message was clear: Joseph, the young brother, would be honored and obeyed by his older brothers. The reaction was very negative. They hated him even more for his dreams and for his words.

There is a play on words in the Hebrew. What is translated as "even more" in "they hated him even more" is a play on Joseph's name. Joseph's name in Hebrew conveys the idea of adding. It reflects God's call on his life, because during a time of life-threatening famine, Joseph would collect and add his birth family to the adopted position he attains in Egypt. The brothers would grow to be glad. But the brothers saw it differently at first. They saw his name as appropriate for adding to their hatred, bringing it to even deeper levels. They "Josephed" their hatred, meaning they added to it more and more.

The hatred didn't thwart God's ability to grow Joseph into his name. In part through the brothers' mean actions, Joseph rose to a position where he could add his family to his home in Egypt, saving all their lives. No one can thwart God's plans!

Lord, may I walk in your will and see your will done! In your name, amen.

Joseph's brothers "sold him to the Ishmaelites for twenty shekels of silver. . . . Then they took Joseph's robe and slaughtered a goat and dipped the robe in the blood. And they sent the robe of many colors and brought it to their father [Jacob] and said, 'This we have found; please identify whether it is your son's robe or not.'" (Gen. 37:28, 31–32)

The Jewish rabbi and Christian apostle Paul wrote, "You reap what you sow" (Gal. 6:7). Four thousand years ago, it was "The sins of the father are passed on to his children" (Exod. 34:7). Genesis shows this problem over and over, challenging us to break the cycles that can too easily continue in our own lives.

Today's passage is one of many examples in Genesis where sin comes back to haunt, generations later. Joseph's father, Jacob, had used a goat skin to deceive his blind father, Isaac, into believing that he was actually his brother, Esau. Through that deception, Isaac was able to improperly receive blessings that belonged to his older brother. Decades and decades passed. Jacob had grown old and had a dozen sons. Those sons didn't all get along, any more than Jacob had with his brother, Esau. Jacob favored his son Joseph, just as his mother had favored him while his father had favored the older Esau.

Now, in his old age, a goat is used to deceive Jacob, only with a twist. It isn't simply that wearing a goat skin and smelling like the fields made a blind father think he was dealing with a different son. This time, the goat was slaughtered and the blood was smeared on the special garment that belonged to the favored son, Joseph. The garment set Joseph apart. It was a special gift from his father. Upon seeing the garment in blood, and being told it was found in that condition, Jacob became the deceived father. Convinced that wild animals had killed his dearest son, Jacob went into mourning. For over a decade, Jacob lived out his old age, believing his son dead. He found out the truth only shortly before passing away, getting to reunite with his son in Egypt.

These stories make me sad. I know that bad actions beget bad actions. I know that sin begets sin. I can see visibly that how I behave affects others. All parents know the way they rear their children will affect how their children parent. I want to live more carefully, more deliberately. Taking this lesson to heart, I want to thoughtfully consider my actions more than ever before. I want to break the cycle of sowing and reaping, both for my sake and that of those I love.

Lord, please help me be careful in life. Let me make choices that reflect your love and goodness. Forgive me my sins, and help me make things right. In your name, amen.

FEBRUARY 28

Judah said to his brothers, "What profit is it if we kill our brother and conceal his blood? Come, let us sell him to the Ishmaelites, and let not our hand be upon him, for he is our brother, our own flesh." And his brothers listened to him. Then Midianite traders passed by. And they drew Joseph up and lifted him out of the pit, and sold him to the Ishmaelites for twenty shekels of silver. They took Joseph to Egypt. (Gen. 37:26–28)

In life, negative things that will happen to us. Some we may deserve, but many we won't. They may be minor, unexpected curveballs that throw us for a loop. But sometimes, there are much worse things, which we should never have to endure. When these things do occur, we should always remember that our God is able to take the worst and turn it into the best. Even when bad things happen to good people, God can use that for his good purposes as well as for ours.

Today's story illustrates the point well. Joseph's brothers hate him intensely. They finally decide that the occasion is right to kill him. Whether they were drunk or simply fueled by their intense hatred, the story doesn't say. But they are planning to leave Joseph in a pit to die, until Judah suggests another plan. "Why kill the brat, when we can sell him into slavery? It gets him out of our hair, *and* we can make money off him!" The brothers agree and pull Joseph from the pit. They sell him for twenty shekels, an amount ancient records indicate was the going rate for a male slave age five to twenty. Divided among ten brothers, who would generally make eight shekels a year as shepherds, that became a rich bonus. Abused by his brothers and torn from the rest of his family, Joseph ultimately becomes a slave in Egypt.

The story isn't over; it is just beginning. By selling Joseph into Egypt, his brothers have apparently disposed of him for good, but unwittingly they have actually helped the fulfillment of his dreams. Joseph had dreamed that he would be raised up over his older siblings. In his dreams, Joseph had seen that even his parents would bow to him. Joseph rose to a high place of authority in Egypt, and he foresaw the need for a savings program that Egypt would need to survive an intense seven-year famine. Joseph's family would seek refuge in Egypt during that famine, and decades after this fraternal abuse, Joseph was able to save the lives of all his kin.

What his brothers meant for ill, God used for good. God molded Joseph into the man needed for a special task no one else was fit to do. Joseph was where he needed to be and who he needed to be to do God's will, in spite of the horrible treatment. No one is going to get the best of God.

Lord, protect those I love, but even more, use the events in this life to bring about your will. Help us to see life through eyes of faith. In your name, amen.

FEBRUARY 29

But Er, Judah's firstborn, was wicked in the sight of the Lord, and the Lord put him to death. (Gen. 38:7)

Everyone has a closet where they keep things they wish kept out of sight. The expression of "having skeletons in the closet" references people with dark secrets they want to keep hidden. For some, the closet may not harbor skeletons, but it at least has some out-of-date clothes! In other words, we all have things we'd like to keep to ourselves, without letting them be seen by the larger world. Although this is part of life, we must never be deceived into thinking we can hide anything from God.

Today's passage makes this point in a subtle and fascinating way. The passage, on its face, at least in English, speaks of Er, the son of Judah and grandson of Jacob. Er was "wicked" or "evil" in God's eyes, and God put him to death. There is not much to this passage in the English translation, but we unlock its significance if we consider the Hebrew original.

"Er" in Hebrew comes from a root word meaning "one blinding another." "Er" is formed by two Hebrew letters: ע and ר. Look at them for a moment. These are important because the Hebrew text reads that while Er was one who might try to keep others from seeing, God saw him for who he was. Er could not blind God. The Hebrew text says God saw Er as wicked. "Wicked" or "evil" is a palindrome when combined with "Er." It is the same two letters, just spelled backward! "Er" is ע and ר while "wicked" is ר and ע.

So it is with God. He sees things truly. We can pretend to be one thing, but he will see us truly. We can't blind him or hide from him. We should never be deceived into thinking we have a closet where we keep things from him. God knows our actions and he knows our thoughts. He knows our innermost secrets and desperations. We cannot hide from him, and we shouldn't pretend otherwise.

Accepting this, the question then arises, "What shall we do?" How should we live before this God? The answers lie in honesty. It doesn't matter how Er spelled his name; God knew who he was. We need to be honest before God and admit who we are. We need to confess our sins and short-comings to him. We should repent of our actions and attitudes that are not what they should be. Once we become honest with God, we can seek his help to grow past what we are into what we can be. He will help us clean out our closet!

Lord, I am a sinner in need of your help. I don't act or think as I should, and I ask you for forgiveness and help in growing. In your name, amen.

MARCH 1

Judah said, "Bring her out, and let her be burned." As she was being brought out, she sent word to her father-in-law, "By the man to whom these belong, I am pregnant." And she said, "Please identify whose these are, the signet and the cord and the staff." Then Judah identified them and said, "She is more righteous than I, since I did not give her to my son Shelah." (Gen. 38:24–26)

Life changes us, sometimes for better, sometimes for worse. Genesis, a book of beginnings, illustrates this over and over. Rebellious sin changed Adam and Eve for the worse. We read of changes in characters as even their names are changed. Abram (meaning "father") responds in faith to God and becomes "Abraham," meaning "the father of multitudes." Jacob (meaning "deceiver") changes and becomes "Israel," meaning, "God fights." In this passage, we see a growing maturity and change in Judah, one of Jacob's sons.

The story is difficult for today's readers because it is steeped in the cultural mores of a people and place thousands of miles and thousands of years away. Judah's son Er died, leaving a widow named Tamar. Culture dictated that Judah give Tamar to one of his other sons in marriage, which he did once, but after the second husband died, Judah left Tamar an unmarried widow. Meanwhile, Judah's wife died, and while on a business trip, he came across what he thought was a temple prostitute. The woman was actually Tamar in disguise. Judah negotiated his dalliance with her, and she requested payment. Judah had nothing with him for payment, so he offered to send her a goat. She wanted something to hold as collateral, and he gave her his signet, cord, and staff. Judah later tries to send a goat, but the "temple prostitute" is nowhere to be found. After the tryst, Tamar became pregnant.

Judah finds out his widowed daughter-in-law is pregnant but never dreams he is the father. He pronounces a death sentence on her for sexual impropriety. She then produces his paraphernalia, indicating he is the father. Judah then confesses his own wrongs. Here his change is shown. This was the Judah who used a goat to deceive his father about whether the favored son Joseph was dead (dipping Joseph's robe in blood before showing it to his father). More character change is on the way in Genesis, getting ready for the story of Moses and the massive character change God calls for from his people. In warm-ups to the Moses story, however, one gets nuggets like this one. It moves me to consider my own actions and ways I need to change rather than sitting in judgment on others, thinking of how *they need to change*. This is a good time for an attitude adjustment.

Lord, forgive me of my sin and change me into a better person. In your name, amen.

MARCH 2

The LORD was with Joseph, and he became a successful man, and he was in the house of his Egyptian master. (Gen. 39:2)

The road of life is far from straight. With twists and turns unforeseen, at times we seem far from what we hoped for or planned. In those times, we need to remember that God controls our path, and as we acknowledge him and seek him, we can trust that he will make our paths straight.

Joseph learned this through tough times. His brothers hated him. His parents didn't understand him. His career path as a family shepherd/bedouin was abruptly interrupted when he was stolen from his homeland and shipped off to Egypt to be a slave. Sold into the household of Potiphar, the captain of Pharaoh's guard, Joseph had every reason to be despondent. His life was a wreck. He went from "favored son" to slave in the blink of an eye. Rescue was not in the cards; his father thought he was dead. His brothers couldn't rescue him, for it would reveal their treachery in putting him in that position. He would wake up in Egypt and stare at each new day with no friends, knowing no one, having no pedigree or position, and going through his day in the lowest position in society. Or so one might think.

Joseph was never alone. He had the Lord with him. God was not some novel concept set aside for consideration one day a week. God was an integral part of each day and night. God was his purpose and his companion. With God at his side, Joseph was never alone. It might seem that fate had sent Joseph into the gutter with a raw deal from life, but such was not the case.

Reality is not always what we see or perceive on earth. There is an unspeakably powerful God who is at work in our lives and in the history of humanity. This God allows humanity to make choices yet is able to weave into our existence his blessings in ways that transform history. God was working through Joseph. God's plans needed Joseph in a certain position at a certain time, and the dastardly deeds of his brothers fit snugly into God's designs. God blessed Joseph; he didn't strand him. With God as his provider and protector, Joseph didn't survive—Joseph thrived!

The same God reigns on high today. He still has plans, and his plans involve each of us. Our goal needs to be walking with him, trusting his will, and giving him glory in all the twists and turns of life.

Lord, thank you for your love. Bless me today as I live for you. In your name, amen.

MARCH 3

His master saw that the LORD was with him and that the LORD caused all that he did to succeed in his hands. So Joseph found favor in his sight and attended him, and he made him overseer of his house and put him in charge of all that he had. (Gen. 39:3–4)

People are watching. They watch what we say and watch what we do. They also watch what happens. This is especially true for those who claim to be faithful believers in the Lord. This can be a good thing or a bad thing, depending upon how we choose to live.

Joseph had every worldly reason to be in rebellion against God. His life had not turned out to be the life he dreamed (literally). Joseph had grown up in the safety of his home, believing he was heir apparent to the blessings of firstborn status, even though he was born eleventh of twelve sons. Though adored by his father, Joseph was hated by his brothers, and their hatred led him to be abandoned, sold in slavery in Egypt with his father thinking him dead. This wasn't the twenty-first century, when the Internet and a small world help locate those lost. In the world's eyes, Joseph's future was hopeless.

But the world doesn't see reality the way the faithful do. The faithful know there is one who made the world, one who can reach his finger into space and time and twirl things around to the result needed. This is the truth about God, and Joseph knew it. Joseph didn't abandon his dreams or the God that sent them. Joseph walked faithfully in spite of hopeless circumstances.

The Lord was at work on a subtler level than most could think. God was with Joseph. Joseph's world wasn't ending in slavery; it was only beginning. Joseph's consistent obedience and walk with God placed him directly in the path of God's blessings, even though he was a slave. And God blessed Joseph. Everything assigned to Joseph, he did well and God blessed. This was seen by his owner, Potiphar. Being a wise man himself, Potiphar put more and more under Joseph's care.

That's the way it is in this world. We are called to walk in faith with our Lord. As we do so, circumstances may not always seem to be a blessing. After all, Joseph *was* sold into slavery. Yet God is still at work, and even the stumbles and falls in life will work to the Lord's good purpose for his kingdom and for his followers. We can be confident of that and live accordingly. As we do so, we can know that the world is watching and will change course based on what is seen in us.

Lord, thank you for being involved in my life. Help me be faithful to you in thought and deed, and bless the work of my hands to your glory. In your name, amen!

MARCH 4

And Joseph's master took him and put him into the prison, the place where the king's prisoners were confined, and he was there in prison. But the LORD *was with Joseph and showed him steadfast love and gave him favor in the sight of the keeper of the prison.* (Gen. 39:20–21)

There's something about faith that at times makes it hard to exercise. Faith in God and his promises, at its core, is trusting in him. Yet that is often hard to do. We can trust him in small things, and we can trust him in eternity and things outside our control. But trusting him in real things of life isn't always easy. Today's passage shows the difficulty and also demonstrates God's faithfulness.

The backstory highlights the passage. Joseph had been given promises from God through his dreams. These promises put him in a place of authority and provision for his large extended family—his brother, half-brothers, parents, and more. Yet this dream seemed shattered when his siblings betrayed him and sold him to slave traders. Ending up in Egypt, Joseph was slave to Potiphar, a high-ranking official of Pharaoh. Joseph rose high in Potiphar's household. Joseph also caught the attention of Potiphar's wife, who sought him as a lover behind her husband's back. Joseph fled the sexual immorality, and the spurned woman claimed he had molested her. Potiphar stripped Joseph of his positions and threw him into prison.

Here was Joseph's challenge of faith. He had meticulously followed God's instructions for life and was falsely charged. His reward? Prison! This isn't the way it's supposed to be, is it? Shouldn't the righteous walk from one sunbeam to the next? Shouldn't the righteous live on at least Comfort Street, even if not Easy Street? The answer is embedded in the story's unfolding events. In prison, Joseph met certain servants of Pharaoh. Joseph had a chance to show them that God placed extraordinary wisdom with Joseph. Joseph could interpret dreams. There came a day where Pharaoh needed someone with that ability, and only Joseph measured up. Joseph was released from prison and became number two in the land of Egypt, second only to Pharaoh himself. From this position, Joseph was reunited with his family, supplied the needs of countless people in a severe famine, and was God's person at the right time.

This is how it is with faith. Faith should be part of every day, days of sunshine and rain. Faith is not a magic pill that gives immediate results. It is a life choice that brings us through the messes and sets us where we need to be.

Lord, give me faith, especially in the struggles of life. In your name, amen.

MARCH 5

Joseph answered Pharaoh, "It is not in me; God will give Pharaoh a favorable answer."
(Gen. 41:15)

Joseph was a wise man with great abilities and insights. But his greatest insight was knowing that his gifts were from God. Humility accompanies those who understand this.

Pharaoh had scores of Egypt's wisest counselors at his disposal. Egyptians believed in priests with special powers to communicate with the gods and with the dead. Court magicians were not understood as performers deft with sleight of hand. They were actually considered conjurers, able to do the miraculous through their insights and skills. Into this culture and mind-set came Joseph.

Pharaoh had dreams, and he knew they were important. His wisest counselors were not able to interpret the dreams, but certain members of his court knew of Joseph's accuracy at interpreting dreams. Pharaoh brought Joseph out of prison to see if Joseph could actually do this feat. Joseph had every reason to claim a special skill, just as the magicians of Pharaoh's court did. After all, if Joseph had the skill, then Joseph had the job! His ability to interpret dreams wasn't simply a "get out of jail free" card; it was a comfortable life in Pharaoh's court.

Joseph was confident he would be able to interpret Pharaoh's dream, but he didn't plan to take any credit for his ability. He wouldn't succeed because he was a wise man. From the beginning, Joseph made it clear that any interpretation would be God's gift to Pharaoh. Joseph "didn't have it in him!"

Pharaoh told Joseph his two troubling dreams, and Joseph gave Pharaoh the interpretations from God. Additionally, Joseph gave Pharaoh wise instruction on how to use the knowledge God imparted through the dreams. Pharaoh was impressed. He didn't send Joseph back into the prison but kept him as an adviser. Joseph rapidly became second to Pharaoh in the land, and through him, God would work marvelous wonders for the Israelites as well as the people of Egypt and surrounding areas.

Humility and wisdom go hand in hand. Anyone who is self-important doesn't see things wisely. The wise one will understand that our gifts come from God, our opportunities come from God, our success comes from God, and the credit and praise should certainly go to God. To think otherwise is vain and deluded. It might make us feel good, but only in a needy way that constantly needs reinforcing. If one sees God as the source of blessing and achievement, the "good feeling" at being used by and in sync with the Creator of all far exceeds the artificial puffery of one's own ego.

Lord, may I humbly pursue your agenda in this world and give you all praise and honor for any success. In your name, amen.

MARCH 6

"There will come seven years of great plenty throughout all the land of Egypt, but after them there will arise seven years of famine, and all the plenty will be forgotten in the land of Egypt. The famine will consume the land." (Gen. 41:29–30)

The Bible is *loaded* with practical advice. Some of it comes in the form of proverbs. Some as commandments. Some as morals built into stories and narratives. If we were to look for a proverb that echoes the idea in this narrative, we would do well to consider Proverbs 6:6–8, "Go to the ant, O sluggard; consider her ways, and be wise. Without having any chief, officer, or ruler, she prepares her bread in summer and gathers her food in harvest."

Consumerism runs rampant in our culture and age. Many people live paycheck to paycheck and have already spent their money before it gets in the door. It's hard not to. There are so many things and opportunities that shout at us, all for a price. Yet the Bible teaches a different way. Money should not all be spent as it's earned. There is wisdom in setting aside money for emergencies, for times of drought, and for the unexpected. Many people think that the time to do that is once the "immediate crisis" is over. Yet too often, that immediate crisis simply runs into another immediate crisis, followed by another, and so on.

What is it about this life that drives us so? Perhaps first, it is misplaced priorities. The simplest and highest joy in life comes from an intimate walk with God. From a human perspective, that comes free. God is the one who heavily invested in turning the possibility of walking with God from wishful thinking into a reachable reality. When one's heart finds true peace in God, it brings contentment, joy, love, patience, kindness, and self-control. As we center our daily life in God's love, we will seek God's directions. This will turn one away from consumerism, which is laden with unsatisfied desires and selfish concerns.

This will also prompt one to see money and resources as gifts and tools from God. No more will the question be "What do I want?" or "What can I get?" The new concern will be "What would God have me do with this?" Some of the time, the answer might be "Get a new sofa!" But sometimes it might be "Help another in need." Almost always there will be a recognition that we ought to set some aside for a day when it is needed.

The practical advice of the Bible shouldn't be overlooked or relegated to a day gone by. It is still practical and will make for a better life if followed today.

Lord, thank you for instructions for living. Help my day be one focused on you, your will, your instruction, your desires, your goals, your mission, and your kingdom. Help me use what you've entrusted to my care for your good deeds. In your name, amen.

MARCH 7

And Pharaoh said to his servants, "Can we find a man like this, in whom is the Spirit of God?" Then Pharaoh said to Joseph, "Since God has shown you all this, there is none so discerning and wise as you are. You shall be over my house, and all my people shall order themselves as you command. Only as regards the throne will I be greater than you." (Gen. 41:38–40)

The blessings of God can be intense! Consider Joseph, a young man who was the apple of his father's eye. He was stripped of his family and life because of jealous brothers. He went from being free to being a slave. He was falsely imprisoned because he stood firm in God's morality, refusing the opportunity to sleep with his owner's adulterous wife. Yet in the midst of that life, God brought him to a position of great authority, being second only to Pharaoh in Egyptian life and society.

With that blessing, Joseph was in a unique position. He was given great authority, and he was expected to discharge that authority in ways that blessed Pharaoh and the Egyptians. Jesus said it this way: "To whom much is given, much is required" (Luke 12:48).

What have you been given? How might you best use it? Some have extra time on their hands. Shall it be used in recreation only? Some recreation is good for re-creating one's energy and focus, as the root of the word *recreation* indicates. However, extra time can also mean opportunities for prayer, for contemplation, and for service to others. What talents have you been given? Are there ways you can use those talents not only to generate income but also to bless others and show God's love and compassion? If you can cook, do you cook for those who need a show of kindness? If you can fix a car, do you find chances to help the elderly or those in need of car care and without the resources to get it? If you can mentor, have you found someone to mentor? If you can encourage, are you looking for those in need of encouragement?

All of us have been given much. Sometimes the biggest obstacle to our meeting expectations is our failure to see ourselves properly. We all need to ask the question "What have I been given?" so we can better answer "What can I do with it?" Examine yourself in terms of your talents as well as your resources. Then prayerfully consider how to best use them for God.

Lord, thank you for making me as you have. Thank you for the good in this life, and help me to wisely use it in ways that bring you glory and honor. Thank you also for not letting the evil and bad in this life define me or my purpose before you. Take the negatives, and turn them around. Help me live in devotion to you in the midst of all things, good and bad. In your name, amen.

MARCH 8

"Let Pharaoh select a discerning and wise man, and set him over the land of Egypt." . . .
This proposal pleased Pharaoh and all his servants. And Pharaoh said to his servants,
"Can we find a man like this, in whom is the Spirit of God?" (Gen. 41:33, 37–38)

How do you select your friends? I don't mean people you are nice to or with whom you socialize. I mean those intimate people who know your heart and speak counsel into your life. We choose the people to whom we listen, and our choices have deep ramifications. We need to choose wisely.

Joseph was called in to interpret Pharaoh's dreams, but Joseph went a step further. After accurately interpreting the dreams, Joseph gave Pharaoh some important and practical advice—Pharaoh needed to make sure that he and his kingdom were ready for a coming famine. To get ready, Pharaoh needed an administrator to oversee the proper precautionary preparations. Where was Pharaoh to turn? Undoubtedly, Pharaoh was aware that his usual advisers had fallen woefully short at interpreting his dreams. Why would he trust them to act consistently with the dreams when they couldn't even understand them? Pharaoh saw wisdom in appointing Joseph as the adviser, empowered to enact the measures necessary to overcome the imminent challenges.

We all need advice. We face difficulties with children, spouses, extended family, work, social relationships, where to live, where to work, what to do, how to do it, and more. Proverbs teaches, "Where there is no guidance, a people falls, but in an abundance of counselors there is safety" (Prov. 11:14). Advice is easy to come by; the key is getting *good* advice. For that, one needs godly counsel. Godly counsel comes from someone who has an intimate walk with the Lord, someone who spends a good bit of time in God's word, in prayer, and in effectively walking through life's challenges, leaning on God. These people are ones who will have good insight into situations, able to weigh things by using godly priorities and principles.

Knowing the value in such counsel should drive us toward two goals. First, we should seek to cultivate intimate relationships with people like this. Second, we should strive to *become* people who are godly, seeking to be friends to those who need godly counsel. As we spend time growing intimate with God, studying his word and prayerfully living life in godliness, we become the counselors that can help others on their way.

Life is a challenge. We can better live it when we live it in cumulative godly wisdom. We need to have friends who offer that, and we need to supply it to others too. This is being both discerning and wise.

Lord, put godly people in my path, and help me to give godly counsel. In your name, amen.

MARCH 9

"May God Almighty grant you mercy before the man, and may he send back your other brother and Benjamin. And as for me, if I am bereaved of my children, I am bereaved." (Gen. 43:11)

Sometimes days seem bright and rosy. Our moods are good; smiles brighten our faces, and a song is in our hearts. Those are the days where we should gaze upward into the heavens and bless God for his goodness to us. Of course, not all days are like that. There are also days at the other end of the spectrum. These are the days where we feel impending doom. We dread what is to come. Maybe the dread is vague or maybe specific, but there are times of foreboding, where we worry about the future. During these times, we can and should lean on God's mercy, trusting the future to him.

Jacob experienced both kinds of days. Jacob knew bright and rosy days. Jacob fell in love with Rachel, and while he had to work fourteen years to win her hand in marriage, he readily agreed to those terms. When Rachel gave Jacob children, again his joy was overwhelming. Rachel and Jacob's first son together was Joseph; their second was Benjamin. Jacob had ten other sons from other women, but Joseph captured his heart.

Jacob's life was one of irony, however. Jacob had been born a trickster (also the meaning of his name). Jacob deceived his own father in the blindness of old age, pretending to be his twin brother, Esau. Jacob's legacy of deception came back to haunt him as his older sons deceived him into thinking his treasured Joseph was dead. Living for decades believing Joseph dead, Jacob was faced with the dread of losing his other son through Rachel. Trying to survive an intense famine, Jacob had sent his sons to Egypt to buy grain. Unknowingly buying grain from their long-lost brother Joseph, the brothers had to leave one brother as collateral and were told that they could not buy any more unless they brought Benjamin back.

At first Jacob would not hear of it. Having lost Rachel's firstborn, he wasn't about to risk her only other son. Yet hunger can force choices people would prefer not to make. Finally, with fear, dread, and foreboding, Jacob agreed to send Benjamin with his older brothers to get necessary food. By this stage in life, Jacob the deceiver had learned to lean on God. It was the only solace he had as he sent out his sons with Benjamin.

This life is a whirlwind of days where we experience highs and lows. We need to be sure that when the bad days come, when we face uncertainty, when we fear that what is about to come is going to hurt and be harmful, we can lean on God. As Jacob recognized, he isn't merely "God," he is "God Almighty." He can handle what is coming our way. And with him, we can handle it!

Lord, give me strength to face days of difficulty. In your name, amen.

MARCH 10

Then Joseph hurried out, for his compassion grew warm for his brother, and he sought a place to weep. And he entered his chamber and wept there. (Gen. 43:30)

Treasure relationships. Invest in them. Protect them. Make them genuine and meaningful. Then be thankful for them and experience them wholeheartedly.

Joseph had an interesting history with his brothers. The older brothers were jealous, vindictive, angry, selfish, antagonistic, and dangerous toward Joseph. They had caused him extreme harm and were the source of much suffering in his life. His younger brother, Benjamin, was different. Born from the same mother, Joseph had a close affection for his younger brother. Joseph hadn't seen Benjamin in years. Undoubtedly Benjamin had grown from a youth to almost a middle-aged man by the time Joseph saw him in Egypt. It moved Joseph to tears. Not wanting to reveal himself as Joseph to his brothers, Joseph wept in private.

One might think that Joseph's tears and affection for his younger brother were understandable, though Joseph properly stayed emotionally cold and distant from his older brothers. But that would not be the full read of the story. Joseph loved his older brothers with affection, in spite of their evil bent toward him. Reading the story in Genesis 45 reveals that Joseph forgave his brothers and loved them just as he did his younger brother. Joseph brought his entire family to live in Egypt. By uniting his family, Joseph brought them blessing and hope during a difficult season. Joseph's name came from a Hebrew verb that referenced the idea of one who added or joined others together. That was Joseph. He didn't do it haphazardly. He did it out of love.

Love for others bears abundant fruit. It requires us to turn our eyes out from ourselves and seek the good of others. Joseph could have maintained his focus on himself, his career, and his success, but that would have left him emotionally crippled and empty. Joseph needed his family as much as they needed him. The relationships brought him meaning, even as he brought blessings to others.

I have found this true in life, and I hope you have as well. When we invest our time, energy, resources, and industry in others, we find our hearts growing in love for them. It means that our capacity for love and being loved grows as well. We become better people. Think about the people around you that God has put into your path. Are there chances to invest in those relationships? Take those chances. It is a good thing.

Lord, thank you for friends and family. Thank you for the chance to bond with others in this life. Help me to be a good friend, living to show your love to this world. In your name, amen.

MARCH 11

Portions were taken to them from Joseph's table, but Benjamin's portion was five times as much as any of theirs. And they drank and were merry with him. (Gen. 43:34)

How do we react when others receive good things? Are we thankful for their good fortune? Or does jealousy stir our hearts, prompting our often secret thoughts, "Why doesn't that happen for me?" or "Why don't I get that?" This is an area where most everyone could use some improvement.

Jacob had twelve sons, and all could see that Joseph was his favorite. Joseph came from the "favorite wife." Joseph was almost the youngest and undoubtedly had fewer adult responsibilities than his other brothers. Joseph's father gifted him a special coat, a visible reminder that he was Daddy's favorite. His brothers were bitter. When Joseph then had dreams indicating his life would succeed beyond that of all his family, dreams that his brothers and parents would all seek his favor and bow before him, it crossed a line. The brothers sought to ruin, if not end, Joseph's life.

Time bore out the truth of the dreams. After decades of separation, the brothers went to Egypt, desperate for food during an intense famine. There, the brothers unknowingly bowed to Joseph, seeking his favor and his resources. Joseph sold grain to the brothers but was working toward a reunion. Joseph needed to know if the brothers had changed their hearts. The lesson came in an interesting way.

When the brothers made a second trip to Egypt for food, Joseph refused to sell any more unless the brothers brought the youngest and other favorite son, Benjamin. The brothers knew that Benjamin was favored. Their father gladly sent the older brothers, but Benjamin was practically pried from his grip. Their father feared that something might happen to him. Once the starving brothers all arrived in Egypt seeking food from Joseph, they were sat down for a banquet. Each brother got food, but the youngest, Benjamin, got five times the portion of the others. Undoubtedly Joseph was eyeing his brothers' reactions. Were they jealous? Were they happy for a tragedy to befall him, as they had been about Joseph decades before? No. Instead they were merry. Joseph tested them further, hiding a cup in Benjamin's pack and bringing him back to punish him as a thief. The brothers didn't delight over Benjamin's downfall but sought to protect him. The brothers had changed. They had grown up. This moved Joseph to tears, and he revealed himself to his brothers. The goodness and joy spread around more.

When good things happen to others, we should be thankful, not jealous. We should be content with what we have. Anything less is simply a form of coveting, a sin.

Lord, help me to be thankful and content with what you've given me. Let me rejoice for others when they are blessed by you. In your name, amen.

MARCH 12

Then Judah went up to him and said, "Oh, my lord, please let your servant speak a word in my lord's ears, and let not your anger burn against your servant, for you are like Pharaoh himself." (Gen. 44:18)

How do we treat people? Are we challenging and in their face? Are we silent, fearful of speaking out? Do we expect others to shape their choices around us and what is important to us? Do we ignore people and just live on our own, doing our own thing?

There certainly isn't one answer and one approach to how to treat others, but that doesn't mean that Scripture doesn't teach us important approaches for life. In the passage quoted above, Judah had a problem. There was a high governmental official (Judah didn't realize that it was his brother Joseph) who held power of life or death over Judah and his brothers. This powerful official was issuing a decree that would greatly damage people Judah loved. Judah didn't sit idly by and let the consequences fall where they might. Instead, he spoke out in kindness, with respect, and truthfully recounted his concerns. There wasn't immediate resolution, but shortly thereafter, the problems were resolved and all worked out for the best.

This story doesn't tell us that things will always have a happy ending if we speak as Judah did. But it certainly gives guiding instructions for how we should deal with others in the midst of turbulent times. How we deal with others is not always a matter of getting what we want or need, but it always speaks to who we are. That is something we should care about.

The rabbi and Christian apostle Paul explained that our dealings with others should be in line with our growth before God. This growth Paul termed "fruit of the Spirit." It includes love, joy, peace, patience, kindness, goodness, faithfulness, gentleness, and self-control. These are traits that will produce the best results, even if the results aren't those we desire. These are traits we should cultivate in our lives. They aren't "tape-on" fruits we can buy at a store and wear on appropriate days. To be real, they need to grow from our walk with God and become part of who we are. They become the language we speak and the treatment we show others. This is related to the instructions from Jesus that we should "treat others as we would like to be treated" (Matt. 7:12). Or as other rabbis in Jesus' day said, "Don't do to others what you would not want done to you."

Judah spoke with honesty and in peace. His words were kind and his request plain. His approach won favor that day. It should draw our attention to how we treat others.

Lord, please give me the fruit of the Spirit. Teach me love, joy, peace, patience, kindness, goodness, faithfulness, gentleness, and self-control. May those traits be my natural reaction in the way I treat others. In your name, amen.

MARCH 13

"Now therefore, please let your servant remain instead of the boy as a servant to my lord, and let the boy go back with his brothers. For how can I go back to my father if the boy is not with me? I fear to see the evil that would find my father." (Gen. 44:33–34)

People are fairly good at looking backward and seeing the consequences of actions and choices. The problem is often *looking forward*! How often people think or say, "If I had known this would happen, I never would have . . ." Or when a problem arises because of a past choice, they reflect, "I wish I hadn't . . ." That is the way of life. However, Scripture teaches that what one sows in life is reaped later. It is an affirmation that the choices we make do have consequences, and while we don't always know whether the results will be A or B, we can be assured that good deeds bring good results and sin brings negative ones.

So it was with Judah nearly four thousand years ago. Judah wasn't the oldest of Jacob's twelve sons, but he was a vocal one. The older sons were pasturing the family flocks several days' journey from the tribe's bedouin tents when the young brother Joseph was sent to them. Jealous of Joseph, the brothers conspired to kill him until Reuben intervened and urged them to leave Joseph in a pit. Reuben figured he could rescue Joseph later. After they threw Joseph into the pit, Judah was the brother who decided to take a different course. He convinced his brothers to pull Joseph out and sell him to slave traders. Judah's idea sent Joseph away, sold into slavery.

As years turned into decades, the family lived thinking Joseph dead. No one dreamed that God had his hand on Joseph and had raised him up to be Pharaoh's right hand ruling Egypt. When Jacob and his tribe needed food, Judah led the brothers into Egypt to buy from Joseph. Of course, Judah did not know he was dealing with Joseph. Dressed as an Egyptian, speaking a foreign language, and well into middle age, Joseph was incognito.

In the ironic story, Judah becomes the one who is in trouble with Joseph. While Judah had sold Joseph into slavery, Joseph now held power over Judah and his brothers. Judah recognizes the crisis and with the haunting memory of what he had done to Joseph, he decides to try and rescue the youngest brother from the Egyptian's (actually Joseph's) wrath by becoming the slave. It is one of many places where Genesis teaches that even a short road usually has a turn in it! The deceptive plans Judah executed became the net that entrapped Judah later.

Fortunately, the story doesn't end there. Joseph revealed himself to his brothers and instead of judgment offered forgiveness and mercy. We, the readers, are left impressed by the justice meted out to Judah and yet touched by the mercy that followed. May it inform how I live.

Lord, help me make good choices. Help me show mercy to others. In your name, amen.

MARCH 14

Joseph said, "I am your brother, Joseph, whom you sold into Egypt. And now do not be distressed or angry with yourselves because you sold me here, for God sent me before you to preserve life." (Gen. 45:4–5)

The life of faith sees things differently. It doesn't remove the cause and effect of the world, but it understands that God reigns over the world. Cause and effect don't operate in a vacuum; they operate in God's plans.

Joseph was perceptive and a man of faith. God had laid dreams upon Joseph's heart that his family would bow and serve him, even though Joseph was a young brother. The idea of older brothers or parents serving a younger brother/son was 180 degrees contrary to his culture. This dream was a tipping point with the older brothers. They got rid of Joseph, selling him into slavery to be carted to a far-off land. Joseph ended up a slave in Egypt, and his life got worse. Joseph was falsely accused when he refused to sleep with his owner's wife, and he wound up in prison.

Yet through these events, Joseph made contacts that later brought him before the mighty pharaoh. God gave Joseph insight to interpret Pharaoh's dreams, and because of his insight, Pharaoh made Joseph his right hand. Then, decades later, a horrid famine brought Joseph's brothers back into his life. The brothers mistook Joseph for an Egyptian. They bowed before Joseph, just as Joseph's dream had forecasted. Joseph put his brothers to the test to see their motives, to see if they had changed, to see how his younger brother was being treated, and to hear about his father's life.

Finally, there was a big reveal where Joseph showed his brothers his true identity. The middle-aged man standing before them was the teenager they had sold into slavery decades before. The brothers surely felt guilt, fear, and a host of other emotions. Then Joseph spoke profoundly as a man of faith. The cause and effect of the real choices made by his brothers—wicked and immature choices—should not be understood in a vacuum. God was at work. God placed Joseph in the right place at the right time to do the thing needed in God's plan.

This is the challenge for people of faith. We make our choices in this world, and we try to make right choices and do the right thing. But this world allows everyone to make choices, and those choices aren't always good ones. Bad things happen around us and to us. The eyes of faith, however, understand that whatever happens, God is not asleep. He is not uncaring. He hasn't lost control. God can and will work through all things for his good plans and purposes. In that truth, his people can live in trust and confidence, even when life is rough.

Lord, give me eyes of faith. Work in my life for your good purposes. In your name, amen.

MARCH 15

"God sent me before you to preserve for you a remnant on earth, and to keep alive for you many survivors." (Gen. 45:7)

How are you feeling today? You might be on top of the world—the sun is out, the wind's behind you, and you sense nothing but pleasant sailing ahead. Or you might be at the other extreme, wondering if you're even alive. Maybe you feel dead inside, your spirit down and your heart sad. Maybe your health is failing. You might also be somewhere in the middle, just moving minute by minute, figuring things could be better or worse, and not too preoccupied with your personal state of affairs.

There is an important and core truth that applies to each of us, regardless of how we feel. As long as we are alive, we can be assured that God has plans for us. God has things he wants us to do. He has a specific role for you and me to take in our world today. We may not feel important, valuable, or able to achieve much, but that is far from reality. The truth is simple. God has full knowledge of our capabilities and limitations, and he has directions for us to walk in ways that serve him and his kingdom.

Joseph saw God's plans for him. He knew that God had a purpose for him that superseded anything that Joseph had planned. Egypt and the surrounding countries were in the midst of a severe drought and famine. Food was scarce, and things were not about to get better. They would go from bad to worse. In the midst of this economic crisis, God was using Joseph to sustain his family and countless others. God gave Joseph the wisdom, the tools, and the opportunities to achieve this important task. By God's foresight, Joseph had seen the famine coming. Pharaoh put Joseph in charge of devising and implementing a solution to the crisis. Joseph did so.

Folks may read the Joseph story and think, "Well, that was Joseph. He's a famous man in the Bible. Of course, God had plans for *him*." But that is not the biblical teaching. There aren't a handful of "special people" that God uses. Everyone is special. Everyone has a role to fill in God's plan and kingdom. What we need to do is first *realize that*, and second, try to uncover what it is God has for us to do.

Some get too dejected and don't think God can use them. Some are physically disabled and even homebound, but that doesn't preclude God setting them up as prayer warriors. Some are so preoccupied with worrying about their own circumstances that it never occurs to them that God has prepared some good works for them to do. Yet he has—for all of us.

Lord, please clear away any distractions that would take me away from seeing your purpose in my life. Thank you for your personal interest, and help me to walk in your will. In your name, amen.

MARCH 16

"Hurry and go up to my father . . . Hurry and bring my father down here." (Gen. 45:10–13)

Are you ever in a hurry? Does the speedometer of your life run fast or slow? Biblically, we are taught that there are times we need to do things quickly and times we need to be slow and patient. The key is knowing which is which!

Today's passage is in the narrative of Joseph revealing himself to his brothers. Joseph had grown up with an especially close relationship with his father. As a teenage boy, Joseph was sent on an errand by his father to assist his older brothers. Having said goodbye for what was supposed to be a brief outing, Joseph wound up not seeing his father again for decades. Joseph was accosted by his brothers, sold into slavery, and shipped off to Egypt. This was before cell phones, the Internet, or calling 9-1-1. There was no hotline for missing children, and no real chance that Joseph would ever see his father again. Joseph's father was misled into thinking Joseph was dead, so there was no search party seeking to find Joseph. To further complicate matters, Jacob, the father of Joseph, was elderly when Joseph was born. Jacob did not have many years left on earth.

Now likely in his forties, Joseph had reunited with his brothers, although the brothers did not recognize Joseph at first. Joseph learned that his aged father was still alive. Joseph then had a big reveal where he showed his brothers his true identity. Joseph was ready to see his father. His brothers needed to hurry and bring their father to Egypt.

No wonder Joseph was in a hurry. Time was lost. No one could register the years of anguish and heartache. Jacob had missed Joseph's wedding, the birth of Jacob's grandchildren through Joseph, Joseph's success in the business world, and so much more. Intensifying this lost time was the sadness of Jacob thinking he had lost his son. Jacob likely blamed himself for sending Joseph on the errand. Like most fathers, he must have played over and over in his mind his seemingly poor parenting choice. No doubt the brothers that sold Joseph into slavery and covered up their misdeeds, letting their father think Joseph dead, were not enamored with the idea of telling Dad the truth! But Joseph was. He wanted to see his dad soon.

There is a time when things must be done quickly. Patience is a virtue, but time is a precious thing as well. We shouldn't waste time and dawdle. We should recognize that each moment is priceless and cannot be repeated. Life doesn't have a rewind button. The key to pacing in life is recognizing the importance of time. We need to appreciate each moment and use it as fully as God allows.

Lord, give me wisdom to appreciate the fleeting nature of life. Let me fill my minutes wisely, making the most of the time you give me. In your name, amen.

MARCH 17

Joseph gave wagons to his brothers . . . and gave them provisions for the journey. To each and all of them he gave a change of clothes, but to Benjamin he gave three hundred shekels of silver and five changes of clothes. To his father he sent as follows: ten donkeys loaded with the good things of Egypt, and ten female donkeys loaded with grain, bread, and provision for his father on the journey. Then he sent his brothers away, and as they departed, he said to them, "Do not quarrel on the way." (Gen. 45:21–24)

What is it about human nature, that we can have a really good life, be in a really good situation with blessings and reasons for joy, and yet succumb to something as childish as quarreling with those close to us?

Look at Joseph's brothers. They were facing starvation and economic devastation because of a pervasive famine and drought. They were having to travel a great distance to Egypt and beg powerful people for the mere chance to buy food at exorbitant prices. Their families were hungry, and for a while, it looked like they might lose their youngest brother to an authoritarian and harsh Egyptian overlord. Then, presto! In a moment, everything changed. The harsh Egyptian turned out to be Joseph, their long-lost brother. And while Joseph had every reason to hate them for a betrayal years before, he didn't. He showered them with love and attention. He gave them huge gifts for themselves and for the extended family. Joseph was setting up a future, providing for his family so they needn't fear or want for the important necessities of life.

The brothers should be on their way rejoicing. They should be looking to the heavens and thanking God, their provider. They should be celebrating the redemption of restoring their relationship with Joseph, the brother they last saw when they had sold him out with no regard for him or his future. Joseph the betrayed showed love and care for his betraying brothers. Yes, the brothers had lots of reasons to rejoice as they returned to deliver the best conceivable news to their aging father. Yet in the midst of this, Joseph fittingly told his brothers, "Don't quarrel on the way."

We might judge the brothers too harshly unless we think carefully about our own tendencies. Grumbling, fussing, quarreling—all of these are not too far from any of us, regardless of how well our lives are going. They are traits that can manifest at any time, especially when hungry, sleepy, or distracted by life. But we are not animals with no control over how we act. We do not have to let our emotions dictate our actions. We can make decisions about how we behave and treat others. This ability is called self-control, and it is a virtue we should prayerfully seek and develop. Let's be deliberate about living and work on the way we behave!

Lord, I need help. I need your strength and insight to grow in self-control. Help me learn to treat others with kindness and respect. In your name, amen.

MARCH 18

So Israel took his journey with all that he had and came to Beersheba, and offered sacrifices to the God of his father Isaac. And God spoke to Israel in visions of the night and said, "Jacob, Jacob." And he said, "Here I am." Then he said, "I am God, the God of your father. Do not be afraid to go down to Egypt, for there I will make you into a great nation. I myself will go down with you to Egypt, and I will also bring you up again, and Joseph's hand shall close your eyes." (Gen. 46:1–4)

Sometimes, I especially need to know God's presence and concern for me. Jesus assured people that if we seek God, and if we ask of him, then we will find God and receive from him. Jesus' teaching was not new. It is found throughout the pages of the Old Testament, including today's passage.

God had assured Jacob, also called "Israel," that the land in Canaan would belong to him and his offspring, but events turned a bit differently. It appeared that Jacob was about to abdicate his possession of the land and move everything he had to Egypt. This was disturbing. This was a time and place where possession was the key to ownership. There were no title offices where deeds of ownership were kept on record. There was no government that oversaw a structured transfer of property rights, and there were no courts where such rights could be enforced. God promised the land to Jacob and his descendants, but history and society showed they would have the land because they possessed the land. That was all about to change if Jacob and his entourage moved to Egypt.

With this heavy concern, Jacob went to Beersheba and offered sacrifices to God, who had made the promise not only to Jacob but also to his father, Isaac. Jacob drew his focus to God, setting aside his selfish concerns (indicated by his sacrifice) and seeking God's wisdom and direction.

God came to Jacob and answered him. Through visions, God explained to Jacob that the move was God's move. It wouldn't invalidate God's promises. It was one part in how God would fulfill his promises. God will always be faithful to his word.

I find this reassuring and also a bit challenging. It drives me to come to God for reassurance of his presence and guidance but to do so in a sacrificial state of mind. I need to lay down what I have and what I want, to follow his will and direction. My relationship with God is not like mine with a concierge at a grand hotel. I don't call him for tickets or reservations. He isn't there to heed my beck and call. I need to seek his plan. I need to want the desires of his heart, not my own. Then in the midst of that, I have an assurance that God will be present. That is more than enough.

Lord, help me put aside my agendas and desires and focus on you, your will, your desires, and what I can do to further your plans. In your name, amen.

MARCH 19

And when the time drew near that Israel must die, he called his son Joseph and said to him, "If now I have found favor in your sight, put your hand under my thigh and promise to deal kindly and truly with me. Do not bury me in Egypt." (Gen. 47:29)

What do we have in common with Jacob? He lived three thousand years ago; fathered twelve sons; lived as a nomad in the area of modern Israel; and had no modern conveniences, no formal education, and of course no social media presence. He spoke not only a different language but an entirely different type of language from the English being written here. His music was different; at best, he read and wrote only minimally (the alphabet wasn't developed yet). Yet despite all those differences, there is something major we hold in common with him, something that should shape how we live: we all have a destiny with death.

Most of us don't like to think about it. If we are on the younger side of life, perhaps death is the last thing on our minds. But that doesn't make it less real, and it may not be as far in the future as we think. If we are older, we might be more reflective on death. Regardless of our perceived distance from death, there is a certain wisdom in living in such a way that we are prepared for the inevitable.

In today's passage, Jacob realized he was close to dying and he made preparations for that inevitability. For him, it involved making some last wishes known to his son Joseph and getting assurances that those wishes would be honored. Today your death may be drawing very close. Preparing for imminent death might involve very different things than preparing for death in the distant future. But even recognizing a distant death can help us live differently today, if we live in preparation for that death.

I am not writing this from my deathbed, I don't think. Yet I still see that today my life can be different because I recognize my days are numbered. I don't want to squander my time. I want to do things that show my family I love them. I want to sow faith in the Lord to those in my circle of influence. I want my children to recognize the lessons of life and the Lord that I've learned over the years. I want my house to be in better order. I want my sweet wife to know that she is important to me. I want to live in a way that makes my passing a time of rejoicing before the Lord, even as people may mourn my departure from this field of life.

Living with an eye toward the end is not a morbid thing. It can help propel us into wiser decisions today. Jacob knew he was going to die. We are too! Let's live like it!

Lord, thank you that I do not live this life alone and I do not leave it alone. Thank you for being not only my creator of life, my sustainer of life, but also my assurance of eternal life. May I live for you today and every day. In your name, amen.

MARCH 20

And he said, "Swear to me"; and he swore to him. Then Israel bowed himself upon the head of his bed. (Gen. 47:31)

Most of us like to think of ourselves as honest people. But honesty goes deeper than simply not telling someone a lie. Honesty includes not making promises or assurances that you can't keep. In many respects, honesty and reliability are joined at the hip.

Today's passage falls in the final stages of the story of Jacob's life. He knew his days were numbered, and he had given his son Joseph important instructions on what to do after he died. Joseph had said he would follow his instructions, but his father reinforced the importance of follow-through, saying, "Swear to me." Joseph did so. Having received that assurance, Jacob was at peace. He knew he could rely on Joseph to keep his word.

The importance of honesty and reliability flows in two directions. We need to be reliable and honest, but it is also important we recognize others who are reliable and honest. Jacob had twelve sons. The responsibilities in his patriarchal society were clearly defined. They belonged to the father of the clan and, upon his passing, to the oldest son. That was NOT Joseph. For Jacob to get to Joseph involved skipping over ten sons. The text doesn't say with clarity, but common sense dictates that Jacob thought that he could rely on Joseph the most to follow through and do as Jacob wished.

Joseph is a model for the faithful today. We need to be careful when we make representations to other people about what we will or will not do. People need to see by our actions that we will keep our word, even when it is difficult to do so. A lot of people make commitments, but when economic circumstances change, they find the lure of money greater than the value in keeping their word. Or others find that saying one thing and doing another seems to be justified when no one will really know the difference. But someone who will do what he or she says, even when no one is looking or will know the difference, is a reliable person who will become known for her or his integrity.

I want to be that person. I want not only for my words to be true but for my actions to be honest and reliable. If I am uncertain that I will be able to do something, rather than affirm I will do so, I need to use phrases like, "I will try . . ." or "I will do my best!" Of course, this is not a "get out of jail free" card that dismisses me from achieving what I have said I would try to do. But it changes my responsibility from achieving to trying or doing my best. I want to be honest and reliable, even in the small things like time. If I say I will be somewhere at five, I want people to know I will be there at five.

Lord, please help me see the importance of being honest and reliable, then give me the strength to be one who keeps my word. In your name, amen.

MARCH 21

And it was told to Jacob, "Your son Joseph has come to you." Then Israel summoned his strength and sat up in bed. And Jacob said to Joseph, "God Almighty appeared to me at Luz in the land of Canaan and blessed me, and said to me, 'Behold, I will make you fruitful and multiply you, and I will make of you a company of peoples and will give this land to your offspring after you for an everlasting possession.'" (Gen. 48:2–4)

Every minute you have been alive, God has been present. He preceded you, me, our parents, and our grandparents. He preceded the entire human race. He preceded the planet and the universe. Not only does God predate everything, but everything is under his oversight. God is involved in this planet and its goings-on. Whether we believe in God or not, God still deals with you and me. That is one of life's ultimate truths. In light of this truth, what a pity it is that we are so slow to tell others about it. We often hesitate about informing people of God's love and role in our lives, even though it should be our natural thought and behavior.

In today's passage, Jacob was elderly and ill. Thinking his father was about to die, Joseph took his two sons in to see him. Upon their arrival, Jacob summoned the strength to sit up in bed and visit. Jacob had little strength, so the visit would be short. Jacob used the little time available to speak of God. Jacob testified as to how God had worked in his life. He spoke of God's promises to him, his father, and his grandfather. With limited time and energy, he explained: God is at work! God is not a passive spectator to human history.

Why is it often hard for us to tell people about the work of God in our lives? Perhaps it is because no one sees God. In the Western world, we tend to think of things as materialists. We like the tangible—things we see, touch, smell, and taste. We readily credit those we see. I have a computer I am using to type this because Steve Jobs and his crew started a company that made what has evolved into a MacBook Pro. I had a great breakfast this morning because farmers farmed, ranchers ranched, drivers drove, sellers sold, chefs cooked, and waiters served. I can readily talk of them, give credit where credit is due, and find ways to share my experiences with others. But God is not material. I believe in him because it makes sense, and I certainly am aware of how he has worked in my life. But sharing it is different from telling someone about a great restaurant or your computer.

We must not let our material society or anything else inhibit us from telling others of God. I love my wife and children, and the fact that love is not a material thing doesn't preclude me from speaking of its importance, its power, and its influence in my life. God should be no different.

Lord, teach me to tell others of your work in my life. In your name, amen.

MARCH 22

Now the eyes of Israel were dim with age, so that he could not see. . . . And Israel said to Joseph, "I never expected to see your face; and behold, God has let me see your offspring also." (Gen. 48:10–11)

How good is your vision? Do you need glasses to read this? Do you need glasses to drive or to see at a distance? I wear glasses for seeing at a distance, and it can be a bit frustrating to be unable to make out writing, faces, and so on without first putting on glasses.

In today's passage, Jacob's eyes were not good. He was basically blind. But while Jacob's physical sight was lacking, his spiritual insight was 20/20. In contrast to his physical limitations of sight, he saw a spiritual truth that we shouldn't miss.

The backstory is helpful. Jacob had twelve sons, and Joseph was second to youngest. Joseph was Jacob's favorite son. Joseph's older brothers were jealous of his relationship with Dad, so they sold Joseph into slavery, deceiving their father in the process. They led Jacob to believe that Joseph had been killed. Over three decades later, Jacob learned the truth and was reunited with Joseph. By that time, Jacob was an old man, and today's passage comes shortly after their reunion. With Jacob believed to be on his deathbed, Joseph brought his two sons in to see their grandfather. Jacob was uncertain who was in the tent with him, and Joseph had to verbally identify everyone.

Jacob was overjoyed that he not only got to "see" Joseph after three decades when he thought Joseph dead, but he also got to "see" his grandchildren through Joseph. This was stunning to a man whose eyes were "heavy" or "dim" with age. While Jacob couldn't really see physically, he did have strong spiritual insight. Jacob *saw* that God had worked this out. God's hand was behind this immense blessing.

Jacob could have cursed God for not having Joseph in his presence for three decades. Jacob could have called God to account for not clarifying the other sons' deceptions. Jacob could have credited fate for the reuniting with Joseph, finding it an amazing set of coincidences. But that would have been a spiritually blind thing to do. Jacob wasn't blinded spiritually. Age may have dimmed his vision, but it sharpened his faith. Jacob knew to give God the glory for the good. Jacob knew that God had brought about a blessing in the midst of pain and misery that had proceeded from evil decisions of others.

My eyesight might not be great, but I can live with that. But my real concern is my spiritual insight. I want that to be sharp! God, give me eyes to see you and your works in my life and in this world. To your glory and in your name, amen.

MARCH 23

Jacob blessed Joseph and said, "The God before whom my fathers Abraham and Isaac walked, the God who has been my shepherd all my life long to this day, the angel who has redeemed me from all evil, bless the boys." (Gen. 48:15–16)

Look carefully at your life. Who has God put in your sphere of care and influence? Who are the people whose lives you touch? Those are people for whom you can and should seek God's blessings. Seeking God's blessings for others is not simply following a sneeze with a "God bless you." It is much more than that. It involves how we live, how we treat them, and how we seek God on their behalf.

Today's passage has Jacob blessing Joseph, his son. Jacob blesses Joseph first by recounting the goodness and faithfulness of God. Jacob is instructing and reminding Joseph of the role God has played in Jacob's history and life. Jacob was not the first in his family to believe in God; his father, Isaac, and his grandfather Abraham had walked with God before him. The success of the forefathers was evident and well known. Jacob gave credit for their lives to God. On a more direct and personal level, Jacob also credited God for his own life. God had been Jacob's "shepherd" all his life.

Jacob knew what a shepherd was. Jacob came from a family of shepherds. Jacob got his own start as a shepherd and had been one his entire life. It was the family occupation. Shepherds protected their flocks from marauders and wild animals. Shepherds sought out places of water and food for their flocks. Shepherds tended the sick and wounded. Shepherds stayed with their flock day and night, in good weather and bad. Shepherds knew their animals intimately, caring for them as family.

This was God to Jacob: one who had been with Jacob from the beginning, protecting him, providing for him, tending to him in times of crisis, and never departing, even when Jacob was less than honorable himself. God was faithful and reliable in his care and love for Jacob. Telling Joseph about God's faithfulness was a large part of Jacob blessing Joseph. The blessing was not simply to call upon God on Joseph's behalf, but it was to attest to Joseph who God was and what God had done. This, in conjunction with calling God to bless and shepherd Joseph, was the blessing.

Let us consider those in our care and circle of influence. Let us decide to bless them today—not simply by seeking God's touch in their lives but by telling them how God has touched us. Give God glory and see God bless them!

Lord, may I proclaim your love to those around me today. And may you bless them richly. In your name, amen.

MARCH 24

Then Jacob called his sons and said, "Gather yourselves together, that I may tell you what shall happen to you in days to come. . . . Reuben, you are my firstborn, my might, and the firstfruits of my strength, preeminent in dignity and preeminent in power. Unstable as water, you shall not have preeminence, because you went up to your father's bed; then you defiled it . . . The scepter shall not depart from Judah, nor the ruler's staff from between his feet, until tribute comes to him; and to him shall be the obedience of the peoples."
(Gen. 49:1, 3-4, 10)

We are blessed with one grandchild so far. She is amazing! For the first eighteen months of her life, she lived overseas, and while we saw her as frequently as we could, often we had to settle for the marvelous pictures and videos her mother posted. The photos were always amazing, showing this expression or that and bringing oohs and aahs as well as laughs and silent appreciation. The videos had a different impact than the pictures. The videos showed ongoing movement, sound, and personality beyond the simple picture. Life can be that way. We can live life as a picture, each day or moment being a snapshot of a fuller time. We can also consider life a movie, knowing that today is one of many, recognizing that tomorrow will be different and the following day different again. Even if death visits us tonight, the movie continues tomorrow, although without us.

Today's passage has Jacob's last act as a father. Immediately before his death, Jacob calls his twelve sons to him for his final words. He announces blessings and curses, reciting much of what the future movie holds for the various sons and their offspring. The firstborn, Reuben, is cursed for his sexual deviancy. For Judah, the pronouncement is one of blessing. The tribe of Judah will be a leader and ruler among the Israelites, one from the tribe becoming even greater than the others from the tribe.

History showed Jacob's words prophetic. Judah's progeny included the great King David, not a perfect king but perhaps Israel's greatest. Solomon and the kings of the kingdom of Judah proceeded forth as prophesied by Jacob. Yeshua (in Greek, "Jesus") himself was from the tribe of Judah, recognized by Christians as the King of Kings. Jacob understood that his life was passing. He knew the lives of his sons would one day pass as well. But Jacob saw a bigger picture. He saw the movie that was being played out over the centuries.

If we see that life is a movie, then we begin to have greater concerns than just the moment. Our actions involve ourselves and also those who come after us. We can live in ways that bring blessings or curses. We make a difference, not only in our own lives but in the lives of those who come after us. Let's live wisely!

Lord, give me wisdom in discerning right and wrong and strength to do right. In your name, amen.

MARCH 25

When Joseph's brothers saw that their father was dead, they said, "It may be that Joseph will hate us and pay us back for all the evil that we did to him." . . . But Joseph said to them, "Do not fear, for am I in the place of God? As for you, you meant evil against me, but God meant it for good, to bring it about that many people should be kept alive, as they are today. So do not fear; I will provide for you and your little ones." Thus he comforted them and spoke kindly to them. (Gen. 50:15, 19–21)

America is a game-playing society. Whether card games, board games, or sports, most Americans (and many other societies) find some activity that requires keeping score. Maybe that is why it's so common for people to keep score in life. America's President Nixon was famous for keeping his list of enemies, people who had slighted him and given him cause to even the score. There are even sayings rooted in this idea, like "Vengeance is a dish best served cold!" But if we look at the holy life of Joseph, and other profoundly holy people, we see the triumph of mercy over scorekeeping.

Joseph had every right to hate his brothers and plot his revenge. His brothers had abused him growing up. The brothers started to kill Joseph, their younger teenaged brother. They changed their minds only when presented with a chance to sell Joseph as a slave, disposing of him from the family while making some money in the process. The brothers never seemed to repent. They let their father think Joseph was dead, eliminating any chance for a search and rescue mission. Then the unthinkable happened. The brothers found the family's life reintersecting with Joseph, and this time Joseph was immensely powerful. Joseph held all the aces. The brothers and all their loved ones were dependent on Joseph's goodwill. Joseph treated them fine while their father lived, but today's passage focuses on what happened after their father died.

The brothers feared for their lives. Joseph was the second most powerful man in Egypt, and the brothers were nothings. They had no connections, no power, no real right to land or anything else. There were no common rights like civilized countries have today. With a snap of his fingers, Joseph could turn his brothers and all those they loved into slaves, confiscating their goods. The brothers feared Joseph was keeping score and might just do it. But Joseph did not. He was filled with love and mercy. He looked beyond the rigid scorekeeping and knew that God's hand was at work, even in the brothers' treachery. Joseph could have mercy and leave any retribution to God.

I may live in America. I may like playing games and sports. But I need to be wary about keeping score with others. A life based on revenge is a life of wasted energy. I need to learn to love even the undeserving.

Lord, teach me to forgive others, even as I seek and receive forgiveness from you. In your name, amen.

MARCH 26

But the midwives feared God and did not do as the king of Egypt commanded them, but let the male children live. . . . So God dealt well with the midwives. And the people multiplied and grew very strong. And because the midwives feared God, he gave them families. (Exod. 1:17, 20–21)

Today and tomorrow are filled with countless decisions. Some are as light as what we might eat, while others are much more significant: how we treat others (words of kindness or harshness), whether we build or destroy, how hard we work, how much we play, what we do with our spare time, or whether we spend time in prayer. All of these involve decisions. Sometimes our decisions are influenced by others. Peer pressure isn't limited to those of school age. As when we are in a social circle that gossips, speaking ill of others, so many decisions are often influenced by the behaviors and attitudes of those around us.

None of our behaviors operate in a vacuum. Decisions have consequences. They always have. In the Old Testament book of Exodus (or *Shemot* in Hebrew), we read about the population explosion of Israelites living in Egypt. Centuries before, God had promised Abraham innumerable offspring, and it was rapidly becoming true. The pharaoh ruling Egypt had no love for the Israelites. The days of Joseph were long gone, and the Israelites were becoming too numerous for Pharaoh's comfort. So, Pharaoh ordered the male children to be killed as they exited the birthing canal. The midwives had decisions to make. They could obey the pharaoh or, at great personal risk, defy his orders and let the male infants live. The midwives made the right choice. Doing the right thing trumped the command of Pharaoh.

The consequences of the decisions were profound. Moses survived his birth, ensuring the survival and history of the Israelites as a nation. More directly, however, there were consequences for the midwives. God saw their decisions not to destroy families, and as a result, God gave them families. As the women exhibited mercy to the Israelites, God extended mercy to them.

There is an active principle that good things bring about good things and bad things bad. It may not be immediate. Our vision may show us bad things happening to good people, but in the grand scheme of life, people will reap what they sow. Those who sow good things will find blessings, even in the midst of difficulty and pain. Those who sow evil will reap a whirlwind of destructive negatives in life, even if circumstances seem positive.

I have decisions to make. I want to make the right ones, even if no one is looking.

Lord, please give me wisdom to discern right from wrong and strength to choose the right. In your name, amen.

MARCH 27

When she could hide him no longer, she took for him a basket made of bulrushes and daubed it with bitumen and pitch. She put the child in it and placed it among the reeds by the river bank. (Exod. 2:3)

Do you have days that are tough? Days that seem to challenge your faith? Days where you wonder, "Where is God?" Days where you desperately cry out to God for salvation? Everyone who lives very long will answer each of those questions yes at one time or another. Yet the promise of Scripture is that there is a watchful God who stands ready to save his people. God is faithful to his word, and he will not leave his people forsaken or abandoned.

Today's passage and storyline in Exodus 2 actually hearken back to the story of Noah and the flood! No, you won't read about Noah in Exodus 2 in the English Bible, but it is there in a subtle reference in the Hebrew text. Remember Noah? Noah was saved from the judgment of the wicked world. God instructed Noah to build an "ark" to save him from the judgment coming on the world. An obscure Hebrew word was used for Noah's ark. The common word for "ship" or "boat" (*anniya*) was not used. (That is the word used in the story of Jonah, among other places.) Instead Noah builds an "ark"; the rare Hebrew word *tevah* is used. This word is used in only two stories of the Bible—Noah and here in Exodus 2.

In Exodus 2, the Israelites are in bondage to Egypt's pharaoh and are subject to a most violent and hideous imperial decree. All newborn male Israelites males are to be slaughtered. Pharaoh's violent order reminds one of the wickedness and violence on the earth at Noah's time. But while in Noah's day God instructed Noah to build an ark, here Moses' mother builds one.

The "ark" or *tevah* in Exodus 2 is the reed basket into which Moses' mother placed him so that he could float from Pharaoh's harsh judgment into a place of safety and salvation. Ultimately, Pharaoh's daughter finds Moses in the "ark" and rears him to become the man that God will use to bring judgment on Pharaoh and to lead his children out of slavery and bondage into the Promised Land. God saved not only Moses but also Israel through this ark.

The times were dark, yet God was not absent. In the darkness, God provided the ultimate deliverance. This is our God. This world has many who thrive in darkness, who hurt others, and whose lives reflect the worst of humanity. But God *never* abandons his people. That is the promise, and that is the truth.

Lord, please give me eyes of faith to see your hand in the midst of difficulties. May I find your deliverance in my day of need and give you all the glory. In your name, amen.

MARCH 28

Now the daughter of Pharaoh came down to bathe at the river, while her young women walked beside the river. She saw the basket among the reeds and sent her servant woman, and she took it. When she opened it, she saw the child, and behold, the baby was crying. She took pity on him and said, "This is one of the Hebrews' children." Then Moses' sister said to Pharaoh's daughter, "Shall I go and call you a nurse from the Hebrew women to nurse the child for you?" And Pharaoh's daughter said to her, "Go." So the girl went and called Moses' mother. And Pharaoh's daughter said to her, "Take this child away and nurse him for me, and I will give you your wages." So the woman took the child and nursed him. (Exod. 2:5–9)

I find God amazing in many ways, and one is especially prominent in this passage. God cares, and he pours out lavish love in ways that should leave us all stunned if we only open our eyes to see it. God's care goes far beyond anything we could ask or even think.

An Israelite couple, Amram and Jochebed, had a son during the time when Pharaoh had ordered the Israelite males killed. They were able to keep the son alive at home for three months. The infant reached a point where he would no longer stay quiet and hidden, so Jochebed decided on a long-term solution. She would need to give her son up and trust that God would be able to protect him. Jochebed had a fitting name for one who trusted God: her name was Hebrew for the "LORD is glory."

Jochebed took reeds and made what is today called a Moses basket. It was a basket of bulrushes covered with pitch to make it waterproof. Jochebed placed the infant in the basket in the reeds on the banks of the Nile. She instructed her daughter, the infant's older sister, to hide and watch to see what happened to the baby. This was the backstory to today's passage.

Pharaoh's daughter found the basket and, feeling pity for the child, decided to keep the baby as her own, naming him Moses. Of course, not having given birth, Pharaoh's daughter would not have been able to breast-feed the baby. Enter Moses' older sister. She asked Pharaoh's daughter if she should find a Hebrew mother who could breastfeed Moses. Pharaoh's daughter said, "Yes!" Moses' sister went to Jochebed and told her the events. Pharaoh's daughter then gave Moses back to his real mother to nurse him.

On its own, the story is incredible, but the kick that puts it over the top? Pharaoh's daughter *paid* Moses' mother to take care of him! What an amazing God! Blessings even beyond our ability to conceive. It makes me excited to serve God and see his plans!

Lord, thank you for your extravagant love and attention. May I never take it for granted but be stirred to love and give to you as best as I can. In your name, amen.

MARCH 29

During those many days the king of Egypt died, and the people of Israel groaned because of their slavery and cried out for help. Their cry for rescue from slavery came up to God. And God heard their groaning, and God remembered his covenant with Abraham, with Isaac, and with Jacob. God saw the people of Israel—and God knew. (Exod. 2:23–25)

I like things to run on my clock, and my clock isn't slow! Waiting has never been easy for me. Yet I am constantly faced with a certain truth: God's timing is not my timing.

The Israelites were hurting. Their status in Egypt had changed: they had been blessed while Joseph lived, but now they were slaves. The people grew in number, but their servitude and difficulties grew as well. They cried out to God. They needed rescue. This wasn't overnight; it went on for "many days." It was a long time. Centuries passed.

Where was God? What happened to his promises to Abraham, Isaac, and Jacob?

God heard the cries of the people, and God was true to his promises. He was involved and moving things toward his crescendo. But it would be in God's way at God's time. Removing the people from Egyptian slavery wasn't God's only objective. There was much more involved.

God was preparing the Canaanites for invasion. God was populating the Israelites with the right numbers and the right people. God was setting up an Exodus that would produce a Passover to be honored and remembered as long as time exists on earth. Was there misery in the meantime? Certainly. But God had made clear since the rebellious choices of Adam and Eve that this world was no longer paradise. Curses and discord, pain and misery entered into the lives of humans through sinful and rebellious choices, and God rectifying that situation was in his plan and in his timing. People are people, and when people are involved, paradise is far away. So God went about his majestic, centuries-in-the-making plans, keeping his covenant made with Abraham, Isaac, and Jacob but letting it unfold in ways consistent with his greater plans.

I read this passage, I write this devotion, and I am still impatient. I still want things when I want them. It is a true struggle for me to find patience with God's timing. This is a good thing for me to work on; I just wish I could hurry up and learn it! Oh, well—God is faithful, and I will work with his timing!

Lord, teach me to wait patiently and prayerfully for you and your will. Help me to accept your timing and focus on the lessons I need to learn in the meantime. In your name, amen.

MARCH 30

God called to him out of the bush, "Moses, Moses!" And he said, "Here I am." Then he said, "Do not come near; take your sandals off your feet, for the place on which you are standing is holy ground." (Exod. 3:4–5)

There are eight billion people on the planet. Can you think of anyone who, if standing next to you for a conversation, would make you nervous? Would you easily talk to the president as if he were just another person? If you met a superstar in sports, music, or movies, would you have slight apprehension or be starstruck? For most people, the answer is probably "yes." Moses, however, had an encounter unlike any you or I could ever have with anyone on earth. Moses encountered God in a physical appearance.

When Moses was on the run from Pharaoh and the Egyptian powers, before he returned to Egypt on God's mission to lead the Hebrews out of slavery, he had a holy encounter with God on Mount Sinai in the wilderness. The scene is dramatic. Moses sees a bush that is on fire but isn't burning! Moses gets nearer to investigate, and a voice comes from the bush, calling him by name and telling him to come no farther but to take off his sandals because he is on holy ground. The voice then identifies itself: "I am the God of your father, the God of Abraham, the God of Isaac, and the God of Jacob" (Exod. 3:6).

This was not the typical nomadic day of Moses the shepherd. Being in the presence of God is not like any other encounter we could have. Moses had been reared in Pharaoh's house, and Pharaoh was considered a god by the Egyptian people. Doubtless, Moses had spent considerable time before Pharaoh, his adopted grandfather, but this was something more. Moses had a personal encounter with the creator of the universe. This was the one who placed the stars in the sky, who wrote the laws of physics. This was the author and sustainer of life. Moses had no business being in the presence of one so wholly holy. Yet God was there because God was calling Moses. God wanted Moses to be aware, though, that this was extraordinary. Moses had to take off his shoes. The ground where God made himself manifest was too holy for the man-made shoes that had trodden through excrement, dirt, and the commonness of the ground.

Sometimes I fear I don't adequately perceive God in his holiness. I tend to reduce God to what I think of him (or don't think of him). I want the awe of realizing he is wholly holy. I want the trepidation that comes from understanding his greatness. I want to learn who he is, not who I think he is. I want to see him, not what I imagine him to be. I want a genuine encounter. As a Christian, I am taught that we have a strong vision of who God is when we see Jesus. If I spend much time thinking prayerfully, I realize this is no president or rock star. God is far beyond that.

Lord, please let me better see you in your holiness and greatness. In your name, amen.

MARCH 31

Then Moses said to God, "If I come to the people of Israel and say to them, 'The God of your fathers has sent me to you,' and they ask me, 'What is his name?' what shall I say to them?" God said to Moses, "I AM WHO I AM." And he said, "Say this to the people of Israel: 'I AM has sent me to you.'" God also said to Moses, "Say this to the people of Israel: 'The LORD, the God of your fathers, the God of Abraham, the God of Isaac, and the God of Jacob, has sent me to you.' This is my name forever, and thus I am to be remembered throughout all generations." (Exod. 3:13–15)

During the encounter Moses had with God at the burning bush, an interesting dialogue took place. God made it clear that he was charging Moses with being the point person in bringing the Hebrews out of their Egyptian slavery. Moses was reticent and tried to get out of the assignment, but God was persistent. Moses was his man.

In the midst of the dialogue, Moses told God that the Israelites would want to know God's name. Having lived for four hundred years in Egypt, the Israelites for generations had heard about the Egyptian gods. There were well over a hundred of them, all with expressive names. Egyptian gods' names were tied to their roles and powers. For example, the god of war, Anhur, had a name that indicated one who "leads back the distant one." The goddess of the sky, Nut, had a name that referenced the sky.

Egyptian gods had names that expressed their roles on earth—not so the true God. God replied to Moses, but not with a limited name as though he were just another Egyptian god. God told Moses, "The LORD, the God of your fathers" was his "name forever."

The Hebrew here is very important. The word our translators give as "LORD," using all capital letters but in a smaller font for the last three, is a special Hebrew word/name. In Hebrew, it has the letters we would pronounce as "yod," "hey," "vav," and "hey" (read from right to left—יהוה). We would transliterate that into the Roman alphabet as YHWH.

This is the right "name" for the God of Abraham, for when God was explaining his promise to Abraham, God said, "And he said to him, 'I am the LORD [יהוה or YHWH] who brought you out from Ur of the Chaldeans to give you this land to possess'" (Gen. 15:7). God gave insight into the meaning of this name in the comment to Moses just preceding. God explained in Exodus 3:14, "God said to Moses, 'I AM WHO I AM.'"

This is God. He isn't limited to the sun, the moon, the sky, or any other element or idea like one of the well over one hundred Egyptian gods. God simply is. Now and for all time. Whether I like it or not. Whether I believe it or not. God is. That changes things for me.

Lord, may I worship you as the God who is, right here, right now, forever. In your name, amen.

APRIL 1

But Moses said to the LORD, "Oh, my Lord, I am not eloquent, either in the past or since you have spoken to your servant, but I am slow of speech and of tongue." Then the LORD said to him, "Who has made man's mouth? Who makes him mute, or deaf, or seeing, or blind? Is it not I, the LORD? Now therefore go, and I will be with your mouth and teach you what you shall speak." But he said, "Oh, my Lord, please send someone else." (Exod. 4:10-13)

Do you ever dread your day? Are there things you put off doing because you don't want to do them? Do you sometimes feel like you're not up to the task? Everyone does! Parents often feel as if they aren't prepared to parent (especially when their children hit certain "stages"). As a lawyer, I can't count the times I have wondered if I am up to the task of lawyering, in whatever courtroom I am. The key for everyone—and I mean EVERYONE—is to realize that there is a God who has made us, who knows our strengths and weaknesses, and who has prepared us for the tasks that are before us.

Maybe that doesn't sit well with you. At times we all wonder about it. We are in good company. Look at Moses. God's task for Moses was no small one. God was sending Moses to Pharaoh, the most powerful man alive, to demand that Pharaoh free the Israelites from slavery. Do not lose the importance of what Moses was demanding. As slaves, the Israelites were Pharaoh's property—just like his horses, his gold, and everything else he owned. The Israelites were also the workforce for Pharaoh's grandiose building projects. Moses was going to demand that Pharaoh *give away*—not even sell—a massive amount of his property and net worth. That was not going to be an easy task!

Moses told God that he was not up to the task. Moses was not a great speaker. Maybe he stuttered; we don't know. But Moses was acutely aware of his speech problems. Moses reminded God, as if God didn't already know. Moses instructing God about his own limitations also indicates that Moses was a bit short in the theology department! Didn't God know these things? God explained, "I made you, Moses. I determine whether you can speak at all! This isn't about you. You aren't the one to get Pharaoh to give up his slave force. This is about me! I will do it through you!" Even still, poor Moses begged God to use someone else.

When we dread our days, when we feel insufficient for the tasks before us, when we don't want to do what is right for us to do, we need to quit making excuses, go to God, make sure we are doing what he wants us to do, invoke his help, and then *do what is before us in his strength and to his glory!* Then when we are done, at the end of each day or task, we should thank him for working in us.

Lord, equip me, empower me, and use me to your glory and in your name, amen.

APRIL 2

"I have heard the groaning of the people of Israel whom the Egyptians hold as slaves, and I have remembered my covenant. Say therefore to the people of Israel, 'I am the LORD, and I will bring you out from under the burdens of the Egyptians, and I will deliver you from slavery to them . . . I will take you to be my people, and I will be your God, and you shall know that I am the LORD your God" . . . Moses spoke thus to the people of Israel, but they did not listen to Moses, because of their broken spirit and harsh slavery. (Exod. 6:5–9)

There is an interesting anomaly I've seen over and over again in the lives of others and in my own life. There are times of intense struggle, times of outright misery and sadness that often drive people from their faith in God—and those very times are opportunities in which God intends to show his love and faithfulness.

It was that way with the Israelites. When Moses went and demanded that Pharaoh release them from slavery, Pharaoh reacted harshly. Rather than release the Israelites, Pharaoh intensified their work. Things didn't get better; they got worse—much worse. The people rebelled against Moses and his brother, Aaron, and saw them as enemies rather than the tools of God. God told Moses to tell the people not to despair, that God was at work, and that at the right time, Pharaoh would indeed release the people from slavery. But when Moses so informed the people, the reaction wasn't faith. It was disbelief. The people didn't listen because their spirits were "broken" and the slavery had just gotten harsher.

I suspect that some of the Israelites had their hopes up. They started out encouraged and trusting. They heard Moses had come to free them and was going in to meet with Pharaoh. Could the promises come true? Could the slavery finally end? Then their hopes were dashed once Pharaoh not only said "No!" but punished them for asking.

God was working. His plans were carefully laid out, and Pharaoh's actions were not the setback the people thought. It was all part of God's redemption that would not only free the Israelites but would also bring God great glory in the process. The people didn't react with faith in the moment, but that wasn't going to stop God from what he was about. God had given his word, and he would be true to his word.

This encourages and admonishes me. I am encouraged that the faithful God isn't finished just because things look bleak or aren't turning out as I thought they would. I am also admonished for the times I have let circumstances, even harsh ones, change my level of love and trust in God. He is at work. I need to trust him.

Lord, I hand over my life to your purposes and your designs. Help me grow in trust to live out the commitment I make to you with joy and confidence in your name. Amen.

APRIL 3

And the LORD said to Moses, "See, I have made you like God to Pharaoh, and your brother Aaron shall be your prophet." (Exod. 7:1)

What is this? God made Moses to be like God to Pharaoh? What is this all about? I thought there was only one God and people were *never* to think themselves equal to God. That is tantamount to the greatest sin! Satan's big temptation to Eve was that if she would eat of the tree of knowledge of good and evil, then she would be like God. What is going on in this verse? This is one of the verses that requires us to understand the culture of the day. Once we do that, the verse becomes very instructive for us in our day.

In Egyptian thought, Pharaoh was not simply a king. Pharaoh was a god. The Egyptians had well over a hundred gods, and Pharaoh was one of them. It is one reason Pharaoh got the great tomb with sufficient food and servants buried with him to see him back to his land as a god. In Pharaoh's mind, and in the minds of his servants, priests, army, and so on, Pharaoh was a god, and no man had any right to approach the god Pharaoh and make any demand. Only a god could instruct or deal with Pharaoh on even footing. So God made Moses like God to Pharaoh. Moses was the emissary of the Divine One of Israel speaking to Pharaoh directly, face-to-face. Moses was speaking as an equal, not as a supplicant.

God doesn't take a backseat to anyone. No one holds power over God. No one ranks higher. There is one God only, and he triumphs over all other powers, earthly or otherwise. Anyone who thinks he or she is in a class by him- or herself, anyone who thinks she or he has great power is deluded. God can take a shepherd like Moses out of the wilderness and elevate him to a level that exceeds that of the most powerful man in the world.

What does this mean for you and me? Are we going to be gods? Of course not! Neither was Moses! God made Moses "like God" in the sense that he empowered and authenticated Moses as one who could rightly stand toe-to-toe with Pharaoh. Moses wasn't begging or pleading for Pharaoh to release the Israelites; he was making God's demand for their release.

But this is where you and I need to pay heed. We don't need to walk through this world on our own merit, skill, social status, popularity, or professional position. We need to walk through this world dedicated to God and what he makes of us. Then we can do what God calls us to do, in spite of the obstacles.

So, let's not think too highly of ourselves. But let's think as highly as possible about our God! Don't let anyone or any situation intimidate you when God is at work in you.

Lord, I give you my life. Work in me. Make me who I need to be to meet your plans and will. In your name, amen.

APRIL 4

The LORD said to Moses, "I am the LORD; tell Pharaoh king of Egypt all that I say to you. . . . You shall speak all that I command you, and your brother Aaron shall tell Pharaoh to let the people of Israel go out of his land. But I will harden Pharaoh's heart, and though I multiply my signs and wonders in the land of Egypt, Pharaoh will not listen to you. Then I will lay my hand on Egypt and bring my hosts, my people the children of Israel, out of the land of Egypt by great acts of judgment. The Egyptians shall know that I am the LORD, when I stretch out my hand against Egypt and bring out the people of Israel from among them." (Exod. 6:29, 7:2-5)

A lot of people don't like this passage. It seems to fly in the face of who they think God is, or at least who he should be. More than one person has said to me, "How can God blame Pharaoh? God hardened Pharaoh's heart!" The comments have gotten worse, especially with the unbelievers who have asked me, "What kind of God would send Pharaoh to hell when it was God who hardened Pharaoh's heart?" These people have not read this and similar verses carefully enough!

This isn't a passage talking about whether Pharaoh would go to heaven or hell. It isn't a passage that contemplates whether Pharaoh was going to become a believer in the God of Israel. This is a passage about God's glory in triumphing over the bondage of Egypt. Pharaoh didn't want to give away his slave workforce. Through Moses, God worked miracles, and in reply, Pharaoh at times wavered in his decision to hold Israel captive. But God knew that his wavering was not final. God would need to show his power more completely before Pharaoh would bend adequately. God would harden Pharaoh's heart to hold firm his control over Israel so that God could eventually work through all the steps to show Israel and Pharaoh the great majesty and absolute power of God. Even then, after Pharaoh finally let the Israelites go, he changed his mind and sent his army to destroy them.

Don't let a passage like this beguile you into thinking that God is not compassionate or does not want the best for his people. The passage actually says the exact opposite. It shows that those set against God and his people will not triumph. God will work in their hearts in ways that bring about God's glory and plans.

In my life, I have encountered many who have set themselves against God and what I perceive to be God's plans and purposes. Of this one thing I am sure, however: God will not be thwarted. He is at work in the hearts of everyone—me, you, our family, our friends, and even enemies of God. No one will stop his love and glory from being demonstrated in our lives and world.

Lord, I worship you as the God who knows my heart and mind. Please soften my heart to your voice, and work in the world to your glory. In your name, amen.

APRIL 5

Then the LORD said to Moses, "Go in to Pharaoh and say to him, 'Thus says the LORD,
"Let my people go, that they may serve me. But if you refuse to let them go, behold, I will
plague all your country with frogs. The Nile shall swarm with frogs that shall come up into
your house and into your bedroom and on your bed and into the houses of your servants
and your people, and into your ovens and your kneading bowls."'"... So Aaron stretched
out his hand over the waters of Egypt, and the frogs came up and covered the land of
Egypt.... Then Pharaoh called Moses and Aaron and said, "Plead with the LORD to
take away the frogs... and I will let the people go to sacrifice to the LORD."... So Moses
cried to the LORD about the frogs... And the frogs died out in the houses, the courtyards,
and the fields. And they gathered them together in heaps, and the land stank. But when
Pharaoh saw that there was a respite, he hardened his heart and would not listen to them,
as the LORD had said. (Exod. 8:1–15)

We live in a world that doesn't honor God as God. Many may give him lip service but do not truly believe him to be the God he is. Many don't even give him lip service. They seem to have no need for him. They have their jobs, families and friends, bank accounts, car, house, and food to eat. What can God give them? What need do they have for God?

These thoughts are directly addressed in today's passage, especially if we understand it within its historical Egyptian context. Among their many gods, the Egyptians worshipped Heqet, the goddess of life and fertility. Heqet brought life to the people, sustained life, and not only gave the people offspring but was responsible for the fertility of their livestock. In Egyptian art, Heqet was represented by the frog. Frogs were symbols of her presence and power. Frogs represented her divine power over life and fertility. God had Moses turn that power on its head.

At first Moses brought such an abundance of frogs that there was a plague from "life and fertility" out of control! Too much of a good thing is not always a good thing! Then when Pharaoh asked Moses to take away the frogs, it seems Pharaoh expected them to return to the Nile from whence they came. But it didn't happen that way. God killed the frogs where they were—in homes, in the courtyards, and in the fields. God killed the symbol of Heqet, and the stench rose. Everyone knew it. Israel's God triumphed over the Egyptian goddess of life and fertility. What Egypt thought worthy of worship for bringing life was stinking up the world with death.

So it is in our world. Those things that seem to us to be reliable resources for our lives aren't really. They are idols. Whether it's our money, our education, our job, or anything else, it is nothing before the real God. Give it time and it will stink too!

Lord, let me put nothing before you. Be my all in this life. In your name, amen.

APRIL 6

And the LORD said to Moses and Aaron, "Take handfuls of soot from the kiln, and let Moses throw them in the air in the sight of Pharaoh. It shall become fine dust over all the land of Egypt, and become boils breaking out in sores on man and beast throughout all the land of Egypt." So they took soot from the kiln and stood before Pharaoh. And Moses threw it in the air, and it became boils breaking out in sores on man and beast. And the magicians could not stand before Moses because of the boils, for the boils came upon the magicians and upon all the Egyptians. But the LORD hardened the heart of Pharaoh, and he did not listen to them, as the LORD had spoken to Moses. (Exod. 9:8–12)

I never served in our military, but I have the greatest respect for those who have. I always find it interesting to talk to them, to hear of their experiences and how service changed their lives. I have a number of military people who work for me, including two Marines (never an "ex-Marine!") who years later embody the best of what we see in people. One of the things that I find interesting is a description of what happens in boot camp. Boot camp isn't just about getting in shape and learning how to disassemble, reassemble, and fire a rifle. In boot camp, the military goes about disassembling and reassembling the recruit! The military tears down and builds up. It makes the servicewoman or serviceman.

There is a bit of that going on in today's passage, although one needs a little Egyptian understanding to see it. Google pictures of Egyptian priests from around 1000 BC and you will see that the Egyptians were clean-shaven. The Greek historian Herodotus (c. 484–c. 425 BC) wrote that the Egyptian priests actually shaved themselves totally every day (*Histories* 2.37). This was to ensure that their skin was perfect and pure, necessary for them to offer worship in the temples for their gods. But God disassembled the worship of the Egyptians. God brought boils on everyone, including the priests. The skin disease would have stopped the priests from offering sacrifices and attending to the gods, with, Egyptians would have thought, disastrous consequences. In spite of God's work and the disruption of Egypt's idolatrous worship, Pharaoh did not get constructive in his actions. He didn't seek the God who had power over the Egyptian religious system, and he sure didn't let the Israelites go. Opportunity missed! Things were going to get worse for Pharaoh and Egypt.

I don't worship the idols of Egypt, but that doesn't give me a pass from this passage. I still place other things where I should place God. When I rely on my insight or cleverness, when I think that I have the strength to handle a situation or the economic resources to be secure, I am placing idols where I should place God. I know God is able to disassemble me from my connection to the idols in my life. When he does it, I need to keep my heart soft and work on his mission.

Lord, disassemble me when I put anything in your place and reassemble me according to your plan. In your name, amen.

APRIL 7

Then the LORD said to Moses, "Rise up early in the morning and present yourself before Pharaoh and say to him, 'Thus says the LORD, the God of the Hebrews, "Let my people go . . . For this time I will send all my plagues on you yourself . . . and your people, so that you may know that there is none like me in all the earth. . . . But for this purpose I have raised you up, to show you my power, so that my name may be proclaimed in all the earth."'" (Exod. 9:13-17)

We all long for perfection. We want a perfect day, a perfect workplace, a perfect spouse or friend, perfect health, a perfectly just society (except where we need perfect mercy in place of justice)—heavens, I often hope for the perfect donut! (Hot, tender, and flavorful.) But this world is a war zone, not a place of perfection. If we aren't careful, we fall victim to the idea that an all-powerful God should ensure that this world is perfect. But that is not a fair assessment of the world or the way God interacts with it.

God was working in the events of Egypt with a long game in mind. His goal was not simply to bring his people out of Egypt but, in the process, to establish clear victory over the gods of Egypt, including Pharaoh himself. God's work would show his glory and power, show that nothing on this earth can stand in the way of his might, and show that he will faithfully fulfill his promises, regardless of the opposition.

At this point, the plagues moved from being an inconvenience to Pharaoh to actually affecting Pharaoh himself. God was about to take over the weather, defeating all the gods of the sky, sun, moon, stars, and so on. This was to show God as the true God. It would let everyone know that the God of Israel was like nothing ever before seen. Israel should have confidence in its God. This plague should have sent Pharaoh to his knees, not only obeying the commands of God but also asking how to worship the true God. Pharaoh should have set aside his "god" status and found humble faith before God Almighty.

But such was not the case. This world isn't perfect. People aren't machines where God dictates their actions. People make choices, and the choices have real effects. For God to accomplish his will, he must maneuver around and through the choices of people. I want this world to be perfect, but it isn't. I want my loved ones perfectly healthy, but they're not. I know the truth is that the world is broken, people are broken, society is broken, and God is the only answer. He doesn't answer by turning people into machines and making everything perfect. But he shows his glory, we honor him as God, we follow him, and we trust that *in the end* things work out for the best for his people. He also promises a day *will come* when things are made aright.

Lord, be lifted up in my life today. In the midst of my own imperfection, be glorified in your name, amen.

APRIL 8

Then Pharaoh sent and called Moses and Aaron and said to them, "This time I have sinned; the LORD is in the right, and I and my people are in the wrong. Plead with the LORD, for there has been enough of God's thunder and hail. I will let you go, and you shall stay no longer." Moses said to him, "As soon as I have gone out of the city, I will stretch out my hands to the LORD. The thunder will cease, and there will be no more hail, so that you may know that the earth is the LORD's. But as for you and your servants, I know that you do not yet fear the LORD God." . . . So Moses went out of the city from Pharaoh and stretched out his hands to the LORD, and the thunder and the hail ceased, and the rain no longer poured upon the earth. But when Pharaoh saw that the rain and the hail and the thunder had ceased, he sinned yet again and hardened his heart, he and his servants. So the heart of Pharaoh was hardened, and he did not let the people of Israel go, just as the LORD had spoken through Moses. (Exod. 9:27–35)

The blame game—it's something we all play at times. Part of it is innocent enough. We live in a scientific age where we are taught from an early age the law of cause and effect. Most things don't happen at random. The lights come on in my room because I turned on a switch that completed an electrical circuit, lighting a bulb. It's cause and effect.

Similarly, we can see cause and effect in the actions of others. In today's passage one reads a critical fact about Pharaoh's actions. Importantly, a risk of devotionals like these is that because I segment the passages into daily devotions, we might miss the context provided by reading an entire story at once. Today's passage, for example, provides insight that fills out our understanding of other passages in the overall story.

Pharaoh is taking actions that bring God's judgment on him and his people. Over and over in the larger narrative we read that "God hardened Pharaoh's heart." That is the cause for Pharaoh refusing God's command. Yet here we read that Pharaoh hardened his own heart as part of his sinning. Which is it? Did God harden Pharaoh's heart or did Pharaoh? Did God do it one day, and Pharaoh the next? We know cause and effect; we play the blame game. Who's to blame? God or Pharaoh?

The passage makes a clear point. *Pharaoh sinned*, and his sin hardened his heart. In a sense, we can also say God hardened his heart because God made us in such a way that sin is destructive to us. Both aspects of the narrative are true. And there is an important lesson here. Sin not only affects our actions; it affects our hearts. It is one reason God instructs us not to sin. Sin is a bad and evil thing that may seem right, may seem pleasurable or profitable, but results in bad consequences, including a hardening of our hearts to God. I read this, and instead of playing the blame game on Pharaoh's actions, I need to turn from my own sinful ways and seek a soft heart to God!

Lord, please forgive my sinful ways, and soften my heart to you. In your name, amen.

APRIL 9

Then the LORD said to Moses, "Go in to Pharaoh, for I have hardened his heart and the heart of his servants, that I may show these signs of mine among them." (Exod. 10:1)

Bad things happen to good people. Everyone experiences it. While nature can cause bad things to happen to good people (earthquakes, floods, fires, etc.), often the cause is directly human. Humans can be thoughtless and also downright mean and evil. History shows it. We experience it. Sometimes we seek help or counsel from a friend or professional. Other times we live with the effects of evil, bottling up the hurt and nursing the pain.

Today's passage speaks to the pain in this life caused by the actions of others. The language is easily taken out of context to indicate that the blame for these bad events should fall on God's shoulders, but the true thrust of the passage is very different.

Moses has sought the Israelites' liberation from Pharaoh's ownership and slavery. Pharaoh has repeatedly refused to free the Hebrews. Instead, Pharaoh has made the burden on the Hebrews even rougher and more abusive. The larger storyline has explained that this was sin on the part of Pharaoh, and that Pharaoh's sin caused Pharaoh to harden his own heart. That is the way of sin—it hardens our hearts to God and his will. It feeds defiance, not holiness. That much of the storyline, most people accept. The problem is these passages that seem to indicate that GOD WAS THE ONE BEHIND THE ABUSE, that God was responsible for hardening Pharaoh's heart.

We must read these passages within the larger context. Then we see that they are actually giving assurance to those who are hurt by the actions of others. People sin of their own volition, not because God forced them to sin. But when there is sin, even though sin is contrary to God's will, God is still able to work through the sin to show his love for his people. God worked through Pharaoh's hardening of his own heart. We can, in a sense, say God hardened his heart, but the point isn't that God forced Pharaoh to an action. Rather, God worked through Pharaoh's sin to bring about a greater good. God would not only win release of his people, he would also shower them with awesome wonders and signs that would shout of God's love for generations to come.

This is our assurance when bad things happen. We can always shake our fists and blame God. After all, if God is God, he is powerful enough to stop bad things from happening. But that's not the world where we live. We live where people can make choices, even ones that hurt us. We can live with confidence, however, that God is there. He is active. He will work to his glory in showing his love to us. In our hurt, we need to see his hand bringing redemption and rescue.

Lord, draw me in faith in the midst of difficulty and pain. Work to your glory in your name, amen.

APRIL 10

"Tell in the hearing of your son and of your grandson how I have dealt harshly with the Egyptians and what signs I have done among them, that you may know that I am the LORD." (Exod. 10:2)

Are you good at saying "thank you" to those who are kind to you or do a service for you? Are you quick to bring them praise and tell others? My wife is one of the kindest people I have ever met. She is not only great at thanking people but amazing at building them up in the eyes of others. Bring up someone before my wife, and the odds are that she will tell you something great about that person.

Becky has reared our children to be the same way. Often one or the other will gently remind me when I am caught up in a moment and forget to thank someone for something. They will also readily lift up those who have done something marvelous, saying good things about others. This is an important feature of life. We need to be people who give praise where it is due. It is important not only for our own development but also for those who follow us down life's road.

Moses was told that God was acting on behalf of his people in bringing about stunning miracles to win the Hebrews' release from Pharaoh's ownership. This was not only a once-in-a-lifetime experience; it was one for the ages. God was working in ways that few in the history of humanity would get to witness. It was important that Moses and the people not only see the hand of God at work but also give thanks to God and then sing, tell, proclaim, preach, and SHOUT that God was at work! God had done what no one thought possible. God brought freedom to the chained. God brought hope to the despondent. God put a song of joy in the mouths of those singing of bitterness. God gave a future to the hopeless. This was unfolding daily right before the Hebrews.

God told Moses to proclaim it. God wanted all the Hebrews to proclaim it. As they told the next generation what God had done, the next generation would know of God's love and faithfulness. Then when the next generation faced days of difficulty and times of temptation, they would have something deeply ingrained in their memories reminding them God is at work. God cares. God is not absent or asleep. God is active and involved. Each generation is responsible for seeing the hand of God, thanking God for his care and love, and telling the next generation.

We live in such a cause-and-effect world, we need to be careful not to lose the eyes of faith that enable us to see God and praise him. Yes, we have food today because somewhere a farmer farmed, a rancher ranched, a deliverer delivered, a cook cooked. But there is more. God is behind it all, providing lovingly and tenderly. Give him credit!

Lord, thank you for your care and concern for me. May I tell others! In your name, amen.

APRIL 11

So Moses and Aaron went in to Pharaoh and said to him, "Thus says the LORD, the God of the Hebrews, 'How long will you refuse to humble yourself before me? Let my people go, that they may serve me.'" (Exod. 10:3)

Most anyone reading the story of the exodus will at some point say internally, "Wow, Pharaoh was an idiot! Why didn't he let the people go a whole lot sooner? These were major miracles he was ignoring!" This verse lets us in on a reason. Pharaoh was blinded by his pride.

Pride is a dangerous sin. Pride can be defined as thinking more highly of oneself than one should. When we do so, it affects how we treat ourselves, how we treat others, and how we treat God. We build ourselves up and become the center of our universe. Things begin to revolve around us, or so we think. We look at events in terms of how they affect us. We make our decisions based on what we want or what is comfortable for us. It becomes all about us.

Pride doesn't stop with how we treat ourselves, however; it grows outward in our actions to others. When we think too highly of ourselves, others become tools. Their lives are seen as important because of what they do for us. It also drives us to treat others selectively. Those who seem to be like us, or perhaps even better, we treat differently than those who are "lesser." The lesser, we overlook or disregard.

Pride also changes how we see and treat God. We might not acknowledge him at all, confident that we have it all figured out. There are many who proudly proclaim (or proclaim from their pride) that they have the insight and knowledge to dismiss this silly superstition of God. After all, only losers and those who are lesser believe in such. Anyone with the sense of the proud would know better. Even if we acknowledge God in spite of our pride, it will still change the way we treat him. In subtle ways, it will still be about us, not him. God will be expected to do the things that make our lives what we want them to be. We become like God, seeking to direct his will rather than searching to discern it.

Pharaoh had a major pride problem. It was his stumbling block. In the end, it brought him great misery and ruin. That's the thing about pride. It is built on deception. I can't brag on where I was born or my DNA. I really didn't earn it or choose it. Furthermore, we are not God, and we shouldn't pretend to be. We are not of greater value than our neighbors. All of us are made in God's image and all of us are valuable. I want to learn humility, treating others as more important and looking for ways to build them up and learn from God.

Lord, help me to learn humility. Forgive my pride. In your name, amen.

APRIL 12

Then Pharaoh's servants said to him, "How long shall this man be a snare to us? Let the men go, that they may serve the LORD their God. Do you not yet understand that Egypt is ruined?" So Moses and Aaron were brought back to Pharaoh. And he said to them, "Go, serve the LORD your God. But which ones are to go?" Moses said, "We will go with our young and our old. We will go with our sons and daughters and with our flocks and herds . . ." But Pharaoh said to them, "The LORD be with you, if ever I let you and your little ones go! Look, you have some evil purpose in mind. No! Go, the men among you, and serve the LORD, for that is what you are asking." And they were driven out from Pharaoh's presence. Then the LORD said to Moses . . . (Exod. 10:7-12)

My grandfather told me at an early age, "If you are going to do something, do it right. Doing something halfway is not acceptable." He was rough in his teaching, but his message was strong. His words are especially true when it comes to honoring God.

Pharaoh's counselors were tired of the destruction from God's plagues. They implored Pharaoh to honor the demand of God and let the Hebrews leave—at least some of them! Pharaoh called in Moses and Aaron and told them that he would allow the older people to leave but not the younger people. Moses replied that God wanted full obedience. God wanted all the people released. God wasn't picking and choosing where he would keep his word. God wasn't selling out the next generation. God is a 100 percent God, and he was going to redeem every Hebrew, just as he promised.

Pharaoh's temper got the best of him. He had offered a compromise, but Moses refused to negotiate. Moses insisted it be God's way all the way. Rather than be obedient, Pharaoh again put his back up and in fury sent Moses and Aaron away. The Hebrew verb form (the "piel" form) indicates that Moses and Aaron were not simply asked to leave. They were *driven out.*

Once Moses left Pharaoh, God gave his next instructions to Moses. God told Moses to go on with the next plague. This is the way with God. He calls us to his will, and his will is not negotiable.

I need to note this. Of course, no one is going to perfectly obey God or follow him. Yet I want to! It should be my goal and desire. I want to give God 100 percent of my life, not the parts I select. I am in no position to negotiate with God how much I will do of what he wants versus of what I want. I need to be all in!

Lord, I give you my life. I give you my choices, my loves, my desires. I want to pursue your will and pledge myself to you. In your name, amen.

APRIL 13

So Moses stretched out his staff over the land of Egypt, and the LORD *brought an east wind upon the land all that day and all that night. When it was morning, the east wind had brought the locusts. The locusts came up over all the land of Egypt and settled on the whole country of Egypt, such a dense swarm of locusts as had never been before, nor ever will be again.* (Exod. 10:13–14)

Locusts were never a strange thing in the land of Egypt. They were regular pests. But the locust experience in today's text was different from the norm in two notable ways.

First, the locusts came from the east, carried on an eastern wind. The locusts in Egypt would generally come in from modern Libya or Ethiopia. That would be a south or south-westerly wind. When the locusts come in on an easterly wind, from Arabia, it is rare but not unheard of. Note, however, that the wind blew for a day and night before the locusts arrived. This shows the locusts came from far away, far beyond the land of Egypt or its borders.

Second, the locusts were not confined to a part of Egypt but covered the entire land. This differed from the normal outbreaks, which cover a region but not the land in its entirety.

What would these differences mean to the person in Moses' day? Both differences speak to the power of God in a clear way. In a day when gods were deemed to be "regional"—in other words, one god for this region and another for that one—Israel's God was different. He commanded the winds and could call up locusts from far away. His power was not limited to a region. It was far and wide. Further, God's power wasn't narrow in its focus either. God focused his efforts on the entire country, and it was evident. No one could escape from the power of Israel's God. His reach was long and deep.

I read this and I am both comforted and warned. I am comforted because I am assured that there is nothing beyond God's reach and power. He has the ability to confront my needs, whatever they may be. He can reach around the globe, if need be, to accomplish what he determines to accomplish. He can galvanize resources beyond what is available to me. He can marshal whatever is necessary to fulfill his will.

But I am also warned. God is no God to be trivialized. Do not trifle with God. Do not suppose you are ever outside his watchful eye or out-stretched hand. You may not see him and you may not feel him, but he is God. He is present. He is powerful. He is active. That is reassuring and yet a bit scary.

Lord, open my eyes to see your power, and align me with your will to work through me. In your name, amen.

APRIL 14

And the LORD gave the people favor in the sight of the Egyptians. Moreover, the man Moses was very great in the land of Egypt, in the sight of Pharaoh's servants and in the sight of the people. (Exod. 11:3)

Reputation is a funny thing. Everyone develops a reputation. It is basically what people think of us—our character, strengths, and weaknesses. It is frequently based on our accomplishments and failures, the actions we have taken, the motives we demonstrate, and our reliability and trustworthiness or lack thereof. Not always, though. Sometimes our reputations are based on others' perceptions of us, which may or may not be reality. I like this passage because it speaks to Moses' reputation in ways that inspire my life.

Moses had been working for the release of the Hebrews from Pharaoh's ownership and slavery. There had been a long battle where some harsh curses were brought upon the land. Pharaoh's house suffered, but so did many ordinary people in Egypt. Each step along the way, however, Moses gave clear warnings and gave Pharaoh every opportunity to avoid the curses. Pharaoh refused to walk as he should, and while many paid the price, the reputation of Moses didn't suffer with the Egyptian populace. It increased.

The people saw Moses as a man with deep conviction, doing what he must to stand up against the most powerful man in Egypt, a man that most considered a god among the mortals. Moses never backed down. Moses was faithful to his calling.

So the time came when the people were finally about to be released. God told Moses that the coming tenth curse would be the last one. After this curse, Pharaoh would not only let the people go; he would order them out. God gave the Hebrews an unusual instruction. God told them to ask their Egyptian neighbors for silver and gold jewelry. God had the people get the materials that would be necessary for building the ark of the covenant and other items pertaining to the tabernacle and Israel's worship of God. "The plundering of the Egyptians" is the phrase most used for this event. To achieve it, God gave the people "favor" in the eyes of the Egyptians.

Yet for Moses, greatness was already achieved. His reputation was very great, even among those in Pharaoh's immediate service. This both amazes and teaches me. I am amazed that after all the calamity Moses brought on the people, they looked favorably on him. I would expect them to take out a hit on him! I am also inspired and learning. I need to be God's person, following God's lead and doing God's will. Too often those who claim godliness live lives that are anything but godly. I don't want people to see me as a hypocrite.

Lord, may I live today in a way that demonstrates my love for you. May people see in my life the truth of who you are and what you are about. In your name, amen.

APRIL 15

The LORD said to Moses and Aaron in the land of Egypt, "This month shall be for you the beginning of months. It shall be the first month of the year for you. . . . On the tenth day of this month every man shall take a lamb . . . without blemish, a male a year old . . . and you shall keep it until the fourteenth day of this month, when the whole assembly of the congregation of Israel shall kill their lambs at twilight. Then they shall take some of the blood and put it on the two doorposts and the lintel of the houses in which they eat it. They shall eat the flesh that night, roasted on the fire; with unleavened bread and bitter herbs they shall eat it. . . . In this manner you shall eat it: with your belt fastened, your sandals on your feet, and your staff in your hand. And you shall eat it in haste. It is the LORD's Passover. For I will pass through the land of Egypt that night, and I will strike all the firstborn in the land of Egypt . . . and on all the gods of Egypt I will execute judgments: I am the LORD. The blood shall be a sign for you, on the houses where you are. And when I see the blood, I will pass over you, and no plague will befall you to destroy you, when I strike the land of Egypt." (Exod. 12:1–13)

Practicing Jews, and many Christians who seek to better understand and experience the Hebrew roots of the Christian faith, celebrate the Jewish festival of Passover or Pesach. It is a most holy time and a celebratory time as well. God was set to redeem Israel from slavery, redeeming them by the blood of an unblemished lamb. The lamb was slain, the blood was put over the Israelites' doors, and the death that came with God's judgment on the unbelievers would not visit those living under the blood. Those with the blood's protection would be released from their slavery to be taken to a Promised Land of redemption.

For Jews, Pesach is a time of remembrance. It is confirmation for all generations that no matter how dark the night, no matter how genuine the fears, no matter how bleak the prospects, God is a redeemer who will faithfully seek out his people.

For Christians, the message is much the same but with an added historical event. Jesus was celebrating Passover when he instituted what is commonly called "the Lord's Supper." Jesus told his disciples that the redemption of God from the toils of life and the slavery of sin would come from a true pure lamb's sacrifice. The lamb of God who would take away the sin of the world, atoning for it in a complete, once-for-all event, was Jesus. So for Christians, the Passover in Egypt is not only a historical reality but also a prophetic vision.

I am in awe of the God who secures his people. Life still has very rough and difficult periods. This is not the garden of Eden, but God is faithful, and in that I rejoice.

Lord, thank you for your deliverance from the travails of sin in this world. In your name, amen.

APRIL 16

When Pharaoh let the people go, God did not lead them by way of the land of the Philistines, although that was near. For God said, "Lest the people change their minds when they see war and return to Egypt." (Exod. 13:17)

Pharaoh had had enough. Plague after plague peppered his land, and he endured them all until the final plague cost him the life of his firstborn. Pharaoh was defeated. He sent Moses and the Hebrews packing. He gave away his enslaved workforce. The Israelites went free.

But God knew it was just a matter of time before Pharaoh's grief turned to anger and hostility. Pharaoh would rouse his army, his generals, his charioteers, his foot soldiers, and all his military might to teach Moses and Israel a lesson. Pharaoh would attack and attempt to destroy Israel. Of course, the later student of history reading the story knows what God can (and did) do to Pharaoh's army. He and his troops would be washed up! But that isn't the pressing concern of the moment.

There is a short way out of Egypt to where God intended to take his people, but that way would cause the Israelites to run into Pharaoh's military outposts. The northern route from Egypt to Israel was packed with Egyptian fortresses one day apart from each other. The people would be faced almost immediately with warring Egyptian forces, and God knew the people's faith was tenuous and not up to the confrontation. The Israelites would capitulate before they could see the saving hand of God.

So God took them by a less direct route. The journey would be longer. The travel would be more difficult. Anyone knowledgeable about the terrain would be able to see that God wasn't doing things in a normal way. God chose the more challenging route. But this wasn't because God's GPS was out of order. It wasn't because God liked watching his people rough it. It was because it was what the people needed.

I've seen God do this in my life on many occasions. He has put me on a route that is challenging, difficult, circuitous, and even painful. But it was that route that got me ready for the tasks in front of me. Looking back, I would never want to endure some of those times again; however, I am thankful for how those times put me where I am today. I appreciate that God used less-than-pleasant events to mold me into a better person. He has kept my heart tuned to him when, if left to my own devices, I might have wandered far away.

I need to focus on God's direction and not my own GPS for my life. I want to pray for this for my children and loved ones as well.

Lord, lead us in the ways that are best for us in living for you. In your name, amen.

APRIL 17

Moses took the bones of Joseph with him, for Joseph had made the sons of Israel solemnly swear, saying, "God will surely visit you, and you shall carry up my bones with you from here." (Exod. 13:19)

How good are you at keeping your promises? When you tell someone you are going to do something, do you do it? Is honesty a trait or a stranger in your life? How about when timing makes honesty difficult? Can we "honestly" say we are good at keeping true to our word?

Today's passage has always stood out to me as really cool and a bit surprising. Joseph was the son of Jacob. Jacob had been told that Canaan was a land God was giving to him and his offspring. Jacob's father was Isaac. God had told Isaac the same thing. Isaac's father was Abraham, the first to receive God's promise of Canaan. Even though all of Israel was in Egypt as Joseph was dying, Joseph knew that God wouldn't break his promise. Joseph knew that God would bring the Israelites out of Egypt and give them the land promised to his forefathers. So Joseph made his offspring promise to take his bones with them when the day came for them to return home.

But Joseph lived in Egypt four hundred years before Moses! Think about how long ago that was. That is the equivalent for me today to a promise made in the early 1600s, long before the United States became a country. Who keeps that promise? Moses hadn't made the promise himself, nor had anyone who was headed out of Egypt with him. That promise was made ten generations back.

Yet Moses was faithful. Moses and Israel kept the promise made four hundred years prior.

This entire passage and the story surrounding it are wrapped up in promises kept. God had promised well over four hundred years before that he would bring the Israelites out of Egypt and deliver them to the Promised Land. God was keeping his promise. The Israelites promised Joseph they would take his bones when they left. Moses saw to it that Israel kept its promise. This verse will take on greater significance as the journey unfolds and we read of the Israelites failing to keep many promises they make to God and suffering because of it.

But that is for another day. This is a day of promises kept. It is a strong day of honesty and resolve. I want to live in today and be a person who keeps my word. If I say, "Yes," I want it to be so. If I say, "No," may it be true as well. Let those who know me know I will keep my word, regardless of how much time passes.

Lord, help me to have integrity and to keep my word, even when it hurts. In your name, amen.

APRIL 18

And the LORD went before them by day in a pillar of cloud to lead them along the way, and by night in a pillar of fire to give them light, that they might travel by day and by night. (Exod. 13:21)

Some people live their lives tied to a calendar. Today I have to wake up at X o'clock to have time to get ready and be at ABC place by . . . whatever time. Then I have to do seven different things before getting home and having dinner. Then it's study time, or maybe relaxation time, as I get ready to sleep and go after my schedule tomorrow. Pretty soon the days add up to weeks, the weeks to months, and the months to years. Then looking back, the days may be long, but the years are short. Time passes.

I don't want that life. Now I'm not advocating schedule anarchy, where I go where I want, do things when I want, and do what I want. I don't want that life either. I want a life of purpose, but the purpose needs to be something grand—something eternal! I want to live my life in a way that is beyond my own vision and thought. I want to be part of something greater than I could schedule on my own.

Today's passage points to what I want. God has a mission. God has a plan. I can choose to ignore his plan and pretend it doesn't exist or doesn't involve me. Or I can buck his plan, knowing it is there but deciding to go my own way. Or I can seek to follow his plan. The passage teaches that God leads his people. He doesn't simply exist on his own, doing his own thing, and leaving his people to fend for themselves. He goes before his people, leading them where they should go. He's not letting them ramble around, cleaning up their messes. He is showing them the way they should go.

When I was young, I considered this and decided I would follow God, but I needed him to be a clear leader. I wanted that pillar of cloud by day and pillar of fire by night. I would pray to God, "Tell me what to do," fully planning on doing it if I could simply hear his voice or read some writing on a wall. But no, that is not what happened. In my study, I came to understand that God is not making us puppets, so overwhelming us with direction that he is really just pulling our strings. God gave us minds, and part of what he is doing is teaching us to use them properly! That means we need to read and consider what he has told us (the Bible), seeking to apply it in our lives.

Over time, I have found that Scripture teaches me what to do and where to go 90 percent of the time. Beyond that, I need to pray for God's guidance, seek to do his will, and trust that he is not leaving me alone. My days may be tied to a calendar, but I want my calendar tied to God's will.

God, please lead me in the way I should go and help me to follow. In your name, amen.

APRIL 19

When Pharaoh drew near, the people of Israel lifted up their eyes, and behold, the Egyptians were marching after them, and they feared greatly. And the people of Israel cried out to the LORD. *. . . . And Moses said to the people, "Fear not, stand firm, and see the salvation of the* LORD, *which he will work for you today. For the Egyptians whom you see today, you shall never see again."* (Exod. 14:10, 13)

When I was young, about five or six years old, I awoke from a good night's sleep frozen. I had phased into awakening from a dreamy sleep where a vampire was about to bite my neck! I was lying on my side, and I was confident the vampire was behind me. I couldn't move. It took me an eternity to work up the courage to turn and see whether the vampire was real. (It wasn't!) One of our daughters went through a phase as a young girl where she was scared to death that a train would come through her room in the night and run her over. I had a difficult time explaining train tracks!

Now I am older. My fears have changed. I haven't feared vampires for some time. Instead I fear things that seem reasonable at my age. Of course, to a five-year-old, a vampire was a reasonable fear, so maybe while my fears have changed, I haven't changed too much.

What do you fear? What is coming to get you? Do you fear death? Life? Failure? Success? Loneliness? Company? Whatever you or I fear, we can take some comfort in today's passage.

The people of Israel had been miraculously set free from a harsh and bitter slavery. It was God fulfilling his promise made over four hundred years earlier. Then, in a turn of emotion, the pharaoh that God had so defeated that he let the people leave decided that he would pursue and kill the Israelites. He called his army, the most fearsome one known in his day, and he brought it in full force to annihilate Israel. The people had been rejoicing in their freedom, only to look up and see the coming army. The noise of the chariots and the soundings of battle horns made it clear that the might of Egypt was descending on what seemed to be a defenseless civilian group.

But the Israelites weren't defenseless. They had God Almighty as their defender. God was the answer to their fears. With God on their side, what could some mere man with a bunch of chariots do? Could the forces of Pharaoh do anything against the protective wall of God? Of course not! Pharaoh was no more to be feared than my vampire many years ago or my problems of today. God is victorious. Nothing will happen outside his control.

Lord, give me faith. Let me trust you to rescue me, and when bad things happen, let me wait patiently for your delivery. In your name, amen.

APRIL 20

Then Moses stretched out his hand over the sea, and the LORD *drove the sea back by a strong east wind all night and made the sea dry land, and the waters were divided. And the people of Israel went into the midst of the sea on dry ground . . . The Egyptians pursued and went in after them into the midst of the sea, all Pharaoh's horses, his chariots, and his horsemen. And in the morning watch the* LORD *. . . threw the Egyptian forces into a panic, clogging their chariot wheels so that they drove heavily. And the Egyptians said, "Let us flee from before Israel, for the* LORD *fights for them against the Egyptians."* (Exod. 14:21-25)

When I read this story, one thing jumps out at me in capital letters: I WANT TO FOLLOW GOD, NOT WORK AGAINST HIM!

The Israelites were in a tough position. Their lives were on the line. They were under attack, and they didn't have the means to defend themselves. This means that there were fathers who couldn't defend their wives or children. There were mothers who were helpless. Children were about to watch their helpless parents fall as they were also slaughtered. The events would be gruesome. Everyone knew it. Panic was in the camp.

Then God stepped in, and the world was changed. God did what no one could do. God parted the sea, dried the land, and guided the Israelites to safety. Anyone following God that day was safe and sound. They witnessed something contrary to the laws of nature as God, the author of those laws, intervened.

Consider the Egyptian side of things that day. They were driven by an angry pharaoh who was considered divine. Their god pharaoh gathered his best charioteers and horsemen, and they galloped in angry pursuit of the Hebrews. Believing they been duped into letting the slaves go, the army was set to exact a bloody revenge. Their eyes were blind to the hand of God. They overlooked and conveniently forgot or explained away the miracles that had brought about the Israelites' release. With military training, they were set to unleash fury and devastation on the Israelites. It wouldn't be hard. The silly Israelites following Moses and their "God" had placed themselves in a stupid trap, surrounded by the sea and the Egyptian forces.

Then God stepped in, and the world was changed. The waters parted, the Israelites began to cross, and the Egyptian chariots and horsemen pursued. Only things began to change. The dry land was muddy. The wheels were getting stuck. Then the waters collapsed and the forces drowned.

I WANT TO FOLLOW GOD, NOT WORK AGAINST HIM. He can change the world.

Lord, may I follow you as you change the world for your glory. In your name, amen.

APRIL 21

Then Moses and the people of Israel sang this song to the LORD, saying, "I will sing to the LORD, for he has triumphed gloriously; the horse and his rider he has thrown into the sea. The LORD is my strength and my song, and he has become my salvation; this is my God, and I will praise him, my father's God, and I will exalt him." (Exod. 15:1–2)

Do you have a song to sing to the Lord? Are you able to tell people, with the joy and excitement that comes in a song, about how God has worked in your life?

The people of Israel did! They were rescued from Pharaoh and his army through God's miraculous parting of the waters at the Re(e)d Sea. God turned the dark day of fear and panic into a day of excitement, rejoicing, victory, success, and a promise of brightness for what would come.

Maybe you read this story and you think, "Yes, well, if God parted the sea for me or God worked some other supernatural wonder for me, then I would be singing too! But I never seem to get my needed miracles from God." If that is your thought, think again! First, be fairer to the Israelites that day. Yes, we twenty-first-century students of science and the world order understand that the fluidity of water, the law of gravity, and the limits of wind make the parting of the sea an unexplainable event beyond divine intervention. But in the pre-science days of long ago, there were many events that defied the understanding of the people. They didn't understand thunder, lightning, and so many other weather phenomena. For them, the parting was an unexplainable miracle, but such unexplained things happened all the time. It wasn't the miracle that brought the song of praise. It was the salvation!

God saved his people. Did God do so in a powerful way? Certainly! And they rightly praised him for that. But the key is this: God did not leave his people to the apparently certain destruction. *How* God did it was magnificent, but that God *did it* was the key!

So now you and me. Maybe you have seen God do what could be explained no other way. Or maybe you have seen the hand of God work through the natural order of this world. Either way, are you able to see that God has answered when you have turned to him in need? Have you seen that God hasn't abandoned you and left you to the destruction of the world? If so, sing to him a song of praise! Tell the world about the faithful and loving God of your salvation.

If you haven't experienced this, have you sought God? Have you sought him on his terms rather than your own? Have you put yourself on his team rather than hiring him to work with your team? That is the place to start!

Lord, I give you my life. Use me, and may I sing your praise. In your name, amen.

APRIL 22

"You have led in your steadfast love the people whom you have redeemed; you have guided them by your strength to your holy abode." (Exod. 15:13)

What a mighty God we serve! What a marvelous God we serve! What a loving God we serve! What a reliable God we serve!

Look carefully at today's passage. Read it again slowly. This is a verse in the "Song of Moses" sung by the Israelites after God saved them from Pharaoh's army by parting the Re(e)d Sea. The song was for a moment in time, but this verse sets out some eternal truths about God and his work with his children.

God's love is "steadfast." This is the Hebrew word *chesed*. It is hard to put it into an English word. The semantic range includes a loyalty to promises made of covenants entered. To quote Bob Dylan, "God don't make promises that he don't keep." God's love isn't temporary. It isn't conditional. It is constant and steadfast. That doesn't make it a soft and gentle love. It can be stern. He can discipline his children as a loving parent might discipline a child, but it is out of love. God's love is reliable.

Jesus told the story of the father who had two sons. One son was rebellious, and he wanted to go out on his own. He asked his loving father for his share of the inheritance, and getting it, he went out and wasted it on wine, women, and a sinful lifestyle. Left destitute, the renegade son finally came to his senses. He figured if he got a job with his dad, he would have a better life than what he had having wasted everything. So he went back to ask his father if he could live as a slave or servant in his father's house. Seeing the son on the road, the father *ran*, not walked, to embrace him, love him, clean him up, and restore him as a son. Jesus was explaining the "steadfast love" or *chesed* of God the Father.

God in his steadfast love "redeemed" his people. He brought them out of slavery, redeeming them from Pharaoh through mighty acts because of God's promises to Abraham and so many more. Having redeemed them, God continued to express his steadfast love as he guided them to *his* holy abode.

That was God then, and it is God today. God has a steadfast love for his children, and he expresses it in redeeming us, saving us, and guiding us! What an amazing God!

Lord, I bless your name. You have loved me and redeemed me, and I am eternally grateful. You guide me in love, and may I always seek to follow you! In your steadfast love and name we pray, amen.

APRIL 23

The next day Moses sat to judge the people . . . from morning till evening. When Moses' father-in-law saw all that he was doing for the people, he said, "What is this that you are doing for the people? . . ." And Moses said to his father-in-law, ". . . when the people have a dispute, they come to me and I decide between one person and another, and I make them know the statutes of God and his laws." Moses' father-in-law said to him, "What you are doing is not good. You and the people with you will certainly wear yourselves out . . . You are not able to do it alone. Now obey my voice; I will give you advice, and God be with you! . . . Look for able men from all the people, men who fear God, who are trustworthy and hate a bribe, and place such men over the people as chiefs of thousands, of hundreds, of fifties, and of tens. . . . Every great matter they shall bring to you, but any small matter they shall decide themselves. So it will be easier for you, and they will bear the burden with you. If you do this, God will direct you, you will be able to endure, and all this people also will go to their place in peace." (Exod. 18:13–23)

I have two good friends. One is able to delegate; one isn't. The one who delegates gets a lot more done. The one who doesn't delegate remembers a time he delegated a task, and the task was messed up. He decided delegation was for the birds. Maybe it was the bad experience, but I suspect deep down, my friend doesn't delegate because my friend is a bit of a control freak. He wants to do everything.

Today's passage relates the story of Moses trying to resolve every dispute among the people, no matter how small. It was wearing Moses out, although that was hard for Moses to see. Once Moses' father-in-law, Jethro, arrived on the scene, however, he spotted the burnout potential quickly.

Jethro gave Moses good counsel. He urged Moses to delegate, warning Moses that he needed to be sure to delegate to good people who were up to the task. Finding those people would be a chore, overseeing those people would be a chore, and fixing the mistakes of those people would be a chore, but through delegation, Moses would accomplish much more, there would be peace among the people, and Moses would have the energy to do the high-priority items that required his personal touch.

This passage teaches me that I need to watch over-controlling, but I also need to be careful at delegating. More than that, this passage teaches me that I need to be ready to learn from others, even when they are teaching me that I am not doing the best I can. Jethro spoke into Moses' life as a concerned father-in-law, and Moses listened. Rather than being defensive or defending his turf, Moses saw the wisdom in Jethro's comments and radically changed his approach. I need godly people to speak into my life, and I pray I will listen with discernment, choosing what is best.

Lord, teach me to listen to others and make good decisions. In your name, amen.

APRIL 24

"'You yourselves have seen what I did to the Egyptians, and how I bore you on eagles' wings and brought you to myself. Now therefore, if you will indeed obey my voice and keep my covenant, you shall be my treasured possession among all peoples, for all the earth is mine; and you shall be to me a kingdom of priests and a holy nation.' These are the words that you shall speak to the people of Israel." (Exod. 19:4–6)

My friend Louis says, "People are people, and the church is full of them." My friend Bernie says, "God made all kinds . . . and they're all here." I tend to say it less poetically but more descriptively: "I can't believe how stupid we often are!"

Does that sound harsh? Maybe. But let me explain. Look carefully at today's passage. Having worked miracle after miracle to redeem Israel from Egyptian slavery, having defeated Pharaoh's army without Israel having to raise a sword, having rained down manna from heaven for a starving people to have food and nourishment in the wilderness, having provided quail for protein and diversity at the table, having promised to deliver the people to a Promised Land, God has to issue this warning. God tells the people who have been borne "on eagles' wings" that they will be blessed if they obey God and keep his covenant.

Doesn't it seem a bit absurd that the God who did all those things would need to be concerned about his delivered people's devotion? People who have experienced what they had should be grateful to their dying breaths and follow of anything and everything the Lord asks.

Yet God knows people. He knows that people are people, and the nation of Israel was full of them. He knew that deep down, we are often selfish, inattentive to him, and caught up in our own worlds. We tend to seek him out when we are desperate for help, but on the good days, God can be far from our minds. We might be more careful about following him when we are living on a sharp edge of life, but when life seems smooth sailing, our attention to his details seems less important.

Yes, I stand by my words. I can't believe how stupid we often are. God has rescued me from horrible circumstances. God has brought me into a wonderful life. He has borne me on eagles' wings to heights I could never achieve on my own. I want to be careful to honor him as my God by the way I live and follow his teachings. It is the smart thing to do!

Lord, thank you for the love and attention you have shown me. Thank you for pursuing me in love and bringing me into your circle of fellowship. Help me to be attentive and careful to obeying your voice and keeping your commandments. In your name, amen.

APRIL 25

"On the third day the LORD will come down on Mount Sinai in the sight of all the people. And you shall set limits for the people all around, saying, 'Take care not to go up into the mountain or touch the edge of it. Whoever touches the mountain shall be put to death.'"
(Exod. 19:11–12)

When I am trying to teach a jury a new concept, I often use a tool psychologists call *anchoring*. The idea is that you tie something new to something someone already knows. You anchor it, and he or she learns it more easily and more readily remembers it.

The brain works well with anchoring. But that same mechanism can wreak havoc on our understanding of God, at least if we aren't careful. We all tend to anchor who God is and what he is like to what we already have in our brain. We tend to think of what seems "good" to us and think that is what God must be. Or maybe we think what we would do if we had unlimited power and then we either assume God would do the same or challenge him because he doesn't measure up to what we think he should be.

Scripture teaches us something altogether different. God isn't something we make in our image. He isn't something we manufacture out of what seems right or sensible to us. God exists on his own. He is who he is, not who we think he should be.

God was making this point clear to the Israelites. They needed to understand that he was no trifling God. God is not a supersized human, as the Greek gods were. God is not a step up from the human race. God is something altogether different. God in his greatness, God in his grandness, God in his majesty is a being we aren't even able to touch, much less comprehend. God told Moses not to let the people so much as get on the mountain or even touch its border elevation lest they die. People need to understand, God is unlike anything else we could ever encounter. The theological word is that God is *holy*. He is special in an awesome and even frightening way.

Because we are made with an imprint of God, being made in his image, we are hardwired to seek him out, to try to find the meaning in our existence. But that doesn't qualify us to create what kind of being God is. We know about God because he has chosen to reveal aspects of his character to us. We know his power over creation, over life, and over death. We know his love and care because he has not abandoned us to our own devices, but he seeks us out to restore a relationship with us that has been lost through our sin and willful disobedience. We know his holiness because he taught us that he is not like any other. We can anchor an understanding of God with traits he has revealed to us, but we need to be careful that we are acknowledging him on his terms, not ours.

Lord, teach me to honor your holiness. Forgive me for trying to make you something less than you are. In your name, amen.

APRIL 26

And the LORD said to Moses, "Go down and warn the people, lest they break through to the LORD to look and many of them perish. Also let the priests who come near to the LORD consecrate themselves, lest the LORD break out against them." (Exod. 19:21–22)

I spent a few years of my professional life working on cases that involved a pain relief drug. The drug was a kind of super aspirin, belonging to the class of drugs called NSAIDs (or non-steroidal anti-inflammatory drugs), in the same category of drugs as the brand name drugs Advil and Motrin. The company's internal data and studies indicated that unlike other drugs, this specific NSAID increased the risk of a heart attack by 600 percent. Yet the label on the drug gave no warning about that increased risk.

The company pulled the drug, the suits were successful, and ultimately the company settled the litigation. I was on a few national news shows about it, and a constant question that was asked of me was how I felt about people losing the right to buy a drug. My response was always the same: my big complaint was never that the company should or should not sell the drug. All drugs come with risks. My big complaint was that the company's conscious decision was not to warn the public and doctors about the risk. People and doctors have a right to know so they can make an informed decision about whether they choose to take or prescribe the drug.

Good warnings are fair and important. Without them we make decisions we wouldn't otherwise make. Israel could *not* accuse God or Moses of failing to give adequate warnings.

Today's passage belongs to a common type found throughout the Bible. God instructed Moses to warn the people. God was teaching Israel to holiness, so He was setting up holy boundaries. The people needed to know that God was not like the gods of Egypt. God wasn't found in a painting or in the common things of nature. God was not a ball of fire, coursing across the sky. God was not found in the land or water. God was something altogether different and holy. God was so holy that he could only be approached in certain ways, by certain people who were dedicated and prepared for the occasion. God warned them that if they failed to follow these instructions, their lives were forfeit.

The Bible is replete with God's warnings. He warns us about behaviors that will bring blessing and behaviors that will bring negative consequences. We should be honest, for example, and not tell lies. We should not envy but wish the best for others. There are many instructions we are given with a warning. We worship a good God who wants us to make good decisions.

Lord, may I hear and heed your warnings as I live for you. In your name, amen.

APRIL 27

God spoke all these words, saying, "I am the LORD your God, who brought you out of the land of Egypt, out of the house of slavery. You shall have no other gods before me. You shall not make for yourself a carved image, or any likeness of anything that is in heaven above, or that is in the earth beneath, or that is in the water under the earth. You shall not bow down to them or serve them, for I the LORD your God am a jealous God, visiting the iniquity of the fathers on the children to the third and the fourth generation of those who hate me, but showing steadfast love to thousands of those who love me and keep my commandments." (Exod. 20:1–6)

In today's passage we begin the most famous legal code in the history of humanity. These verses are the beginnings of the Ten Commandments. Some regard these commandments as the "really important" part of the law God gave to Moses. This assessment is undoubtedly true in some sense, yet it isn't fair to say that this is the "most important." What makes these commandments unique is that they are ones that God himself wrote on a tablet for Moses to take to the people and keep with the most holy treasures in the ark of the covenant. The other commandments are basic applications of the principles in these ten.

The commandments begin with God giving his own authority as Law Giver. God is the one who brought the Israelites out of slavery. He is the one responsible for Israel as its own nation. God is the one who should be giving Israel the laws by which they live.

After proclaiming his own authority, God then sets up the importance of the Israelites honoring *only* God as God. We err if we think that God's prohibition of putting other "gods" before him speaks only to having some carved idol for worship. There are plenty of things that we place in front of God where we shouldn't. For some, the pursuit of money is more important than the pursuit of God. For those, money or possessions become their idol or god in violation of this commandment. Others might place social status as a greater drive and achievement than living with God as the first priority. Again, this is idolatry. There are even those who make food an idol, pursuing the satisfaction of pleasing their stomach over pleasing God.

Idolatry is losing focus on God. God should be our starting point and our goal. We should orient our choices around him. We should make him our chief desire. He should help us understand how to treat others. Our goals should be built around pleasing him. Our first desire should be finding his will in our lives. We should strive to know him, relate to him in love and dedication, and live for him. This is the foundation for not only the laws of Israel but also our behavior today.

Lord, I honor you as the one true God. Inform my mind as you inspire my heart. May I seek you above all else. In your name, amen.

APRIL 28

"You shall not take the name of the LORD your God in vain, for the LORD will not hold him guiltless who takes his name in vain." (Exod. 20:7)

This is my favorite of the Ten Commandments, if one is allowed a favorite! My reason for placing this one into a unique category is simple. I believe it is the most misunderstood of the commandments, and yet, when properly understood, it is one of the strongest ones for helping us in life.

The key to understanding this commandment lies in the word *name*. It is the Hebrew word *shem*. In our twenty-first-century lives, *name* is simply a label. It is what we put on our headings in school when we were first learning to write. Before that, it was put by our parents on our birth certificate so we had a label for people (and the government) to use in identifying us. Our parents picked out our name, perhaps because it ran in the family or maybe because it sounded good. But our names are labels, no more and no less.

With the twenty-first-century "name is a label" mentality, this commandment gets reduced to an instruction not to say God's name lightly. We aren't to invoke his label absent intentional meaning. We don't say "God" or some variant of it in a haphazard fashion or as part of an ordinary expression.

But that is not what *shem*, or "name," meant in biblical times. Your name wasn't simply your label. It was a statement of who you were, your reputation and your character. In a modern sense, we can more closely relate it to your resume, not simply your label. It stood for what you had done. In fact, if your name didn't align with your character, in biblical times, they would change your name!

In light of this, reconsider this commandment. The Israelites were instructed not to take God's *shem*, or name, in vain. When we see that this is a reference to more than pronouncing a name wrongly, we get a glimpse at the moment-by-moment importance of this command. We see why God put it so early among the Ten Commandments. The Israelites, and we, are not to take God's character lightly. We aren't to overlook the importance of his resume or curriculum vitae. We should see him for who he is, and we should honor him. We should remember his deeds, and we should have confidence in his steadfast love.

We violate this commandment when we fear God can't help us, when we doubt his love, when we believe we have to find our own way out of a mess, when we turn to others before turning to him, and so on. We should never take God lightly. He is a great God.

Lord, forgive the many ways I fail to regard you in your greatness. Forgive me for taking your "name" in vain. I pray this in light of who you are, in your name, amen.

APRIL 29

"Remember the Sabbath day, to keep it holy.... Honor your father and your mother.... You shall not murder. You shall not commit adultery. You shall not steal. You shall not bear false witness against your neighbor. You shall not covet." (Exod. 20:8–17)

These final commandments are important ones for society and the ways we interact with others. Yet at the same time, they are very personal. I find some of these GREAT and some of them difficult, especially when understood as conditions of the heart, not simply actions of the body.

For the Sabbath day, God instructs us to find a day a week to rest from ordinary work. This helps us keep perspective on who he is, how he made us, and what he requires of us. It gives us time for recharging our batteries. It gives us time to focus on our families. Like all the commandments, it is actually a great benefit to us if we follow it. However, we live in a day of cell phones, email, and 24/7 access to our jobs and obligations. That makes this an easy instruction to ignore. I need to work on this one!

Honoring one's parents can seem a bit ambiguous. It might seem easy to those of us with great parents and hard to those with difficult ones. The idea of "honoring" parents means to hold them in regard. When we are young, it means to obey them if they are godly. (If they aren't, we honor them by doing what is right, even if they don't. We should not teach children to obey molesting or abusive parents, nor does God expect them to.) When we are older, it means to help take care of them. It says that our parents are important at each stage of life, and we need to show them love.

Murder, adultery, and stealing are three commandments that many people feel they can check off the list. As in, "Well, at least we didn't do those!" Not so fast, however! Jesus explained that these are commandments not only of the body but also of the heart. We are not to murder *or* hate or wish ill for others. We aren't to commit adultery *or* even lust or commit sexual infidelity in our minds. We aren't supposed to take what doesn't belong to us, but that isn't just breaking into another's home or lifting a wallet or purse; it means taking the change given to us by the clerk in error. It means getting refills when they weren't part of the purchase price. It means taking or doing what we want when we aren't entitled to it.

Bearing false witness is a technical courtroom idea, but the commandment is deeper. We are not to lie. We are to be honest people. When we speak, people should be able to rely on our honesty. We aren't to covet. We should be glad for others' success rather than jealous. Like the other commandments, this is a goal not always easily achievable!

Lord, I fail in so many ways. Please forgive me. Help me to grow. In your name, amen.

APRIL 30

"Now these are the rules that you shall set before them. When you buy a Hebrew slave, he shall serve six years, and in the seventh he shall go out free, for nothing." (Exod. 21:1-2)

Slavery was the economy in the days of Moses. Every culture had slaves. These were those who worked without property ownership. They belonged to the wealthier people in society. From our vantage point in history, it is not unusual for people to look back and be appalled, thinking, "How could a good God allow or endorse slavery?" We need to be careful to read these passages in their historical context as well as their context in the entirety of the Bible. This passage about slavery is a good example.

Without a doubt, the slavery of our modern era is one of the most abhorrent aspects of our history. That gross injustice and sin that blights our past is *not* what Scripture spoke to as God put forward these laws to Moses and Israel. The differences are profound. This was an economic model vastly different from the slavery of America, for example.

God gave clear instructions that slaves were to be held only for six years. They were then to be released. Only if the slave chose to remain would the slavery continue. Furthermore, the slaves were to be treated incredibly well. They were to work only six days a week, honoring the Sabbath as all Hebrews were ordered to do. They were not to be abused or treated as chattel but were to be respected and treated with care. They had rights in the courts. To call them slaves as we know that word is not necessarily even the best translation. The word we translate "slave" (*ebed* in Hebrew) might just as well be translated "servant."

Rather than concentrating on how appropriate the economic class of servants or slaves might be, and I am quick to say and applaud that society has outgrown this economic model, we need to see the lesson in God's instructions. For God gave the Hebrew nation instructions that were a major leap forward from other societies. Not only did God give slaves rights and ultimately freedom, but God charged the owners with the responsibility to treat their workers properly!

We live in a different economic time, but the charge for employers to treat employees well has not evaporated. Employers should show care and concern for employees. They should give them pay and wages that will enable their employees to eventually retire. They should give them jobs where they have time off. The treatment should show respect and honor people's core rights. This commandment is a positive commandment about treating people well, even if they are at the bottom of the working class.

Lord, help me to see the least of my human brothers and sisters as worthy of attention and rights. Help me to seek to enforce fair and good treatment of others wherever I see abuse or unfairness. May I do this in your name, amen!

MAY 1

"Whoever strikes a man so that he dies shall be put to death. But if he did not lie in wait for him, but God let him fall into his hand, then I will appoint for you a place to which he may flee. But if a man willfully attacks another to kill him by cunning, you shall take him from my altar, that he may die. . . . Whoever steals a man and sells him, and anyone found in possession of him, shall be put to death." (Exod. 21:12–16)

My grandfather believed in God, but he wouldn't go to church. He said the church was filled with hypocrites. There was a fellow who attended church who my grandfather believed had swindled him of some money. I tried to talk my grandfather into changing his mind or approach, but I was never successful. I can't judge the other man, but I have seen as I have aged people who use religion for purposes other than worshipping and serving the Lord. Some see it as a business opportunity, some a social network. I even know some who go to services to be seen and enhance their community profile.

Into these circumstances come passages like today's. It is seemingly unrelated, as it prescribes capital punishment for those who intentionally murder another. In the event that the death was accidental, the responsible party is given a chance to make a defense. He does so by fleeing to a city of refuge and embracing the altar of God. But here is where the passage gets interesting! Once one is secured in a place of refuge, the refuge only works if the person fleeing didn't intend to kill the other. If the killing was purposeful, the killer cannot escape justice by availing him- or herself of religion! Religion is not a crutch or tool. Our interactions with God are to be genuine.

The passage then speaks of one who steals a person and sells him as a slave. Not only is that person subject to death, but *so is the person purchasing the slave.* Again, the law makes clear a principle about making excuses. Not only is "religion" not an excuse, but we should never think that we can let someone else do our dirty work while we escape the consequences personally. At least not before God.

I have seen the temptation of wanting to do something wrong, of seeing how it might be helpful and excusing it because someone else does it rather than me. I suspect you have too. Am I being too harsh? People don't bat an eye about receiving a phone call and having their assistant tell the caller, "She (or he) isn't in right now. May I take a message?" We should never think that having someone else do something wrong for us makes us any less culpable for the wrongdoing.

Gamesmanship in religion is not acceptable before God. We need to weed it from our lives.

Lord, I have a long way to go in growing before you. Help me in your name, amen.

MAY 2

"If a man gives to his neighbor money or goods to keep safe, and it is stolen from the man's house, then, if the thief is found, he shall pay double. If the thief is not found, the owner of the house shall come near to God to show whether or not he has put his hand to his neighbor's property. For every breach of trust . . ." (Exod. 22:7-9)

I have had the pleasure of working with some really exceptional people in my life. Some have sparkling personalities. Some are brilliant minds. Some have all the social graces. Some are driven and ambitious. Some have excellent qualifications. With all of these different people, however, one consistent trait causes folks to rise to the top in my work life: they are reliable. They are are diligent people I can entrust with anything, knowing that they will be careful and take care of what is entrusted to them.

This strength and character trait is not something new. It has been recognized as a virtue for thousands and thousands of years. In the law given by Moses, the issue of trust is dealt with in many ways. One aspect is found in today's passage. The issue arises from entrusting a neighbor with money or other valuables. If the neighbor handles the valuables properly, then all is well. If something happens to the property and it is stolen, then the neighbor entrusted with the valuables is to be examined. The examination hinges on whether the person was trustworthy or not. Was the person responsible? Did the person play a role in the valuables disappearing? If the person did, then the person will be held accountable.

I want to be a trustworthy person. By that, I don't mean I don't want to steal someone's property. That is a given. But I want to be more than that. When someone entrusts something to my care, and I agree to take it on, I want to do so responsibly. I want to be diligent and accomplish the task I've agreed to do. The importance of trust cannot be overstated.

I am also motivated by thinking through the importance of trust to consider my work for God in his kingdom. How shall I go about keeping the commitments I have made to him? How seriously do I take the valuables he has entrusted to my care? I have a marvelous wife and five children. I need to teach them about life, faith, morality, and more. Do I take that responsibility seriously? Am I trustworthy with those treasures? My health is a valuable gift. Do I keep trust with that by my lifestyle and choices? I want to be a trustworthy person in all areas of my life.

Lord, help me to see the importance of being trustworthy and reliable. Teach me those traits and strengthen me to do better. In your name, amen.

MAY 3

"You shall not wrong a sojourner or oppress him, for you were sojourners in the land of Egypt. You shall not mistreat any widow or fatherless child. If you do mistreat them, and they cry out to me, I will surely hear their cry, and my wrath will burn . . . You shall not pervert the justice due to your poor in his lawsuit." (Exod. 22:21–24; 23:6)

I love passages like today's. I also squirm when I read them. They touch me and make me uncomfortable, all at the same time. God cares for the poor, the downtrodden, and the helpless. God doesn't teach his people "survival of the fittest," where those less fit to make it are relegated to second-class citizenship, are taken advantage of, or are treated poorly.

The court systems in Western civilization are built on passages like this. When operating at their best, they provide a level playing field, where everyone has a fair day to have grievances heard and where a widow can stand toe-to-toe with the largest company in the world. Of course, courts don't always operate at their best! There are times when the resources of the rich and powerful strip the rights of the poor and defenseless. But in those instances, the faithful of God should recoil. Injustice should make us seethe. It isn't right, and it incurs the wrath of Almighty God.

This passage, however, isn't limited to how people are treated in court. It equally applies to treatment in general. How do we respond to those who are oppressed or in need? Do we look for ways to show them God's care and blessing? Or do we ignore them, knowing we can't always understand where people are in need or where they are not being personally responsible? This can be a practical question about how to help people.

I was walking the streets of Oxford one day with our son, who had lived there for six years, moved away for two, and then returned for several years. We saw a person begging on the street with a sign saying he had just lost his job and asking for help for bus fare. Will commented that the sign must be effective, since the person had used it for years during our son's first sojourn in Oxford and he was still using it when our son returned from a two-year absence. How does one know when someone is truly helpless versus when asking for help has become his or her full-time job?

One of our daughters was concerned that giving money to beggars only fueled their alcohol and tobacco problems. Her solution was keeping and handing out gift cards to fast food places.

These aren't easy problems to answer, but I know it is important to God that I address them. I need to care for those less fortunate, not ignore them or run from them.

Lord, teach me your compassionate heart and give me direction in your name, amen.

MAY 4

"If you lend money to any of my people with you who is poor, you shall not be like a moneylender to him, and you shall not exact interest from him. If ever you take your neighbor's cloak in pledge, you shall return it to him before the sun goes down, for that is his only covering, and it is his cloak for his body; in what else shall he sleep? And if he cries to me, I will hear, for I am compassionate." (Exod. 22:25–27)

WHAT? This is in the Bible? Does the Bible really instruct us to lend money without interest? Sort of! Read this passage carefully.

The passage is speaking of how we treat the poor. When the poor need something, we are to step up and help them. If they need money, we loan it to them. But we aren't to be loan sharks and exact interest. The goal is to help the poor person with a solution, not compound the problem. The same idea permeates what one takes as collateral. Don't take collateral on a loan when that collateral is needed for life. If someone has a coat, you don't take the coat as collateral, leaving the person cold through the night.

We read this law, and we can certainly see how Israel would and should take it literally; however, I believe the heart behind the command is worthy of greater attention than the mere letter of the instruction.

The heart of today's passage is the importance of helping those in need. If the passage were only concerned with charging interest to the poor, then the answer for the lender would be simple: only lend money to people who can afford to pay interest. In other words, you don't have to worry about taking the coat for collateral if you just say, "No!" to someone who asks you for help.

This is why we must understand this passage as saying more than, "Don't charge interest to the poor." Built into this passage is the understood but unstated command to HELP THOSE IN NEED!

Jesus told the story of a traveler who was set upon by robbers. The traveler was left naked by the side of the road, stripped of all he had. Many people passed by the wounded traveler, and only one stopped to help. Jesus taught his disciples to be the helper.

This needs to be my story. Not everything is about my interest or what I get out of the relationship. When I see those in need, I need to help them. It is God's heart.

Lord, give me eyes to see those in need and the resources to aid them in your name, amen.

MAY 5

"You shall not delay to offer from the fullness of your harvest and from the outflow of your presses. The firstborn of your sons you shall give to me. You shall do the same with your oxen and with your sheep: seven days it shall be with its mother; on the eighth day you shall give it to me." (Exod. 22:29–30)

When I was a young law student, I made the moot court team. It was my law school's competitive team that went up against the teams of all the other law schools. Our coach was an adjunct professor, meaning that he coached the school's moot court team but made his living practicing law, not as a law professor.

At our first team meeting, Coach Hunt told our team of three, "I want a time commitment from you. Here is what I demand of you and your time. First, you put your faith. Second, you put your family. Third, you put your schoolwork. Then I want every second of every day you have left." Coach Hunt understood priorities. There is a proper ordering of things, whether in hunting ("ready . . . aim . . . fire," not "ready . . . fire . . . aim") or living. We are always to put God first.

Today's passage speaks of the law that the first of everything is to be dedicated to God. Dedicate to God your firstfruits from harvest. Or in modern language, give God from the first of your income, not what's left after your bills and Starbucks. Beyond your money, dedicate to God your family, teaching all of your family the importance of giving back to God. When the passage speaks of giving your firstborn son, it is something that the whole family would see and understand. You are dedicating to God's service first! Then everything that follows is no less God's.

An interesting part of the passage is the first phrase, "You shall not delay . . ." There is to be no hesitancy. There are to be no second thoughts. When we receive anything, our first thought should be "This belongs to the Lord." We put meaning into this thought by offering it and giving it in a real fashion.

Another intriguing part of the passage is the recognition that for animals, oxen and sheep, you don't sacrifice them to God until after seven days. This alleviates lactating pain for the milk-producing mother, and it allows the mother to cycle through the hormonal response to birthing. In other words, the command takes into account what is best for the party, even while securing a proper devotion and dedication to God.

Practically speaking, what does this mean to me today? I am going to recognize that God gets the first and best of me. My time, my thoughts, my resources, my opportunities—they all belong to him. Without delay, I want to serve him fully today.

Lord, all I have is yours. Put me to work in your service today. In your name, amen.

MAY 6

"Behold, I send an angel before you to guard you on the way and to bring you to the place that I have prepared. Pay careful attention to him and obey his voice; do not rebel against him, for he will not pardon your transgression, for my name is in him." (Exod. 23:20–21)

Growing up, I can remember times when my parents would be telling me something and my mind would be a million miles away. I can see my dad saying, "Are you paying attention?"

Today's passage is a strong admonition of a simple truth: pay attention to God! God has a purpose in this world and a purpose in our lives. He doesn't lead aimlessly, and we shouldn't follow haphazardly. Lest we think this is not important, the passage underscores that there are consequences to how we live and follow God.

We live in an era of multitasking. We can listen to music, type on a computer, and keep a text chain going on a smart phone, all while eating lunch. Distractions come easy in this world. We need to make sure, in the hustle and bustle of life, that we never get sidetracked from the major focus we should all maintain. That is a focus on God.

What is God doing? How does God want us involved? What are God's priorities and missions to be accomplished? These are the questions that should be foremost in our minds as we go through our lives. They will help us train and equip for doing God's work. They will help us spend our energy and resources doing things that count, things that make a real difference. They will focus our desires on things of value. They will make our lives productive in eternally significant ways.

What is the other option? Distraction? Self-serving living? Heaven forbid that the God of the universe should take time to lead us and instruct us, and we give him only half our attention. May we not choose to follow any other. May we not give to any other attention that belongs to God.

This all makes sense intellectually, but how shall I live it? It begins with the mental recognition: I am going to focus on God. It includes quiet time of prayer and reflection. That is one purpose of this book—to draw the reader into a focused moment each day to reflect on who God is and what that should mean in each of our lives. This enables me to make the mental decision to live today following God as best as I can, seeking his leading. It may not be what my self-interest wants, but if it is right, it is what I choose! I want to pay attention to God!

Lord, thank you for today. May I follow you wholeheartedly. In your name, amen.

MAY 7

The LORD said to Moses, "Speak to the people of Israel, that they take for me a contribution. From every man whose heart moves him you shall receive the contribution for me." (Exod. 25:1–2)

Whether we like it or not, we live in a society that values *things*. It's not fun to write that, and it doesn't feel good to admit it, but if we are honest, we see it. People value assets. Money can provide for necessities. It can give a measure of security. Some think it can make life more interesting.

This is not a new thing. It has been a struggle and issue for people throughout history. It was in the hearts and minds of the Israelites who were coming out of Egypt. God was having Moses collect from the people to build the tabernacle, the altar, the ark of the covenant, and various other pieces to be used in Israel's worship of God in the wilderness. Of course, God could have had the materials already available. God could have placed the gold in the mountains where Israel encamped. God could have set jewels into the rocks for the picking. But God didn't do that.

Alternately, God could have ordered Israel to give. After all, most of the treasures held by the ex-slaves were those given to them by the Egyptians when they fled. God could have assessed a tax to build the worship materials. All it would take is for Moses to say, "Everyone must give X percent." But God didn't do that.

God did something altogether different. God had Moses ask the people to give "as their heart moved them." These were "contributions," not taxes. The goal wasn't for God to have a beautiful house of worship. God could have accomplished that by placing the gold and gems in the mountains. The goal wasn't for God to make the people give. That could have been ordered.

Israel was building a house of worship. That means that Israel was recognizing that God had greater worth and value than material things. To build something that declared such a truth, the material things would need to be given of a free and willing heart. These structures and items being built were expressions of worship as well as locations for worship. Here the people showed they valued God more greatly than their possessions.

There are multiple lessons here for me. I want to have a willing heart that shows I value God more than things. I want to instill in my worship for God a genuineness that shows he far exceeds the value of mere things. In this, I can also see how my worship might bring others into a relationship with and worship of God also. Finally, this casts possessions in a new light. They have value in how they can be used for God, not for me.

Lord, may I have a generous heart toward you. Use what I have in your name, amen.

MAY 8

"They shall make an ark . . . And you shall put into the ark the testimony that I shall give you." (Exod. 25:10, 16)

Today's passage contains a simple instruction with a profound implication.

Moses and the Israelites were to build the ark of the covenant. Made famous in the Indiana Jones movie, this ark was a chest carried on poles. On the chest was a lid with two angels cast on top. This ark was the meeting place where God would, from over the ark, meet with Moses and interact for the sake of Israel.

Inside the ark, Moses was to put the tablets that had God's commandments inscribed on them. These were commands that God revealed to Moses and the people. They were rules for living in harmony with God and each other.

By placing the testimony inside the ark, God was making a statement. God demonstrated to the people of Israel that their relationship with him was based on God's revelation and testimony. God relates to us on his terms, not ours.

We don't always see this. We often think our relationship with God is based on our terms. We expect God to be the kind of God we think he should be. We expect him to approve of the things we approve. We expect him to make decisions we would make. We want his compassion where we have compassion. We want his judgment where we place our judgment. We want him paying attention when it is convenient for us. We want to be able to ignore him for much of life but call him into play when we are desperate for his help.

But that is not the way of God. God made it abundantly clear. God will relate to us on his terms. God is God. He is not what we make him out to be. He is what he is. It's always been that way, and it always will be that way. If we want to understand him, we will need to do so on his terms. If we want to relate to him, we will need to do so as he sets it out.

We need to move away from making life about us, especially where God is concerned. Life is about *him.* We need to learn of him, seek him, understand him, and then join him in lives of praise and service.

The Christian understands that in the life of Jesus (Yeshua), we see most clearly the face of God. We want to see Jesus to see God better—the God who meets us on his terms, not ours!

Lord, please reveal yourself to me so I can better see and serve you. In your name, amen.

MAY 9

"You shall make a mercy seat of pure gold. . . . There I will meet with you, and from above the mercy seat." (Exod. 25:17, 22)

I remember one time when I was in college. I was in church, and we were singing a song of praise to God. I felt very unworthy to sing the song, much less address the God of the Universe as if he and I were in the same room. It didn't seem right.

My experience was reminiscent of Israel's prophet Isaiah, who saw the Lord in a vision. The Lord was sitting on his throne, and Isaiah fell to the ground lamenting his unworthiness to even be in the presence of God, much less address him. Isaiah's experience was moving:

> I saw the Lord sitting upon a throne, high and lifted up. . . . And the foundations of the thresholds shook. . . . And I said: "Woe is me! For I am lost; for I am a man of unclean lips, and I dwell in the midst of a people of unclean lips." (Isa. 6:1–5)

This was me. I was the lost man, unworthy of seeing or speaking to God. But then my thoughts turned to this passage. God didn't say he would meet with Moses, the representative of the people, on the basis of Moses being a good guy or the Hebrews being righteous. God was going to meet them above a "mercy seat" of pure gold. The mercy seat was the covering on the ark of the covenant. Each Day of Atonement, the high priest would sprinkle the blood of a sacrifice to symbolically atone for the people's sins.

God never meets with us based on our merit. We aren't worthy. The holy God must first address and resolve the problem of our sin and iniquity. To meet God, we must be purified. The purification takes place at the mercy seat, which was made of pure gold, the most valuable thing the Israelites possessed. The seat had to be the greatest and most valuable, for this was the atonement location. Many other tools used in Israel's worship were made of gold-covered materials. But not this seat. It was pure gold.

This speaks to me as a Christian of the purity of the sacrifice of Jesus, whose sacrificial blood became the basis for my relationship with God. Jesus the pure died for Mark the impure, and God meets me there. I see this as the altar of God. Even Isaiah was purified to speak with God by an angel touching Isaiah's mouth with a coal from God's altar—God's sacrifice. "Then one of the seraphim flew to me, having in his hand a burning coal . . . from the altar. And he touched my mouth and said: 'Behold, this has touched your lips; your guilt is taken away, and your sin atoned for'" (Isa. 6:6–7).

Lord, please forgive my sins and bring me peace with you. In your name, amen.

MAY 10

"And you shall set the bread of the Presence on the table before me regularly."
(Exod. 25:30)

In this book, I put 366 days of devotions, one for each day of the year with an extra one thrown in for leap year. Why? Why not 52 days of devotions, one for each week of the year? Can't devotionals be like the joke on the exercise videos? There used to be a bestselling video called *8-Minute Abs*. Then someone said they would beat the product in the marketplace by selling a video called *7-Minute Abs*. It would be a minute faster each day, and, as the joke went, how much of a difference could that one minute make in results?

Today's passage is one of the driving forces behind a *daily* devotional. The Israelites were receiving God's instructions for how they were to worship and relate to God. There were animals to be sacrificed, money to be given, grain to be burned, and more. One of the things Israel was to do was to keep "the bread of the Presence" before the altar of God each day.

"The bread of the Presence" is more literally "the bread of the Face." It was symbolic of the presence of God among the people. There would be twelve loaves put out each week, one for each of the twelves tribes of Israel. This was a holy recognition of God's presence with the people and God's covenant. It was placed before the Holy of Holies. The loaves were there every day, replaced with fresh each Sabbath. The replaced loaves were too holy to be thrown away. They were to be eaten by the priests within the sanctuary grounds.

I need a daily reminder of God. I need my focus each day, sharpened to God and his presence. He is more vital to me than food that I eat. This daily recognition of my need for God fuels my desire to write these devotions and also to read them! I want God to inform my day today. I want to see his presence in all I do. I want to thank him for the food I eat, the safety I enjoy, the family I love, the friends I love, the health I have, the opportunities to serve him and others, the blessings of liberty, and so much more. I also want to seek him today. I want to know him more fully. I need his help to make it through my day. I need his wisdom to live as I should. I need him to grow fruit in me, teaching me love, joy, peace, patience, kindness, goodness, gentleness, self-control, and many other virtues.

So there are 366 devotions in this book. As I write them, I pray that they will bless you and everyone who reads them. May we all seek God's presence each day.

Lord, please bless me and those who read this book with a closer walk with you. Be present with us. In your name, amen.

MAY 11

"You shall make bars of acacia wood, five for the frames of the one side of the tabernacle, and five bars for the frames of the other side of the tabernacle, and five bars for the frames of the side of the tabernacle at the rear westward. The middle bar, halfway up the frames, shall run from end to end. You shall overlay the frames with gold and shall make their rings of gold for holders for the bars, and you shall overlay the bars with gold."
(Exod. 26:26–29)

Do you ever feel lonely? Do you ever feel as if no one understands you? Perhaps you feel like no one really knows you; they only know the part of you that you show. Do you ever fear that if people knew your darkest secrets, they might not care too much for you? Put those fears to rest! There is a reality, a simple truth in this life. God made you and me. God knows our darkest secrets and deepest fears. And in spite of that, God wants to be in an intimate relationship with you and me.

Today's passage might seem unrelated to this devotion, but it's not. Look at it. God is directing Moses on how the Israelites are to make one aspect of the tabernacle. The tabernacle was an enclosure, a bit like a tent. It was the place of worship for Israel while they were a people on the move. It housed the ark of the covenant. It was the location for the sacrifices offered by the priests as directed by God. It was the place where God would meet with Moses. It was the physical location of God's relationship with his people.

The tabernacle was not designed by humans. God designed it. God set up the meeting place for his relationship with people. The tabernacle was the result of God's decision to relate to us, not our feeble attempts to find and gain his audience.

This was never because God thought we made ourselves worthy of his time. History shows the opposite to be true. We tend to ignore God or to limit him to the places in life where we are comfortable with him—places where he helps us or where he doesn't get in the way too much. Often, we are outright challenging to him and disobedient in our actions. Israel was that way. Yet even as Israel rebelled against God, God was at work preparing a place for relationship, a place to interact.

This is the way of God. He is the bloodhound who seeks out the lost. He is looking for the lonely to give them company. He is fighting to restore life to those who feel dead and abandoned. He gives value to those who feel valueless. He offers peace to those who are in turmoil. He forgives the worst sins. He redirects the wayward life. He offers hope to the hopeless. God meets his people in the wilderness, and he stays with them throughout life's journey.

Lord, thank you for your love. Thank you for seeking me out. May I have the wisdom and foresight to walk with you. In your name, amen.

MAY 12

"You shall hang the veil from the clasps, and bring the ark of the testimony in there within the veil. And the veil shall separate for you the Holy Place from the Most Holy. You shall put the mercy seat on the ark of the testimony in the Most Holy Place." (Exod. 26:33–34)

I like the idea of an immediate God. I like that God is approachable and near. It feels nice to know that God cares for me and reaches out to me. To me, God as father and friend is warming and secure.

But if we see God only in that light, we are not seeing God in his fullness. God is not human—not on any scale. God isn't of the human race. He isn't what we can fully comprehend with our minds. Our brains are the size of our fists. That much gray matter cannot really behold the being that is able to create the countless stars and galaxies, to keep track of them as well as the subatomic particles that make an atom look big. God knows the thoughts and future of all nearly eight billion people on the planet. The kind of being that is "God" is not something we can readily define or understand.

Even beyond his power, though, there is much more that makes God ungraspable. God is pure, 100 percent good. His morals and ethics are what drive us to define "right" and "wrong." God doesn't lie. God is just. God is unlike any other.

This is part of the import of today's passage. God instructed Moses that part of the tabernacle, part of the place of worship where the people honored God as God, was to be "the Most Holy Place." This was a room within a room where only the High Priest would be allowed to go. Once a year, on the Day of Atonement, the high priest would enter the Most Holy Place and offer atonement for the people, sprinkling blood on the mercy seat that sat atop the ark of the covenant.

This reflected the awesomeness of God. God was not the mundane God who just sort of hung around waiting for people to pray to him. God was the holy and special God. Approaching him was a reverent activity. It was to be held in the highest regard. God was to be recognized as unlike anything on earth. God was truly unique in power and purity.

I would do well to recognize this about God. Yes, he is my father and friend, but he is so much more. I should never forget that God is an awesome God, and it is my honor to know him. It is amazing that he knows who I am, cares for me, calls me by name, and seeks intimacy with me. God's love is warm and secure, but I must never forget the power and perfection of God.

Lord, I am amazed at you. I am amazed that you love me. Thank you for your love. May I always love you in return and honor you as God. In your name, amen.

MAY 13

"You shall make the court of the tabernacle. On the south side the court shall have hangings of fine twined linen a hundred cubits long for one side . . . And likewise for its length on the north side there shall be hangings a hundred cubits long . . . And for the breadth of the court on the west side there shall be hangings for fifty cubits . . . The breadth of the court on the front to the east shall be fifty cubits." (Exod. 27:9–13)

One of my favorite psalms is Psalm 139. In it, the psalmist asks, "Where can I go, where God is not already there?" The answer is, "Nowhere!" God is at the farthest point to which we could travel. That is true not only physically but mentally! God is in our thoughts as well as present in the world. God knows our thoughts. God knows the words on our lips, even before we form them. God has always been that way. It is not new.

In today's passage, God is giving Moses instructions for the dimensions and constructions of the tent-like walls that will be part of the tabernacle. This was the site of Israel's worship of God, the one who rescued them from Egypt. The people were used to Egyptian gods that had a presence that was restricted to certain areas. The Nile god was present at the Nile River. The sun god was in the sun and its rays. It wasn't only Egypt; the neighboring people also had territorial gods, who had certain boundaries where they ruled and were present.

God was teaching Israel something very important. God was not in one place. God was not limited in where he was present. God was everywhere. Everywhere Israel went, they were to assemble the tabernacle, for God was there. The tabernacle was an earthly meeting place, and it was portable. God was not found only in Egypt. He wasn't only in the wilderness. He wasn't limited to Sinai. Wherever the people went, God was there.

The tabernacle walls served another important purpose and lesson for the Israelites, even as God was everywhere they went. There was a holiness of God that set him apart from the mundane everyday existence. God was in the midst of the people, but God was holy. He was still set apart.

I like what this says to me. I find it reassuring. God is present in everything I do. He knows my heart and my mind. I never need fear that I am out of his thoughts or presence. Yet I also know that God is something more. God is beyond special and unique. God is alone in majesty, power, love, and purity. Only God is worthy of my praise and attention.

The tabernacle went everywhere, yet it still showed God was unique. I need to know this.

Lord, thank you for your holy presence. May I always honor you. In your name, amen.

MAY 14

"You shall command the people of Israel that they bring to you pure beaten olive oil for the light, that a lamp may regularly be set up to burn. In the tent of meeting, outside the veil that is before the testimony, Aaron and his sons shall tend it from evening to morning before the LORD. It shall be a statute forever to be observed throughout their generations by the people of Israel." (Exod. 27:20–21)

Google became a worldwide sensation, then a worldwide crutch, and ultimately a worldwide economic power. How? By offering insight to those surfing the web for answers. Google can find you a product you want, a news account you need, the location of an individual, or the website for just about anything. Google is the index for all things Internet. I must say, however, that not everything Google finds is right! The Internet is rife with falsehoods, and Google will lead you to any of them.

God is a quite different from Google. God knows all the answers to life's questions, but God doesn't deal in false information. God has quality control. God only dispenses the best insight and wisdom. Importantly, God doesn't do so at the command of our fingertips, responding after we hit the "enter" key. God will answer our questions, but he engages our minds, he makes us use discernment, he makes us process and grow while we hear his answers. That he does so should never make us doubt that his answers are nonetheless there.

We see this in today's passage. God as a source of insight is seen in the metaphor of the lamp in the temple. The lamp shines forth light, as God shines forth presence and light for life among the Israelites.

Earlier, God instructed Moses on how Israel was to build the menorah (candle stands) for the tabernacle worship. In today's passage, Moses is told two things of note for this devotion: what oil to use in the lamps and how often to have the lamp lit.

The oil for the lamp is to be "pure"—or more clearly translated, "clear"—oil of "beaten olives." No twigs, no leaves, no big millstone—these olives are ground by hand with a mortar and pestle to keep the olive oil the purest possible. The light is also to be kept on constantly. It should never go out.

This passage speaks to the purity of God's light. God speaks through Scripture with absolute purity. It also speaks to his constancy. His light never goes out. He instructs, trains, and gives wisdom through the illumination of his word 24/7.

What shines in your life? I want to spend time in the pure word of God each day.

Lord, shine your light in me. I'm too blind without it. In your name, amen.

MAY 15

"And you shall make holy garments for Aaron your brother, for glory and for beauty. You shall speak to all the skillful, whom I have filled with a spirit of skill, that they make Aaron's garments to consecrate him for my priesthood." (Exod. 28:2-3)

When I was a young lawyer, I had great personal doubts. I wasn't sure I had what it took to be a good lawyer. I was worried my writing wasn't up to par. I didn't know things I should know for success. I feared I had chosen the wrong career. It was odd to me, because I had believed I was doing what God called me to do when I chose law school, but doubts crept in once I began to practice.

Passages like today's brought me reassurance. The Israelites were given new tasks to do, things they had never done before. They were to create the special ornate robes and accoutrements for the priests to wear. If that order had simply been given to Moses, Moses might have wondered, "How on earth are we to pull this off?" But God gave the instruction to make the garments with an assurance. God filled certain Israelites with the skill to do the job. All Moses needed to do was give them the instruction on what was to be made and what it should look like upon completion. Those God imbued with skill would take it from there.

It is a biblical principle and a core truth to life: God equips us for our tasks. God doesn't call people to do things that he hasn't made provision for them to do successfully. If God calls you to be a teacher, he will ensure you have what it takes to teach. If God calls you to be a parent, he will be your source of the skills, patience, wisdom, economics, and everything else it takes to parent successfully. If God calls you to speak to someone about him, he will give you the words to do so.

None of this means that we don't work hard. Nor does it mean we need no training. To the contrary, God could have made us puppets had he chosen to do so, but he didn't. God made us real people with real choices. We should choose to follow his direction, and that means that we seek his help. We learn how to do things to the best of our ability. We take advantage of the opportunities he puts in our paths to develop skill. We practice. We work diligently, seeking to do our best.

But all of this should be done with faith in God's promise to equip us. It should also be done with gratitude for his hand in our lives. How great is it to know that we are tasked with good works that God wants us to do? How magnificent that he will equip us to do those works! I might not have thought I could be a trial lawyer, but that is part of what God called me to do, and he equipped me to do it. Thank you, God!

Lord, put me to work! Give me the skills to do the job! In your name, amen.

MAY 16

"You shall take two onyx stones, and engrave on them the names of the sons of Israel, six of their names on the one stone, and the names of the remaining six on the other stone, in the order of their birth. . . . You shall enclose them in settings of gold filigree. And you shall set the two stones on the shoulder pieces of the ephod, as stones of remembrance for the sons of Israel. And Aaron shall bear their names before the LORD on his two shoulders for remembrance." (Exod. 28:9–12)

Let me tell you something very valuable: GOD KNOWS YOUR NAME. It doesn't matter who you are or how you live. It doesn't even matter whether you believe in God or not. He knows your name. He knows your parents' names. He knows their parents' names, and so on. This is a game changer.

As an integral part of Israel's work to outfit its priests as God instructed, Israel was directed to have a jeweler engrave the names of each of the twelve tribes on two beautiful onyx stones. The stones were then to be set in gold and attached to the breast piece worn by the high priest.

These stones served as a reminder to the people and a recognition of God's awareness that the people weren't simply numbers or warm bodies. They were named individuals, descended from the children of Jacob through his twelve sons. The people needed to know that God saw them as individuals—personal, named, with heritage and a place before him.

Some people today feel lost in the crowd. Some wonder if there is purpose in life. Some wonder if anyone truly knows them. Some wonder if there is a God and figure if there is, then he likely doesn't give a hoot about them (or any of us). Some are just beginning to realize that God is there and that he cares, but they are unsure how much.

This passage speaks to all those people. This passage was a fundamental instruction to Israel that God knew them all. By expressing their tribe on the garment worn by the high priest, God informed everyone that he knew them, where they were from, and they never left his sight.

This is an affirmation for living. It gives encouragement to the depressed. It gives direction to the aimless. It gives peace to the distraught. It gives meaning to those who are hollow and empty. God cares deeply for each of us, all day, every day.

God knows your name . . . DON'T FORGET THAT!

Lord, I am touched that you know me and care for me so. Thank you. May your love move a responsive love in my heart. I want to know you better. In your name, amen.

MAY 17

"For Aaron's sons you shall make coats and sashes and caps. You shall make them for glory and beauty." (Exod. 28:40)

There are some chores in this life that I don't really care for. I may need the results, but the process isn't always great. Example: taking out the garbage. It's not my idea of fun. It can be a smelly task. It can be a dirty task. Once when one of our daughters was taking out the trash, she burst into tears, exclaiming, "I got garbage water on me!" It was the first time I had heard the term, but I embraced it. Yes, taking out the garbage isn't fun, especially when you get garbage water on you! But it is necessary.

There is something different about our service to God. God gives us chores to do in this life. There is no doubting that. Some of the service we give him involves how we treat others. Some involves how we treat ourselves. Regardless of the chore, however, when we do it for God there is a glory and beauty to it.

The Israelites had a full list of things to do in preparation for their worship of God. Today's passage includes instructions for making coats, sashes, and caps for the priests to wear. These items were to be made "for glory and beauty." God wasn't interested in the priests simply having the clothing. God was interested in the process of making it as well as the end use. Making it and wearing it were both part of Israel's service to God. Service to God is wrapped up in glory and beauty. We must not lose track of that.

Israel's priests were wearing these garments "for glory and beauty" every time they served in the tabernacle. This wasn't just something done on days of fair weather. They truly wore them when the sun shone and when the rain clouds gathered.

So on sunny days, when we've had a good night's sleep, when birds are singing, the food is plentiful and tasty, and everything is going our way, we can serve God with glory and beauty. That is a good thing. But we also need to know that God is served with glory and beauty when the rain is pouring down, the car is stuck in the mud, and everything seems to get messed up.

Knowing I am doing something for God has a way of changing my perspective. I think even the mundane taking out of trash shines differently if I realize that I am doing it for God. If it is part of his plan for me to do that task, then I want to do it the best I can, whistling in gratitude at such a thing of beauty and glory. Even if I get garbage water on me!

Lord, may my service to you be real and a thing of glory and beauty in your sight. In your name, amen.

MAY 18

"You shall bring Aaron and his sons to the entrance of the tent of meeting and wash them with water. . . . You shall take the anointing oil and pour it on his head and anoint him. . . . Then you shall take part of the blood that is on the altar, and of the anointing oil, and sprinkle it on Aaron and his garments, and on his sons and his sons' garments with him. He and his garments shall be holy." (Exod. 29:4, 7, 21)

I loved the years I took Hebrew in college. It taught me a new alphabet and language. I learned new grammatical structures, so different from anything else I'd studied (including Greek, Latin, and a smattering of Spanish). It also opened my eyes to matters of Scripture that I had never seen. Today's passage is a wonderful example.

In this passage, God is instructing Moses on how to prepare Aaron and his sons (the priests of Israel) for their service to God. First, they were to be immersed in water. Subsequently, in daily service, they would simply wash their hands and feet. Then Aaron, the high priest, was to be "anointed" with oil. The Hebrew word for "anointed" has the root *m-sh-ch*. It is the root for "messiah." To be anointed with oil was to be a messiah.

In this passage, before Aaron comes to fill his role as high priest, intervening and atoning for the sins of Israel, he is to be immersed in water and then anointed as a messiah. Only then could he fulfill his role.

Intervening for sin is no ordinary task, and it can't be done by any ordinary person. God showed that through the rituals he instituted for the work of Aaron and the other priests. No one has a righteous forgiveness through anything ordinary. God was pronouncing that righteousness and forgiveness are something that must be done by someone else. Even the high priest had to be anointed by others before he was allowed to serve. Aaron needed to be cleansed of his own sin through the blood of a sacrificial ram.

For me as a Christian, this takes on a special meaning beyond the direct one. Christians understand that Yeshua (in Greek, "Jesus") was the final and ultimate Messiah. He was fully immersed in water (as he explained, "to fulfill all righteousness"—Matt. 3:15), and he was the anointed high priest who truly took on the sins of the world, once for all, when he was sacrificed on our behalf. We are cleansed of sin by his sacrificial blood.

I need to know that I am at peace with God. I can't get there on my own. I need someone to intercede on my behalf. I need a messiah. I need to know that the just God can forgive my transgressions and sinful heart in a righteous judgment.

Lord, please forgive my transgressions. I have sinned before you, and without your salvation I am utterly lost. Lead me to your rock. Let me know your salvation. Then may I ever sing your praise. In your name, amen.

MAY 19

"You shall take the breast of the ram of Aaron's ordination and wave it for a wave offering before the LORD, and it shall be your portion. . . . It shall be for Aaron and his sons as a perpetual due from the people of Israel, for it is a contribution. It shall be a contribution from the people of Israel from their peace offerings, their contribution to the LORD."
(Exod. 29:26, 28)

Do you go to church or synagogue? Do you watch ministers on television or the Internet? If so, you see those who serve God as their day-to-day job. It is right and fitting that those serving God in such capacities get paid for their service. This isn't a part of God needing to sell tickets or dispensing his grace for a price. Neither is it a justification for outrageous amounts of money to be taken by those in service to God. It is a simple fact. God makes provision for those working for him.

In today's passage, God is laying out the ways that the priests are to carry out various sacrifices. The whole animal (or grain) was not to be burned as a sacrifice to God. A share of it was to be taken by the priests as sustenance. The rest of Israel could farm, shepherd, or work in some other capacity, but the priests were called to serve in the tabernacle and temple. This was how they spent their days. Because they had families and needs, God made sure they had food on the table.

It is notable that God gave them a portion, not the whole beast! This should make some who see God's ministry as a profit center beware. God is not about selling his grace. He is about making sure those who serve him have adequate provisions.

This extends beyond those in full-time ministry. God provides for all his children as they have need. God is the reason we have food and shelter. God sets our jobs before us and equips us to do them. Like the priests, this is not so we can hoard money and take more than we should. Anything we have is God's gift to us. We are to use what we need and give back into God's service the rest. That means from those to whom much is given, much is expected. We are to be responsible with what we have.

With passages like today's, I get reflective. I want to have a heart of gratitude for what God has given me. I also want to be responsible with it, seeking to give back to him with a conscious recognition that I am a steward of *his* resources. These are not my own. I have God's provisions for my life and for me to use in his service.

Lord, thank you for my daily provisions. Help me to use the resources you've given me to your glory. In your name, amen.

MAY 20

"I will dwell among the people of Israel and will be their God. And they shall know that I am the LORD their God, who brought them out of the land of Egypt that I might dwell among them. I am the LORD their God." (Exod. 29:45–46)

When I was in middle school, we moved from Rochester, New York, to Lubbock, Texas. When I moved, I had no idea I would meet the beautiful Becky Smith, who would one day become the beautiful Becky Lanier. I just knew that I didn't know anyone else in the whole town, save my two sisters, mom, and dad. The school year was halfway gone already, and all the cliques were firmly in place. They would be hard to crack open!

But I was fine with that—more than fine, actually. For there was a God who was everywhere, including Mackenzie Junior High School, and that God was my friend. I was acutely aware that God was in my heart, and it made a real difference then, as it does today.

This was not something new and unique to Lubbock. When God brought the Israelites out from Egyptian slavery, it wasn't simply to improve their difficult lives. God wasn't calling them out, giving them core instructions, setting them up in the Promised Land, and then leaving them on their own, perhaps checking in occasionally to make sure they were alright. To the contrary, God brought them out to be their God. God brought them out to dwell among them.

God is a God of relationships. There are two sides to that. One side is that he is God. We must never lose sight of that. We must always guard against making him a supersized human. When we do so, we lose sight of truth and reality.

The other side is that God wants involvement with us and our lives. He seeks out a relationship with us. He brought Israel out to "dwell with them." What a waste when we ignore him. We miss out on the relationship of a lifetime. We miss out on the comfort of a compassionate friend, the presence of a true companion, and the leadership of an encouraging and empowering leader. We miss out on the strength we need to make it through the day. We miss out on the wisdom to discern what is right and wrong. We miss out on someone to dry our tears. We miss out on someone to keep us in line and hold us accountable. We miss out on so much we need in this life!

I want God to dwell with me. It is my pleasure and joy.

Lord, abide with me. Be my shelter from the storm, my vision in the night, my rock among shifting sands, my water in times of dryness, my strength when I am weak, my confidence in times of doubt, my all in all times of life. THANK YOU! In your name, amen.

MAY 21

"When you take the census of the people of Israel, then each shall give a ransom for his life to the LORD when you number them, that there be no plague among them when you number them. . . . You shall take the atonement money from the people of Israel." (Exod. 30:12, 16)

How do you treat money? Are you careful with it? Some people budget and watch every penny they spend. Some people are less attentive. Yet most everyone sees the value of money, and I know very few people who throw it around with no regard for it. Money is, by its very definition, a thing of value. This becomes an integral part of Israel's sacrificial system installed by God.

Today's passage comes in the context of things that God required of Israel to account for their sins. Already God had laid out certain animal sacrifices, explaining that a price of sin is death. Additionally, the people were required to give what became an annual fee as "atonement money." This was a sacrifice of money given to atone for sins.

Inherent in this instruction is the recognition that sin costs us. We might not think of it that way, but it does. Many people think of sin as angering God or getting on his bad side. It is as if God made up some arbitrary list of taboos that we are to avoid or else he gets upset. That is not the biblical teaching, however. Scripture teaches that God himself is a moral being. For example, God is truthful; he is not a liar. Just as God has morality, so he has made us in his image with morals hardwired into our brains. No one disputes that certain things are wrong. For example, I have never found anyone who earnestly believes it is good to molest a child. So, sin will always come at a price because it violates our programming. It does damage to our moral fiber.

Sin is also costly, beyond distorting our moral character. It can and does affect ourselves and others. Many of God's instructions are for our own good, individually and societally. For example, if a husband fails to honor his wife, the husband will suffer, the marriage will suffer, and society will suffer. Or if I drink to excess, I destroy my liver and brain cells; I can disrupt my relationships and even damage or kill others by driving under the influence of alcohol.

There is an interesting twist on this given by the first-century Jewish rabbi and Christian apostle Paul. Paul told a group in Corinth, Greece that they were "bought with a price," so they should live like it. Paul explained the Christian understanding that Christ paid the debt of sin not with a shekel but with his entire being. This was an atonement cost beyond measure, and we should recognize that and live accordingly.

Lord, may I take sin seriously and avoid it at all costs! I am thankful for your atoning for my sins. In your name, amen.

MAY 22

The LORD said to Moses, "Take sweet spices, stacte, and onycha, and galbanum, sweet spices with pure frankincense (of each shall there be an equal part), and make an incense blended as by the perfumer, seasoned with salt, pure and holy. You shall beat some of it very small, and put part of it before the testimony in the tent of meeting where I shall meet with you. It shall be most holy for you. And the incense that you shall make according to its composition, you shall not make for yourselves. It shall be for you holy to the LORD. Whoever makes any like it to use as perfume shall be cut off from his people."
(Exod. 30:34–38)

When I was taking an anthropology course at a secular university, my professor discovered that I was a Christian. In discussions with him in his office, he began mocking my beliefs, asking me to show him God. He told me if there was a God, all that God needed to do to prove himself was appear. God's failure to do so was, to this fellow, proof of God's nonexistence. My suggestion to the professor was that I would be shocked if God's daily activity included visual appearances for all the unbelievers or doubters in the world. I thought rather that the evidence of God's reality was itself present for any who thoughtfully considered the world and humanity. On that we disagreed.

God has always given indications to us of his real presence. Scripture teaches that God created the physical world; God isn't a part of the physical world. Not being a physical form, God has still used physicality to indicate to us his real existence and presence among us. Today's passage is a good example.

God was explaining to Moses the recipe for a special blend of incense to be used in the tabernacle, and later in the temple, as part of Israel's abiding in the presence of God. God could have had the Israelites manufacture some idol as a representative of him. The Greeks did it. So did the Romans, the Egyptians, and most every other contemporary culture. But not Israel. God instructed Israel not to make some image of him. That would limit God, and the people would never grow in understanding him as they should.

Instead God used things like fragrance. Never to be mistaken as God, the fragrance nonetheless was a physical reminder that God was real and God was there. As they smelled the incense, people could mentally acknowledge God through their senses.

I don't need incense to tell me there is a God. He shows himself in many ways. He doesn't give me a physical show, but he is here nonetheless.

Lord, I thank you for your presence. Help those who doubt, and make yourself real to them. In your name, amen.

MAY 23

When the people saw that Moses delayed to come down from the mountain, the people gathered themselves together to Aaron and said to him, "Up, make us gods who shall go before us. As for this Moses, the man who brought us up out of the land of Egypt, we do not know what has become of him." (Exod. 31:1–2)

We have five children. Several are particularly time sensitive. Several aren't. Those that are expect things to occur within the time allotted, and when things don't, they spring into action, installing an appropriate Plan B to use the time. Fortunately, as they grew up, our children learned a very valuable lesson. God has his own timing. He doesn't fit into our schedules.

Israel needed to learn that lesson. Today's passage recounts what happened when Moses went up on Mount Sinai to receive God's instructions for the people. Moses had been gone for some time, much longer than the people projected. When Moses failed to appear as expected and failed to bring to Israel God in some form or another (God appeared in the form of his laws and instructions), the people turned to their Plan B. They decided to make their own idol as God.

We read the story and think, "Foolish Israelites. Did they really think God would be pleased by them making an idol?" Of course, we have the benefit of knowing what was going on up the mountain. We know that, among other things, God told Moses, "The people aren't allowed to make an idol!" I'm not fully sure we are being fair to the Israelites when we judge them harshly. Here is why.

We often expect God to show up on our time schedule. We pray for him to do XYZ or to teach us A or B. We pray for him to lift us from despair, yet we find ourselves still stuck. We pray for him to solve a wounded relationship, yet the wound still festers. We pray for him to help sell our house or find us a job, yet we wait and wait with seemingly no results. There are countless times when we project our schedule onto God.

Then the question becomes, what do we do when God's timing isn't ours? Do we turn elsewhere? Do we find substitute gods or manufacture some made-up god? Where do we turn when we are waiting on the Lord?

I suspect sometimes I am not really waiting on God to show up or answer my prayers, but I just don't like the answer he gives me! He might want me to do something to get a job when I'd rather him drop it in my lap. He might want me to move to restore a relationship when I want him to get the other side to move! I have a lot to learn here, but I know that God's timing is always the right timing.

Lord, may I live by your schedule and not try to put you on mine. In your name, amen.

MAY 24

Aaron received the gold from their hand and fashioned it with a graving tool and made a golden calf. And they said, "These are your gods, O Israel, who brought you up out of the land of Egypt!" When Aaron saw this, he built an altar before it. And Aaron made a proclamation and said, "Tomorrow shall be a feast to the LORD." And they rose up early the next day and offered burnt offerings and brought peace offerings. And the people sat down to eat and drink and rose up to play. (Exod. 31:4–6)

We read passages like today's and can almost laugh at the Israelites. There they were, in the wilderness, saved miraculously from Egypt. Fed with God's manna and quail, given water to drink, the Israelites had experienced God in ways few in all of history would rival. Yet in the midst of that incredible experience, Israel starts freelancing, making up its own religion and ideas of God.

This was man-made religion at its finest, or maybe at its worst. While we may deride it as the silliness of the old superstitious Israelites, I think it isn't that far removed from what we do today. People are famous for building up their own religious ideas about God. We manufacture our own ideas about God, convinced they must be true.

Generally, man-made religion takes a truth and distorts it in some way. For example, God is loving and compassionate. That is true. Some people then think that God could never judge sin, because as loving and compassionate people, they would never judge sin. Therefore, they create a God that would behave as they would, without regard to figuring out who God really is.

Another example stems from recognizing that every human has value and merit. Some people take this to mean that all people who pursue God on their own terms are just as acceptable to God as those who pursue him consistently with a biblical understanding of him.

I don't think too much of man-made religion. I certainly want to weed it out where I might have it. I want my understanding of God to be based on how he has revealed himself in Scripture. I want to relate to him on his terms, not those I dream up. I want to conform my beliefs to those of the Bible. I want reality, not a fiction of my own making.

There is a real God. Learning of him and discerning him is my goal—not making him up as I go along.

Lord, please reveal yourself to me. May my time in your word be time spent learning who you are and changing my heart and mind to align with your reality. In your name, amen.

And Moses said to Aaron, "What did this people do to you that you have brought such a great sin upon them?" And Aaron said, "Let not the anger of my lord burn hot. You know the people, that they are set on evil. For they said to me, 'Make us gods who shall go before us. As for this Moses, the man who brought us up out of the land of Egypt, we do not know what has become of him.' So I said to them, 'Let any who have gold take it off.' So they gave it to me, and I threw it into the fire, and out came this calf." (Exod. 32:21–24)

One of our daughters is famous for her line, "It wasn't my fault!" This daughter saw humor in the line but invoked it often growing up. The situation might have been as simple as coming home with a bad grade on a test. "It wasn't my fault!" Or maybe it was the time she failed to get her chores done. "It wasn't my fault!" One of my favorites was when she ate some of a sister's Easter candy and when caught exclaimed, "It wasn't my fault!" Of course it was!

It seems Moses' brother, Aaron, had this same trait. Moses had been gone on Mount Sinai, receiving God's commands for Israel. The people had gotten restless because it was taking Moses so long. So the people got Aaron to agree to make them an idol for worship and revelry. Aaron collected gold from the people and fashioned for them a golden calf. This idol became God for the people, and they commenced a raucous celebration and party. Moses came down in the midst of the dancing and was rightly furious.

When Moses challenged Aaron over the actions, Aaron first set to blaming the people. "They are set on evil," he explained. In more common language, he said, "Hey, you and I both know these people are trouble! They wouldn't leave me alone, so I finally said, OK!"

Here is where Aaron's story got even more preposterous as he tried to deflect personal responsibility. Aaron said he melted the gold and the calf came out all on its own! Like a certain second-grader in our home caught with the candy in her mouth, Aaron was saying, "It wasn't my fault!"

Aaron needed to own up to the truth and take responsibility. It was his fault. Not only his, but certainly he had fault. We all need to recognize and accept responsibility for our actions. We teach that to our second-graders and hopefully have learned it by the time we are mature enough to read this devotional. I have sinned against God in thought, word, and deed, and I should confess that sin, not run from it. It is an important stage on the way to living with God's forgiveness.

Lord, I am a sinner. I have sinned and continue to sin. I confess that sin, even as I pray for your forgiveness. In your name, amen.

MAY 26

Moses said, "Please show me your glory." And he said, "I will make all my goodness pass before you and will proclaim before you my name 'The LORD.' And I will be gracious to whom I will be gracious, and will show mercy on whom I will show mercy. But," he said, "you cannot see my face, for man shall not see me and live." And the LORD said, "Behold, there is a place by me where you shall stand on the rock, and while my glory passes by I will put you in a cleft of the rock, and I will cover you with my hand until I have passed by. Then I will take away my hand, and you shall see my back, but my face shall not be seen." (Exod. 33:18–23)

This story of Moses has always held me in fascination and awe. If God were a genie God and I were given three wishes, my first wish would likely be to see God. I want to see God and behold his glory. How incredible would that be?

Moses had the desire. He asked God for the chance to see God's face. God kindly explained to Moses why that couldn't happen. No human being can behold the true face of God in our current state of being and live through it. God is not a physical God. Our word to describe him is *spiritual*. Even describing him thus, however, is somewhat vague. Realistically, we cannot see or know what kind of being God is beyond the fundamental ways he has revealed himself to us.

Stephen Bullivant likens our ability to understand God to a drawing he did of his mother when he was three years old. His mother had a big smile and was standing by a flower. To an adult, it might look like his mother had a pig's snout as a nose; however, that is just the way a three-year-old drew a nose. His mother doesn't have a pig's snout! Stephen drew his picture the best he could with the tools he had.

In much the same vein, we should consider our efforts to see God. We don't really have the tools. We know what things we see look like, but to describe the appearance of one so unhuman and unphysical can't be done. In his naïveté, Moses thought he could see God, but God explained such wasn't possible. What Moses could see was God's goodness. God said Moses would see his "back," and we can see why. We see where God has gone. We behold his works. We see the execution of his thoughts. We experience the expression of his words. We behold God in action, even as we don't physically see the unphysical God.

Yes, I want to see God. I don't get to see his face, but I can behold his wondrous works. And all that is within me should cry out, "Glory and honor to the Lord of lords and King of kings!"

Lord, I praise you as most amazing and beyond comprehension. You are kind and loving, even as you are awesome in power. In your name I pray, amen!

MAY 27

"The LORD, the LORD, a God merciful and gracious, slow to anger, and abounding in steadfast love and faithfulness, keeping steadfast love for thousands, forgiving iniquity and transgression and sin, but who will by no means clear the guilty, visiting the iniquity of the fathers on the children and the children's children, to the third and the fourth generation." (Exod. 34:6–7)

I love this passage for each of its heavily laden words and ideas. It begins with the name of God (YHWH), shown in our English Bibles as "LORD," written in all uppercase letters. In the Hebrew, that name is written twice, followed by the word "God." It immediately commands your consideration: YHWH, YHWH, El . . . What drives this blunt, attention-grabbing start? The descriptors that are about to follow!

The LORD God is "merciful" and "gracious." These two Hebrew synonyms are almost always found together in the Old Testament, and they always refer to God's traits of compassion and kindness. God doesn't treat us as we deserve, but he looks for ways to show his love and care. God cannot do that in a way that changes his holiness or condones the disease of sin. But even within his justice, God is looking for ways to care for and nurture his children. This is the LORD God, merciful and gracious.

The LORD God is "slow to anger." This is a good thing, a *very* good thing. I have known some short-tempered people, and they are difficult to be around. You have to walk on eggshells or face their wrath. When there is an all-seeing and all-knowing God, and when he is all-powerful and with a slight notion can destroy me, my world, and all I hold dear, I am glad he is slow to anger. I know I am guilty of disregarding him, disobeying him, disbelieving him, and more. These aren't onetime mistakes I've made. They often seem to be my pattern and practice. I desperately need the LORD God to be slow to anger.

The LORD God is "abounding in steadfast love and faithfulness." When I am inadequate in my love for him, he loves me. When I fall short in my faith, he is faithful. He meets me where I am and takes me to a higher place. He doesn't wait for me to deserve his love; he loves me first. This is the LORD God, abounding in steadfast love and faithfulness.

The LORD God forgives my sin, but there is still a consequence. Sin is like a fire. You can stick your finger in the fire, and you will get burned. That is the nature of sin. It is also one reason God teaches us and warns us to avoid sin. He wants to save us from its harsh consequences. Some sin doesn't stop with the sinner. We can commit some sins that affect our children, our grandchildren, and future generations.

Lord, I praise you for who you are and pray to grow in purity. In your name, amen.

MAY 28

Moses assembled all the congregation of the people of Israel and said to them, "These are the things that the LORD has commanded you to do." (Exod. 35:1)

Moses assembled the congregation, not just some but "all" of the people of Israel. He did it to give them instructions from the Lord.

This was in a day before churches or synagogues. Israel had no temple. We know of no ritual weekly gathering for the ancient Hebrews as they dwelt in Egypt or as they were called out of Egypt. Temple, synagogue, and church come much later.

Yet even in these early days as Israel was coming together as a nation, there were times when Moses called all the people together. He could have divided the people into groups, assigning some to inform others, and those to inform others, and so on, but he didn't.

There is a power in a group gathering for a common purpose. It is an enriching time for those assembled. There is fellowship, camaraderie, and a commonness that allows sharing and promotes unity. This was no accidental gathering by Moses. It was intentional. As Hebrew thought continued to grow, the Psalms would speak of "how good it is" and "how pleasant it is" when the people dwell *together*, united in purpose and spirit (Ps. 133).

We need togetherness. It serves many purposes. It can bring out the best in us when we gather around a good common purpose. This is the calling of Moses to Israel; it is the calling of Jesus to Christians; it is the calling of God to his people. We find strength in numbers. We find enrichment from fellowship. We get insight from others. We grow in tolerance, patience, knowledge, and joy when we unite with others around the common purpose of knowing and glorifying God.

Corporate worship is a great opportunity for us, and we shouldn't see it as a burden. We need that regular call together. We need others. It will sharpen our focus, strengthen our commitment, and keep us accountable. It is necessary!

Lord, I love my alone time with you and in this world. But never let me think that is sufficient. Please lead me into a vibrant fellowship with others who will stand with me, grow with me, love me, and be a part of my life. Help me to plug into others and befriend them as well. Thank you for fellowship, Lord. Amen.

MAY 29

"Six days work shall be done, but on the seventh day you shall have a Sabbath of solemn rest, holy to the LORD." (Exod. 35:2)

God commanded humanity to rest. One day a week, work is to stop. The Bible calls it "Sabbath."

Sabbath stood out from all other days. In English, most days of the week come from Norse Gods or the solar system. Sunday is named after the sun; Monday is the moon's day; Tuesday is named after the Norse god Tiw; and so on. Romance languages gave Roman/Latin names to the days of the week, adopting the names of heavenly bodies or the gods reflected in those bodies. In Spanish, Monday is *lunes* after the Spanish *luna* for "moon." Tuesday is *martes* after the Spanish for Mars, the planet named after the Roman god Mars, and so on.

Not so with Hebrew! Hebrew names get their genesis from the Bible. The ancient Hebrew Scriptures never named days of the week anything other than an assigned number, with one exception. So, Sunday is simply "day one" or "the first day of the week" (*yom rishon*); Tuesday is "day two" (*yom sheyni*). The exception? The final day of the week. Day seven is given a name—*Sabbath*. This name comes from a primitive root of "rest" or "stopping from exertion." It is what God did after six days of creation. It is what God told his people to do after six days of exertion.

God quit his work after six days because his work was finished. Humans don't finish work, but we are to rest just the same. Rest is necessary for us on many levels. Athletes know the importance of resting our bodies. It gives recovery and growth. Our minds need a day to rest; it is when we rejuvenate and refuel ourselves for good mental health. Spiritually, rest is important. When we cease from what we work on, it gives us time to contemplate God and his work in and around us.

This is a personal issue with me, especially in the age of cell phones that push emails to our attention 24/7. Emails never take a day off. People always think you are accessible for work. I find I need to take a day and leave the emails behind. One day a week, I am to rest, not work. I don't do it well, but I am learning!

God didn't make the Sabbath and then force people to follow it. God made people and then had a Sabbath. Sabbath rest is for us. We should make it a point to enjoy and profit from a day of rest each week. Our maker said we need it!

Lord, rest is not always easy. There is so much to do. Help me to reshape my priorities to align with your instructions. Teach me to enjoy a day of rest. Use it to draw my mind and attention to you and the things you value. Thank you, Lord. Amen.

MAY 30

"Take from among you a contribution to the L<small>ORD</small>. Whoever is of a generous heart, let him bring the L<small>ORD</small>'s contribution . . ." And they came, everyone whose heart stirred him, and everyone whose spirit moved him, and brought the L<small>ORD</small>'s contribution to be used for the tent of meeting, and for all its service, and for the holy garments. (Exod. 35:5, 21)

"Mine!" It is a word learned early by children. As we age we don't lose that word, but we frequently add or hear other common claims, including, "I worked hard for this."

There is a different concept in Scripture. Beginning in the garden of Eden, the provisions of this life are provided by God, not simply earned by people. Do people work? Of course! Adam and Eve were put to work in the garden. But the work was itself a calling or gift of God. God gave people purpose. God gave people skills to achieve that purpose, and God gave people responsibilities to achieve that purpose.

In the midst of it all, however, this giving God has declared that we are to grow and develop a spirit of generosity. As image bearers of God, we are to reflect his giving nature in our interactions with him as well as with others.

Moses speaks here of a "generous heart." That is the heart we need to cultivate. Followers of the giving God should be known as people of a generous heart. This does mean giving back to God, which is a recognition that what we have he has given to us. It also means sharing with others in need. We should not have to be told but should always be on the lookout for how we can take the things he has given us and turn them into blessings for others.

One of my favorite prayers before mealtime includes the request, "Lord, as we thank you for this marvelous blessing of food, please make us mindful of others less fortunate. Teach us ways we can share your love and bounty with them."

"Mine" is fine as we are growing out of infancy, but we need to grow beyond that. We need to learn to turn the "mine" that we learn so early into "his." Then we see ourselves more as stewards in charge of God's things rather than owners and possessors of our things. As we do this, giving becomes a joy and an opportunity to share God's love.

Lord, thank you for the many gifts you have given to me. Please give me a generous heart. Help me learn to use what you've given me to bless you by blessing others. Let me reflect your giving nature. In your name, amen.

MAY 31

And Moses called Bezalel and Oholiab and every craftsman in whose mind the LORD *had put skill, everyone whose heart stirred him up to come to do the work.* (Exod. 36:2)

What are you good at doing? Are you an artist or an accountant? Are you a thinker or a dreamer? Are you super coordinated or a bit clumsy? Maybe you're none of the above. When I left middle school, a few students compiled a "last will and testament" for each person heading on to high school. For me, they put, "Mark Lanier leaves his natural argumentative abilities to . . ." and then they listed a shy student. I'm not sure it is a good thing to say, "I am a good arguer!", but I do know that everyone has a set of gifts, skills, interests, and opportunities in this life. This is at the core of today's passage.

The passage does two things. It teaches us that the skills and gifts we have are gifts from God, and it calls us to use those gifts for him.

I like that the passage teaches us our gifts are from God, especially in the way it is explained. These are craftsmen who are given names, and the explanation is that the Lord put the skill into their minds. This is something deliberate from God. God chose the people and he instilled the gifts. As we read that he put them in the people's "minds," the passage propels us to the second concern. What are we going to do with what we have?

We need the skills and capacities nurtured and developed. We need to exercise our minds to make use of what we have. But then there is something beyond simple skill. There is the decision of the heart. Bezalel and Oholiab had hearts that were "stirred up" to come do work for the Lord. That is the real and best use of the skills God has given us.

We are where we need to be and are at our best when we decide to use our gifts for God. If we are artsy, we should be creative for God. If we are compassionate, we should be compassionate for God. If we are arguers, we should use critical thinking and argue for God!

Do you know your skills? Do you know what God has gifted you to be able to do? If not, ask God. Ask your friends. Search your opportunities. Look for ways to develop at serving others.

Find your skill set, thank God for it, develop it, and use it for good!

Lord, thank you for making me and instilling in me gifts and skills. Help me discover them, develop them, and stir my heart to use them for you. In your name, amen!

JUNE 1

"Then Moses said to the people of Israel, 'See, the LORD has called by name Bezalel the son of Uri, son of Hur, of the tribe of Judah; and he has filled him with the Spirit of God, with skill, with intelligence, with knowledge, and with all craftsmanship, to devise artistic designs, to work in gold and silver and bronze, in cutting stones for setting, and in carving wood, for work in every skilled craft.'" (Exod. 35:30–33)

As Moses saw things, Bezalel was "filled with the Spirit of God" as he was gifted with "skill," "intelligence," "knowledge," and "craftsmanship." It made him artistic, able to conceive pretty things and then make them. I like the way Moses saw it.

"Skill" is the Hebrew word *chacmah.* It is used for skill in technical work or war. It is also the word we typically translate as "wisdom." It conveys the idea of a particular understanding for the task at hand, whether handiwork, battle strategy, or daily living.

"Intelligence" conveys a closely related idea. It is having the "know-how" to go along with the insights of skill. "Knowledge" is a third word Moses used, and it conveys not only mental knowledge but common sense as well.

These three Hebrew words go well together. Bezalel had the technical expertise ("skill"), the intelligence and know-how for using the skill, and also the common sense that makes everything work better. With those talents, Bezalel was able to engage his craftsmanship to make the creative artistic designs that would bless the people of God for many generations to come.

Here is an analogy. In basketball, one needs basic skills: dribbling, shooting, passing, and so on. Additionally, one needs the intelligence of basketball strategy: when to be aggressive, when to conserve energy. With all of these, one also needs knowledge, the common sense to know when to pass or when to shoot. If one possesses all of that, then basketball rises to a whole new level.

This passage challenges me to grow. I want to develop in all these ways as I seek to be useful to God in his kingdom. I want technical expertise that is applied with the know-how and common sense to bring about lasting results. Life is more than a basketball game, and I want my time on this earth to make a difference. I need to be deliberate in growing!

Lord, give me wisdom, skill, intelligence, know-how, knowledge, and common sense. Let me use these abilities in ways that creatively bring glory to you. In your name, amen!

JUNE 2

And all the craftsmen among the workmen made the tabernacle with ten curtains. They were made of fine twined linen and blue and purple and scarlet yarns, with cherubim skillfully worked. (Exod. 36:8)

In 1943, Abraham Maslow, an eminent American psychologist, published his theory that people had to have certain needs met before others could be addressed. For example, if someone is desperate for air, water, or food, she or he concentrates on that to the exclusion of other needs, like social belonging. A person drowning, fighting for oxygen, isn't likely to be thinking, "I have a brilliant idea for a business proposal!"

There is a time and place for things. In today's passage, we read of Moses assigning the children of Israel the task of making curtains. This transpired a good bit *after* their rescue from Pharaoh on the shores of the Re(e)d Sea. When the people saw Pharaoh and his army, they thought they were about to die. It was not the moment for Moses to hand out tasks of making curtains entwined with fine linen threads of blue and purple.

So, recognizing that things have a proper time and place, we get to this verse. Think about this verse for a moment. Curtains can be made in a variety of ways. You can take the nearest yarn available and weave a curtain. That yarn might be roughly made (it is cheaper that way, after all). It might be naturally colored (coloring takes time and dyes, and it is expensive). It can be done rapidly without interweaving designs (again, quicker, cheaper, more efficient). But this verse speaks to a very different kind of curtain.

These were not cheap, quick curtains, rapidly thrown together with whatever might be at hand. These curtains were careful works of art, made with fine linen threads. Linen wasn't bought at the store; it came from a plant. It had to be found, harvested, and made. The yarns were hand-dyed in beautiful colors that flowed well together. Again, dye was not bought; it was made. Intertwined in the curtains were angels ("cherubim"), giving an even greater artistic flair.

Yes, there is a time and place for things in our lives. Maslow has a point. But heaven forbid we not take time for art and beauty. It is a legitimate use of time and money. It might be as small as arranging food on a plate or flowers in a yard, but humans are made in the image of God, and God is a creative, artistic genius! We reflect his glory when we make art!

Lord, thank you for the beauty all around us. Let us value that aspect of our nature and honor you as we make art in our lives to your glory, amen.

JUNE 3

He coupled five curtains to one another, and the other five curtains he coupled to one another. . . . And he made fifty clasps of gold, and coupled the curtains one to the other with clasps. So the tabernacle was a single whole. (Exod. 36:10, 13)

One of the unique features of Israel's relationship with God was the singular nature of the tabernacle and temple. Most of Israel's contemporaries had many places of worship. They would have altars in their homes, create places of worship on hilltops, and build temples in their various towns and cities. Israel would copy many of these practices, always bringing the condemnation of God's prophets. It was not to be so in Israel.

Israel's first place of worship was the tabernacle, or tent, that Moses had built during the time in the wilderness. This was where God would meet Moses, the representative of the people. The tabernacle was built as one. Even the curtains were coupled to each other so that the tabernacle in all ways would be seen as a single whole. God met with his people in one place.

Over time, the moveable tabernacle gave way to a permanent structure for Israel's worship. Known as "Solomon's Temple," this new structure was in Jerusalem and was the designated meeting place for Israel and God. Sacrifices were to be performed only at the temple. As with the tabernacle, it was a "single whole," and God had one place of meeting with his people.

This same singular idea is found in the Christian understanding of Jesus. Jesus was and is the single meeting place for God and his people. Rather than being one of many paths to God, Jesus explained that he was the one meeting place, the one way to God. John explained that Jesus was where God "tabernacled" or "pitched his tent" with humanity. This is translated as "the Word became flesh and *dwelt* among us" (John 1:14). John used the Greek word for "tabernacle" when he said God "dwelt" among us in Jesus. Jesus spoke to the same "single meeting place" of God and people when he said, "I am *the* way, and the truth, and the life. No one comes to the Father except through me" (John 14:6).

God seeks to meet and commune with people. He is not an isolationist God. But he sets up his meeting places where we meet him. It has always been a single location.

Lord, thank you for meeting with us. Thank you for providing for a relationship. May we seek you and find you and grow before you. In your name, amen.

JUNE 4

These are the records of the tabernacle, the tabernacle of the testimony, as they were recorded at the commandment of Moses, the responsibility of the Levites under the direction of Ithamar the son of Aaron the priest. (Exod. 38:21)

A lot of people have Bibles. Some even read them! Even those that don't, however, often have a measure of respect for the book. I've heard people say, "I swear on the Bible." In many courtrooms, I've had judges give the oath to witnesses on a Bible. The Bible is special, but this is not because of the paper or ink in its printing. It isn't the cover or the font used. It isn't the book's antiquity. It is the belief that the Bible isn't just another book. There is something sacred and holy about it.

"Bible" comes directly from the Greek word *biblos*, which was a scroll, book, or record. Through history, our Bibles have usually been called "the Holy Bible," because it isn't an ordinary book. It is exclusive and unique.

The claims of the Bible are that God chose to communicate to humanity through words as well as events. Those are the two core aspects of human learning. We learn from what we hear/read and from what we experience. In the Bible, we have written down accounts of God's interactions with people as well as the words he has used to record those experiences.

In today's passage, we read of Moses instructing certain people to be responsible for recording aspects of God's works. The passage we read is one that sets up the "records" Moses told the Levites to make and keep.

In the earliest days of the Christian church, the Jewish rabbi and Christian apostle Paul was writing to a group of Jewish and Gentile Christians in Rome. Paul posed the question, "What is the advantage of being a Jew?" He then answered that there were many, not the least of which was that God had "entrusted" to the Jews the Scriptures, the holy words of God (Rom. 3:1).

In the Bible we find words of instruction, words of encouragement, words that inspire trust and faith, words that feed our hearts, minds, and souls. I want to take the Bibles off my shelves and learn to read them. By God's grace and direction, many people have worked for millennia to make that possible. I need to spend more time in it!

Lord, thank you for Scripture. Teach me to read with understanding. In your name, amen.

JUNE 5

From the blue and purple and scarlet yarns they made finely woven garments, for ministering in the Holy Place. They made the holy garments for Aaron, as the LORD had commanded Moses. (Exod. 39:1)

When I first got out of law school, I went to work in an old, established, and highly esteemed law firm. It was the first time in my life I was expected to wear a suit every day. We were a "suit and tie" law firm: no trousers with a sports jacket. No open-collar shirt. Over time, the firm loosened up, but I had left and started my own firm before that. Without a boss, I could wear anything I wanted. No one could fire me if I went to work in gym shorts and a t-shirt.

In my firm, I was fine in my normal clothes. Most law firms have now pursued similar casual dress, at least on Fridays. Still, there are times when I see certain clients, lawyers, or judges or go into court and wear a suit and tie. This is a show of respect. It says, "You are important, and what we are about is important, and my clothes will show it." It is an outward showing of an inward belief.

This is not limited to law or any work arena. How many weddings have a bride in a bridal gown? How many black-tie dinners or formals have you seen or attended? Even in school, we see proms and homecomings with hair done, fresh manicures, and stellar dresses. Our clothes and dress speak to the solemnity of occasions. Funerals might see people in black in mourning or in joyous colors to indicate celebration. We convey meaning and attitudes by what we wear.

By God's instructions, the priests who were called to minister on behalf of the people before God were given exclusive and unique clothes to wear. The priests did not approach God wearing their everyday clothes. Street clothes were not allowed. God wanted the priests to realize that they were about something special. There was a holiness in what they were doing, and it showed itself in their holy attire.

I know about wearing my "Sunday best" to church (or Sabbath best to synagogue), and there is some truth to that. But I need to get to the root of this. I shouldn't wear my clothes to impress others. I wear what I wear to show devotion and love to God. Peter taught that people of God should clothe themselves "with humility toward one another" (1 Pet. 5:5). That is going to trump my suit and tie! Better flip-flops with the right attitude than a tuxedo with arrogance!

Lord, in humility may I seek to give you my best, every day, in every way. Amen.

JUNE 6

He made the ephod of gold, blue and purple and scarlet yarns, and fine twined linen. And they hammered out gold leaf, and he cut it into threads to work into the blue and purple and the scarlet yarns, and into the fine twined linen, in skilled design. They made for the ephod attaching shoulder pieces, joined to it at its two edges. And the skillfully woven band on it was of one piece with it and made like it, of gold, blue and purple and scarlet yarns, and fine twined linen, as the LORD had commanded Moses. (Exod. 39:2–5)

I have not always been one who follows instruction manuals well. I tend to think of the instruction manual for putting something together as describing "one recommended way it might be done." I might have another idea. Of course, most of the time, after I finish putting something together and realize I have a number of "spare parts" I didn't use, I go back to the instruction manual to fix what I've done wrong.

In today's passage, we read about some of the extensive work done by the Israelite craftsmen in an effort to build the various pieces God had commissioned. I am impressed in the passage by the phrase that it was done "as the LORD had commanded Moses." It seems the Israelites and Moses were much better at seeing God's instructions as offering something more than one recommended way they might go about things.

Don't get me wrong; there are many times when God gives us guiding principles and we have to figure out how to build lives in accordance with those principles. I understand I am to love my neighbor as myself, and I need to figure out how to do that. I need to use my brain to consciously think, "What does that look like here?"

But there are also times when God makes his instructions quite clear. His instructions are not based on my wishes or inclinations. My decision becomes simple. Am I going to follow his instructions or make up my own? Am I going to treat his instructions as authoritative or am I going to see them as suggestions?

My faith tells me that God hasn't given instructions for arbitrary reasons. His instructions are part of a grander purpose and design, both for me and for the greater good. I am going to work on following directions better!

Lord, please help me focus on your directions for my life. Help me hold to the principles for living you have given as well as the specific instructions. Help me to bring you glory by the life I lead. In your name, amen.

JUNE 7

They made the plate of the holy crown of pure gold, and wrote on it an inscription, like the engraving of a signet, "Holy to the LORD." And they tied to it a cord of blue to fasten it on the turban above, as the LORD had commanded Moses. (Exod. 39:30–31)

I love my wife. She is my wife, not anyone else's. I am her husband. No one else's. She is dedicated to me as I am to her. One of the joys in my life has been performing weddings. In every wedding, one thing is consistently touching: when the bride and groom look at each other, in front of the witnesses, and they take their vows of devotion. They pledge to keep themselves wholly for the other until death. Tragically, those vows are not always kept, but that doesn't invalidate the beauty in exclusive commitment.

In today's passage, we read how the Israelites made the turban for the priests to wear when approaching God on behalf of the people. The priests' turban had a "crown" or "diadem," which was a piece of gold fastened to the top of the turban in the front. This piece was important for what it said, for where it was, and for how it was made.

The piece was engraved with the phrase *qodesh la-yhwh*, "Holy to the LORD." *Holy* is an interesting word of devotion and exclusivity. Much like wedding vows, "Holy to the Lord" conveys the idea of "dedicated exclusively to God." The service being brought by the priest was not partly dedicated to God, partly dedicated to the people, partly dedicated to—fill in the blank. It was exclusively dedicated to God.

Knowing what the phrase said is only part of the story in today's passage. The location is also important. This phrase of dedication was on the headdress, fastened to the front. As such, it was on the top of the priest. It covered everything, head to toe. It was also in the front so that anyone who saw the priest in his service saw this affirmation of exclusive dedication.

The plate that was engraved and fastened was made of pure gold. This was Israel's most precious metal, in its purest, most valuable form. The exclusive dedication to God was not one of anything less than the very best Israel had to offer.

My question after reading this is, What do I bring to God? Am I exclusively dedicated to him? Do people see that when they see me? From head to toe, do I give him the very best that I have? Are there areas in life I carve out from his lordship? I have some work to do!

Lord, help me purify my service to you. May I learn to give you my best. Head to toe, may I bring my whole life into dedicated service to you. In your name, amen.

JUNE 8

He also made the robe of the ephod woven all of blue, and the opening of the robe in it was like the opening in a garment, with a binding around the opening, so that it might not tear. On the hem of the robe they made pomegranates of blue and purple and scarlet yarns and fine twined linen. (Exod. 39:22-24)

Today's passage is a bit scary to me. No, I'm not typically afraid of garments or the making of them. What I find frightening is God's attention to detail!

The people are making the robe for the high priest to wear when performing certain priestly functions for Israel. God had given Moses distinct instructions on how to make it. God had the details down to even instructing them to add a binding around the opening so the garment wouldn't tear when taken on and off. Then, with an artistic flair, God had them make pomegranates to decorate the hem of the robe.

Do you see how incredible this is? In the previous book of Moses, we read that God made all of creation in six days. This God, who is responsible for the moon and stars and all the celestial bodies, who set into motion days and seasons, who saw to the land and water on our planet, who saw that the planet brought forth living creatures and plants for foodstuffs—this same massive God, who has done things that truly transcend our vision and knowledge, took time to explain how one robe was to be made in ways that would last and be beautiful. This is our detailed God.

Jesus taught his disciples that they needn't worry when they put their trust in God. The detailed God knew when a sparrow fell. He knew the numbers of hairs on our heads. He could be trusted not to overlook his followers (Matt. 10:29-31).

When we worry about today or tomorrow, when we fear what may or may not come, we need to remember our God, who takes care of details. He will hear our cries and come to our rescue. That might mean solving our problem. Or it might mean teaching us how to walk through our problems in his care. Either way, we are never in danger that he might overlook us, forget about us, or simply not care. Not this God. He gives great attention even to a priest's robe!

Lord, I do not always live in faith before you. I doubt, I worry, I get anxious about what is before me. Instill in me greater faith in you. Please watch over my life, lead me in your ways, and strengthen my faith in you. I pray by your great name, amen.

JUNE 9

Then the cloud covered the tent of meeting, and the glory of the LORD filled the tabernacle. And Moses was not able to enter the tent of meeting because the cloud settled on it, and the glory of the LORD filled the tabernacle. (Exod. 40:34–35)

Four buddies and I were having dinner in a hotel in Beverly Hills when we noticed that several tables over was Glenn Close. Ms. Close was a famous actress, having been in countless movies and television shows. We were all a bit stunned. She was sitting alone, eating and reading what turned out to be a script. One of our group said, "We gotta meet her!" Then another added, "No! That wouldn't be right, just to go up and interrupt her." I suggested the best thing to do if we wanted to meet her was to have her come introduce herself to us.

I called the waitress over and told her we wanted to pay for Ms. Close's meal. When asked who paid, she was to say us and explain we were fans but expected nothing in return and simply wished her a great evening. After finishing her dinner, Ms. Close came and introduced herself, thanked us kindly for her dinner, and talked to us for a good bit before leaving. We had quite the tale to tell when we got home.

That was fun. Ms. Close was impressive. But we had no problem being in the same restaurant with her. There are some very important people on our planet, people most of us are not likely to ever meet. People like presidents, prime ministers, chief justices, and more are removed from normal encounters with people. However, if a famous or notable person *was* in the same room as we were, we might be nervous, we might even not say anything, but we would live to tell the story.

Not so with God. In today's passage, we read about the "glory" of God entering the tent of meeting. This wasn't the fullness of God; it was simply his glory (in Hebrew, *cavod*). This was his honor or splendor. Simply a reflection of his awesomeness was so great that Moses could not even enter the tent. Moses, the best of Israel, was unable to be in the same room as the glory of God.

I fear we often make God into a little god of our own liking. My mom always warned us that God was not to be trifled with, yet how often are we dismissive of him? That is our error. God is not what we want or make. He is a being so great that even his glory is beyond our ability to bear. May God have mercy on us.

Lord God, I praise your greatness in my own feeble way. May I see you more clearly and bring ever greater praise to you. Humbly I pray in your great name, amen.

JUNE 10

Throughout all their journeys, whenever the cloud was taken up from over the tabernacle, the people of Israel would set out. But if the cloud was not taken up, then they did not set out till the day that it was taken up. (Exod. 40:36–37)

Boy, I wish I had that cloud today! The passage speaks of a cloud that covered the tabernacle while the Israelites were in the wilderness. When the cloud lifted and moved, the Israelites knew God was moving, leading them somewhere else. When the cloud remained, God was guiding the Israelites to remain. I can't count how many times I have wished God would be so clear in giving me instructions where to go, when to go, and when to stop.

Reflecting on my life, I can remember wondering where God wanted me to go to school, what career choice I should make, what job I should take, whom I should marry, where to live, where to go to church, how to rear our children, and more. I needed the cloud (the biblical kind, not the Internet kind)!

My reflections also drive me to two distinct realizations. First, there are times when I have known what God wanted me to do or not do, yet I haven't followed his wishes. Some things are very clear in his word, but I mess up often and am not able to follow instructions that couldn't be clearer. I'm not sure the cloud would always be a help. I might just ignore it on certain days.

Second, the wilderness was a unique time and place in history. God had yet to reveal much of himself, and the Israelites were only beginning to receive the revelation of Scripture. These thousands of years later, we have millennia of history and revelation to help us understand God and his ways. Part of the insight he has given us over the centuries is found in the wisdom literature of the Bible. We read in Proverbs 3:5–6 that to "trust in the LORD with all [our] heart, and do not lean on [our] own understanding. In all [our] ways acknowledge him, and he will make straight [our] paths."

This is an amazing teaching. It entails that God never wanted us to be his puppets. His goal isn't to pull our strings, having us dance to the tune he dictates. He wants us to grow up in our thinking, be mature in our motives, and seek him and his will. The assurance from him is that as we do so, he will *make* our paths straight, whether we could have done so on our own or not! God is at work renewing our minds!

Lord, thank you for teaching me. Forgive me when I fail to accept your will. Help me find your direction in life and acknowledge you in what I do today. In your name, amen.

JUNE 11

The LORD called Moses and spoke to him from the tent of meeting, saying, "Speak to the people of Israel and say to them . . ." (Lev. 1:1–2)

I have a friend named Ernest who has a rule about telephone calls. I learned it when he called me one day, and after we exchanged greetings, I began to ask him some questions. Ernest stopped me and said, "Mark, you don't have telephone etiquette down!" I asked what he meant, and he said, "I called you. By telephone rules, that means we talk about why I called you first. You have to wait for your questions." I think to some degree, Ernest was being funny, but the more I thought about it, the more logical his point seemed.

Ernest's telephone rules apply well to today's passage. God called Moses and spoke to him. This was God telling Moses what God wanted Moses to do. The agenda was God's agenda. We see that God instructed Moses to be his mouthpiece in speaking to the people of Israel.

This is the charge of God that brought forth much of what we call "the books of Moses," or the first five books of the Old Testament (the Jewish law, or Torah). These books form the foundation of this year's worth of devotions. The reason what we read is worthy of our devotional consideration is that it is what God instructed Moses to convey. This is God's agenda.

None of this should be taken in a way that indicates God cares only about what God has to say. All of the Bible makes clear that God wants to hear from his people. God wants a relationship that is two way. He speaks to us, but we also speak to him. Moses repeatedly talked to God, praising him, complaining about life and relationships, commiserating about frustrations, expressing joy, interceding for those in need, and more. God was always responsive and always wanted to hear Moses, and he gives the same attention to us that we are to give to him.

So, in today's passage, I ask myself, am I paying attention to God through these passages from Moses? Am I ready to let it affect who I am and what I do? I want to apply the Ernest rules of telephone conversation. I want to stick to God's agenda that he gave first and *then* lay out my own concerns to him.

Lord, I pray that I will be attentive to hearing your message and concerns. Tune my ears to hear your voice. As I listen and grow, help me engage you, fully pouring out my own concerns of life to you. In your name, amen.

JUNE 12

"If his offering is a burnt offering from the herd, he shall offer a male without blemish. He shall bring it to the entrance of the tent of meeting, that he may be accepted before the LORD. . . . If his gift for a burnt offering is from the flock, from the sheep or goats, he shall bring a male without blemish." (Lev. 1:3, 10)

Sacrifices are big in the books of Moses. Over and over one reads very particular instructions about when to sacrifice and how to sacrifice. In some ways today, this seems such a primitive and ancient practice that it is hard for us to relate to it.

That is why I stop at this passage. I want to understand it better. I want to seek its ancient roots and consider why it seems so primitive today. When considering these ancient practices, two important questions arise to me: first, why did the ancient Israelites sacrifice? Second, what did the ancient Israelites sacrifice?

The "why" of sacrifices is rooted in the idea that something about God has been offended. Pagan societies worshipped arbitrary and capricious gods that might be offended over next to nothing, but Israel's God was not like this. He showed himself righteous and just, attentive to the actions of his people. He laid down very specific instructions for holy living, and the people were never able to live up to God's level. For this reason, the people would offer sacrifices. It showed repentance before God as they gave up something in order to let him know their remorse. It showed recognition that they had fallen short of God's standards, as they offered up something to help make a difference. In a similar vein, it showed a respect for and fear of God as they sought to appease his just response to their disobedience.

The "what" of sacrifices varied tremendously. Many times, the sacrifices were on a wage adjusted scale, to use twenty-first-century economic terms. Those who could afford a lamb sacrificed a lamb. If one could only afford a bird, then it was to be a bird. Regardless of the level of the sacrifice, the point was in part that an innocent was given up for the sins of the guilty. The prophets knew and said over and over that the blood of a goat really achieved nothing on its own. That never made up for sin. Christianity teaches that those sacrifices foretold a real substitutionary sacrifice in the person of Jesus.

There is something real about our inadequacies before a holy and just God. I can't make it right on my own. I need God's mercies; I need God to make it right, even as I repent and try my best.

Lord, have mercy on me, a sinner. In your name, amen.

JUNE 13

"If his gift for a burnt offering is from the flock, from the sheep or goats, he shall bring a male without blemish." (Lev. 2:8-10)

One aspect of sacrifices in the law of Moses is that of a "gift." There is an idea that in sacrificing to God, one is making a gift to God. Think about giving God a gift! It is the ultimate task of "What do you give to someone who has everything?" After all, God created all we see about us. What do we have to give him?

For me the answer lies first in the heart. Simply wanting and seeking to give God something speaks volumes about us and our view of him. We want to give to people and causes we love. I love my wife and take great joy in giving to her. The fun of Christmas in our house includes the joy of giving to others and showing our love in our gifts. I think our love for God should propel us to give him gifts.

Then we ask, what do we give to him? Surely he's not that interested in me killing a goat. Granted, giving a goat in the Old Testament achieved a good bit we don't always associate with the gift. The meat was butchered and most of it given back to the giver. Some of it was burned, but some of it was also there to feed the priests and their families. By giving to God, the people were furthering God's work among his people, just as contributions to churches and synagogues today go to helping the ministers and the efforts on God's behalf. Still, there is more to give to God than goats.

I think what God most wants is my heart. God made humanity for a relationship rooted in love. God wants our love and our trust. He wants a relationship with us. He wants us to open ourselves up and allow him to father us. In some ways, this is simple; in some ways, it is complicated. God has done the work to make the relationship valid. He stands at the door of our hearts and knocks. Our response is what is lacking.

We need to respond in faith, love, and trust. We need to respond in ways that allow him to be who he is, Lord and God, and not some concierge to help us get dinner reservations. Here is the complication. Our relationship with God must be based on truth. His truth. If we try to make him anything less than God, we aren't interested in God as God. This is the root of our giving. We give to God as our Lord. That means *automatically* that God gets all we have. A physical gift is merely a representation of that truth. It checks whether we really mean that we give our all to God.

Lord, thank you for seeking me out. May I give you my all as I live in the joy of being in a relationship with you. In your name, amen.

JUNE 14

"If anyone of the common people sins unintentionally in doing any one of the things that by the LORD's commandments ought not to be done, and realizes his guilt, or the sin which he has committed is made known to him, he shall bring for his offering a goat, a female without blemish, for his sin which he has committed. And he shall lay his hand on the head of the sin offering and kill the sin offering in the place of burnt offering . . . And the priest shall make atonement for him, and he shall be forgiven." (Lev. 4:27–29, 31)

Unintentional sins? Am I responsible for those too?

I have enough concern over the sins that are intentional. Unintentional sins seem to pile it on too deep for anyone to climb out! This passage teaches us that sin has its consequences, whether we are aware of the sin or not. Those consequences need dealing with, whether we know of them or not. Sin is not an arbitrary list of dos and don'ts that God has placed in our lives. It is something much more significant.

Sin is living in violation of the character and morality of a moral God. God is a being that has moral corners, in a manner of speaking. For example, God is a God of truth, not of lies. God is a just God, hating injustice. God is righteous, and what he does is righteous by definition. Sin is a choice, a behavior, an attitude that is UN-God, or "ungodly," as we would say in everyday language.

As humans, we exist in the image of God. This means a lot of things, including that we are moral beings, as he is moral. Morality is hardwired into our minds. We know that there is right and wrong. From an early age, we say things like "That is not fair!" because we know that fairness is a virtue. It is the value we should seek. We are moral creatures as God is a moral being.

So, now we get back to this passage. What does it mean to have accountability for unintentional sins? It means that sin drives a wedge between us and God. When we make immoral choices, when we harbor immoral thoughts or motives, we set ourselves up against God and his character. That has bad effects for this life, and it disturbs our fellowship with him.

This calls for accountability and his forgiveness. To the Christian, there is just forgiveness in the sacrifice of Christ. These Old Testament sacrifices are seen as foreshadowing that ultimate satisfaction and atonement for sin. Something must be done for sin, whether intentional or not!

Lord, have mercy on me, a sinner in thought and deed. In your name, amen.

JUNE 15

"If anyone sins in that he hears a public adjuration to testify, and though he is a witness, whether he has seen or come to know the matter, yet does not speak, he shall bear his iniquity." (Lev. 5:1)

The lawyer in me wants to stand up when reading this passage, delivering it out loud in a clear voice. The passage says that when a matter is being called to a public trial, or when people are making a decision about a matter, those who have relevant testimony are sinning if they fail to let their knowledge be known.

This might strike some as bizarre. After all, "I don't want to get involved" may not be the most admirable attitude, but is it sin? Surely not! Well, actually, yes, it is.

Why? What lies behind this passage? A lot, actually. First, we see here the importance to God of justice. God cares about things being right, fair, and just. It matters to him whether fairness is implemented in our society, whether it is a dispute among friends or family or a major crime in a court. God cares about things being right.

A second implication is the importance of truth. Justice depends upon true and accurate information. We are to be honest people. When we speak, we are to speak truthfully. When we act, we are to act without deception. People need to be able to rely on our honesty. If we see things going awry and if we have knowledge or information that can help set things right, we have a responsibility to speak up or act. We need to be people who care about justice.

This is not limited to speaking up when the people at risk of injustice are our friends and families. If we see something or know something that helps make things right for a stranger, we need to be godly and say what we know.

Let the people of God be known for mercy and also for caring about truth and fairness. We need to let the poor know the people of God will speak out for their justice. We need to let the disadvantaged know we will not let others take advantage of them by our silence or by ignoring events.

Let us speak out for God's truth and justice!

Lord, give me insight in holiness to be a person of truth who cares about justice and fairness for everyone. In the midst of this, also keep me merciful when people need your mercy. In your name, amen.

JUNE 16

"If anyone utters with his lips a rash oath to do evil or to do good, any sort of rash oath that people swear, and it is hidden from him, when he comes to know it, and he realizes his guilt in any of these; when he realizes his guilt in any of these and confesses the sin he has committed, he shall bring to the LORD as his compensation for the sin that he has committed, a female from the flock, a lamb or a goat, for a sin offering. And the priest shall make atonement for him for his sin." (Lev. 5:4–6)

A "rash oath"? How many people make oaths, anyway? Actually, quite a few! One is making an oath when he or she says, "I swear . . ." It doesn't have to be, "I swear to God . . ." or "I swear on my mother's grave . . ." It is also an oath when one says, "I promise . . ."

Of course, there is no magic to the words "swear," "oath," or "promise." The core idea is whether or not one is honest in one's speech. When I commit to something, am I reliable? When I affirm something, am I truthful?

At the core of this instruction in the Old Testament is the root idea that our commitments need to be real. We are warned against giving commitments "rashly," because often they turn out to be ones not easily kept.

There is a lot of practical life advice wrapped into this passage. When asked to do something, I need to be thoughtful before responding. I need to think about it, pray about it, and not be fearful to answer "I'm not certain right now" or perhaps even "No, thank you!" When asked about a situation, I need to be thoughtful in reply. Sometimes the fast answer that can roll off our lips is not really the accurate answer. It is the easy answer instead. That kind of rash response is not one rooted in truth and needs to be avoided.

In trial and depositions (sworn testimony), we always teach our witnesses to be thoughtful before responding. It is important the answer be truthful, and that means reflection is an imperative before answering.

At the office, I find that those people who say they will do something and then follow through are invaluable. I trust them with big and more important things. Those people that prove untrustworthy, however, scare me to death. I am hesitant to give them anything important to do. I fear it won't be done, in spite of what they say.

I don't want to be rash in what I say or where I commit. I want people to know that when I say, "Yes," it means "Yes!" This is a good way to live.

Lord, I am guilty of making rash commitments and vows, even to you. Help me learn and grow in this. Help me to be reliable to others as one who keeps my word. In your name, amen.

JUNE 17

The LORD spoke to Moses, saying, "If anyone commits a breach of faith and sins unintentionally in any of the holy things of the LORD, he shall bring to the LORD as his compensation, a ram without blemish out of the flock, valued in silver shekels, according to the shekel of the sanctuary, for a guilt offering. He shall also make restitution for what he has done amiss in the holy thing and shall add a fifth to it and give it to the priest. And the priest shall make atonement for him with the ram of the guilt offering, and he shall be forgiven." (Lev. 5:14–16)

In book 2 of his *Republic*, Plato wrote a story about a mythical ring discovered by an shepherd. The man stole the ring off a giant corpse. He learned that when he adjusted the ring, it allowed him man to become invisible. The invisibility became a moral trap, and the shepherd used it to seduce the queen; with her help, to murder the king; and then to become king himself.

The story, which inspired Tolkien to write his Lord of the Rings saga, asked the question of whether anyone is so virtuous that they would be virtuous if the penalty of immorality was removed. In other words, are we only good for fear of getting caught and the resulting punishment or penalties?

Doubtless, penalties and punishment are deterrents of bad behavior. However, there is hopefully something beyond that. Somewhere in humanity is the virtue of doing right, even when no one is looking. Somewhere in the faithful, there is a confidence that God is watching, even when the world isn't. My actions may be invisible to the world, but they aren't to God.

God's instructions to the people of Israel in today's passage deal with the importance of restitution. When we do wrong, even if we don't mean to, we are to try and fix the wrong, adding "interest" to whatever we've done (the "fifth" in the text).

This doesn't mean we give restitution only when we are caught. Faithful to God, we should recognize our sins and shortcomings, and when we wrong someone, we should try to make it right. The idea of "interest" may be as simple as restoring money we've wrongfully taken. But more often, it will be giving the extra effort to restore trust, fix feelings, mend brokenness, and so on. This makes life more complicated, but it is the right way to live.

Lord, many are the ways I've violated your trust and that of others. As I seek forgiveness, help me to work toward making things right again. Give me chances to restore what I've harmed. In your name, amen.

JUNE 18

The LORD spoke to Moses, saying, "If anyone sins and commits a breach of faith against the LORD by deceiving his neighbor in a matter of deposit or security, or through robbery, or if he has oppressed his neighbor or has found something lost and lied about it, swearing falsely—in any of all the things that people do and sin thereby . . ." (Lev. 6:1–3)

We often take for granted certain ideas that have become part of what we know and believe. A close examination of history, however, often illuminates the basis for beliefs that we never knew. In college in Tennessee, I had a friend who told me of his mother always cutting two inches off a ham when she would bake it. He asked his mother once why she did it. She replied, "It's just something that's done. My mother did it and I do it." My friend was overly inquisitive and said, "But why?" Unable to give an explanation, they got his grandmother (the mom's mother) on the phone. When asked why she always cut two inches from the end of a ham, the grandmother replied, "It's the only way to make it fit in my pan!" It can help to know the roots of ideas!

Here we see an important root of an idea that pervades most of those who will read this book: immoral acts are sins against God. It is an understanding that made Israel stand out from its neighbors. For most early societies, there were certain obligations owed to the gods, but most of daily life was simply fitting in with the cultural rules. The gods little noticed and had no real care about such things.

For Israel, however, the law given to Moses was not simply a legal system for society. It wasn't a law code that said, "Do this and that or pay your price to society." For Israel, the law was also a moral obligation to God. Taking someone's money was not just a crime of society, mandating a criminal penalty. It was a sin against God. It was an offense against God.

The book of Genesis teaches that people are made as moral beings in the image of a moral God. Therefore, people are expected to live morally before this moral God. While my stealing from you may be wrong in society, the real truth is it's a sin before God. This is why I should refrain from doing it, even if I can get away with it.

My friend's mom found out she was cutting two inches of a ham for no good reason. If we look at the root of our moral code, you have a very good reason to follow it! God is a moral God. When we commit a wrong, we are sinning. That means something.

Lord, may my actions be tuned to your morality. May I care for the things you care about and live consistently with your character. In your name, amen.

JUNE 19

The LORD spoke to Moses, saying, "Command Aaron and his sons, saying, 'This is the law of the burnt offering. . . . Fire shall be kept burning on the altar continually; it shall not go out.'" (Lev. 6:8, 13)

It seems common that children go through a growing stage where they challenge authority. It's that stage where a parent might instruct a child to do ABC, but the child thinks of the instruction more as a recommendation or suggestion! God made it very clear to his people that his instructions were not suggestions. They were commands.

In today's passage, God speaks to Moses and sets out the way the Israelites are to tend to the fire used in sacrifices. That might be something that seems open to suggestions. People make and tend fires differently. I was taught to make a fire with three logs, placing the kindling in the base and then setting the three logs to burn. Others have told me there is a better way. I have had debates on this!

God wasn't making suggestions, though. He was telling the Israelites exactly how he expected them to maintain their fire. He gave them instructions on removing the ashes, where they were to be put, and more. God was not about micromanaging. God wanted the Israelites to see the need for constancy in sacrifice. The sacrifices of animals and foodstuffs were never a sufficient sacrifice that took care of all the people's transgressions. The people would sin over and over, and the sacrificial fires had to be maintained twenty-four hours a day, seven days a week, 365 days a year.

I get this. I personally know the presence of sin. Sinfulness is ubiquitous. It is in every area of life. There are many times I see myself sinning over and over. Some sins are so sticky, I can't seem to get clean from them. They are like a subdivision with only one entrance. Everywhere you turn, they seem to take you back to where you were. Even when I am doing good things, my attitude is far from perfect. I understand the need for continual fire prepared for sin offerings.

Christianity teaches that Jesus was an offering for sin that was different. In contrast to the continual fires for bulls and goats, Jesus was a one-time sacrifice, adequate to atone for the sins of all for all time. His sacrifice was of a quality necessary to truly atone for the sins of humanity. The blood of a goat or bull isn't really a fair exchange. It was continually offered to show the continual need until something complete came along!

Lord, I confess myself a sinner, and I ask for your forgiveness. I am not worthy of your love, but I couldn't exist without it. I need your mercy. In your name, amen.

JUNE 20

"And this is the law of the grain offering. The sons of Aaron shall offer it before the LORD *in front of the altar. And one shall take from it a handful of the fine flour of the grain offering and its oil and all the frankincense that is on the grain offering and burn this as its memorial portion on the altar, a pleasing aroma to the* LORD." (Lev. 6:14–15)

In law, we often speak of whether testimony or an idea will "pass the smell test." The expression is not new. Throughout the world today and back into antiquity, people would determine if something was good or not by smelling it. This human trait is also used to express the way God finds an obedient sacrifice pleasing.

Today's passage speaks to Israel's grain offering. This was an offering that Israelites would bring to God for burning on the altar. The grain was ground into flour, mixed with oil and spices (frankincense), and burned as a memorial. The grain offering was not simply taking the harvested grain to the priests for burning. It was an end product. The grain was picked, threshed, and ground into "fine flour." This was the best of the best. It was the result of hard work. The key for God was not the ingredients but the work that went into the sacrifice.

We should never make the arrogant mistake of misreading passages like this as simply reflecting a primitive view of God where he needed to sniff an aroma to be happy. Certainly, this primitive view of the gods were held by many of Israel's neighbors, but that is not the God of Israel. The pleasing aroma to God was an obedient sacrifice, the result of hard work given out of dedication and commitment to God.

Psalm 51 speaks of this truth. In repenting before God for his blatant sin, the writer said, "For you will not delight in sacrifice, or I would give it; you will not be pleased with a burnt offering. The sacrifices of God are a broken spirit; a broken and contrite heart, O God, you will not despise" (Ps. 51:16–17).

I need to inspect my life and look at how I live before God. Do I sacrifice to him my obedience? Do I choose his ways over my own? Do I let his priorities trump my own? Do I seek to serve him with my time, energy, thoughts, and plans? These decisions I make daily are my chances to offer obedience as a sacrifice. I can give God the best of my best. That will "pass the smell test." It will be a pleasing aroma to my God.

Lord, may I live consciously, putting the best of my life to you to use as you see fit. I want to please you in all that I am and all that I do. In your name, amen.

JUNE 21

The LORD spoke to Moses, saying, "Speak to Aaron and his sons, saying, This is the law of the sin offering. In the place where the burnt offering is killed shall the sin offering be killed before the LORD; it is most holy. The priest who offers it for sin shall eat it. In a holy place it shall be eaten, in the court of the tent of meeting." (Lev. 6:24–26)

I was deposing a doctor recently and during a break, he looked at food that was set out and said, "Eat this, not that." I replied that I try to be careful about eating, but I'm not always as good as I should be. His reply was "You dig your grave by your teeth." I thought for a moment to soak it in. He had a new way of expressing the old maxim, "We are what we eat."

The priests in Moses' day were taught this maxim, but in a different sense. The Israelites were charged with a need to sacrifice for sin. This was putting to death an innocent animal in recognition that the people had sinned and the price for sin was death. We can equate sin to cancer that needs radiation to kill the cancerous cells. Sin leads to death most assuredly. God set up a system where the people were instructed to sacrifice an animal rather than themselves. This was something very important. It was to make the people holy in spite of their actions and sins proving them unholy.

Holy in this sense means that the offering was set apart for God. It is the opposite of *profane*, which meant "ordinary" or "everyday." The point of the sin offering was that it was not ordinary. It was something being done for God and before God. There was no inherent value in killing an animal; the value was showing God recognition that sin is wrong, that it bears a punishment of death, and that even though inadequate, a price was being paid for sin.

The priests were to perform the sacrifice in a most holy way in a holy place. Then the priests were to eat the sacrifice in the holy place. Even four thousand years ago, people realized that food was sustenance. "You are what you eat" is not a novel concept. This was another way to show that the holiness of God was something that was to be a part of the people. In Christianity, this sacrifice and eating takes on another dimension. Jesus is seen as the ultimate sacrifice for sin. Jesus taught his followers that they would "eat his body" through the elements known as the Eucharist or Lord's Supper. The people become what they eat. As Jesus is holy, the followers of Jesus are holy. I want to take in all that God has to offer. I want to feast on his word (and "Word").

Lord, I confess myself a sinner and ask you to make me holy. May I partake of your holiness as you manifest it in me. In your name, amen.

JUNE 22

"Flesh that touches any unclean thing shall not be eaten. It shall be burned up with fire." (Lev. 7:19)

A dear friend of mine once pointed out to me that as we age, a lot of what we see as black and white becomes gray. I have found that to be true. But I have also found the opposite true as well. As I age, a lot of what I have seen as gray has become black and white. Holiness and purity are important at any age.

Today's passage comes from the instructions given the priests for handling sacrifices. Generally, a priest would be given an animal to sacrifice, and the priest would first slaughter the animal. Then, in butchering the animal, certain fats, entrails, and other parts were offered as burnt offerings on the altar. Other more choice pieces were given to the priests as food. Then the bulk of the animal was returned to the ones offering it.

While normally the priests would eat a measure of most sacrifices, there were some limitations built into this system. One of the most prominent concerned the priest's portion being touched by something or someone unclean. In that event, the portion became unclean, and it was burned up, not eaten.

Two aspects of this speak to me. First, I take an admonition in the way uncleanness spreads. It is the opposite of holiness. Holiness comes from how something is set apart and dedicated. But one holy thing touching another holy thing doesn't spread the holiness. Uncleanness, however, is spread by contact. In this way sin and uncleanness are like sickness. We share sickness; disease is transmitted. Health, however, not so. I can give you a disease by sneezing in your space. I can't give you health the same way. This passage and principle teach me to be careful about uncleanness. Whether evil thoughts or deeds, uncleanness spreads like a disease.

My second concern is that uncleanness is not profitable for use. I do not make myself better for God's service by dabbling in or touching things that are not right and good. As my mom taught our children about watching movies that were garbage, "Do you really want to feed your mind *that*? That is the equivalent of eating dog poop and thinking it's a brownie!" (Grandmothers can use that language.)

I need to stay away from garbage!

Lord, give me wisdom to discern right and wrong. Help me see what is profitable and what is destructive, and give me strength to choose right. In your name, amen.

JUNE 23

"Speak to the people of Israel, saying, 'Whoever offers the sacrifice of his peace offerings to the LORD shall bring his offering to the LORD from the sacrifice of his peace offerings. His own hands shall bring the LORD's food offerings.'" (Lev. 7:29–30)

Sacrifice and obedience should be personal. There is no value in my sending someone else to sacrifice on my behalf.

Today's passage includes God's instructions for the Israelites to bring their sacrifices personally to the priests. Living under the law of Moses, I couldn't get my parents to take my sacrifice. It wasn't adequate to send it through my spouse. My children were not an adequate conduit for my obedience to God. I had to bring it personally. Sacrifice and obedience were first and foremost personal responsibilities, not communal.

When my sisters and I were very young, my dad was fond of noting when one of us might leave the room to go to the restroom. His general comment was the question, "Would you go for me while you're up?" As children we giggled most every time. His point, aside from humor, was the simple notion that some things you must do for yourself.

That is a point in this passage. We are personally responsible for our relationship with God. We can't pawn that off on someone else. It is often said, "God doesn't have grandchildren. He only has children." There is merit to that saying. We come to God on our own, or we don't come at all. My friend Bob teases that he is going to be fine with God because his wife is tight with the Lord. Bob figures that God isn't going to let his wife be disappointed, so by taking care of his wife, God will have to take care of Bob. Bob secretly knows better, but his comment always makes me walk back through the teaching of personal accountability and responsibility.

One of the positive aspects of this is our ability to take our cares and concerns to God. As we personally go to God with our sacrifices, we take him our cares and concerns as well. We have access to him on a personal basis.

This ready access to God gives me reflection in two directions. I get to serve him loyally and faithfully, and I get to take him my problems. We never need to wonder about whether God is interested in a relationship with us. He gave clear instructions that he wanted a relationship with *each individual.* He meets me and in his loving mercy receives me. I am grateful.

Lord, thank you for hearing my prayers. Thank you for asking and even instructing me to come before you personally. There can be no doubt about your care. In your name, amen.

JUNE 24

Aaron and his sons did all the things that the LORD commanded by Moses. (Lev. 8:36)

There is power in obedience. When we follow God's instructions, we live in his will and see amazing things come from his hands.

Aaron and his sons were set aside as the special priests for Israel. They were responsible for many if not most of the legal requirements given by Moses. The priests had rules for sacrifices and for upkeep of the tabernacle and temple. The priests were responsible for seeing to holiness in many of the rituals before God throughout all of Israel. There were special garments they wore, special prayers they learned and recited, blessings they pronounced on the people, and more. When the priests obeyed, as they did at first, the entire land profited. When the priests dropped their obedience, the whole land suffered.

Our actions affect our own lives. There can be no real debate about that. If I choose to be a glutton, I will see a difference (and feel a difference). If I choose to look at garbage on the Internet, my mind will think garbage. If I choose to treat people with contempt, I will develop habits that hurt all my relationships. While our actions change who we are, they do much more than that. Our actions also affect others.

Should I choose to text while I drive, I risk ruining not only my life but also the lives of others on the road. Even ruining my own life would have an effect on the lives of my loved ones. By how we live, whether we are holy and obedient or unholy and disobedient, we change the world around us. Here is the power of obedience.

All of this is true in not just a negative sense of sin but also a positive sense of obedience. When I show my wife God's endearing love, her life brightens, and she is better able to bless others. When I demonstrate God's love to the less fortunate, they are in a better position to live profitable lives to the benefit of everyone.

We need to learn and believe that the instructions of God are more than arbitrary lists of dos and don'ts based on the mood of God at the time he gave them. His instructions are part of his will. They are the living values that, as we follow them, make the world a better place. When I show love and compassion to others, God is working good and important things in this world. When I refrain from gossip, I am preventing a destructive course of action with negative repercussions. God's will is found and enacted through doing all the things the Lord commanded.

I need to listen for God's instructions and obey them. God will work wonders when I do.

Lord, give me eyes to see your will and strength to follow it in my day-to-day walk. Let my obedience make a difference. In your name, amen.

JUNE 25

"This is the thing that the LORD *commanded you to do, that the glory of the* LORD *may appear to you." Then Moses said to Aaron, "Draw near to the altar and offer your sin offering and your burnt offering and make atonement for yourself and for the people, and bring the offering of the people and make atonement for them, as the* LORD *has commanded." (Lev.* 9:6–7)

Most everyone I've met, and likely everyone reading this devotional, knows the pain associated with sin. We know that doing wrong, and even thinking wrong without acting on the thoughts, has negative consequences and is something over which we wish we had better control. God is not silent on this subject.

Today's passage has Moses explaining God's commands for the priests to offer atonement for the people. *Atonement* is a word that speaks to paying a ransom price or appeasing one who has been wronged. It conveys the idea that sin is not simply something that is disturbing to the sinner. Sin also is an obstacle that inhibits one's relationship with God. Sin is an affront to God. Rather than simply turn his back on the sinner, however, God seeks to make the sinner whole and righteous again. The law of Moses included the instruction that some price must be paid for the sin. This was the atonement. It was a recognition that sin has consequences. It was a visual reminder that sin costs the sinner something. Sin comes at a price.

When I reflect on the sin in my life, I can see the consequences. Sometimes they aren't so obvious, but the sin affects how I feel, how I interact with others, and how I interact with God. Some sins are so powerful that they harden my heart to God. I can almost say I ignore him and shut him out of part of life. Other sins can bear dire and real consequences to relationships. After all, how good can a relationship be when one person treats another one poorly? Some sin seems to settle in our hearts and minds like a piece of rotten food, starting to stink and fester while attracting flies. Not pretty, I admit, yet in a graphic way, this is mild compared to what goes on.

Sin is mighty serious stuff. So is atonement. God doesn't want us saddled with our sin. God wants us to find his forgiveness and he wants to empower us to live better. The Christian understanding is that Jesus became the ultimate ransom or atonement for our sin. He had no personal sins that needed an atonement, but he was sacrificed nonetheless on behalf of others. God redeemed humanity this way and now works among his children to grow them in holiness. I don't want my sin. It serves no good purpose.

Lord, please forgive my sin. Help me learn to be a better person. In your name, amen.

JUNE 26

Then Aaron lifted up his hands toward the people and blessed them, and he came down from offering the sin offering and the burnt offering and the peace offerings. (Lev. 9:22)

Get in a crowded room and listen for a sneeze. If you hear one, you will likely hear at least one person affirm "Bless you!" or even "God bless you!" It is a practice with people today. Blessing after a sneeze has been around for almost 1,500 years. It was instituted by Pope Gregory in 590. He was concerned at the ravages of the plague in the early Middle Ages. Sneezing was seen as an early plague symptom, and so he ordered that when one sneezed, others pronounce a blessing on them. In its rudimentary form, the blessing was a prayer. It was a request that God look upon a person and be good to him or her.

Today's passage shows that the idea of blessing another goes back far beyond any pope. Over 1,500 years before Gregory, Aaron was taught to bless the people. Aaron was dealing not with the bubonic plague but with the plagues of life and sin. Aaron was a "high priest." More than any other priest, the high priest was charged with ministering on behalf of all the people of Israel, including the other priests. The law set out a fundamental truth. Everyone needs the blessings of God. There is no exception.

We need his blessings in many ways. *Need* is the operative word. We need his blessings through life's difficulties. We need God's blessings in our families, our studies, and our jobs. Even more, we need his blessings on our hearts.

This is the problem: we have a sickness for which, like the plague in the Middle Ages, there is no known cure. Even the best of us aren't as good as we should be. We do things we know we shouldn't do, or we fail to do things we should do. A few folks might think they are fine, with irreproachable lives, but those folks are overly proud. *Haughty* is the word. In other words, they are sick and just don't realize it! When I was a young man, I asked a fellow, "How are you doing?" His reply, given with a knowing smile, was "Better than I deserve, but not as good as I'd like!" He had it right.

Since we all need God's blessings, I've decided to start praying them over people, and not just when they sneeze. As I type this, I pray that God will bless the reader. In restaurants, I am writing "God bless you!" on the check. (Don't do that and leave a poor tip! You reflect badly on God!) I am adding "God bless you!" to people in conversation and when leaving. Importantly, as I say it or think it, I am praying it to the Lord.

Lord, please work in and through me, and may I give you glory for the work you do. Bless those around me today. In your name, amen.

JUNE 27

Fire came out from before the LORD and consumed the burnt offering and the pieces of fat on the altar, and when all the people saw it, they shouted and fell on their faces. (Lev. 9:24)

We have a few expressions in English for particularly stunning times. "I'm speechless!" "I'm at a loss for words!" One time, before a particularly surprising jury verdict was going to be read, a court deputy who knew the result told me, "You'd better be sitting down!" Most of our expressions are just that—expressions. Rarely are they literal.

Today's passage surpasses all of our modern expressions, and it seems it was a literal occurrence, not hyperbole. The people of Israel had gathered before the constructed tabernacle. It was their first time to offer the sacrifices instructed by God. The priests were dressed in their splendid regalia, specially made for the moment. The high priest wore the turban with the gold plaque devoting him to the Lord. He wore the gold breast plate with stones engraved with the names of all twelve tribes of Israel. The glimmer of the sun's rays off the gold was undoubtedly unlike anything the people had seen before. The incense was offered, and fragrant smells lay heavy over the assembly. The animals were sacrificed, their parts laid on the altar, and then, in a flash, fire came forth from God and the burnt offerings were consumed.

Everyone was beyond stunned. They fell on their faces. Undoubtedly a mixture of awe, fear, and amazement combined with the unexpected and unknown to produce such a reaction. Falling on their faces was an expression of deep and reverent worship. There was no doubt that a holy moment was transpiring with a holy God. No one felt worthy to stand. There were no casual observers.

Have you ever fallen on your face before God? Admittedly, I haven't seen God come forth in such a manner, but God has not been absent in my life. He has rescued me when I was stuck. He has lifted me from despair. He has sustained me through times of weakness. He has forgiven me for deliberate and unconscious sin. He has blessed me with family, friends, purpose, mission, opportunities, joy, favor, and things I don't even see or know. I have *every reason* to fall on my face before God.

If I tend to be more a casual observer and less a reverent worshipper, shame on me. I should know better. God is stunning. He should leave me speechless and at a loss for words. When I see the Almighty, I shouldn't just be sitting down; I might need to fall on my face!

Lord, may I see you in my day-to-day living. You have blessed me beyond measure, and I am thankful. May I grow in my worship of you. In your name, amen.

JUNE 28

Now Nadab and Abihu, the sons of Aaron, each took his censer and put fire in it and laid incense on it and offered unauthorized fire before the LORD, which he had not commanded them. And fire came out from before the LORD and consumed them, and they died before the LORD. . . . And the LORD spoke to Aaron, saying, "Drink no wine or strong drink, you or your sons with you, when you go into the tent of meeting, lest you die." . . . Now Moses diligently inquired about the goat of the sin offering, and behold, it was burned up! And he was angry with Eleazar and Ithamar, the surviving sons of Aaron, saying, "Why have you not eaten the sin offering in the place of the sanctuary, since it is a thing most holy and has been given to you that you may bear the iniquity of the congregation, to make atonement for them before the LORD? . . . You certainly ought to have eaten it in the sanctuary, as I commanded." And Aaron said to Moses, "Behold, today they have offered their sin offering and their burnt offering before the LORD, and yet such things as these have happened to me! If I had eaten the sin offering today, would the LORD have approved?" And when Moses heard that, he approved. (Lev. 10:1–2, 8, 16–20)

This is a crazy story, and to get the entire context, I have quoted an unusually large portion of Scripture. Many students of Scripture are surprised and even frightened by the story of Nadab and Abihu, two sons of Aaron assigned to the Lord's priestly service. The two men offered unauthorized fire before the Lord, contrary to God's command. The result was not a warning, a scolding, a reprimand, or even removal from God's service. They were killed. Immediately. That seems harsh!

Then we have at the end of the reading the story of Nadab and Abihu's brothers, Eleazar and Ithamar. These brothers were commanded to eat the sin offering and they disobeyed. They were not killed, however, but excused. Their failure to eat was because they mourned the deaths of their brothers.

What explains the different treatment? Why does God kill one set of disobeying brothers, while the other set is excused? The answer seems to lie in the verses that sit between these two stories. After the death of Nadab and Abihu, Aaron is told, "Don't you or your sons serve the Lord when you are drunk!" That seems to explain the rather terse account about the first two sons' demise. They didn't simply offer unauthorized fire as some mistake. They flippantly disregarded the God they were serving and went in drunk. God's holiness is real, and we take it lightly at our own risk.

I need to rethink how I treat God.

Lord, I confess I don't always treat your holiness as I should. Please forgive me and help me grow in this. In your name, amen.

JUNE 29

"I am the LORD your God. Consecrate yourselves therefore, and be holy, for I am holy." (Lev. 11:44)

We are taught at an early age to behave. From home, in school, and even from friends, we learn which behaviors are acceptable and which are not. As we get older, we begin to question morality as taught to us. Children decide what they will embrace from their upbringing and what they will reject. This is a normal part of aging as our minds engage and we weigh the reasons behind our ethics and behaviors.

Into this picture comes religion and faith. Most religions, and certainly those based on the Bible, teach an ethics that prescribes behaviors and attitudes as right and virtuous or wrong.

The motives for doing right and avoiding wrong also develop. When we are young, the motivation is often seeking to please our parents or seeking to avoid their displeasure. There is frequently a negative consequence associated with wrong behavior, and this can motivate our actions. As we get older, our motivations can also change. Often adolescents modify their behavior as they desire to be independent and free from the restraints of childhood. There is also a stage where people change their behavior to fit in, to be part of a group.

Hopefully our motivations for behaving continue to grow from these stages. Today's passage gives a mature motivation. God instructed the Israelites that they were to be holy because the LORD God was holy. This is an altogether different motivation.

God gives a simple instruction to behave as he commanded, basing his instruction on the nature and character of God. God is a holy God. God is a moral God. God is a righteous and just God. God is a loving God. As we learn and see God, as we watch his hand work in our history, in our present, and in our futures, we are to bring our actions into alignment with him.

This is not because God is a narcissist, making it all about him. It is because it is the right, smart, and mature thing to do. God knows best, God behaves best, God has all the plans and foresight, and God is acting for our best good. Anyone who understands this will seek to be who God instructs her or him to be.

I want to say, "Yes, Lord! I will be holy because you are!" Regrettably, however, I find it isn't as easy to do as it is to say! But I am working on it.

Lord, teach me holiness. May my life echo yours to your glory and in your name, amen.

JUNE 30

"For I am the LORD who brought you up out of the land of Egypt to be your God. You shall therefore be holy, for I am holy." (Lev. 11:45)

Yesterday's devotion explained the reason for being holy as a desire to follow God's character and morality. We are holy because he is holy. Today's passage continues the theme of holiness, but today, there is a slightly different slant on why we are to live holy lives.

God says that his children should be holy not only because God is holy but also because of what God has done. The acts of God should motivate our lives choices and behaviors.

At the time the Israelites received this commandment, they had notable experiences upon which they could reflect. God had saved Moses through the quick thinking of his mother, his sister, and the intervention of Pharaoh's daughter. God then called Moses through a miraculous encounter in a burning bush, sending him back with his brother to demand Pharaoh's release of Israel. Pharaoh refused, so God worked miracle after miracle over the gods of Egypt and the land of Egypt until finally, Pharaoh drove out the Israelites. When Pharaoh had a change of heart and sent the military after the Israelites, God intervened most miraculously, parting the Re(e)d Sea for the Israelites, then using it to drown Pharaoh's elite army. As the Israelites wandered in the wilderness, God showered them with manna and quail and even supplied fresh water as needed.

Israel had every reason to follow and obey such a God as this. After all God had done, how could Israel do anything but follow him in obedient holiness? Of course, then the question turns to us.

What has God done that should influence our desire to serve him and be obedient in holiness? Each of us needs to answer this personally, but if we are honest, the list is long. I start my list with the joy of life and God giving me an incredible family, working up the family tree (parents, sisters, grandparents, etc.), across the family tree (my sweet wife, Becky), and down the family tree (children, grandchild, with hopefully more to come). Beyond my family, God has given me a great job, great friends, a country with freedoms galore, a super church home, food, shelter, safety, education, health—the list goes on and on. How can I be anything other than grateful? How can I choose any course of conduct besides what my Father instructs?

I should be and *want* to be holy because of what God has done.

Father, make me holy. Aid my life. Teach me. Correct me. Guide me. In your name, amen.

JULY 1

This is the law about beast and bird and every living creature that moves through the waters and every creature that swarms on the ground, to make a distinction between the unclean and the clean and between the living creature that may be eaten and the living creature that may not be eaten. (Lev. 11:46–47)

When I was growing up, I confess I didn't do much laundry. Then I went to college. Oh my, laundry once a week! Worse yet, clothes have rules about washing. It isn't as simple as throwing them in a machine and adding quarters. There are temperature choices. There are different cycles. Most important, there are rules about which clothes can go with which. I found out these rules are very important. It turns out that I wasn't supposed to wash my blue jeans with my white shirts!

Thousands of years ago, God taught his people a similar lesson on the importance of separating one thing from another, but he didn't use laundry to teach it. He used something even more commonplace than weekly laundry. He used food, something we consume multiple times a day. God used this constant activity that for every person—young or old, rich or poor, educated or not—would be something encountered over and over every day of life to teach a very important lesson about separation.

God had very specific dietary laws, allowing his people to eat beef, lamb, and goat but not pork or camel! They could eat perch and bass but not shrimp or catfish. The laws were very specific and fairly complicated, but the reason was straightforward. God labeled the forbidden foods "unclean" and the acceptable foods "good" and "clean." God wanted the people to remember every day, multiple times each day, that cleanness is part of the life of his children. We should shun and run from anything unclean. The lesson was taught with food, but the importance lay far beyond that.

There are things in this world that we consume—mentally, emotionally, spiritually—as well as things we eat. We need to be constantly mindful that the followers of God should work to consume things that are clean. I can't nibble trash on the Internet and expect it to have no effect. I can't imbibe gossip and not have it work negatively on my mind and heart. I can't eat with darkness and have my soul filled with light.

When our children were young, my mom would make brownies with them. She would ask if they wanted to add dirt to the batter. They would say, "No, Mimi! That's nasty!" Mom would reply, "You are right. That is why we don't watch garbage. We don't want to mess up what God is cooking in our lives." Mom was right. God taught the lesson well. We need to remember. We are God's, and we should feed ourselves accordingly!

Lord, please purify my life. Give me insight and discipline to separate the good from the bad. In your name, amen.

JULY 2

The LORD spoke to Moses, saying, "Speak to the people of Israel, saying, If a woman conceives and bears a male child, then she shall be unclean seven days." (Lev. 12:1-2)

Our children played a lot of sports growing up. In weekend tournaments, there were often brackets set up where the teams played elimination games but where your first loss moved you into the consolation bracket. If you won out, you won the bracket, but it was still the consolation bracket. You could be joyful about winning that bracket, but no one needed to walk around bragging about winning the whole tournament. It was the consolation bracket!

This sports idea is a small analogy that lays the groundwork for today's passage and devotion. There are a considerable number of Torah verses that set out the uncleanness of a mother after giving birth. People are often stumped about the idea of uncleanness, but there is an important lesson that God taught through this. It is the lesson of focus.

Childbirth is a marvelous and joyous occasion. Scripture teaches that. Children are a gift from the Lord, and we rightly rejoice over their births. In the days of Moses, those births were much more precarious than they are today, both to the newborn and to the mother. Infant and maternal mortality rates were much higher then, and a healthy mother and child were cause for a huge party. Yet in the midst of this, the mother was declared by God "unclean" for a period of time. That seems rough, unfair, and maybe even misogynistic today. But that's likely our bringing modern thoughts and prejudices into the text rather than understanding the text in its original context.

Childbirth was tied back to the original sin of Adam and Eve. Satan had tempted Adam and Eve to sin, even though the result of their sin was rightfully death. Adam and Eve had been told that ahead of time by God. As Satan became the leader to death, God pronounced that there would be another course for humanity. God would unfold a savior through the offspring of woman. There was a curse. Humanity would suffer. But in the end, there would also be a deliverance and a deliverer.

So when giving birth, a mother is defying the death grip of Satan and sin. Birth was a victory over death and promise of what would come. Yet it wasn't the final defeat of evil. There was residual uncleanness to be remembered. In the joy of childbirth, we must not forget the consequences of the sin in the garden. That said, God still used the reminder of sin and death to the good of the mother! As a result of the status of "unclean," the mother had time from work and many wifely duties to spend recuperating from birth and nurturing her newborn.

Lord, thank you for the enjoyable blessings of life. May I not forget the tragedy of sin. In your name, amen.

JULY 3

"When the days of her purifying are completed, whether for a son or for a daughter, she shall bring to the priest at the entrance of the tent of meeting a lamb a year old for a burnt offering." (Lev. 12:6)

I have been blessed in this life with a marvelous son (our firstborn child), followed by four fantastic daughters. Each of my daughters loves the Lord and is accomplished in this life. We sought for each to have education such that she could lead any kind of life she chose. Like my wife, who has multiple graduate degrees, our daughters have been taught to know they can succeed wherever they choose to walk. Their gender does not determine their worth or make it less in any way than that of their brother.

Some people think that the Bible teaches that women are lesser than men in the eyes of God. Such is not true. One of the best examples comes from passages like today's. The mother who gave birth to a child was deemed unclean for a period of time. As explained in yesterday's devotion, this may sound bad to today's ears (who wants to be "unclean"?), but that isn't a fair reading of the passages. The important point being made today is what followed the period of uncleanness.

The mother was commanded by God through Moses to offer a sacrifice for the child that was born. That the woman was instructed to offer the sacrifice is itself notable. It shows the importance of the woman as well as her direct responsibility to God. As the Jewish rabbi and Christian apostle Paul would write to a group in Corinth over a thousand years later, women are responsible to God directly. They don't report to God through their husbands.

Beyond the instruction to the woman to sacrifice, however, we should note what she sacrificed. It was the same whether the child born was male or female. Whether a son or a daughter, the child had the same value in God's eyes.

I think our society is getting better at seeing equality between genders, but not always. At the time I write this, there is still disparity in what the genders are paid, even when doing the same job. It is the responsibility of believers to set this record straight. Even for those who view roles of men and women as being different, there is no difference in value. Both male and female are made in the image of God, and both are equally worthy of honor and respect.

I am thankful for the women in my life and pray that they are treated appropriately by others.

Lord, thank you for the magnificent ways you have made us. May we all, male and female alike, reflect your glory to an often unbelieving world. In your name, amen.

JULY 4

"And if she cannot afford a lamb, then she shall take two turtledoves or two pigeons." (Lev. 12:8)

Money and wealth are unusual things. They are often associated with power. It seems the "haves" in society are almost always more highly regarded than the "have nots." We often treat the wealthy with a greater measure of respect and honor. It starts at a young age, with those growing up in wealthy homes able to afford and wear the most stylish clothes, drive the best cars, have the nicer jewelry, and afford the better education. Those who aren't so wealthy learn early on to look at the wealthy with admiration, longing, and even envy. We even use words that ascribe value to the wealthy, calling them the "upper class."

God doesn't have room for any favoritism for the fortunate. If anything, God teaches the opposite. As Jesus explained, "To whom much is given, much is expected" (Luke 12:48). Over and over in the prophets, the wealthy are warned about God's coming judgment should they continue to use their power to slight the poor. (For example, see Amos 4, where the wealthy are called "cows of Bashan" who oppress the poor.)

In this passage, Moses has set out God's instructions for the mothers to offer sacrifices after the births of their children. God tells them to sacrifice a lamb unless they can't afford it. In that event, they need to sacrifice two birds. This is God making provision for the poor. It is a reminder to all that God is not impressed with wealth. The rich don't make God stop in awe, amazed at their spiffy clothes.

Jesus was watching a group of people go by the temple treasury. A contribution box was by the door. Many wealthy people went by and deposited large sums of money. Then a poor widow came up and deposited two small copper coins. The coins were one sixty-fourth of a day's wage, a pittance. Yet it was all the woman had. Jesus commented, "This poor widow has put in more than all those who are contributing to the offering box. For they all contributed out of their abundance, but she out of her poverty has put in everything she had, all she had to live on" (Mark 12:43–44). Wow. Of course, it is also notable that Jesus didn't come from a wealthy family either. His mother, Mary, after giving birth to him, offered two birds for sacrifice. She couldn't afford a lamb.

Many people want to be wealthy. Many people want to be associated with the wealthy. As Proverbs says, "The poor is disliked even by his neighbor, but the rich has many friends" (Prov. 14:20). But this is not the way of God. God sees the poor and provides for them. They are no lesser than those of wealth. Everyone, rich or poor, is in need of God.

Lord, I need you today and every day. Help me honor all people in your name, amen.

JULY 5

The LORD spoke to Moses and Aaron, saying, "When a person has on the skin of his body a swelling or an eruption or a spot, and it turns into a case of leprous disease on the skin of his body, then he shall be brought to Aaron the priest or to one of his sons the priests, and the priest shall examine the diseased area on the skin of his body. And if the hair in the diseased area has turned white and the disease appears to be deeper than the skin of his body, it is a case of leprous disease. When the priest has examined him, he shall pronounce him unclean." (Lev. 13:1–3)

Let's get really practical for today. God cares about community health!

Today's passage reflects a section of many verses in the Torah that concern how the community handled the outbreak of what might be a contagious disease. The sick person was brought to the priest. The priest examined the person, and if certain symptoms of disease were seen, the person was isolated until either the disease passed or the diagnosis was confirmed. If the diagnosis was confirmed, the contagious person was quarantined until she or he recovered. Then there was a process for coming back from quarantine.

There are a lot of spiritual realities expressed in this process, as several coming devotions will note, but one key is God's concern for community health. God set up a process to protect others from catching disease.

Cynics recoil at this and suggest, "Well, if God is God, why this elaborate process? Why didn't he simply heal everyone?" This is actually a legitimate and important question, for God certainly had (and has) it in his power to say the word and heal the sick, allow the lame to walk, and restore sight to the blind. The answer is as important as the question: God didn't make this world a Harry Potter world, where the right incantation or request suspends the laws of nature. God made this world a cause-and-effect world. It is true spiritually (my sin brings damage) and physically (when I drop a glass, gravity pulls it down).

This doesn't mean that God doesn't do something about disease. He does. This is what drives science. God has made this cause-and-effect world, so we can discover the cause of disease and find the tools that can fight it. This also doesn't mean that God isn't able to suspend cause and effect and intervene miraculously. He can. But that isn't the norm. It's not the world where we live.

What does this mean to me today? I need to pray for God's hand in the simple cause and effect of the world as well as the miraculous. For the sick, I pray for doctors, medicine, and treatment, as well as divine healing.

Lord, thank you for medicine. Use everything to bring health to my loved ones as you see fit. In your name, amen.

JULY 6

"The leprous person who has the disease shall wear torn clothes and let the hair of his head hang loose, and he shall cover his upper lip and cry out, 'Unclean, unclean.' He shall remain unclean as long as he has the disease." (Lev. 13:45–46)

When it was determined that someone suffered from a contagious disease, the process God had put in place had that person quarantined from interacting with the larger community. When the sick person was near someone who was well, the sick person was supposed to cry out, "Unclean, unclean." The law required the person to say it twice, emphasizing that it was to be loud and clear. This would allow the person who was well not to come into the contagion zone.

Because the person shouted, "Unclean," it is common for readers of the text to spiritualize these instructions. It is also common for the reader to limit these instructions to the disease of leprosy (*tzara'* in the Hebrew). I think both of these approaches are missing a significant mark. The text does clearly talk about skin disease, but rather than limit it, as if God would give a complete medical compendium on how to treat every possible malady, it is more proper to see this as an instructive approach to dealing with disease. You have it examined. If it seems contagious, you confine the person until they are well.

The bigger error, however, lies in overspiritualizing this and losing the emphasis on physical health. Here is what I mean. Some read these commandments and ask, "How is this relevant to me?" They might say, "It isn't!" Or they might say, "Well, the leper had a physical malady, but we have a spiritual malady that makes us 'unclean' in a spiritual sense." There is a validity to seeing an analogy to the spiritual world, and that is done in coming devotions. But if we only see it relevant there, we miss a first level of application: God really had concern over the physical health of his people.

If we fail to note that God is concerned with the whole person, we risk minimizing an entire area of our lives. We think there is more merit to praying than to eating right. We think that attending church or synagogue is more important than attending to our physical needs. We think that telling the beggar in the street, "God loves you," is more important than helping the beggar find sustenance.

God is concerned with the whole person, and we should be as well. True spirituality addresses the whole human. We know it is important to rear our children knowing about God. It is also important to rear them knowing about eating right, exercising, and taking care of themselves.

Lord, help me to find the balance in this life. May I never fail to address how you wish me to live, both spiritually and physically. It is hard to find that balance, and I need your wisdom and insight. In your name, amen.

JULY 7

"When there is a case of leprous disease in a garment, whether a woolen or a linen garment . . . or in a skin or in anything made of skin, if the disease is greenish or reddish in the garment, or in the skin or in the warp or the woof or in any article made of skin, it is a case of leprous disease, and it shall be shown to the priest. And the priest shall examine the disease and shut up that which has the disease for seven days. Then he shall examine the disease on the seventh day. If the disease has spread in the garment, in the warp or the woof, or in the skin, whatever be the use of the skin, the disease is a persistent leprous disease; it is unclean. And he shall burn the garment, or the warp or the woof, the wool or the linen, or any article made of skin that is diseased, for it is a persistent leprous disease. It shall be burned in the fire." (Lev. 13:47–52)

Today's passage calls forth two independent devotional thoughts to me.

First, there was an elaborate process for checking on mold and other growths that might infect clothing. The clothing wasn't simply thrown away. It was carefully examined by an expert. Then it was isolated to see if it grew and got worse. If it did, then it was burned and destroyed. I read this and think, "Why take a chance? They didn't have microscopes to determine exactly what the growth was or wasn't. You see what looks like mold, throw the clothes away!" In part this might be because clothing is relatively cheap and readily available today. But in this passage, we see that God is not a wasteful God. There is an element of economic care in these instructions. God doesn't condone waste, nor should we.

A second and more intimate thought to me lies in the analogy likening the moldy disease to sin in our lives. The analogy is fair. The Hebrew word (*tame'*) is used by the prophet Isaiah as an analogy to those who were spiritually unclean to God (Isa. 52:1). The Jewish translators of the Hebrew scriptures into Greek used the Greek word *akathartos*, a word that was also used for those who were devious (Prov. 3:32) and arrogant (Prov. 16:5).

So using the analogy, we see that we should not flirt with sin in our lives. Left to itself, sin grows. The effect it has on our lives is unmistakable. It sickens us spiritually and can even affect us physically. God's instructions for sin are important. We should examine ourselves, and where we (or others) point out sin, we need to make every effort to not only isolate it but destroy it. We should burn it. We should do everything in our power to rid ourselves of sin.

Much of sin is sticky and isn't so easily removed from daily life. This is going to take divine help. So we turn to God, conscious of what needs doing.

Lord, help me identify and get rid of sin in my life. In your name, amen.

JULY 8

This is the law for a case of leprous disease in a garment of wool or linen, either in the warp or the woof, or in any article made of skin, to determine whether it is clean or unclean. (Lev. 13:59)

Today's passage is a summary passage for the treatment of unclean disease discussed in the previous day's readings. The emphasis I draw from this summary is the recognition of how uncleanness spreads. It makes me want to examine those with whom I associate, recognizing that I will affect them and they will affect me.

Most people are social. We find friendships and embrace them. The ancient Greeks had an expression, "One person is not a person." In modern times we have a similar expression: "No man is an island." We live in community. We want friends and seek them out.

As with much of life, this can be a good thing or a bad thing. It is a blessing and a curse. Both sides of the coin stem from the truth that, like it or not, we tend to become like those with whom we are intimate. It isn't just that "birds of a feather flock together," but birds that flock together start to grow similar plumage! (I'm not saying that happens with real birds!) When we are young, this process can unfold through peer pressure. As we age, peer pressure isn't as great, but the effect of becoming like those with whom we surround ourselves is still real.

When we surround ourselves with people who gossip, we tend to gossip. When we are around people who eat or drink to excess, the temptation is to eat or drink to excess. When we are around people who value possessions, the temptation is to value possessions. It is how we are.

This calls for care in choosing our friends and those close to us. We need people who are good influences. We need people who bring out the best in us. We need people who point us in the right direction, helping us grow before God and walk in his will and plans. We don't need distractions, nor do we want those who feed our darker sides.

This also calls for us to be the kind of people who influence others for good. We should ask ourselves, What can we do to be that kind of person? What are good habits that we not only develop but encourage in others? If a devotion speaks to you, share it. If you find a good personal habit, like daily quiet time, go out on a limb and let others know. You can influence others in positive ways.

Lord, help me to be a positive influence on others. Help me also to choose my friends and close associates wisely. In your name, amen.

JULY 9

The LORD spoke to Moses, saying, "This shall be the law of the leprous person for the day of his cleansing." (Lev. 14:1-2)

I grew up in the sixties. I wasn't old enough for the free-living, anything-goes lifestyle that was prominent, having been born in 1960, but I remember watching it, and it certainly influenced me and others my age. We grew up valuing freedom—freedom of expression, appearance (hair length, etc.), career choice, and more. Sometimes we forget the differences that happened in society. Before the sixties, women were relegated to very few career choices. They could be secretaries, nurses, and teachers, but that was about it! After the sixties, women could be doctors (two of my sisters-in-law) and lawyers (my wife and at least one daughter so far!), or they could succeed in business. They could choose careers based on interest and talent, not the strictures of tradition.

As the sixties brought about greater freedoms, not all the results turned out to be good. We need some boundaries in life. For example, unbridled sexual freedom brought about increased rates of venereal disease, rapidly escalating abortions, and destruction of families. A longer example of a freedom that can have negative consequences concerns guns. The United States has long had the Second Amendment, ensuring people that the government cannot inhibit their right to bear arms (own guns). There is a strong reason for this right, yet the proliferation of guns has left horrible scars on families where schools have been shot up, and communities face deranged people killing indiscriminately. Everyone recognizes that there needs to be some level of legal control, and the debate over the level of that control rages.

Into this push and pull of freedom and law comes today's passage. God gave Moses laws for the community of Israel. These laws weren't mere suggestions. They were instructive laws with consequences should the community fail to follow them.

If we trace the history of American politics and the legal system, there is a direct line back to Moses and the legal code God dispensed. The United States uses a legal system that has developed from that of the British. The British system was based on the biblical teachings of law. It has only been in the last 125 years that law schools have moved from using Blackstone's *Commentaries on the Laws of England* as a textbook. In that law book, property rights were based on the Jewish Torah. Many other laws were similarly explained biblically.

Freedom is important, but unbridled freedom doesn't work well with the human penchant for sin. God gave Moses law. We need to understand the importance of living within appropriate laws, even if we impose them on ourselves. Just because something is allowed doesn't make it profitable for me!

Lord, give me wisdom to live in good and profitable ways. In your name, amen.

JULY 10

"And he who is to be cleansed shall wash his clothes and shave off all his hair and bathe himself in water, and he shall be clean. And after that he may come into the camp . . ."
(Lev. 14:8)

Have you ever messed up? Have you ever let someone down? Have you ever not kept a promise? Have you ever made a huge mistake? If you didn't answer yes to all of these, then I ask you one last question: Have you ever failed to be honest? Yes, we have all failed miserably, sinning against God and violating the trust we have with our friends, families, and community. Thankfully, we worship a God of second chances!

Today's passage continues the series in Leviticus that deals with contagious disease. It does so in language that makes the disease an appropriate analogy for our sin and moral disease. The passage today explains how people would be welcomed back into the community once their disease was cured. It is an appropriate analogy to the forgiveness we should express to others who are repentant as well as to ourselves! (We often more readily forgive others than we do ourselves.)

Forgiveness is part of God's nature. To be sure, God's unchanging character cannot be violated while he finds mercy and forgiveness. In other words, God can't "just let it slide." There must be justice for sin. But God has always promised he would work a just forgiveness for sin. In the Torah, this was foreshadowed through animal sacrifice. To the Christian, this was fulfilled through the sacrificial death of Jesus.

People are aware of the saying "To err is human, to forgive divine," and there is a strong truth embedded in that. When the Israelites were returning from their captivity in Babylon, a removal from Palestine for seventy years that grew out of unrepentant rebellion by the Jews against God, God still forgave them. The prophet Nehemiah wrote of God, "But you are a God ready to forgive, gracious and merciful, slow to anger and abounding in steadfast love" (Neh. 9:17).

God not only models forgiveness, but he teaches us to follow his example. Forgiveness as a concept should be part of our lives. Jesus taught his followers to forgive others, just as we desire to have God forgive us (Matt. 6:12–14). The Jewish rabbi and Christian apostle Paul also wrote a similar point to a group in Ephesus: "Be kind to one another, tenderhearted, forgiving one another, as God in Christ forgave you" (Eph. 4:32).

It is appropriate for us to ask, "Whom do I need to forgive?" This doesn't mean subjecting yourself to abusive people, but it does mean letting go of the vengeance you might feel in your heart!

Lord, please forgive me my sins, and help me to forgive others in your name, amen.

JULY 11

"And he shall offer, of the turtledoves or pigeons, whichever he can afford." (Lev. 14:30)

I was brought up in a home that taught generosity. Before food banks became common, my mom started one of the biggest and best. We were taught from the earliest age to give what we could to those in need, even if we didn't have a lot to give.

Recently our church began a campaign to try to raise money for a number of worthy projects. During the campaign, I had a chance to visit with our lead pastor. We were speaking of this verse and something particularly profound in what it says about God.

The Israelites were being given instructions for the sacrifices they were to bring to God. By the very meaning of the word, a sacrifice was to be something that to the giver was *sacrificial.* It wasn't just something that was going to be thrown away anyway. It was something that meant something.

Now some Israelites could offer their sacrifices out of their plenty. When you have hundreds of lambs, the loss of one is not so great. But when you have only one, then losing it might not be sustainable. When God laid out the sacrifices required of his people, he had an option for those who didn't have the resources to pay the full sacrifice. They could instead offer something lesser, birds instead of livestock. This was based on "whichever they could afford."

Importantly, God didn't set the standard for what income level or asset level justified the lesser sacrifice. It was left up to the individual. It isn't much different today. When we look to give in the name of God, whether to church, synagogue, or some other godly endeavor, we are to give as we can afford.

But giving what we can afford is not a free pass to give nothing at all. If we are strapped for cash, then perhaps we give services. If we haven't something readily available to give, perhaps we skip a meal and give the money that is saved.

Sacrifices are important in this life, as are giving and generosity. If we fail to give, more than anything or anyone else, we are cheating ourselves. We want to cultivate giving spirits because it changes our natures. We become more godlike. We become better people. We find how it really is more blessed to give than to receive.

God is a giving God, and he calls us to be giving followers. I want to focus on this today and seek where I can give to my God, even as I can afford it!

Lord, show me the places where I can give to you. Give me a generous spirit. Change me from being one who grasps to one who offers. In your name, amen.

JULY 12

"The priest shall make atonement before the LORD for him who is being cleansed." (Lev. 14:31)

"They go together like oil and water!" We're all familiar with that phrase. Oil and water don't mix. There's a chemical reason. On a molecular level, the two substances don't "get along." Soap, on the other hand, does a great job binding to oil *and* to water. Therefore, when you wash your hands with soap (or use soap in cleaning dishes), the soap will adhere to the oil on your skin or dish and also adhere to the water. Soap is the key to bringing the oil and water together.

Sin and God do not go together either. God is like pure light. Sin is like darkness. You can't find light and darkness coexisting. By definition, they don't occupy the same space. Israel didn't always understand this. I'm not sure we do either.

God taught Israel in a number of ways, including by instituting a system where there would be a priest intervening with God on behalf of the Israelites. Because God called the Israelites into a relationship, one might think that everything would be fine. But Israel was sinful, and God is pure. This was oil and water. Left to themselves, the two do not coexist. So God put into place a priest who would serve as an intermediary.

The priest was responsible for coming before God on behalf of the people, offering a sacrifice to atone for the people's sins. Of course, the priest also had sin, so he had no right to go before God and atone for the sins of the larger group of Israelites. So God required that an atonement first be made for the priest! The priest had to be declared clean before he could approach and make the people clean. In a sense, the priest became the soap that would enable the people to have a relationship with God.

There are many lessons we draw from this system. First, we find out that God really is unique and sin really is a problem. Sin is not some arbitrary list of "rights" and "wrongs," but it is something contrary to the essence and character of God. We should never be making light of sin. We should regard it with great seriousness.

Additionally, this system shows the importance of finding purity, something no person can really achieve on one's own. Purity will always have to come from another. The priest provided the purity in the Mosaic code. To the Christian, Jesus as Messiah became the ultimate priest who provided purity for his people and access to God through that purity.

Lord, please help me understand the severity and realness of sin. Please wash me from my sin and make me clean in your sight. In your name, amen.

JULY 13

The LORD spoke to Moses and Aaron, saying, "When you come into the land of Canaan . . ." (Lev. 14:33–34)

I was getting ready to try my first case, and I was concerned. I wasn't worried about talking in front of people; I'd already spent a good bit of my life in public speaking. I wasn't afraid of cross-examining witnesses; I'd done plenty of cross-examination in high school and college debate. My worry was that I didn't know all the rules I needed to know. I wasn't sure I was prepared *legally*. Now this isn't a knock against my law school; it was more a concern with how my education would translate into real courtroom action.

Over the years, I learned how to prepare not only for the facts but for the law. I learned what I needed to know to be able to proceed with confidence that I wasn't going to trip up over some unknown legal procedure or rule. Preparation makes all the difference in the world.

I know that there are things in this world that you and I are to do for God. When we go into God's service, when we pledge ourselves to him and his plans, we can be certain that he will be setting us in places where we have things we need to do. It is the way of God. He works through his children.

As we think about what we are supposed to do for God, we can be certain of something. God has prepared us and the factors at play. God is a God of preparation. This world does not live in some scattershot, helter-skelter manner. Life is not a roll-the-dice affair. God, with his divine foreknowledge, knows what is coming and prepares us to take part in it.

In today's passage, God is speaking to Moses and Aaron. God is laying out what they need to know to prepare the people of Israel for conquering the Promised Land. It would be decades before Israel would move into Canaan, but God was already at work, preparing them, their leaders, and the people they would drive out from Canaan. The preparing God was preparing.

God does the same with you and me. God gets us ready. Sometimes this is a simple thing, but oftentimes it is difficult. In some ways our preparation is painful. Ask anyone who has trained for a marathon. It isn't always joyful running ten to fifteen miles on a Saturday. Yet if you are going to run 26.2 miles, you'd better prepare by running a lot in the buildup. So enjoy today and be blessed, knowing God is at work getting you ready!

Lord, prepare me for your works in my life. I want to serve you faithfully and fully. In your name, amen.

JULY 14

"So he shall make atonement for the house, and it shall be clean." (Lev. 14:53)

Atonement is not a word most people use each day. We know about the Jewish Day of Atonement (Yom Kippur). A lot of churches talk about Jesus being the "atonement for sin." Beyond that, we hear the word occasionally, but it not in common use.

The Hebrew word translated "atonement" consists of the Hebrew letters *k-f-r* (or *k-p-r*). These letters speak of a payment that is made for a life. They include the idea of pacifying one who has been wronged or covering over one's guilt. The word can reference legal rites for covering over one's transgressions.

In today's passage, the uncleanness is in the context of leprosy, a contagious skin disease that is written up in ways that are analogous to sin. Both set one apart as unclean. Leprosy creates an unclean skin condition. Sin creates an unclean soul condition.

All uncleanness must be atoned for. There is a price to be paid. When we consider our sin before God, we must remember the justness of God. As a just God, he can't close his eyes to sin. Sin isn't merely violating rules; it is rebellion against the character and person of God. It is wrapped up deeply in choosing ourselves over him. It is charting our own courses rather than trusting his. It is ignoring his direction and walking as we wish. It is spiritually thumbing our noses at him.

As certainly as fire will burn your hand, sin will bring destruction. Since God is life, anything in rebellion to God is death. God has to deal with this sin in an appropriate way. There must be an atonement for sin.

Under the Mosaic code, this atonement took the form of animal sacrifices, analogizing an animal to an innocent who took on the sins of the person. Then the animal bore the punishment of death. Another atonement occurred through the payment of money, although this was limited in its use.

For the Christian, the atonement in Moses' day was a prophetic act that spoke of Jesus as Messiah coming to give his life on behalf of sinful people. As a perfect messiah, Jesus was undeserving of death, and so his death can be appropriated for others. It is a human life paying the penalty for other humans.

Atonement speaks to the character of God, the seriousness of sin, and the need of forgiveness for us. It is the key to both the Old Testament law and the understanding of the core of Christian faith.

Lord, please teach me to understand your atonement for my sin. In your name, amen.

JULY 15

"Thus you shall keep the people of Israel separate from their uncleanness, lest they die in their uncleanness by defiling my tabernacle that is in their midst." (Lev. 15:31)

I have been accused of being a germophobe, a germ freak. The accusation doesn't seem fair to me. I am not afraid of my own germs; I only fear those foreign germs! I am the weird one who will wash his hands in a public restroom and then use the paper towel to open the door. The mere thought of someone's flu germs on the doorknob is enough to send me around the bend.

When I read chapter after chapter in the Torah speaking about uncleanness and God's instructions, it resonates in my soul. YES! We need to deal with uncleanness. We need to wash it clean. We need to stop the germs before they spread!

Of course, the Old Testament wasn't concerned so much with physical germs. The concern is first and foremost a concern with cleanness in heart and body before God. Like a sickness, spiritual depravity leads to worse and worse things. Furthermore, it contaminates those around it.

When I sin, I do so not only to my own detriment but to that of those around me as well. As when a pebble is thrown into a still pond, the reverberations of my sin influence others. If I am dishonest, how will my wife trust me? If I can't control my anger, what will my children grow into as adults? If I gossip about others, what damage do I do to their reputation and relationships? If I eat gluttonously, how does it affect my health? When I defy God and his reality, how does my influence bring others down?

I need some deep cleansing. I need scrubbing beyond what I can find with a loofah and hardy soap. I need to find God's cleaning. In the words of King David, I need God to "wash me thoroughly from my iniquity and cleanse me from my sin" (Ps. 51:2).

I wish this was a onetime need, but regrettably, I need it constantly. As much as I try, I do not seem to be able to conquer sin. It is like washing my hands; it only lasts so long! So what I really need from God is a permanent cleansing. I need him to purify me once and for all.

This is a daily struggle. In God's eternity, I understand the forgiveness he gives me. It is part of my faith as a Christian. It is the trust Abraham gave God. But I still want some help in the here and now. My sin works misery and destruction here and now.

Lord God, please clean me up. Wash me through and through. Create in me a clean heart, and renew a right spirit within me. For your name's sake, amen.

JULY 16

The LORD said to Moses, "Tell Aaron your brother not to come at any time into the Holy Place inside the veil, before the mercy seat that is on the ark, so that he may not die. For I will appear in the cloud over the mercy seat." (Lev. 16:2)

Every fall, observant Jews recognize a set of holidays considered the "High Holy Days." These days are built around the most holy Day of Atonement. This day, known in Hebrew as *yom* ("day") *kippur* ("atonement"), is set forth in detail in the chapters including today's devotion and that of the next several days as well.

The focus of Yom Kippur was atoning to God for the sins of the Israelites. The concept is rooted in a distinction of Israel from other societies and cultures of the day. For most every other culture, the behavioral codes of the nations were societal codes, based on how to live and get along with others under the jurisdiction of a ruler. If someone violated the law, then the consequence was a legal one. The punishment was set into the code or established by the ruler.

The uniqueness of Israel was that its legal code was given by God, and a violation of the code was not simply breaking the law. It was breaking faith with God. Violating the legal code was considered open rebellion against God and a moral issue, not just a criminal or societal issue.

This stemmed from the Hebrew recognition that people were made to be in a relationship with God. This truth was set forth in the creation account of Israel, where God made people in his image, able to reflect godliness and able to relate to God. God then placed Adam and Eve into the garden of Eden, walking and talking with them daily. When Adam and Eve violated God's commands, they set themselves up as rebellious, and the sin destroyed their relationship with God. That sin contaminated future humanity. People are born not into Eden but into the sinful and cursed world of estrangement from God.

From the earliest days when God pronounced the price for Adam and Eve's sin, God also promised that he would redeem humanity from the curse, giving, in a sense, a "do-over." God promised that this deliverance would come from the woman's offspring. Then the promise was further refined as being through Abraham, Isaac, and Jacob. God promised a chance to atone for sin, and in the rites associated with Yom Kippur, those sins are front and center. Something needs to be done to make people right with God.

Our sins are not mere social failures; they are an affront to the God of the universe.

Lord, teach me your atonement for my sins. I want to be right with you. In your name, amen.

JULY 17

"In this way Aaron shall come into the Holy Place: . . . He shall put on the holy linen coat and shall have the linen undergarment on his body, and he shall tie the linen sash around his waist and wear the linen turban; these are the holy garments. He shall bathe his body in water and then put them on. And he shall take from the congregation of the people of Israel two male goats for a sin offering, and one ram for a burnt offering. Aaron shall offer the bull as a sin offering for himself and shall make atonement for himself and for his house." (Lev. 16:3–6)

You can't wash your hands clean with muddy water. It seems logical, doesn't it? If you want to wash something clean, you need clean water to do it. It isn't very different for your soul. You can't get clean washing your soul with muddy water.

Aaron was Israel's first high priest. God put the high priest in charge of the rites to cleanse Israel of its their sins. As long as the sins of Israel were not really a big deal, as long as the ceremony was perfunctory, with no real purpose other than busy work, Aaron's actions might not matter much. But if the sins were real and if they were a serious matter, then there was an immediate problem. The high priest suffered from the same problem as the people. The high priest was also a sinner in need of atonement.

The question then arises, How can a "dirty" high priest offer cleansing for a dirty people? You can't wash clean with dirty water! The solution put in place involved the high priest first sacrificing for himself. Then, once he was purified, he was able to sacrifice and purify the people.

Aaron's purification began with bathing himself, no easy task in the wilderness before the advent of the bathtub or mikvah (a Jewish baptistery or pool for ritual bathing or cleansing). Once Aaron had washed, he would put on the white linen clothing special for the occasion. With a clean body, wearing holy clothes, Aaron would then take a bull and sacrifice the bull to atone for his own sins. Only then—bathed, specially clothed, and having received a sacrifice—could Aaron perform the ceremony to cleanse the people of sin.

To modern Jews, there are no animal sacrifices since the destruction of the temple. To sacrifice in another location is deemed disobedient. Atonement is more contrition and less sacrifice. To Christians, there are no more animal sacrifices because the death of Jesus is seen as the final, ultimate cleansing. Understanding that Jesus was perfect, he would have no need to clean himself with special sacrifices, bathing, or clothing; he was fully qualified to be the sacrifice for humanity's sin, atoning for the sins of others through his death.

Lord, teach me to take sin seriously. Cleanse me in your righteousness. In your name, amen.

JULY 18

"Then he shall take the two goats and set them before the LORD *at the entrance of the tent of meeting. And Aaron shall cast lots over the two goats, one lot for the* LORD *and the other lot for Azazel. And Aaron shall present the goat on which the lot fell for the* LORD *and use it as a sin offering, but the goat on which the lot fell for Azazel shall be presented alive before the* LORD *to make atonement over it, that it may be sent away into the wilderness to Azazel. . . . Thus he shall make atonement for the Holy Place, because of the uncleannesses of the people of Israel and because of their transgressions, all their sins. . . . The goat shall bear all their iniquities on itself to a remote area."* (Lev. 16:7–16)

There is something liberating about trash day. It is a chance to throw out and be rid of garbage. Some of the garbage is just paper and junk that gets in the way, causing clutter. But some of the garbage smells. It is refuse from cooking and eating, from personal living, and it is good to be rid of it. No one likes a smelly house.

The ceremonies around the Hebrew Day of Atonement (Yom Kippur) are called "rites of riddance." The ceremonies are built around the idea that the sins of the people need disposing of. The ceremonies included taking two goats, one of which would be killed as a sin offering, the blood of the goat being deemed a substitute for the blood of the Israelites, which would have been the proper price for the sins of the Israelites.

The sins of the people were deemed transferred to the second goat by the high priest laying hands on the goat. Then the goat, with the sins of the people, was driven out from the camp. This became the genesis of our expression "a scapegoat." The goat bearing the sins of Israel was "sent away into the wilderness to Azazel."

While some scholars have attempted to find interesting interpretations for "Azazel," most Jewish and Christian scholars agree that Azazel was a demon that was associated with rebellion against God. Sins of rebellion were sent into the wilderness of rebellion to be with the forces of rebellion, leaving the people atoned for.

Christians see in this the transfer of sin onto Jesus, who was driven out from God and society to be consigned to death and Hades before his resurrection into a new life. For the Christian, this becomes not only a matter of serious reflection over the cost of sin but also a matter of rejoicing at the liberty and freedom that comes from forgiveness.

Getting rid of garbage is refreshing, especially when it is the garbage of sin.

Lord, I am a sinner in need of serious cleansing. Please teach me your atonement and bring your cleanness to my heart. In your name, amen.

JULY 19

"No one may be in the tent of meeting from the time he enters to make atonement in the Holy Place until he comes out and has made atonement for himself and for his house and for all the assembly of Israel. Then he shall go out to the altar that is before the LORD and make atonement for it, and shall take some of the blood of the bull and some of the blood of the goat, and put it on the horns of the altar all around. And he shall sprinkle some of the blood on it with his finger seven times, and cleanse it and consecrate it from the uncleannesses of the people of Israel." (Lev. 16:17–19)

I'm a lawyer. Three years of law school and over thirty-five years of practice have taught me certain truths. One is popularized in the phrase, "Don't do the crime if you can't do the time." The idea is built into our legal system. If you violate a law, there is a just punishment. For parking tickets, you pay a fine. For robbery, you are incarcerated. Either way, once you have fully paid the price, you are deemed free. There might be some residual penalties—for example, you lose the right to vote if convicted of a felony—but paying the penalties puts an end to the crime.

Israel was unique in this regard. The legal code set up penalties and consequences for societal wrongs. If your ox gored someone, there was a penalty you had to pay. But beyond that, Israel's law had a moral implication. Breaking the law wasn't simply a civil or criminal matter. It was also a moral matter. Breaking the law violated a code with God.

Because Israel understood violating the law as a moral wrong against God, even though the law breaker had paid the civil or criminal price to the community at large, the crime or conduct wasn't "over." There was still a moral price to be paid before the moral God who ruled Israel.

This idea that breaking the law was more than a community offense still permeates the mind-set of people of faith today. When I violate the standard for conduct, I do more than live contrary to a community law or standard. I sin against the moral God. At issue is handling not just the earthly consequences of my bad actions but also the divine consequences of my immorality.

This places God at the center of my life. I am not just guilty of poor conduct to my neighbor; I have true moral guilt before God. This explains my guilt over my actions. It explains my feeble efforts at self-justification, which never really strike a chord as accomplishing anything. I need God to solve this problem of my sin. Should I sin against my wife or neighbor, should I gossip or steal, an apology may make things better in this world, but they do not fix the moral guilt before God. I need a God-given solution.

Lord, I confess myself a sinner and pray for your forgiveness. In your name, amen.

JULY 20

"If any one of the house of Israel kills an ox or a lamb or a goat in the camp, or kills it outside the camp, and does not bring it to the entrance of the tent of meeting to offer it as a gift to the LORD in front of the tabernacle of the LORD, bloodguilt shall be imputed to that man. . . . So they shall no more sacrifice their sacrifices to goat demons, after whom they whore. This shall be a statute forever for them throughout their generations." (Lev. 17:3–7)

The Bible speaks often about motivation. Passages talk about the foolish person who is motivated by money, sex, power, prestige, and ego. Passages talk about the wise person being motivated by love, holiness, and humility. The Bible gives insight into the role of motivation in our behaviors. Often the behavior is wrong *because* the motivation is wrong. Today's passage directs our attention to motivation as it is tied to actions and behavior.

Israel did not come into existence out of nothingness. It wasn't suddenly plopped onto the planet with no history or cultural interaction. The nation was a group of people taken out of four centuries of living in Egypt, having spent many of those years as slaves to the nation. During that time, Israel didn't have the code of Moses, the "law" given by God. That came after the people left Egypt. Not surprisingly, Israel was influenced by the nations around it and the cultural ideas of the pagan people. Part of that influence included sacrificing to the goat gods, termed the goat "demons" by God to Moses.

God said to put a stop to such sacrifices. All our sacrifices should be to God. What or who else is worth our sacrifices? Is it worth sacrificing yourself for your job? Shall you take the things of value in your life, things like your family or faith, and trade them in for success at work? Is it worth sacrificing your family or faith for fame? Shall you sacrifice your relationships for immediate physical or emotional gratification?

No! We need to see sacrifices for what they really are. We need to examine our motivations. If the sacrifice is one God calls for, then the sacrifice is made—hands down. If the sacrifice is one not called for by God, then what is our motivation for doing it? Do we see it as the equivalent of sacrificing to a demon? Do we understand the implications of our choices and actions?

I want godly motivations. I want to readily sacrifice to God and his cause. I also want to make sure I don't sacrifice anything outside of his will. For me to sacrifice to anything or anyone other than God is, in the long run, destructive behavior.

Lord, help me to see my motivations. Help me readily sacrifice to you and no other. In your name, amen.

JULY 21

"You shall not do as they do in the land of Egypt, where you lived, and you shall not do as they do in the land of Canaan, to which I am bringing you. You shall not walk in their statutes." (Lev. 18:3)

What were you like as a teenager? Maybe you're one right now, or maybe you were one so long ago the memory is faint. But regardless of where you are today, you likely realize or remember those teenage years where it seemed so important to fit in. If your friends used a particular kind of dialogue or certain phrases or cadences, you might have picked them up and used them too. If your friends had certain clothing styles or brands, then likely you considered wearing them as well. There is a tendency we all have of being like those we value and with whom we associate. As the saying goes, "Birds of a feather flock together."

The people of God are not supposed to reflect community values and practices. The people of God are to reflect God's values and practices into the community. This is part of what it means to "bear God's image" (Gen. 1:26). We are not only made such that we inhabit God's thumbprint, but we mirror that thumbprint or show it to the world.

Today's passage grew out of the practical truth that Israel was surrounded by pagans. The pagans had different values from those God gave Israel. The pagans had different beliefs about reality, and those beliefs drove different behaviors than those God taught Israel. God drew Israel's attention to these differences with a command to do as God says, not as the other people did.

It is the problem we all face at different times. Will our values be driven by God or by society? Think about it practically. How do you view honesty? If others shade the truth to get where they want to be, does that make it OK? How about gossiping? Maybe we think, "Oh, gossiping is definitely wrong," but then we talk about others behind their backs in ways we would never do to their faces. That is gossip, even if we don't use that name. Do we treat our money the way our credit-addicted society does, or are we following God's instructions?

We need to examine our behaviors to be sure that they align with God. When we do so, people will take notice. They will notice the person who doesn't speak ill of another. They will notice someone who is carefully honest. This lifestyle of walking as God would have us walk not only will bring blessing to our lives and the lives of those around us, but it will also reflect well on God as others see us.

Lord, may I refine my values and choices so they align with your morality and ethics. Help me reflect your glory in what I say and do. In your name, amen.

JULY 22

"You shall follow my rules and keep my statutes and walk in them. I am the LORD your God. You shall therefore keep my statutes and my rules; if a person does them, he shall live by them: I am the LORD." (Lev. 18:4–5)

What does it mean to be a person of faith? Is it a nice thing to tell other people? "I am a Christian!" or "I am Jewish!" or even "I am a Jewish Christian!" Is it a way to rear our children? "Get dressed, we're going to church (or temple)." Is it to have some notion that there is likely something beyond what we see? "Yes, I believe there is something divine." Is it a set of rules to live by? "Yes, I'm religious. I live by the Golden Rule" or "I keep kosher." Is it familial tradition? "Yes, I was born to religious parents. It's part of my family."

I don't think that any of the above are the earmarks of being a person of biblical faith. The biblical faith is deeply rooted in a belief and understanding of who God is. It is taking that knowledge and living the proclamation of the biblical God as the lord of one's life. This moves faith from being simply head knowledge into a relationship. The Lord becomes a true lord over one's life.

Today's passage summarizes God's instructions that his people are to follow the laws he handed out through Moses, but with a twist. They are to be followed because of who God is and because he offers a relationship with his followers. God could have said, "I am the Lord" (the name given by God to Moses when he chose to lead them out of Egypt). The Lord was all powerful and was their redeemer. They could have been ordered to follow his rules. In a sense, they could have traded the slavery to Pharaoh (who claimed to be a god) to slavery to another God, the Lord.

But the Lord didn't become the new slave master. His claim on the people was based on his authority as "God" and the decision of the people to live by the rules and relationship. God didn't take slave ownership of Israel. God gave the Israelites freedom to determine their own course. If the people chose to follow God, then he would lead them in blessings. If the people chose not to follow God, they would suffer life and death outside of God's presence.

Being a person of faith is not simply following rules, being a member of some religious organization, or having a vague notion about who God is or isn't. Being a person of faith means that one has embraced the Lord of Scripture and has decided to walk with the Lord as his or her God. This is reflected in life by the way we think, live, strive, love, rest, and so many other characteristics that accompany those whose God is the Lord.

Lord, I pray that you will be lord of my life. I give myself to your service, not on my terms, but on yours. Teach me what that means. In your name, amen.

JULY 23

And the LORD spoke to Moses, saying, "Speak to all the congregation of the people of Israel and say to them, You shall be holy, for I the LORD your God am holy. Every one of you shall revere his mother and his father." (Lev. 19:1–3)

I count myself among the fortunate. My mother and father were magnificent parents. They weren't perfect, but they loved each other, loved the Lord, and loved my sisters and me. They plugged into our lives, made sure we had as many opportunities as we could afford, and were a constant source of encouragement. My parents did not ignore our behavior or leave us to our own devices. They expected us to behave. We were taught to live up to a certain standard. When we failed, there were consequences. If the failure was deliberate, the consequences were stepped up a notch!

Not everyone is as fortunate as we were. Not everyone has or had marvelous parents. Some parents struggle to do the best they can but don't have all the tools to be really good. Some parents just don't care and are shoddy parents. Regrettably, there are even a few parents who are evil and do monstrous things to their children. Those parents leave a thumbprint that is not specified greatly in this passage. This passage concerns the parents doing their best.

I like what this passage does. It marries the need to revere one's mother and father to the command to be holy because God is holy. God's holiness and our reaction to that are appropriately analogized to our parents and the way we honor them. The idea behind our honoring God is built on who he is and what he has done for us. God had rescued his "children" Israel from slavery to the king of Egypt. God brought them out with miracle after miracle, wielding his great might to save and protect his children. As a result, the children were in a position to honor God and live by the code he taught them.

In the same way, parents are to work to rear their children, rescuing them, supplying their needs, and bringing them up to be productive and useful. The children are then to show honor to their parents, showing them respect and living appropriately.

There are differences, of course. Our parents grow old and die. That doesn't happen to God. Our parents are imperfect. God isn't. Still, God says that how we treat our parents is a reflection of how we respond to God's love for us. We need to honor and show respect to our parents. Again, not knowing the reading audience for this, I underscore that there are parents who are destructive and even evil, and the best way to honor them might be to honor the kind of parent they *should have been* and stay away from them. God is not calling us to abuse. He is calling us to honor our parents appropriately as we honor God.

Lord, thank you for my parents. Help me to be a good parent. In your name, amen.

JULY 24

*"I am the L*ORD *your God. Do not turn to idols."* (Lev. 19:3–4)

When we were young, my older sister went through the stage where she had the "teen idol" magazines. I must confess, I never saw anything in Bobby Sherman or Donny Osmond, but David Cassidy did have good hair. Regardless of what I saw, however, Kathryn and her friends had the magazines, the posters, the latest information, and of course, the records.

Now that doesn't mean that I didn't grow up with people I idolized. Mine just weren't hers! I had Bob Gibson, Willie Stargell, Roberto Clemente, and the other folks whose faces were on my treasured baseball cards.

Now I've grown up (sort of). I'd like to tell you that I've learned that idols are a thing of childhood and adolescents. But if I told you that, I would have to use a pretty narrow definition of *idol.* Moses wasn't writing to teenagers. God wasn't giving this instruction to children. This commandment is dead-on important for everyone, regardless of age.

We need to understand that idols are not simply clay figurines that the ancients would hold up, light incense to, pray to, and so on. Idols are *anything* that we place before God in our lives. Only God is to be worshipped. That means only God has the value and worth that calls for our adoration. Our idols become anything that takes the place of God in our value system: anything we value more highly than him (including anything we pursue with the efforts we should use for God), anything we rely on in ways we should rely on God, or anything we value more highly than we value the commands of God.

What is your idol? Appetite? Popularity? Money? A relationship? A hobby? A possession?

Interestingly, if we pursue God as our first priority, making everything else a distant second, third, fourth, and so on, then we wind up with the things we need *and* we have them in the right measure. They take the right place in our lives. We can pursue God first and find that we still have enough to eat, often sumptuously. We pursue God first and find that our relationships are grounded in him and are most satisfying. We pursue God first and find that our money is fit for our needs. We find we control our money rather than it controlling us.

Pursue God. Seek him and his kingdom first in your life. Run from idols, and he will take care of you.

Lord, may I seek you above all others and all things. In your name, amen.

JULY 25

"When you reap the harvest of your land, you shall not reap your field right up to its edge, neither shall you gather the gleanings after your harvest. And you shall not strip your vineyard bare, neither shall you gather the fallen grapes of your vineyard. You shall leave them for the poor and for the sojourner: I am the LORD your God." (Lev. 19:9–10)

Some people say we live in a dog-eat-dog world. Some people believe that "survival of the fittest" dictates that available resources should go to the cream of humanity, not those who are barely making it. Some people believe that benevolence and helping the poor are the responsibility of government. Some people believe that government should not be in the business of helping the poor. Lots of people have lots of beliefs about the impoverished. I am interested most in what God believes about the issue.

Today's passage gives instructions from God about how we should regard those less fortunate than ourselves. We should first note that what we are reading is not God's request of his followers. This is God's command! This is an instruction. This is part of the law. This is serious business to God.

God told his people that the farmers and vineyard keepers should not work to garner every ounce and scrap of crop available. They should leave some for the poor and indigent to gather. God didn't say to wait for the government to take care of the poor. God didn't say to pick the food for the poor and take it to their doorstep. God made provisions so that those who were less fortunate could go and get the food and drink they needed at the expense of those who had abundance.

I don't think this was a command limited to field and vineyard owners. God set up a principle that all his followers should take to heart. We have a responsibility in our bounty to help those less fortunate. The form it takes can be diverse, but it is generally one where the recipient is involved as well.

Practically, this can become difficult in our age, but that doesn't excuse us from trying to live consistently with God's instructions over three thousand years ago. I do believe that in a democracy, where the government *is* the people, that it is appropriate for the government to be a tool for helping those in need, but it needs to be done responsibly. I also think that the government is not the only answer, and it does not excuse the follower of God from reaching out to help those in need. True help isn't just a handout. It is better to teach someone to fish than to give someone a fish. Still, I fear at times we live blessed lives, without thinking about ways we can show God's love and blessings to those less fortunate. I need to be conscious of this.

Lord, show me people in need, and give me wisdom, resources, and time to help them in your name, amen.

JULY 26

"You shall not curse the deaf or put a stumbling block before the blind, but you shall fear your God: I am the Lord." (Lev. 19:14)

Are you familiar with the phrase, "kill or be killed"? For many, this world is ruthlessly competitive. We are often told, "If you don't look out for your own interests, no one else will do it for you!" These phrases are true for much of the world, but they are not what God expects of his people.

In today's passage God instructs his people not to take advantage of those situated in such a way that it could easily be done. If someone is deaf, we shouldn't say things about him that we wouldn't say if he were able to hear us. If someone is blind, we shouldn't place things in her path that might work to our advantage as it works to her disadvantage.

Moses wasn't giving an injunction only against how we treat deaf or blind people. This injunction was a principle that applies to how we treat others. We row against the stream of most people who live for their own good. Our eyes should be looking out for others. We should see others as valuable, and we should treat them thusly.

Some people are always looking for what they can get out of a situation. The relationships they value are relationships that give them benefits. The time they will invest in others is time really invested for self-gain. Some even go to churches and synagogues to see and be seen, perhaps even to get some business, work, or other valuable result.

God wants his people to invest in others, not for self-gain but for the good of the other. Doing this will redirect some of our actions, but it should also redirect our attitudes. Rather than simply being a chore, treating others well should reflect our learning from God that all people are valuably made. We might not readily see it, and we might not appreciate it, but we should work to find it. As for those who have taken the beauty and value of their lives and destroyed or marred it beyond recognition, we hope and pray for them to find redemption before their lives are over. This is the life of God's children: caring for others in the world. We aren't dogs eating dogs, we are people helping people.

Lord, one of my hardest things is looking beyond myself to others. Give me eyes to see others in need, a heart to value them, and the resources to help them. In your name, amen.

JULY 27

"You shall not steal; you shall not deal falsely; you shall not lie to one another. You shall not swear by my name falsely, and so profane the name of your God: I am the LORD. You shall not oppress your neighbor or rob him. The wages of a hired worker shall not remain with you all night until the morning. . . . You shall not go around as a slanderer among your people." (Lev. 19:9-13, 16)

How do we deal with people? This is a question that goes to the root of daily life. We can examine life through three questions: How do we deal with God? How do we deal with others? How do we deal with ourselves? While these may seem three different areas, the truth as set forth by God is that they are all related.

God tells us how to deal with others, so at their core, our interactions with others reflect on our faith and obedience to God. God tells his followers not to steal, and lest someone think they have a technical way to take advantage of someone without literally "stealing," God adds that we are not to deal falsely with each other, nor are we to lie to each other. God tells his followers not to oppress their neighbor (read that as anyone you deal with in life, not simply who lives next door). God tells us to hand over wages as they are due and to pay our debts and bills on time rather than delay paying another for our own advantage. This can run contrary to the capitalistic bent in many, but it is what God declared right. God instructed us not to slander another. This means that we aren't to speak ill of others, even if we cloak it in nice language ("You need to pray for Johnny because . . .") or in secrecy ("Don't tell anyone, but Johnny . . .").

These instructions for dealing with others are not only part of our relationship with God, but they also speak to our own personage. These are matters of integrity. If we are less than honest, we aren't the kind of person we are called to be. These are matters of honor. If we steal, delay payment, or take what isn't ours, we singe our consciences and distort our vision of right and wrong. If we gossip and say negative things of others, we sin, even if it seems acceptable in the eyes of the world.

I want to work assiduously to follow God here. I want my words to be honest and trustworthy so people can rely on me. I want to safeguard the possessions of others and be someone who is scrupulous, even when no one is looking or will know. I want to speak only positively of others. As my father taught us growing up, "If you can't say something nice, don't say anything at all."

I want to be right with God, right with others, and right with myself.

Lord, give me insight to see where I need to grow in these areas, and help me to be a better person. In your name, amen.

JULY 28

"You shall not hate your brother in your heart, but you shall reason frankly with your neighbor, lest you incur sin because of him. You shall not take vengeance or bear a grudge against the sons of your own people, but you shall love your neighbor as yourself: I am the Lord.*"* (Lev. 19:17–18)

Buried here, in the middle of Leviticus, one of the most challenging books of the Bible to read, lies what Jesus called the second greatest commandment in the law. It should command our attention.

Jesus was approached by a Jewish lawyer who asked him which commandment was the most important of all. Jesus answered that the greatest commandment was the *Shema*: "Hear, O Israel: The Lord our God, the Lord is one. And you shall love the Lord your God with all your heart and with all your soul and with all your mind and with all your strength" (Mark 12:29–30, quoting Deut. 6:4–5). Jesus then gave the lawyer a bonus! He told him the second greatest commandment: "The second is this: 'You shall love your neighbor as yourself.' There is no other commandment greater than these" (Mark 12:31, quoting today's passage). The lawyer agreed.

What makes this commandment so great? It reaches down past our actions into our motives and hearts. We make mental decisions to do what is best, whether it is what we want or not. We rule our emotions rather than letting them rule us. We shun a narcissistic self-focus in favor of one that builds up others. When we follow this commandment, we make the world a better place.

I want to look for ways to do this. As I think through it, one of the simplest rules that one can follow to turn this command into practical advice is the Golden Rule. This was a rule Jesus taught his disciples, but it wasn't original with Jesus. Jesus was quoting a rabbinical teaching of his day. Jesus told his followers, "Whatever you wish that others would do to you, do also to them," proclaiming this a good summary of not just the law but the prophets (Matt. 7:12). The Jewish rabbi Hillel, who was slightly before Jesus in time, summarized the law in much the same way, telling one who asked for Judaism in one sentence, "Do not do to another what you would not wish done to yourself; that is the whole Torah. The rest is commentary; go and study" (*b. Šabb. 31a*).

If we follow this advice, we will grow and mature, blessing those around us in the process. What would the world be like if everyone truly lived by this maxim? I can't always get it right, and I can't make others live by it, but I can be an example and, by God's grace and strength, do better every day!

Lord, keep me mindful of the need to treat others as I would like to be treated. Help me grow into a person of greater love for my neighbor. In your name, amen.

JULY 29

"When a stranger sojourns with you in your land, you shall not do him wrong. You shall treat the stranger who sojourns with you as the native among you, and you shall love him as yourself, for you were strangers in the land of Egypt: I am the LORD your God." (Lev. 19:33–34)

I have a love/hate relationship with politics. It both fascinates and appalls me. It motivates me to be involved with our government, even as it sometimes makes me want to crawl under a rock and ignore it. One area of politics I find especially fascinating is the way it mixes with religion.

I am not one of those who believes that religion should stay out of the political process or political decisions. But I am also one of those who is fairly skeptical of the way religion comes into play. I have seen the Bible and faith abused in the political arena. There have been times when I have wanted to scream because of those who claim the Christian faith while promoting what I believe to be the most unchristian "virtues."

But I have also seen the opposite. I have seen religion do some marvelous things in the political world. Bible believers were some of the strongest abolitionists in the 1800s trying to rid the United States of the scourge of slavery. In the 1960s civil rights movement, many of the strongest proponents of breaking down racial barriers and inequality were doing so because they were moved by their biblical faith. I have seen people of faith move into areas of the world where despots reign, seeking to improve the quality of life of indigent people. I know firsthand missionaries to countries that would have their heads for bringing faith to others.

In the face of these issues comes today's passage, one that would weigh heavily on a debate about immigration. It speaks of how Israel was to treat the "sojourner" (*ger* in Hebrew), or the non-Israelite newcomer or immigrant. Israel was to treat such people with love, encouraging and helping them in their lives.

We have trouble with this today. We live in a nationalistic time, where we are protective of our boundaries. There are fears that many who come to our country come for deceptive and warlike reasons. They come to do harm to our people and institutions. The government has a responsibility to protect our inhabitants, citizens, and immigrants from intruders who seek to harm us. This is why there are no easy answers to the problems. But as we search for answers, seeking to protect as well as love and honor the immigrants here in good faith, we need to be mindful of God's instructions as they guide our policies.

Lord, give our leaders wisdom and compassion in handling immigration issues. In your name, amen.

JULY 30

"Speak to Aaron and his sons so that they abstain from the holy things of the people of Israel, which they dedicate to me, so that they do not profane my holy name: I am the LORD.*"* (Lev. 22:2)

When I was I high school, one of my mentors introduced me to a group called Dogwood. I was never a big fan of country music, but this little-known trio from Nashville had some songs I really enjoyed. One of them was "Remember Whose Child You Are," written and sung by Steve Chapman. The lyrics begin with Steve getting called from his mountain home to serve in the military during the Vietnam War. As Steve was leaving home, his father told him, "Boy, remember whose child you are!"

Steve knew that his actions reflected not just on him but on his family as well. It didn't matter where Steve went, his name went with him. Steve's father was a wise man. He was telling Steve a concept that God told Moses over three thousand years earlier.

In today's passage, God tells Moses to let Aaron know that he and his sons are special among the people of Israel. Aaron and his sons were the priests of God. They were charged with knowing and teaching the law. They were the people's representatives before God. They were the ones who offered sacrifices to God. Their actions were open to scrutiny, and God wanted them aware that they must behave properly. When the priests sinned, it reflected not just on them but on God. Sin on the part of the priests would "profane" or "pollute" God's reputation.

It is no different today. It is a media splash when high-profile people claiming to be Christians are caught in horrible indiscretions. Sexual improprieties, shady financial dealings, violent displays of temper—these types of sin bring disrepute to the practitioner but also to God and the faith.

Even beyond the high-profile people, everyone who holds onto a faith that should be life-changing needs to remember that people are watching. I might tell someone how important God is in my life, but if I live like everyone else, or even worse than many, I bring dishonor on God.

Deliberate living includes taking stock of our actions. We need to build in safeguards so we don't fall into licentious traps. We need to be careful as we act, knowing people are watching. It doesn't matter where we are; we have a name. The children of God need to remember whose children we are!

Lord, please help me to live in ways that reflect your love and goodness. Let people see the positive difference you have made in my life. To your glory and in your name I pray, amen.

JULY 31

"They shall therefore keep my charge, lest they bear sin for it and die thereby when they profane it: I am the LORD who sanctifies them." (Lev. 22:9)

Everyone wants to be special. We see signs of it in the behavior of children and adults. Children act out to get attention. They try hard to fit into whatever crowd they admire. They will change most anything to be special or popular. They will pretend to be movie stars, sports figures, or entertainers. They want to be special.

Adults aren't much different. They want to be special and significant. They work hard to measure up. They will put their best faces on and their best feet forward to impress others. They seek love and attention often in the wrong places to assuage their feelings.

The wild part of it all is, *everyone can be special!* There is no magic way to dress, talk, behave, or achieve. No secret behavior or accomplishment will bring the specialness people crave. This specialness can only come from having a truly great value—not one that is gold-plated but one that is pure. The key to understanding this is in today's passage.

God is explaining to Moses the importance of the priests' role in the law given to the Israelites. The priests *were* special, but not because they had found a great job. They were special because God was making them special. This is the importance of the Hebrew word meaning "sanctify." As God explained to Moses, in "sanctifying" the priests, God was setting them apart as special and sacred, dedicated to God and his service.

It takes the hand of God to lift an ordinary human being into something truly meaningful and eternal. People can give their best efforts at becoming special, but no one can achieve what God can do. God takes anyone who turns to him, whether such a person is strong or weak, educated or uneducated, rich or poor, pretty or unbecoming, witty or not, well behaved or a rascal, or any other set of traits or behaviors one can think of. God can and will take *anyone* who genuinely turns to him, seeking his blessings.

The Jewish rabbi and Christian apostle Paul knew of God's sanctifying power. He wrote of it frequently, tying it to the forgiveness found in the sacrifice of Jesus as Messiah. He addressed one of his letters to the believers in Corinth, noting they were "those sanctified in Christ Jesus, called to be saints together with all those who in every place call upon the name of our Lord Jesus Christ, both their Lord and ours" (1 Cor. 1:2).

Specialness comes from God. It is humbling to find it there and not create it on our own. But it is genuine and satisfying.

Lord, I turn my life to you. Make me what I should be for you. In your name, amen.

AUGUST 1

"Speak to Aaron and his sons and all the people of Israel and say to them, When any one of the house of Israel or of the sojourners in Israel presents a burnt offering as his offering, for any of their vows or freewill offerings that they offer to the Lord, if it is to be accepted for you it shall be a male without blemish, of the bulls or the sheep or the goats." (Lev. 22:18–19)

When I was little, my parents were consistent in teaching me the importance of doing my best. When I made my first football team, I was frustrated that I wasn't given the position of quarterback or running back. (It never occurred to me that I was too slow!) Instead, I was relegated to playing offensive guard. My dad sensed my disappointment and the effect it had on my effort, and he pulled me aside and told me, "Son, you are a guard. It might not be what you want to be, but it's what you are. The key for you is to give 110 percent and be the best guard this coach has ever seen. You get to practice earlier than others. You stay later. You bust your gut on every exercise and every play."

I'd love to tell you that with *all that effort*, by game three, I was moved to running back. But in truth, I played guard the entire year. Ultimately, I decided my strength was in debate!

Today's passage homes in on an emphasis that is greater than football or debate. When God spoke what the Israelites were to sacrifice to him, his instructions were clear: give God the very best you can. Nothing less will do. This was specifically for "freewill offerings," voluntary offerings. God made the point that when we voluntarily give to God, we should still give him the absolute best. God never deserves less.

This is important for us to realize. Whether Jews or Christians, we do not have animal sacrifices today. Jews do not sacrifice without the temple. Christians do not sacrifice because we believe that the death of Christ was the culmination of the sacrificial system. In other words, in Jesus God already received the most perfect and best sacrifice. No animal death can add anything.

But even though we no longer sacrifice animals, it doesn't mean we don't give freewill sacrifices to God. Anything we do for him, anything we give to him, is a freewill sacrifice. We should be giving him nothing but the best. If I give him my time, I give him my best time, not my leftovers. If we help someone in his name, we do the best we can. If we donate to his ministry and work, we give not just from our surplus but as best as we can for the need we are helping.

Whatever we are about, we need to do our best. Especially if we are doing it for God.

Lord, help me to give you my best of my own free will. In your name, amen.

AUGUST 2

And the L*ORD* *spoke to Moses, saying, "When an ox or sheep or goat is born, it shall remain seven days with its mother, and from the eighth day on it shall be acceptable as a food offering to the* L*ORD.*" (Lev. 22:26–27)

Our son is a vegan. He doesn't eat meat or the products that come from meat. He doesn't because he wants no part of animal suffering. I am not a vegan. I am not even a vegetarian. I am an omnivore, with a few exceptions. My reasoning is that God made animals for a purpose, and for some animals, that purpose is to provide food. When an animal is eaten, that animal is actually fulfilling its purpose before God and bringing praise to God, who created it for that purpose. It is no less bringing praise than when you or I fulfill our purpose before God.

While my son and I disagree about that, there is one related matter on which we do agree. We should treat animals with dignity and be sensitive to how they live and die. Why do I believe that? Mainly because of Scriptures like today's.

Over and over in the Torah, God speaks of how animals are to be treated. God always instructed the Israelites to treat animals respectfully. Today's passage is a classic example. When an animal was born and was to be sacrificed to God, the animal was not to be taken from its mother immediately. There were to be seven days while the animal stayed with the mother.

Today science and medicine have taught us the importance of those days after birth in the hormonal response of the mother. It gives time for an adjustment of hormones and the resultant lactation and other physical changes. It makes the mother's life better.

It is notable to me over and over that God cares about creation. God gave animals the ability to feel pain, to process the environment on a very basic level, and to react accordingly. I want to care about God's creation as well.

Animals are not humans. Animals have another purpose in God's creation. Humanity reflects God's image and can walk with God, unlike other creatures. Humanity lives with God's morality hardwired into their brains. Humanity is given charge over creation. All of these are differences. Yet passages like today's make me reflect on something as simple as seeking free-range eggs over those coming from chickens that are born and die never leaving a one-cubic-foot cage. It makes me want to care for our dog, indoor cats, and even the strays that come around the door for a bite. I want to teach our children how to be responsible pet owners and encourage others as well.

Lord, help me to expand my vision of you and your purposes for me. Let me see how you expect me to treat this world, and let me do so in ways that honor you. In your name, amen.

AUGUST 3

"You shall not profane my holy name, that I may be sanctified among the people of Israel. I am the LORD who sanctifies you, who brought you out of the land of Egypt to be your God: I am the LORD." (Lev. 22:32–33)

I was trying a case in Dallas, Texas, cross-examining a witness about some pretty reprehensible corporate behavior. Whenever a doctor spoke out against the company, the standard response of the company was to try to ruin the doctor's reputation in the medical and scientific community. I thought the company's unwritten policy was outrageous. In the heat of the moment, while looking for the right verb to describe what the company did, I used a modern slang term I had never before (or since) used in a trial. I said something like, "This is what your company does . . . You take good doctors and you *diss* them!" Not only had I not used the word before, I'm still not even sure if *diss* in this sense is spelled with one *s* or two!

There is something important about our reputations. More people know us from that than they do from an actual intimate knowledge of who we are. Perceptions of our reputations can become reality to other folks. I write of reputation because it is triggered in my head when I read passages like today's. The passage speaks of God's holy "name" (Hebrew *shem*) being profaned or polluted. We commonly use "name" to refer to the label used to identify or call someone, but the Hebrew word carries a much more significant connotation. In Hebrew, this word for "name" means one's reputation or character. It is one's resume or curriculum vitae (CV, the Latin term used to refer to things relevant to your professional life).

God had a CV. He was the God who brought Israel out of Egyptian slavery. He was the God who created all things. He was the God who called the patriarchs, Abraham, Isaac, and Jacob. The people who followed the Lord were to behave in ways that brought glory to his name. They weren't to *diss* him. God is glorified when we listen to his words. It shows we believe him worthy of our attention. Then as we hear his words, when we trust in him and are obedient to his commands, it means that we have confidence that he is all knowing and caring.

The opposite is also true. When we don't bother to listen to him, we are telling the world we believe he has nothing important enough to say. We are dissing him! When we listen but don't trust and obey, we are telling the world he isn't trustworthy or he doesn't really know about what he speaks. We are dissing him.

I don't want to profane God's holy name. I don't want to diss him. I want my life to reflect my true knowledge—that he is a God above all others, worthy of every ounce of my energy, trust, and praise.

Lord, may my life bring you glory. In your name, amen.

AUGUST 4

"In the seventh month, on the first day of the month, you shall observe a day of solemn rest, a memorial proclaimed with blast of trumpets, a holy convocation. You shall not do any ordinary work, and you shall present a food offering to the LORD." (Lev. 23:24–25)

I enjoyed school, at least a good bit of it. There were some classes that I didn't really care for and even a teacher or two that didn't fit my learning well, but by and large, I loved it. I guess I'm a nerd; learning is one of my joys in life.

There are some courses that aren't offered in school, however, even though they seem important. I've never seen a class on "How to Live Happily and Productively." It seems an important subject, something everyone should want to learn, and it certainly isn't something most people know. Yet I'm not sure of any schools that offer it.

If it were offered in school, I'm convinced one of the chapters in the textbook would include today's passage, or at least the idea in today's passage. Here is what Israel was told to do: annually set aside one day a year for solemn rest and to congregate together to worship the Lord. There was a festive offering of food, which also meant a time of feasting for the people. This was originally a festival in preparation for the Sukkot festival, but over time it became the celebration of the Jewish New Year.

Does this seem bizarre to you? God commanded his people to celebrate and worship him with rest from work, corporate worship, and feasting. This wasn't something God said to do periodically when the schedule allowed it. This was something ordered for a specific day and time. That means the people would need to plan for it, build it into their schedules, and deliberately do it. This was a conscious decision by the people to let following God and celebrating with God trump their work and jobs. This wasn't a substitute for the weekly day of rest each Sabbath. This was in addition to the Sabbath rest!

How could we see this principle being part of our lives? There are days that we celebrate God in worship, days we have off from work, days of sacrifice to God, and days of feasting. But the admonition we can find in this command is that it is important we plan for time like this. We need to plan and prepare to be with others in dedicated worship and celebration of our God: not checking emails, not handling work calls, just deliberately celebrating God with rest and concentration. This will help us live happily and productively!

Lord, teach me to be still and rest before you. Teach me to celebrate you. Teach me to worship you above all else. In your name, amen.

AUGUST 5

"Whoever takes a human life shall surely be put to death." (Lev. 24:17)

I find passages like today's full of layers of significance. They are food for meditation in countless ways. I think they are as life changing as most any passage in the Bible.

A lot of people will ask, "Why?" Some see this passage at first glance merely stating, "Don't kill someone," and it certainly says that. But I believe the passage has a deeper underlying significance. Part of the reason lies in *why* the Bible says not to kill another.

The Bible repeatedly explains why it is wrong to kill another. In Genesis 9:6, God explained it plainly, "Whoever sheds the blood of man, by man shall his blood be shed, for God made man in his own image." The reason we are not to kill another is because every other person is, like us, made in God's image. This instills great value in each person. This is also why the text means so much as we meditate on it.

Because my neighbor is made in God's image, hence having great value, I need to not only refrain from killing her or him; I also need to treat him or her as a person of value in other ways. Have you ever been around shouters and people who have volatile tempers? Today's passage should change the way shouters speak to people. We should all speak to people as ones who are made in God's image and are valuable in God's sight. Have you been around gossips, who speak ill of people behind their backs? Knowing that everyone is made in God's image and deserving of respect should stop me from being a gossip. Have you been taken advantage of or been stomped on for someone else's gain? Knowing that we are all made in God's image should preclude us from mistreating and abusing anyone in this or any other way.

As we reflect on the value of a human life, we must not ever fall prey to thinking only about our obligation not to kill another. We need to take the spirit of this command to heart and treat others the way we would like to be treated. We need to show that we highly regard others. We need to treat others as we would like to be treated. When people are mean and vindictive to us, we need to pray for them, not club them over the emotional head. When people get on our nerves, we need to deal with it respectfully. When someone is in need, and we have the means to help her or him, we need to do so with joy in our hearts at getting to show that we value one who bears God's image.

I haven't arrived on all these points, but I am working to grow in them. I want to do better by being better. With God's help, this is where I am headed.

Lord, please give me insight into these passages so I can better understand how to treat others. Thank you for instilling such value in people. May I bear your image well to the world around me. In your name, amen.

AUGUST 6

*The L*ORD *spoke to Moses on Mount Sinai, saying, "Speak to the people of Israel and say to them . . ." (Lev. 25:1–2)*

We read an amazing thing in today's passage. God spoke to Moses. God gave Moses a message that God wanted Moses to hear and then repeat to the Israelites. This passage meets a big need in my life. I need to hear from God.

Each day, we all face the unexpected. Even with things we know are happening, there is always a layer that is unseen. Using an innocuous example, I may know that I am going to be eating lunch with my wife, but that doesn't mean I know what the precise conversation will be. On a more serious level, I may know that today I will be in court for a hearing, but I don't know what the other side will argue, what the witnesses might say, and how the judge might react.

Along with the unexpected that occurs daily, there are decisions that I must make. Again, on a fairly innocuous level, I need to decide what to eat for lunch. On a more serious level, I need to decide larger things, grand in scope and effect. Where shall I live? What should I do with my life? Then there are everyday decisions that can also have a huge effect. What shall I do with my time today? How shall I deal with certain problems and issues?

In all these areas, it would be extremely nice to hear from someone who knows everything. To have someone who can see through all the variables, who is aware of what is possible and what isn't, who sees behind each corner—this is the kind of resource that would be a game-changer in life.

It would be even better if that all-knowing one loved me and cared about what happened to me. If there was someone who both had this knowledge and also had the best wishes and desires for me and my life, I would be sitting on a gold mine for living.

Reality check: the all-knowing ("omniscient") God *does* care for me, *does* have plans for me, and *does* speak. You and I might think, "Well, I am not hearing his voice!" but if we are thinking that, we are wrong. He speaks in a myriad of ways, and one of the ways we read of today. The Lord spoke to Moses and told him what to say to Israel. These are the words that are recorded in our Torah devotions that we are reading each day. These words are instructive for us. They are insights for living handed down by the divine, all-knowing God. We need to listen and think through these words, seeking to live our lives based on our discernment of the messages and implications.

Lord, please help me to hear you voice. Give me understanding so I may live to your glory. In your name, amen.

AUGUST 7

"The Sabbath of the land shall provide food for you, for yourself and for your male and female slaves and for your hired worker and the sojourner who lives with you, and for your cattle and for the wild animals that are in your land: all its yield shall be for food." (Lev. 25:6–7)

I have a theory on what I call "percentage worrying." I'm not 100 percent sure I am right, but I think I am reasonably close. Here is the theory. Many people have a tendency to worry a certain amount. It may come in certain moods, on certain days, or even in certain seasons, but there is some tendency to worry in some general amount. For example, if I am a 10 percent worrier, then I will generally spend 10 percent of my time worrying about something. You could list all the possible worries I might have, and as a 10 percent worrier, I would only have the time to worry about the first three. However, if you removed those three from my list, if the causes for worry magically resolved, then I wouldn't quit worrying, I would just move on to the next three things on my list. I am going to spend 10 percent of my energy worrying about *something*.

This theory doesn't apply to everyone, but I have seen in my life that we all worry. We worry about our family and how their lives are going. We worry about work or school. We worry about friends. We worry about happiness. We worry about money. We worry about our relationship with God. We worry about our relationships with others. We worry about what we are going to wear, how we are going to fit in, whether we have what we need to do what we need, and on and on and on.

Today's passage speaks to worry. God instructed Moses and Israel to celebrate a Sabbath for their land. This meant that every seventh year, their land was to remain unplanted and their vineyards unpruned. Allowing the land to lay dormant would recharge the soil somewhat (not unlike rotating crops today), but it would also limit what was grown. No bumper crops arise from the unsown field. The crops would be limited to what came up on its own.

This might be frightful to a family living off the land, yet that is where today's passage fits. God told Israel not to worry about that. The God who told them to allow the land to have a Sabbath rest each seventh year would also see that they had enough food if they lived under his instructions. Following God's other instructions would become a key to this. For God instructed the Israelites how to live carefully, how to plan and lay aside, and other habits that would aid and sustain them. But all of this boiled down to trusting and obeying God. That is the solution to life's worries.

Lord, I do worry about [fill in the blank with your worries for today]. Give me wisdom to see how to live and faith to obey your instructions. Lord, please take care of the consequences in life as I trust in you rather than worry! In your name, amen.

AUGUST 8

"You shall count seven weeks of years, seven times seven years, so that the time of the seven weeks of years shall give you forty-nine years. Then you shall sound the loud trumpet on the tenth day of the seventh month. On the Day of Atonement you shall sound the trumpet throughout all your land. And you shall consecrate the fiftieth year, and proclaim liberty throughout the land to all its inhabitants. It shall be a jubilee for you, when each of you shall return to his property and each of you shall return to his clan. That fiftieth year shall be a jubilee for you." (Lev. 25:8-11)

Have you ever been stuck in a situation? Have you ever found yourself in need of rescue? Have poor choices ever left you in bad shape, needing redemption? Have you ever felt trapped by life and responsibilities? If so, today's passage is for you!

God set up a system of Sabbaths for Israel. Everyone was expected to work for six days, but every seventh day was a day of rest, a Sabbath. The Lord also set up Sabbath years. So everyone plowed the land, sowed the fields, pruned the vineyards, and so on for six years. But every seventh year was a Sabbath rest. There was to be no sowing the fields, pruning the vineyards, and so on. Then, every forty-nine years, seven times seven Sabbath years, there was a final resetting of the calendar with a year of "Jubilee." This was a Sabbath year unlike any other! During Jubilee, slaves were set free, debts were forgiven, and property was returned to the family that had sold it. The implications of this were profound. It would mean if you decided to loan someone money, you did so knowing that the debt would be forgiven when the year of Jubilee came around. If someone sold himself into slavery, you knew that the slavery would end at the year of Jubilee. If you bought someone's property, you knew you were only owning it until the year of Jubilee.

People don't keep the year of Jubilee today. We don't have that liberation that I spoke of in the first paragraph of today's devotion, at least not from the hands of people. The concept of Jubilee, however, is one that is from God and can affect all of us. Jubilee was a magnificent concept that expressed a perfect balance of responsibility and grace. It recognized and didn't substitute for people's choices and responsibilities. You could still get in debt that handcuffed your life. You could still make mistakes that hurt. But there was a grace that countered the mistakes. There was forgiveness that restored liberty. This balance was given by God, and we can rest assured that God embodies the instruction he gave.

In God we have a Jubilee. He both holds us accountable and offers his mercy and forgiveness. He will forgive our debts. He will rescue us. He will redeem us! Praise God! May we show mercy and compassion to others, even if it's not Jubilee.

Lord, I have sinned against you and made plenty of mistakes. Please give me your mercy and forgiveness. Teach me your mercy to show others. In your name, amen.

AUGUST 9

"You shall not wrong one another, but you shall fear your God, for I am the LORD your God." (Lev. 25:17)

Have you ever counted how many people you come into contact with each day? I have tried, but it varies widely. Some days it numbers in the dozens. Many days it exceeds hundreds. Occasionally, it gets even higher.

Every time we interact with someone, we rub off on them. If we smile, it has an effect. If we show her or him a cold shoulder, it has an effect. Our words of encouragement, words of warmth and genuine caring, and words of affection all have an effect. Our brusque business as usual has an effect. If we are watching and thinking, we realize that.

Beyond those interactions, we also affect others indirectly. I do things every day that have an effect on those I love, even if I am not around them. My priorities will shape how I treat others in my life. My clients are directly affected by how I work on their cases, even when they will never see the work. My wife will be affected by how I live my life when I am away from her and our home. The list of how our actions affect others could go on for pages. It is what makes today's passage so important and instructive.

God said we should not wrong one another. That surely means not only in our direct interactions but indirectly as well. What is more, God ties how we are to treat others to who God is. In other words, the way I live with my fellow human beings is dictated by who God is and what God is instructing and teaching me.

God genuinely cares about how we treat each other. He cares how others treat us. God isn't some absentee landlord who periodically checks in on his property. He is a loving and just being who is constantly working to bring his will into our lives and world. He wants us to grow up as humans to be better people. He wants us to more clearly reflect who he is to our dark and often unseeing world. He wants us to spread his compassion.

How we treat others reflects both who we are and who God is. This means that we should treat others right, even when only God sees. How we treat others, especially when *no one* will see or directly notice, reflects how much we believe in God. It shows our true belief that God is watching and is a God of his word.

Lord, help me to live conscious of how I treat others. Let me treat them with your love and compassion. Help me not to wrong anyone and, when I do, to make restitution. In your name, amen.

AUGUST 10

"Therefore you shall do my statutes and keep my rules and perform them, and then you will dwell in the land securely. The land will yield its fruit, and you will eat your fill and dwell in it securely." (Lev. 25:18–19)

The most popular baby powder on the market, used by hundreds of millions of people, was made from talc. Talc is a mineral mined from several locations around the world. Talc mines have proven to be laced with asbestos, a well-known cause of cancer. I suspected that the talc podwer had a small level of asbestos, and I had a lab test over fifty bottles. The lab found asbestos in over half the bottles. I tried a case over the product, arguing that the manufacturer had a duty to either sell a formula without talc, or to at least warn the user.

I believed then, and still do, that my argument appeals to people's common sense. If you are going to make something that is hazardous, you need to warn the user of the serious risks of which you are aware. God did that with Israel.

God explained to Israel a simple truth: you will reap what you sow. The Israelites needed to know that God had provided them with instructions for living. These instructions covered everything from devotion to God to how they treated their neighbors. They were instructions that, if followed, would teach them humility and would build a society that would progress and lead the world around them. But this positive held a negative also.

God explained that the failure to follow the instructions would bring negative consequences. The people would suffer individually. Their families would suffer. Their community would suffer, and ultimately, the nation would suffer. Israel was fully warned, but as we often do, Israel didn't always heed the warning. The Israelites' hearts would grow cold, and they would quit teaching God's instructions to the people. Some of the rules became harsh laws that smart people would figure out how to wire around. They failed to see them as God's warnings and instructions that were given to make life better.

I am blessed by thinking through this. I know that God has given me instructions. I know his teachings can set my priorities; modify my attitudes and behaviors; give me better habits; and help me personally, in my family, at work, and in the larger social structure of society. I also know what happens when I shun his directions. God has warned me. He is not deceived. General rule: I will reap what I sow.

Lord, I am thankful for your mercy and pray for your forgiveness in the midst of my errors. I also pray that you will help me sharpen my focus on behaving as you have instructed me. In your name, amen.

AUGUST 11

"The land shall not be sold in perpetuity, for the land is mine. For you are strangers and sojourners with me." (Lev. 25:23)

Every first-year law student takes a course in "property." I had Bruce Kramer as my instructor. He looked a good bit like Groucho Marx, but property was no laughing matter with him. We learned the basics of who owns land and the forms in which it is owned. We learned unusual terms like "incorporeal hereditaments" and obscure legal doctrines like the Rule in *Shelley's Case*. The class was a monstrous five hours a week for a whole semester. I still think of it with shivers.

As God was setting Israel up with a legal structure for its occupation of Canaan, the Promised Land, God had for the Israelites core property laws. The laws were based on an important premise: God owned the land. Everyone else had possession.

God wanted to make it clear that as owner, he set up the rules. God decided who lived where. God was the one who could decide what land could be used as collateral and when debts on land had to be forgiven. No one was ever allowed to say that "God's not being fair!" because God as owner could do as he wished.

This principle of property extends beyond the real estate of Palestine. In truth, God owns everything. I suspect about the only thing he doesn't own is my own will. Yet that is the core thing he asks me to give to him. He teaches us to give of our possessions, but part of that giving is recognizing that what we are giving him is really his to start with. Our giving of ourselves is our real gift.

Once we give ourselves to God, then everything else falls into place. The first and really big issue is *giving ourselves*. This means a willingness to forego what we have let own us beforehand. We must be willing to give up our identities should they conflict with what God wants. We need to be willing to give up our goals and adjust them to goals that God has for us. We need to give up what we deem to be "success" and seek the success that God set out. Our giving of ourselves means that God now owns us as well.

We continue to live our lives, but the life that we live, we live by our trust in God, knowing that we are no longer our own; we belong to him. That may seem scary, but it turns out to be the opposite. God puts us on a path that he secures. Storms will come and go, but we will stand secure on the rock that is higher than any flood waters. God is fully trustworthy.

Lord, I give myself to you. Unequivocally. Teach me what that means and help me to discard anything that stands in the way of my discipleship. In your name, amen.

AUGUST 12

"If your brother becomes poor and cannot maintain himself with you, you shall support him as though he were a stranger and a sojourner, and he shall live with you. Take no interest from him or profit, but fear your God, that your brother may live beside you. You shall not lend him your money at interest, nor give him your food for profit. I am the LORD your God, who brought you out of the land of Egypt to give you the land of Canaan, and to be your God." (Lev. 25:35–38)

Shall we read that passage again?

That is a stunner, especially in capitalistic America. Did God really teach his people that if someone becomes so poor that she or he cannot take care of life's necessities, then we are to take her or him in and help her or him? Isn't that the job of government? Aren't charities supposed to do that?

This is not an instruction to governments or charities, however; it is an instruction to everyday people. What shall we make of this? Are we really supposed to start taking in families that are in need? At the risk of "over-lawyering" this, I suggest yes and no. Let me explain.

First, we do have a form of government where we have elected, since at least the social programs of the Great Depression, to give basic sustenance to those in need. We have food stamps, free education, public housing, Medicaid, and more. We citizens support these programs through taxes, and we believe that the programs provide the necessary safety net for those in need.

But in reality, those governmental programs do not provide an adequate safety net for everyone in need. We have churches, synagogues, and other charitable endeavors that step in to provide more assistance. Even those programs do not always provide the ultimate safety net.

We need to never view our duties before God as discharged, simply because we pay taxes and make charitable contributions. We still find people in need and we have a role to play. We help them get back on their feet. We don't do it because of what we get out of it—that is, we don't charge interest on loans, and we don't sell them food for profit. We step up and help because we have a God who does the same. We should reflect his image in how we treat others. That may not always be a handout (teach someone to fish; don't just give a fish), but it might mean a handout. We do what we can to *help those in need!*

Lord, give me an observant eye and the physical, economic, and emotional resources to help those in need. May I do so in your name, amen.

AUGUST 13

For it is to me that the people of Israel are servants. They are my servants whom I brought out of the land of Egypt: I am the LORD your God. (Lev. 25:55)

Physically take your eyes off this page for a moment and look around you. What do you see? I can't forecast where, when, or how everyone will be reading this devotional, but I think the odds are high that you have seen something that is "yours." If nothing else, as you lifted your eyes, you likely saw part of your body! That is yours, right?

Well, according to the Torah, the answer is yes and no. Yes, we belong to ourselves, and property rights are real. Things are yours, and things are mine. Leviticus 25 lays out various property rights, including the ability to sell ourselves into the service of others. But the answer is also no.

God makes it clear that we are to treat others with honor and dignity. We are not to take advantage of others, especially others in need. We are to look after them, help them, and nurture them back to a place of self-sufficiency. Why are we told to do this? Because we belong to God! That gives God the right to tell us how to treat others and how to behave. But more than that, the "others" we deal with also belong to God. So when we interact with others, in a sense, we are interacting with God's property!

In modern legal systems, there exists a property right called "bailment." This isn't what we might think of as "posting bail" to get someone out of jail. Rather, when we are entrusted with someone else's property, we have certain legal obligations to treat that property well. If you pay me to care for your dog, I can't ignore the dog, fail to feed or water the dog, or kill it without being held accountable.

This is the principle in today's passage. God wants us to see others as his. He wants us to treat others as if we are dealing with his property. This translates into a different mind-set than we might ordinarily have. I look at those with whom I will interact today and must ask myself, How will I treat them if I see them as God's property? Will I be more patient? Less prone to anger or frustration? Will I seek their good or will I use them for my advantage?

People are not tools for my purposes but part of God's grander purpose for which I am to play a role. That role includes me treating others accordingly.

Lord, I readily confess that I am not good at seeing things and people as yours. I tend to think of everything in terms of me, my plans, my needs, and my desires. Forgive me for that and retrain my mind-set. Let me see things as you see them and seek to serve you with my life and with my interactions with others. To your glory, amen.

AUGUST 14

"You shall not make idols for yourselves or erect an image or pillar, and you shall not set up a figured stone in your land to bow down to it, for I am the LORD your God." (Lev. 26:1)

For me, studying ancient Greek was hard. Studying ancient Hebrew was even tougher. Several studying keys helped, especially figuring out a way to anchor what I was learning to something I already knew. Beyond that, though, the most important tool used over and over again was not surprising. It was repetition. Saying the paradigms over and over, writing the paradigms over and over—this approach drilled forms, rules, and concepts into my head. I will likely die before I forget how to conjugate *sh-m-r* (שמר).

God used repetition in teaching the Israelites. He told them over and over again, "Do not worship idols!" This might seem a simple "one and done" kind of commandment. It seems simple enough to simply say, "Don't do it," and then the Israelites should refrain. But it was never so simple. In actuality, even though God told the Israelites over and over, both the Bible and archaeology confirm that Israel still had huge problems, consistently going after idols both in their homes and in public places.

What made this so difficult for them? Does this speak to us in the twenty-first century? It might seem not to. When was the last time you saw someone construct an Asherah pole for worshipping?

A key to understanding both why it was a perpetual problem for Israel and why it is still an issue we should address today is found in today's passage. God told Israel bluntly, "You shall not *make* . . . you shall not *set* . . . to bow down." These idols were creations of the people. Idol creation came from the people using their ingenuity, their learning, their interactions with people they respected or envied to try and understand and construct their understanding of God or gods. It made sense to the people.

Here is the instruction for us. We tend to do the very same thing. We don't call them God or gods, but we construct our ideas of who God is and how we should relate to him. We use the images of God that our friends, neighbors, or those in the media believe true. For example, when we hear that all paths lead to the same God, it sounds good to our pluralistically trained, politically correct ears of tolerance.

But this is not the biblical concept. God told Israel clearly, "You worship me as I have revealed myself to you. You don't decide what the revelation of God should be and worship that. That is simply something of your own creation. That is an idol!" He says it over and over. We need to learn that message.

Lord, reveal yourself to me in your word. Let me worship only you. In your name, amen.

AUGUST 15

"I will give peace in the land, and you shall lie down, and none shall make you afraid." (Lev. 26:6)

When I was young, Heinz 57 Sauce advertised a good bit on the television. The advertisement I most remember dealt with the name. Heinz 57 was a sauce made up of fifty-seven different ingredients. It was the sauce equivalent of V8 Juice (made up of eight different vegetables). These are all-in-one products.

I think there may be a Heinz 57 word in the Hebrew language. It is the word *shalom*. We often think of *shalom* as "peace," and that is certainly a good English word to describe an aspect of *shalom*. But *shalom* has a much larger semantic range. We may not need fifty-seven English words to fully flesh out its meaning, but we need a lot more than one!

Here are some English ideas built into *shalom*: Peace! Wholeness! Soundness! Completeness! Welfare! Safety! Soundness! Health! Prosperity! Quiet! Tranquility! Wellness! Contentment! Friendship!

Now with that fuller semantic range, can we all agree that we need *shalom*? This is what God offered and promised to the Israelites—if the Israelites would live as God instructed. If they would put him first in their lives, shunning idols. If they would offer him sacrifices not as a legalistic merit-based ritual but with hearts that were sacrificial—that is, if they obeyed out of love. If they would love God with all of their hearts, souls, and minds. If they would love each other as they loved themselves. If they would be thankful to God for each morsel of bread, looking to him to meet their needs. If they would be a people of prayer and loyalty. If they would teach their children about God and their children would carry on in purity. Then God would give them *shalom* in the land. Then they would be able to lie down and not fear anyone or anything.

Israel couldn't live that purely. I can't live that purely. As a Christian, I don't believe anyone other than Jesus Messiah can live, has lived, or will live that purely. But the beauty of my Christian faith is that God's justice is satisfied in the death of Christ, and there his justice intersects with his mercy. God can justly forgive me of my sins and bring me *shalom*. The Messiah is the only chance I have for *shalom*.

Even still, I do note that in my life, I most readily lose *shalom* when I sin or transgress God's will. Sinfulness disturbs my soul with a disconcerting foreboding that drives me back to ask for forgiveness and pushes me to seek living right before him. I need *shalom*.

Lord, I confess my sins and pray for forgiveness. Bring me shalom *in your name, amen.*

AUGUST 16

"I will make my dwelling among you, and my soul shall not abhor you. And I will walk among you and will be your God, and you shall be my people." (Lev. 26:11–12)

I don't do tattoos. I know they are popular in many places, but I don't do tattoos. I taught my children, I don't do tattoos. It is understood in our house. Two of my daughters used to prod me on this with a game they played. "Dad, we know you don't do tattoos, but if you *had to get one*, what would you get?" I have always told them, "I wouldn't! I don't do tattoos." They would try for hours to get me to give a different answer: "But if you had to get a tattoo or be shot dead, what would you get?" My answer never wavered: "I don't do tattoos."

Now I will say this, which may delight my children: if I did tattoos, *which I don't*, then this might be what I would have tattooed: "And I will walk among you and will be your God, and you shall be my people."

To have God walk with me is a deep desire in my life and has been for almost as long as I can remember. To have God dwell in me, to be my constant companion, is the highest joy. God does so as GOD but also as friend. It means having someone as a counselor 24/7. It means the best resource in times of trouble. It means pure light in times of darkness. It means compassion in times of hurting. It means solace in times of grief. It means help in times of need. It means joy in the midst of sorrow. It means faith in times of doubt. It means unconditional love. It means mercy. It means peace. Having the Creator God dwell in my heart, walking in my life, means the world.

Wouldn't every sane person want this? Moses spoke of this, but not just Moses. The prophet Jeremiah told a rebellious people that a day would come when God would give the people "a heart to know that I am the LORD, and they shall be my people and I will be their God" (Jer. 24:7). Jesus taught his disciples that "If anyone loves me, he will keep my word, and my Father will love him, and we will come to him and make our home with him" (John 14:23).

Dwelling with the Lord, the Lord dwelling with us—this comes from making the Lord our God. He stands at the door of our heart and knocks. He waits for us to invite him in and allow him, the Lord God, to set up in our lives. When we do so, life takes on a whole new meaning.

I want to walk with God.

Lord, please come into my heart. Be the Lord of my life. Take all of me and put it to use in your kingdom and plans. May I seek you above all others. In your name, amen.

AUGUST 17

"If you spurn my statutes, and if your soul abhors my rules, so that you will not do all my commandments, but break my covenant, then I will do this to you: I will visit you with panic, with wasting disease and fever that consume the eyes and make the heart ache. And you shall sow your seed in vain, for your enemies shall eat it. I will set my face against you, and you shall be struck down before your enemies. Those who hate you shall rule over you, and you shall flee when none pursues you." (Lev. 26:15–17)

We lawyers were visiting with a judge one time after finishing a case. The judge had served in the military during the Vietnam War. The judge told of his young son seeing a television show about the fall of South Vietnam. His son asked him, "Dad, is that the war where you fought?" The judge answered, "Yes." The son said, "Dad, did we lose the war you fought in?" The judge said that he paused at his son's question, uncertain how to answer, and then the answer just came out, "Well, we were winning when I left!"

Regardless who wins, war is a horrible thing. It destroys families, robs humanity of many lives, scars many who serve nobly, and uses up wasteful amounts of resources that could go for building rather than destroying. Certainly, sometimes war is necessary, but it should always be a last resort.

Think about war as we consider today's passage. It raises the question, who would want to go to war with God? Can you think of anything more insane than choosing to go to war with an all-powerful, all-knowing God? Especially if that God is kind, benevolent and loving, always seeking our best? It seems to me that people would choose to war with such a God only if (1) they hadn't really thought it through, (2) they were stubbornly set on self-destruction, or (3) they had played a mind game that God wasn't real. For the Israelites, God set out clear instructions on what to do to avoid war, and he also told them what the casualties of war would be. The Israelites would be inviting war with God if they spurned his commandments, if they abhorred his rules, breaking the agreement they had made to follow him. The results of the war would not be a victory by Israel! Instead, the Israelites would panic as they lost health, heart, and material wealth. God would have neighboring tribes conquer and rule over the Israelites as they lost their status and independence. War would not go easily for them.

Many of us suffer from a stubborn streak. For many there is something inside saying, "We would rather be defeated than serve a tyrant!" But that is not wise thinking. God is no tyrant. God's rules and wishes are best for us. He gave us instructions to help us live productively and happily. Faith teaches us to trust him for that. This brings me back to where I started: Who would want to go to war with God?

Lord, break my stubbornness and lead me into your peace. May I serve and worship you in faith from my heart. In your name, amen.

AUGUST 18

"And if in spite of this you will not listen to me, then I will discipline you again sevenfold for your sins, and I will break the pride of your power." (Lev. 26:18–19)

Something powerful, *very powerful*, scares me. It is pride. Pride is one name for "conceit." Our modern poet (and prophet?) Bob Dylan sings about it, putting into modern language what the Bible says. Dylan says this of pride (conceit): "Comes right down the highway / Straight down the line / Rips into your senses / Through your body and your mind . . . Steps into your room / Eats your soul / Over your senses / You have no control . . . Give ya delusions of grandeur / And an evil eye / Give you the idea that / You're too good to die."

The Bible says it this way: pride keeps us from believing in or seeing God. "In the pride of his face the wicked does not seek him; all his thoughts are, 'There is no God'" (Ps. 10:4). God says he hates pride. "Pride and arrogance and the way of evil and perverted speech I hate" (Prov. 8:13). Many are familiar with what pride brings: "Pride goes before destruction, and a haughty spirit before a fall" (Prov. 16:18). People who are proud generally don't even realize it. The prophet Obadiah wrote, "The pride of your heart has deceived you" (Obad. 3). Jesus taught that people are defiled by the evil things that come from their hearts, including "sexual immorality, theft, murder, adultery, coveting, wickedness, deceit, sensuality, envy, slander, *pride*" (Mark 7:21–22).

What do we do to guard against the power of pride? If pride is so deceptive that we aren't aware of it, how can we avoid it? How can we guard against it? I should first note that if I think I can instruct others in how to avoid pride, then I am probably trapped in it while typing! So with some reticence, I simply make suggestions. For one, we need to have a clear vision of who God is. As we see and understand God for who he is, there is no room for pride in any of us. We will understand our true place in the universe only as we see God on his throne. If we don't see God clearly, then we are left gazing at ourselves, a sure way to self-conceit. Or we might gaze at others, measuring ourselves, another avenue for pride.

There are some other possibilities. We might not become proud but rather defeated and unimportant when we gaze at ourselves or somewhere other than God. But that is not a good thing either. For we are not unimportant to him. He loves us enough to rescue us from our sin and bring us into a walk with him. We have value because he made us valuable. We need to understand that also.

We will do our best if we stay constantly gazing upon God in worship, in study, in prayer, and in fellowship with other believers.

Lord, rid me of any pride, and may I find my worth in you. In your name, amen.

AUGUST 19

"And if by this discipline you are not turned to me but walk contrary to me, then I also will walk contrary to you." (Lev. 26:23–24)

"Don't make me tell you twice!" That was my father's way of telling me something twice without it seeming like he was telling me something twice. At least that's what I thought when I heard it as a young boy. Still, even realizing what Dad was doing, I paid attention when I heard the warning. I knew if I didn't heed it, then what followed was not going to be a good thing. Discipline rode in on the next horse if I failed to respond properly.

Mom and Dad disciplining me was a good thing. Without it, I'm not sure that I would have grown up with a clear understanding of right and wrong, of consequences, and of compassion and mercy. All of those go hand in hand. Certainly, discipline can be abusive, but Mom and Dad lived by the rule that they would use the lowest measure of discipline, knowing if it wasn't heeded, then the next step would be more. They never jumped to the nuclear bomb of discipline if something less drastic would work!

Over and over in the Torah and all of Scripture, God speaks of disciplining his children as a parent. It is a marvelous illustration of what happens. God warned the Israelites early, and as we see in today's text, if they violated the agreed covenant, if they broke his rules and flaunted his lordship, then he would discipline them. God used the language of a parent disciplining a child. In Deuteronomy 8:5, Moses used the same language when he explained, "Know then in your heart that, as a man disciplines his son, the LORD your God disciplines you."

God also made it clear that if the first level of discipline didn't work, then he would make things worse. This would continue until God would turn and "walk contrary" to the Israelites. Failure to honor God's discipline doesn't cause him to give up on his people. God's steadfast love kicks in. But God's love is a tough love. God will pull back and let his people suffer the consequences of disobedience in order to get them to respond as they should.

I would love to live life so obediently that I never received the discipline of the Lord. I would love to say that the Christian experience of the cross removes the Lord's discipline. But I haven't lived thusly, and the cross does no such thing. The writer of the New Testament book of Hebrews quoted the Psalms for the truth that "the Lord disciplines the one he loves" (Heb. 12:6).

The key for me, then, is to be attentive to the discipline of the Lord! I want to learn fast!

Lord, thank you for teaching me and training me. May I learn! In your name, amen.

AUGUST 20

"But if they confess their iniquity and the iniquity of their fathers in their treachery that they committed against me, and also in walking contrary to me, so that I walked contrary to them and brought them into the land of their enemies—if then their uncircumcised heart is humbled and they make amends for their iniquity, then I will remember my covenant with Jacob, and I will remember my covenant with Isaac and my covenant with Abraham, and I will remember the land." (Lev. 26:40–42)

I have a number of friends who have found health and recovery through the twelve-step program of Alcoholics Anonymous. I reflect on that program as I contemplate today's passage because the AA program understands the imperative of confession.

Consider how many of the twelve steps deal with confession in one way or another. Step 1—admission that one is powerless. Inherent in this step is a confession of a problem. Step 4—make a searching and fearless moral inventory. No one can do that without recognizing his or her sins. Step 5—admit to God and others the exact nature of wrongs committed. This is straightforward confession. Steps 8 and 9 both deal with making amends for wrongs committed, which is a confession of wrongs to others. Step 10 involves an ongoing inventory and confession. These steps that have guided countless people from addiction into recovery find their roots in confession.

Scripture teaches that we do not need an addiction to alcohol, narcotics, or any other such physical malady that uses the twelve-step program. Without such addictions the need for confession still exists. God calls his people to confess their sins before him.

Confession starts a process that is vital to honest living. Confession takes what is hidden and secretive and brings it into the open. Left unconfessed, sin becomes a festering sore that can weigh one down, inhibiting not only happiness but growth and development as well. As we confess, we drop the pretense of being someone we're not—a useless pretense before an all-knowing God anyway.

We then set ourselves into a place where God can go to work. He can heal where we are broken. He can nurture where we are struggling. He can restore what we have lost. He can enlighten what has become dark. God can show us the forgiveness he provides as we seek it with an honest need.

Take a moment and think about the dark areas you hide from God. Give them to him in confession. Seek his restoration and forgiveness. Seek how he would have you address these things further, and be willing to follow his lead.

Lord, I confess to you my sins [list some!]. Please restore me and help me make things right. Forgive me in your name, and teach me your forgiveness. In your name, amen.

AUGUST 21

The LORD spoke to Moses in the wilderness of Sinai, in the tent of meeting, on the first day of the second month, in the second year after they had come out of the land of Egypt, saying, "Take a census of all the congregation of the people of Israel, by clans, by fathers' houses, according to the number of names, every male, head by head. From twenty years old and upward, all in Israel who are able to go to war." (Num. 1:1–3)

Growing up, I loved to play chess. As a preteen, I was the young nerd, playing in rated tournaments against all the old folks. There was a lot I liked about chess. It was war without guns and death. I had pieces to bring into battle. The pieces needed to be placed strategically on the board, so they could be called into the right attack at the right time. I also had an opponent. There was an enemy that needed beating. This is the way of war.

Before any chess tournament, I prepared. I studied openings, figuring out lines of play that best fit my style. I worked through positions, learning from other games how to best use the pieces in a concerted attack. This made me a better player.

Many people do not like the idea of war. We think of war as a time where people are hurt and killed. War is destructive. It takes resources that could be used for building and uses them to destroy. We don't want to go to war. It is a tool of last resort. Diplomacy, negotiation, sometimes even appeasement are options we use before war. With all those options, however, war still exists.

Scripture makes clear that there is a war going on, and not one simply of nation against nation. There is a cosmic struggle of right versus wrong, of obedience to God versus disobedience, of light versus darkness, of love versus selfishness. God is the general in the war, and we choose which side we join. No one sits out this war. We are part of the solution or part of the problem.

Today's passage gives us insight into how God wages war. Preparing the Israelites to fight earthly battles, God started by determining the resources to engage in the battle. God had Moses count the people who could fight, putting them into natural divisions by their clans, knowing they would fight best when fighting with their families and friends. (Even military thinkers today explain that in the heat of battle, soldiers are fighting to save those at their right and left as much as a homeland.) God got the people ready for battle and set the chessboard up for victory.

God does the same in the cosmic war for good and evil. He prepares us and places us where we need to be. Our job is to follow his lead and fight for right over wrong, truth over lies, love over selfish hate. We are the Lord's army, and it's a war out there!

Lord, prepare me for battle. May I fight for you. In your name, amen.

AUGUST 22

"And these are the names of the men who shall assist you. From Reuben, Elizur the son of Shedeur; from Simeon, Shelumiel the son of Zurishaddai; from Judah, Nahshon the son of Amminadab . . ." (Num. 1:5–7)

It would be both boring and interesting to produce the entire section from which I drew today's passage. It would be boring because it is a list of name after name of people who lived over three thousand years ago that none of us have heard of or know. It would be interesting for the very same reason! This is a list of dozens of names of people we will never really know anything about. And it is in the Bible! This wasn't done in the age of word processing, where someone could cut and paste a list of names. These were names taking up precious ink on precious parchment, handwritten and copied with eye strain and careful spelling for *thousands of years*! Amazing, right?

Why do I find this amazing and interesting, even inspiring? Because of what it says about God and his people! God is handpicking people to assist Moses in the tasks ahead. God knows the ones he is picking out by name. Even beyond knowing their name, God knows their lineage. God didn't say, "Hey, Moses, go get one or two folks from each of the tribes and enlist their help." God didn't say, "Find twelve of your favorite people that work well with you." God didn't send a test for Moses to use to determine who might fill the job of assistant. God selected each one of them based on his knowledge.

God handpicks people! This wasn't a onetime thing. It is the way of God. God cares about what is happening in our world. He is unfolding his plans for the ages, bringing his will to fruition. Every one of his children has a role to fill, and who better than God knows that role? No one! This has huge implications for me today.

I know that I have a fairly full set of things I will be doing today and tomorrow. Some of it seems rather uneventful (breakfast?). Some of it seems more notable (work meetings). What about you? I suggest that we all need to realize that most of the things before us today are things where God has called us by name to do them to his glory. If they are not, then they are not things we should be doing at all!

Each day presents unique opportunities to answer the call of God and serve him, living to his glory. Who's going to do what you have to do today to God's glory if not you?

Lord, thank you for calling me into your service. I stand ready to serve! Use me in the mundane as well as the glamorous. Put me into your service in all I do. May I do it to your glory. In your name, amen.

AUGUST 23

The LORD spoke to Moses and Aaron, saying, "The people of Israel shall camp each by his own standard, with the banners of their fathers' houses. They shall camp facing the tent of meeting on every side." (Num. 2:1–2)

Business often takes me to London. I have a favorite hotel where I stay, right on the edge of Hyde Park. Half of the rooms look out onto Hyde Park. The other half look out on a bunch of streets and buildings. Occasionally, the hotel will give me a room upgrade where I get a Hyde Park view. It is a marvelous view, although to me not worth the money they charge absent the upgrade! I am amazed at the value put on a good view.

If we shift from hotel views to everyday life, we are barraged by things we see. Driving down the road we see billboards and signs advertising everything conceivable. On our computers we see pop-up ads and suggestions of websites for us to click. Our televisions provide a feast for the eyes, both in the shows and the advertisements. Even in our interactions, we can opt for FaceTiming people or videoconferencing rather than just speaking by telephone. We sit down for face-to-face meetings and visits so we have a greater degree of interaction. We are a visual society, and where we turn our eyes is where we put our focus.

Today's passage sets out the instructions God gave the Israelites for how they were to pitch their camps. Every tribe's tents were to be pitched facing the tabernacle. The tabernacle was the "tent of meeting" where God would meet with Moses. It represented God's presence among the Israelites. By facing their camps toward the tabernacle, all the Israelites, as they came in and went out, as they rose or went to sleep, when they moved or when they stayed put, did so with a view toward God and his presence among them.

This is the way to live. We should live each day with our lives oriented around God's presence. We should behold him in all that we do. God should never be out of our field of vision. He should be our focus.

Practically speaking, this means that in the morning when we rise, we recognize God is already up. As we begin our day, we recognize that God is present in each moment. Whatever we find to do, whether it is a word we say, a thought we think, or an action we do, we should be doing it to God's glory. We need to recognize that every interaction we have with someone is a unique moment God has put in our lives to make an impression on that person, to serve that person in God's name, and to show God's love and attention to that person.

We should do all we do with our eyes to the Lord. We should live facing him.

Lord, create in us hearts of fire to see you and live for you. In your name, amen.

AUGUST 24

Those who were to camp before the tabernacle on the east, before the tent of meeting toward the sunrise, were Moses and Aaron and his sons, guarding the sanctuary itself, to protect the people of Israel. And any outsider who came near was to be put to death. (Num. 3:38)

Israel was told to closely guard the presence/sanctuary of God. In all ages, most kings have kept guards around them so that the king wasn't molested or attacked. In antiquity, even pagan temples kept guards so that the temple (and its god) wasn't subject to robbery or theft. But that is not what was going on with God and his presence. God had a guard set up to protect the outsider who would dare enter! God Almighty doesn't need protecting. The protection was necessary for anyone who would dare to approach him without justification! The God of Israel is no plaything or a creation of someone's imagination. He is a living being, all powerful and holy beyond measure.

Today's passage is one of many in the Torah that speak to this. God set up clear guards around his presence. The guards were for the protection of someone coming before God. They guarded the sanctuary to "protect the people of Israel." God didn't need human protection, but God's holiness would burn through any who came to him casually.

We live in a different age. We live in an age where people can and do often treat God casually. How often do we hear of God being used as an afterthought or in some common slang expression?

This is not going to ruin God. We never have to worry that God is lessened in who he is. But it does have an effect. The people who cheapen God, take him for granted, or use him as a byword or expression will be affected. God sees to that.

I want to be careful here. I don't want to take God lightly, but that isn't just a matter of speech. God's concern in this passage wasn't with people who simply slighted him in speech. God was focused on people's actions and behaviors.

We need to be careful how we approach God in our behavior. Do we approach him in prayer or thought based on our own merit? Do we assert our right to freely go into God's presence? Or are we too scared to ever approach him at all?

Christianity teaches us to approach God meritoriously, but the merit is not our own. It is the merit of Jesus as God's anointed. Christians understand that through Jesus, everyone can approach God purely and justly. God was clear to Moses. There must be some measure for approaching God, lest the one approaching suffers!

Lord, I approach you in prayer on your merit, seeking your love and forgiveness. Show it to me and give me courage to embrace it, in your name, amen.

AUGUST 25

"Aaron and his sons shall go in and appoint them each to his task and to his burden . . ."
(Num. 4:19)

My brother-in-law took over management of my law practice one fine day many years back. We were a midsize firm, about to grow significantly. Kevin had a rule. He wanted to make sure we looked at each employee carefully and made sure that everyone "had the right seat on the bus." He knew that some people were strong doing certain tasks and other people were strong at other tasks. He wanted to make sure that we were as efficient as possible, meaning each person had to be where they could best perform. This was good economics on a practical level.

I often think that God is the world's greatest economist. He was putting people in the right seat on the bus long before it became the textbook business move. Today's passage is a perfect example. After designating certain individuals for certain tasks, God instructed Aaron and his sons to tell the people their assignments. God had picked people to do the chores they were best suited to do, and then saw that the people got to work accordingly.

We do well to think this through. God has work for you and me, good things for us to do. He has prepared the works for us, and he has made us to be what we need to be to accomplish the works. This is an amazing thing to think about.

Take a personal inventory of how you became the person you are today. I do so and find that a lot of it involves where I grew up, values taught me by my parents, interactions I had with my siblings and friends, my schooling, and other interactions that built my character, honed my abilities, and shaped my personality.

But I am not only a composite of those positive building experiences. I am also a product of negative things in my life. The mistreatment I have experienced and bad things that have occurred—unfortunate circumstances, harsh interactions, sin, and many other negatives—have also shaped me.

God knows all of these things. God, the ultimate economist, will not let any of them go to waste. God will use my past—good and bad—that made me who I am today and appoint me to the perfect seat for me on the bus. God will use me to do things no one else is positioned to do. I must confess, I am in awe of this marvelous God. I am also humbled that he would use me.

Lord, thank you for your work in my life. Mold me and make me after your will. Use me in your work. In your name, amen.

AUGUST 26

"They shall not go in to look on the holy things even for a moment, lest they die." (Num. 4:20)

Today's passage sets up a warning from God that only the priests were to come into the holy sanctuary, and parts of the holy area were reserved for the high priest. Even then that holiest of the holy places was only to be entered once a year. God had Israel set a guard so no one would accidently (or purposely) enter in violation of God's decree. God's holiness was not to be taken lightly. To gaze upon it uninvited was death.

Some five hundred years later, a bad Israelite king of Judah named Uzziah (also called "Azariah") in arrogance disregarded this command of God and entered into the temple to burn incense. He claimed to be acting out of reverence toward God, seeking to worship him, but the Bible notes that this was a move of arrogance. God struck Uzziah with leprosy, and he soon died.

In the year that Uzziah died, the prophet Isaiah, fully familiar with the king's error and leprosy, had a vision. In the vision, Isaiah found himself in God's throne room. Knowing what had happened when the king had wrongly come into God's presence, Isaiah was mortified. Isaiah fell on his face and cried out, "Woe is me! For I am lost; for I am a man of unclean lips, and I dwell in the midst of a people of unclean lips" (Isa. 6:5).

After Isaiah's repentance, at the Lord's command, an angel took a coal and touched Isaiah's lips, pronouncing him clean. Then the voice of the Lord called out for a servant: "Whom shall I send, and who will go for us?" Isaiah responded quickly with a servant's heart: "Here am I! Send me," and God did (Isa. 6:8).

Uzziah looked in on God and suffered leprosy and died. Isaiah looked in on God and came out holy and on a mission for God. What made the difference? Uzziah acted in arrogance and pride, while Isaiah acted in humility and submission.

How shall we live? What will be our attitude? Will we be humble people or people filled with self-importance and self-determination? Will we ask to learn God's ways, that we might walk in his path? Or will we follow our own way, walking our own path?

God has warned us. We would do well to heed his warning. Let us humble ourselves before him, setting aside our pride and haughtiness, and exalting him as we seek to serve him to the best of our abilities.

Lord, teach us your ways. Touch us with the coal from your altar and cover us with your sacrifice, so we might be able to stand before you, hearing your voice and living with your mission first and foremost on our minds and hearts. In your name, amen.

AUGUST 27

The LORD spoke to Moses and Aaron, saying, "Take a census of the sons of Kohath from among the sons of Levi, by their clans and their fathers' houses, from thirty years old up to fifty years old, all who can come on duty, to do the work in the tent of meeting. This is the service of the sons of Kohath in the tent of meeting: the most holy things." . . . "Take a census of the sons of Gershon also, by their fathers' houses and by their clans. From thirty years old up to fifty years old, you shall list them, all who can come to do duty, to do service in the tent of meeting. . . . They shall carry the curtains of the tabernacle and the tent of meeting." (Num. 4:1–3; 22–23)

One of my favorite medical terms is *triage*. It refers to the prioritization of patients for treatment, based on the condition of each. If someone has a splinter that needs removing, he or she will be triaged and placed after someone who is having a heart attack. I find the term useful, especially for email. When my time is limited, I triage my email, determining which messages need a reply before others that can wait a bit. Triage is a reflection of how we value things. It indicates our priorities.

Today's passage contains a subtle lesson in triage before God. The passage covers the duties of the sons of Levi. These were priests with various responsibilities. In the previous chapter, the sons are listed by name: Gershon, Kohath, and Merari (Num. 3:17). The sons are also listed out in a census of priests who could work in the Lord's service. As is typically done, the sons are written up and listed in their birth order. Gershon was the oldest and is listed first; then Kohath, the middle son; and finally Merari, the youngest.

But something unusual happens in chapter four. Here the sons are assigned their responsibilities in packing up and transporting the tabernacle, the tent of worship for Israel. While the eldest son is typically listed first, this time the listing begins with the middle son, Kohath. Why? The listing is not by priority of the sons but by priority of the items involved. Kohath and his sons were in charge of the holiest items (the ark, the altar, etc.), while Gershon and his sons were in charge of the tent curtains. Merari and his sons were involved in disassembling, carrying, and reassembling the poles and support structures.

God listed things in order of holy importance, a triage system that trumped human custom. This speaks to us in our efforts to find godliness in our lives. What others might perceive as important may be important, but the greatest importance lies in what God teaches us. The holiness of God should be first and foremost in our consideration of how to live and love as well as what to do and when to do it. This should be how we triage our lives each day.

Lord, teach me to put you and your holiness first in all I do. In your name, amen.

AUGUST 28

"As for the sons of Merari, you shall list them by their clans and their fathers' houses. From thirty years old up to fifty years old, you shall list them, everyone who can come on duty, to do the service of the tent of meeting. And this is what they are charged to carry." (Num. 4:29–31)

There are several tests to see if you are an optimist or a pessimist. The most common one is whether you see a glass half empty or half full. Another similar one is whether you consider yourself as young as you will ever be or older than you have ever been. Age is something everyone has, and aging is something everyone does.

Now that our children are adults, it is interesting to hear their thoughts on aging. As they approach their thirties, they begin to get reflective about age and its implications. I think it is part of the ability to go back in our memory and remember when our parents were the age we are now. That is odd.

When I was in law school, I was asked to go to a retirement home—an "old folks home," as we called it—and give a devotion. There at the Pioneer Hotel in downtown Lubbock, Texas, I spoke to a group of twenty or so people a good six to seven decades older than me in my young twenties. I sure couldn't relate to being their age, but I didn't need to in order to give the devotion that evening.

I spoke to them about the *fact* that God uses us at any age. We know we have reached an age where God can no longer use us when we die. Because as long as we're alive, God has a purpose for us. Those elderly people were not going to be out and about, but every one of them could fulfill a day's purpose before God. God might have been calling them to pray for a younger generation, but everyone who was conscious could rest assured God had tasks ready that only they could do.

Today's passage gives a glimpse of this aspect of God. God was assigning chores for the assembly, disassembly, and transport of his tabernacle of worship. God had already had a census completed of the offspring of Levi suitable for the work, but here he carved out tasks for the sons of Merari who were in a special age group (thirty to fifty). This follows on the heels of God telling Moses to have the sons of Kohath and son of Gershon that were within that age group do certain tasks.

God knows your age and mine. He knows the young and the old. He knows those in the middle. No one's age is lost on God, nor are anyone's skills lost. Everyone at every age is called to serve God, as appropriate. Faith is not a young person's game or an old person's hobby. It is a way of life, serving God at every age.

Lord, put me to work for you today! In your name, amen.

AUGUST 29

The LORD spoke to Moses, saying, "Command the people of Israel that they put out of the camp everyone who is leprous or has a discharge and everyone who is unclean through contact with the dead. You shall put out both male and female, putting them outside the camp, that they may not defile their camp, in the midst of which I dwell." (Num. 5:1–3)

Do you know the Hebrew word *shallach*? Probably not. But if you were reading this in the Hebrew, you would know it when you were done. It is used three times in just verses two and three. Many translate *shallach* as "put out." The way the Hebrew is written draws attention to this word. I could fairly, though awkwardly, translate it, "Put out (*shallach*) of the camp the leprous," "put out (*shallach*) male and female," and "putting them out (*shallach*) of the camp."

We shouldn't lose the importance of this repetition. Most of us are not lepers, but we don't need to be to apply the principle at work here. God's concern is contamination. Leprosy was a highly contagious condition, and one that rendered the sick person unclean. It was readily equated to sin, another highly contagious condition rendering a person unclean. God's solution for lepers was to put them out of the holy community until they could show they were cured.

We all can use a dose of this cure. If we examine our lives, we will see that there are sins that are much more damaging than leprosy. I can take the triply emphatic instruction as a warning to be heeded. I need to remove those sins from my life. I need to put them out from who I am.

Some of this is simply a matter of choice. Other times, however, it isn't so simple. I know many people who want to quit smoking, but the addiction is so strong, they find themselves unable. (My friend Bob used to say, "I am really good at quitting smoking. I've done it twenty times in just the last three months!") Smoking, however, isn't the only thing so addictive. There are sins that people have a tremendous problem conquering. How shall we put these out of the camp?

The answer isn't easy. There isn't a one, two, three that will conquer any addictive sin. But there are some things we can and should do. First, recognize the sin, confess it, and pray for God's help. Second, find accountability friends whom you can be honest with and who will help hold you accountable. Third, spend a lot of time in prayer, worship, and song, seeking the presence of God to drive away the cravings of sin. Fourth, when you fall down, start back over with the first thing given above (confess and pray). Fifth, recognize the circumstances and places that lead to failure and avoid them like the plague! Sixth, stay busy! It's not in the Bible, but it could be: idle hands are the devil's workshop. We need to find all the tools available to put out our uncleanness!

Lord, I am a sinner. Forgive me. Teach me to put away sin. In your name, amen.

AUGUST 30

*And the L*ORD *spoke to Moses, saying, "Speak to the people of Israel, When a man or woman commits any of the sins that people commit by breaking faith with the L*ORD*, and that person realizes his guilt, he shall confess his sin that he has committed. And he shall make full restitution for his wrong, adding a fifth to it and giving it to him to whom he did the wrong." (Num. 5:6–7)*

In today's passage, God instructs Moses about what people should do when they have wronged a fellow person. The wrongdoer, upon realizing the wrong, is to confess and then make restitution.

This makes sense. God cares about justice, and not just in the sense that we need to be right with God; God cares about justice among people on earth. How we treat each other should be based on the character of God just as much as how we treat God.

Centuries later, God sent a prophet to the Israelites to warn them about their failures in this regard. The prophet's name was Micah. Micah delivered three different messages with a common theme: God saw the great injustices the wealthy and elite wrought on the poorer, more common people. God saw the use of judges as courts to propagate these injustices. In the third prophetic utterance, Micah framed God's complaints against the nation in the form of a lawsuit. In this section, Micah asked the question, "What does the LORD require of you?" He then answered, "To do justice . . ." (Mic. 6:8).

God cares how we treat each other. God cares that we are fair to people. If we are to err in this at all, we shouldn't err by being overly strict. Our adjustment to strict justice needs to be one of mercy. In other words, if we have wronged someone, we need to repay and fix it. If someone has wronged us, we don't have to demand restitution; we can show mercy. This is given by the rest of Micah's passage referenced above. After noting that God requires us "to do justice," in his next words, Micah gives the additional requirements "to love mercy, and to walk humbly with your God."

Before leaving today's passage, note two additional things that stand out. First, God required not only restitution but also an additional 20 percent on top of it. In a sense, God noted the interest due on what was owed. The second note is that committing a wrong against another is called by God "breaking faith with the LORD." Here is the sense that we treat others properly because God has taught us to do so and commanded us to do so.

We should examine our lives and, where we have wronged others, apologize and try to make it right.

Lord, give me eyes to see my sins. Help me know the right time and way to make amends. May I live justly with mercy and walk humbly with you. In your name, amen.

AUGUST 31

And the Lord spoke to Moses, saying, "Speak to the people of Israel and say to them, When either a man or a woman makes a special vow, the vow of a Nazirite, to separate himself to the Lord, he shall . . ." (Num. 6:1–3)

Each November 10, my wife and I try to do something special, just the two of us. It is a special day to us. It's not a birthday or our wedding anniversary. It doesn't mark the birth of a child or even our first date. It marks the anniversary of our first date as adults! (We did go out several times in high school.) This is a special time we set aside to enjoy each other and thank God for our marriage.

In the world today, people celebrate all kinds of events and holidays. We set aside time and even certain rituals as a part of those celebrations. Some are shocked to find out that in the Bible, there were specific opportunities for people to dedicate time and activities as a "vow" to God. These were chances to concentrate and focus on God, living in such a way that would draw our attention and interest into our relationship with him.

One of the most well-known vows was called a "Nazirite" vow. The structure and rules of this vow are set out in Numbers 6. The Nazirite vow was taken by a man or woman. God instructed Moses that those who took a Nazirite vow were to abstain from wine, strong drink, and even grape juice, grapes, and raisins. The hair was to remain uncut, and the person with the vow was to avoid contact with any dead person. Jewish tradition imposed these vows for a period of thirty days, unless the person taking the vow specified a different time period (see the Mishnah, at *Nazir* 6:3). Once the time of the vow was over, the person was to shave his head and purify himself before the Jewish temple authorities.

Vows are times when we dedicate ourselves to God for a specific purpose or in a specific way. They are voluntary, but once entered into, they are not to be taken lightly. In Moses' day, vows were treated as contracts. They were not to be violated without penalty. Importantly, vows were not a *quid pro quo*. They were not set out as a "deal" with God, like, "I'll stop drinking for thirty days if you'll get me out of this trouble." Vows are chances to celebrate a time of focus and resolution before God. It doesn't mean we are holier because we make and keep a vow. It should never be a cause of pride on our behalf. But in humility, and even secrecy, if we take the time to dedicate something to God, it will be amazing how he grows us in that. It might be a Nazirite vow or maybe giving something up for Lent or the High Holy Days. But for many it might be simply a vow to take money spent at Starbucks for a month and give it to the poor.

Consider celebrating your relationship with God in a special way.

Lord, thank you for walking in this life with me. In your name, amen.

SEPTEMBER 1

The LORD spoke to Moses, saying, "Speak to Aaron and his sons, saying, Thus you shall bless the people of Israel: you shall say to them, The LORD bless you and keep you; the LORD make his face to shine upon you and be gracious to you; the LORD lift up his countenance upon you and give you peace." (Num. 6:22–26)

Today's passage is one of the most powerful blessings found in the Bible. It was an instructed blessing, meaning that God instructed the priests to pronounce this blessing over Israel. That in itself merits consideration. This was not the best effort of humans to bless one another. This was a blessing God wrote. We should look at it carefully.

The blessing is built around the number three. Three was a symbolic number for the Hebrews and for most of their contemporary cultures as well. This was an age before science and math. It was an age with a very limited vocabulary. These factors led toward numbers having a symbolic meaning as well as a mathematical one. Three was a number that represented the divine. It is appropriate to have a threefold blessing from God to his people. God's name is invoked three times, each time with a blessing: "The LORD bless you . . . The LORD make his face shine . . . The LORD lift his countenance . . ." The priests may have uttered and channeled the blessing, but there was no doubt, the blessing came from the Lord.

The Hebrew of the three blessings reads as a buildup to a majestic crescendo. It begins with the first blessing, consisting of three Hebrew words in fifteen consonants. The second blessing is five Hebrew words in twenty consonants. The final blessings peak with seven Hebrew words in twenty-five consonants. These blessings were to be pronounced upon the "people" of Israel (literally the "sons" of Israel, but that is a reference to all of the Israelites). Yet the blessings themselves are individual ones. The "you" in each of the three blessing phrases is in the singular. God's blessings upon his people are individual blessings upon each, not simply one blessing on the corporate whole.

We can see from this how God wishes to bless his people. God wishes to keep, watch, guard, and preserve his people (blessing one). Blessing two shows that God wishes to shine his face, or show his character and personality, to his people in a way that showers them with favor ("be gracious"). This is the way of God. As we behold who he is, it changes us. It brings us favor as we see him in truth. The final blessing has God lifting his face (translated "countenance") to give peace (*shalom*). This again is the effect of God. He brings peace on those who live under his character and care.

As I write this devotion, I adjust my usual prayer at the end. I offer this prayer for you, the reader, and urge you to offer it for someone else.

May the Lord bless you and keep you. May the Lord make his face to shine upon you and be gracious to you. May the Lord lift his countenance upon you and give you peace. In his name and power, amen!

SEPTEMBER 2

The LORD spoke to Moses, saying, "Speak to Aaron and his sons, saying, Thus you shall bless the people of Israel: you shall say to them, 'The LORD bless you and keep you; the LORD make his face to shine upon you and be gracious to you; the LORD lift up his countenance upon you and give you peace. So shall they put my name upon the people of Israel, and I will bless them.'" (Num. 6:23–27)

Yesterday's devotion looked carefully at this special blessing God instructed the priests to say over the Israelites. Today we move the focus to the final statement God makes at the end: "So shall they put my name upon the people of Israel, and I will bless them."

Do you notice something unusual about that? The priests pronouncing the blessing over the people were putting God's name upon them. Some Israelites still today wear this blessing in an amulet, literally carrying the name of God on their personage. More to the point, however, is the idea behind God's name being on someone. It signified ownership. It is the same type of language used for God's house or temple (Deut. 12:5; Jer. 7:10).

We live in a time where good news is sometimes hard to find. But good news is critical to our frames of mind as well as our world perspectives. Today's passage is a cause for rejoicing and encouragement. Remember that this is a blessing that God wrote for the priests to say over God's people. This wasn't human desire expressed in a prayer; it was God's desire. God wants to put his name on us! God wants us to be aware of that fact. God knows our frailties, errors, and mistakes. Yet he still wants to put his name on us.

God's relationship with his people is not a banking account, set up at the bank that is most convenient or that offers the best terms, then switched when a better bank is found. We are not related to God as to a vendor or service. God wants us 24/7, and when we truly give ourselves to him, we are claiming him 24/7—for life.

This idea of God putting his name on me changes my day, or at least it should. Good news may come today, but that news can't beat God wanting his name on me. Bad news may come today, but that news can't defeat the truth that God has his name on me. I may see people that build me up today, but they can't build me up more than God, who has put his name on me. I may see people bent on destroying me today, but they can't destroy the *fact* and *result* of God putting his name on me. I am rejoicing today, regardless of circumstances. God has chosen to put his name on me. Praise the Lord!

Lord, please bring the reality of this blessing to me. I give you my life and heart and desire you to have your name on me. As I pray this prayer in your name, I also seek to live in your name. Amen.

SEPTEMBER 3

Now the LORD spoke to Moses, saying, "Speak to Aaron and say to him, When you set up the lamps, the seven lamps shall give light in front of the lampstand." And Aaron did so: he set up its lamps in front of the lampstand, as the LORD commanded Moses. (Num. 8:1–3)

In many ways, the modern world is tremendous. The occasional power outage has reinforced the delight of having light at the flip of a switch. No one likes walking around in the dark. I have stumbled more than once over items that I would have been able to see if only there had been light.

Because light is so readily available, we may not fully appreciate the ancient analogies of antiquity. Even our darkness today is rarely as dark as what the ancients knew. At night, our cities put out enough light that we have the term "light pollution." People on the space station can readily identify cities at night because of the lights. For the ancients, light was a precious and vital commodity. Getting light wasn't as simple as flipping a switch or striking a match.

We can see a variety of biblical uses of "light" in a metaphor or analogy. One that today's passage evokes is "light" as illustrative of God's word. Today's passage has God speaking to Moses, giving Moses a word for Aaron. The word concerned the way Aaron would provide light for the tabernacle. The location for worshipping God was to be illuminated as the word of God instructed. This creates a natural understanding of the illumination that comes from the word of God.

In the Psalm 119, the writer uses this same analogy: "Your word is a lamp to my feet and a light to my path" (Ps. 119:105). The Bible uses a marvelous analogy for the word of God. This psalm gives practical application to today's Torah passage. We look to what God has to say to help us see where we are going. We risk stumbling around absent God's direction.

A natural question for many is "How do I find God's direction for today? How do I hear the word of the Lord?" These are important questions. The biblical answers involve spending time prayerfully reading Scripture. These are words spoken by God. As we read them prayerfully, we should ask God to illuminate his words to us. We can also get illumination by speaking to other followers of God whose lives illustrate that they have a good grasp on godliness. The Christian understands that in Jesus, we see the Word of God. We see how God would live as a human, and we can model our lives after Jesus. With all of these considerations, for much of "hearing" God, we need obedient hearts to do those things we read and study. Then God's light becomes much clearer.

Lord, may your words light my path. In your name, amen.

SEPTEMBER 4

And whenever the cloud lifted from over the tent, after that the people of Israel set out, and in the place where the cloud settled down, there the people of Israel camped. At the command of the LORD the people of Israel set out, and at the command of the LORD they camped. As long as the cloud rested over the tabernacle, they remained in camp. Even when the cloud continued over the tabernacle many days, the people of Israel kept the charge of the LORD and did not set out. (Num. 9:17–19)

Whenever I read passages like today's, I do so with the Mississippi Fred McDowell song "You Gotta Move" playing in my head. The song has been recorded by many, including the Rolling Stones in 1971, but in my head, I hear the McDowell version, with its slow blues accentuated by the slide guitar:

> *You gotta move*
> *You gotta move*
> *You gotta move, child*
> *You gotta move*
> *Oh, when the Lord gets ready*
> *You gotta move*
> *You may be high*
> *You may be low*
> *You may be rich, child*
> *You may be poor*
> *But when the Lord gets ready*
> *You gotta move.*

This was the story of Israelites. God dictated where they went and when they went. Their destiny was fully in the hands of God. This was a one-two combination of trusting God and his plans and obeying his call to stay or go.

This is still our call today. When God puts something in front of us, we move. When God stops us, we stop. It doesn't matter who we are. We can be rich or poor; we still need to trust and obey God. We may be high or low, young or old, sick or well—when the Lord gets ready, we move. I want to follow God. If he puts a problem before me, I want him to walk through it with me, unfolding to me his solution. If he allows a tough time to block my path, I long to follow him through the difficulty, knowing nothing stops my God. If he sets me down in a good place or a bad place, I will sit and enjoy it (if good) or endure it (if bad) until God moves me onward. This will be my journey through life!

Lord, may I be ready and alert, moving when you move and stopping when you stop. In your name, amen.

SEPTEMBER 5

And Moses said to Hobab the son of Reuel the Midianite, Moses' father-in-law, "We are setting out for the place of which the LORD said, 'I will give it to you.' Come with us, and we will do good to you, for the LORD has promised good to Israel." But he said to him, "I will not go. I will depart to my own land and to my kindred." And he said, "Please do not leave us, for you know where we should camp in the wilderness, and you will serve as eyes for us. And if you do go with us, whatever good the LORD will do to us, the same will we do to you." (Num. 10:29–32)

I have great brother-in-law whom I have worked with closely over most of my adult life. He has spearheaded business efforts for the law firm and family, and it has been a great blessing. I would like to think that Kevin worked with me because I was smart enough and glib enough to convince him to do so or maybe because he was wise enough to know he could do a great job. But that would not be the real and true story. That would be a very earthly way to see things.

Instead, the clearest truth is that God has made my brother-in-law with the skill set to do this fine work, and God has structured this life in such a way that Kevin and I had this chance to work together, and we both understood it was what God was leading us to do.

My experience readily comes to mind when reading today's passage. Moses has been working closely with his brother-in-law Hobab, a brother to his wife. Hobab wasn't an Israelite, but he was invaluable to Moses nonetheless. As Moses was planning the departure from areas around Sinai, a mountain near where Hobab's family kept their flocks, Hobab was going to stay behind. The Israelites could go to their Promised Land, and Hobab could stay in his. Moses asked Hobab to come with the Israelites, promising that he would be treated like any of the rest. Hobab demurred, but Moses then pleaded, asking, "How else will we know where to go or camp in the wilderness?" Hobab finally agreed.

I like the interplay here. God put Hobab into Moses' life, and it was a major way that Moses knew how to handle the wilderness. Moses could have taken the easy way out and let Hobab go, knowing that God would show the people where to camp and where to stay. Instead, Moses knew that God had a role for Hobab in that regard.

There is an interplay for us between prayerful following of God and personal responsibility. God expects us to do our best, use our resources, think through situations, and live honoring his name. None of us are his puppets. We are his followers and servants. But we are also incredible beings with minds and wills. He wants us to use our minds, growing and renewing them to conform to his will. Don't ever think we are God's puppet show. We are his people. That is different.

Lord, help me to see the resources you give me. May I use them in your name, amen.

SEPTEMBER 6

And the people complained in the hearing of the LORD about their misfortunes, and when the LORD heard it, his anger was kindled, and the fire of the LORD burned among them and consumed some outlying parts of the camp. Then the people cried out to Moses, and Moses prayed to the LORD, and the fire died down. (Num. 11:1–2)

A sitcom in the 1980s called *Newhart* featured Bob Newhart running a small inn in Vermont. Julia Duffy played a spoiled rich girl whose father had given her everything, yet she found herself working as a maid in the inn. She was haughty and clearly never left her expectation of the finest things in life. At one point, the main characters were facing some monumental problems. Meanwhile, something really minor happened to the high-bred brat (akin to breaking a fingernail), and she exclaimed, "Why does everything happen to me?" The absurdity of the comment made everyone laugh.

There is almost the same absurdity in today's passage, but it is no laughing matter. The Israelites have been on the receiving end of some of the most spectacular human interactions with the Almighty God: an unexpected rescue from the powerful pharaoh of Egypt, complete with ten miracles of plagues; a miraculous parting of the Re(e)d Sea, saving the people from Pharaoh's army; miraculous feeding of manna on a near-daily basis; an obvious visible presence of God in their midst; and a physical dispensation of God's laws and commands. All of these things are aside from having one of history's greatest leaders taking charge and guiding Israel through all of this. Yet in spite of this, the Israelites were overflowing with dissatisfaction and discontent.

They complained, grumbled, expressed disrespect to God, and embodied ingratitude. Again, if it wasn't real, if it wasn't a true slap in the face of God, it would almost seem sitcom funny. Another reason it isn't funny, however, is it sometimes hits a little too close to home.

God has blessed me beyond measure. I am breathing. That alone is a blessing. Look at life and start making a list of your blessings. Family? Friends? A job? Food? A song in your heart? Health? Education? Opportunity? A walk with the Almighty? A Bible to read? Entertainment to watch? Maybe you have all of those blessings, maybe just a few. Regardless, you can always know that you have purpose under God's care, and you have his presence available to call on to achieve what he has planned. Yet one thing or another can happen and we suddenly quake. We wonder, "Why does everything happen to me?"

I don't want to be that way. I don't want an attitude of ingratitude. I don't want to be like a tall blade of grass that blows one way and then the other in the wind. I want to be solid in my faith, seeking God's best and trusting him to lead me there.

Lord, forgive my grumbling. Teach me to trust you. In your name, amen.

SEPTEMBER 7

"I am not able to carry all this people alone; the burden is too heavy for me. If you will treat me like this, kill me at once, if I find favor in your sight, that I may not see my wretchedness." Then the LORD said to Moses, "Gather for me seventy men of the elders of Israel, whom you know to be the elders of the people and officers over them, and bring them to the tent of meeting, and let them take their stand there with you. And I will come down and talk with you there. And I will take some of the Spirit that is on you and put it on them, and they shall bear the burden of the people with you, so that you may not bear it yourself alone." (Num. 11:14–17)

Life has heavy burdens. Some are part of life. Some come from our wandering into places we don't belong. Some even come from our best efforts to serve God. Regardless of where the burdens come from, we never have to bear them alone. God wants to take our burdens from us and give us a load that we can bear without strain.

Moses had been carrying a load for a long time. He was the reluctant prophet God sent to confront Pharaoh and the gods of Egypt. It was a strain and something he didn't want to do. Yet he did it, although it took a lot out of him. He then was responsible for leading an entire nation on a very tough journey. Along the way, he had to be the warrior general. He had to be the judge discerning and ruling right from wrong in the disputes of the people. Moses was the one chosen to hear the voice of God and repeat God's instructions to the people. Moses had the burden of taking the people's complaints to God. Moses was overloaded with responsibility. We should note that Moses was no young pup. He was well into old age as he did these things. At an age where most people should be taking naps, Moses was burning both ends of the candle.

At one point, it got too much for Moses. He went to God, and with an ancient form of "burnout," Moses fell flat. "I can't do this alone!" He told God the burden was too great. Moses was finished. He would have been happy if God had taken him then and there. But God wasn't through with Moses.

God wasn't ignoring Moses. God met Moses in his moment of need, and God gave Moses a solution. God explained to Moses how to find those that God had appointed to help bear Moses' burdens. God was always there to help with the load; Moses had just failed to ask.

Jesus explained this attitude of God. He called those who are "weary" and "heavy laden," offering them rest. Jesus had a light yoke, and his followers could trust God to take care of their worries. We can too. God will not let us down.

Lord, I do get weary at times, and I pray that I will never needlessly carry a burden without your help. Please give me faith and strength. In your name, amen.

SEPTEMBER 8

"Say to the people, 'Consecrate yourselves for tomorrow, and you shall eat meat, for you have wept in the hearing of the LORD, saying, "Who will give us meat to eat? For it was better for us in Egypt." Therefore the LORD will give you meat, and you shall eat. You shall not eat just one day, or two days, or five days, or ten days, or twenty days, but a whole month, until it comes out at your nostrils and becomes loathsome to you, because you have rejected the LORD who is among you and have wept before him, saying, "Why did we come out of Egypt?"'" (Num. 11:18–20)

Look up the word *ingrate*. It is a noun from the Latin *ingratus*. It means "ungrateful." If you have a picture dictionary, it might have a picture of Israel at the time of Moses. But don't get haughty over it. It might have a picture of you and me too.

The Israelites had been slaves in Egypt. As slaves, they ate on slave rations and what they could manage to grow or raise on their own. The food would have been meager at best. The work was horrendous. Their rights were few. Their future was more of the same. Then God came to their rescue. He delivered them from Egypt by mighty works. He softened the hearts of the Egyptians such that they gave the Israelites gifts and treasures before the departure. Pharaoh's army pursued, and when all looked lost, God defeated the army miraculously, without one Israelite getting scraped. As the Israelites moved through the wilderness, they were fed manna six days a week, with food for the seventh day coming from a double portion on day six. The Israelites should have been dancing a jig of gratitude each day and night, but instead they started whining and complaining. They wanted meat!

How ungrateful! Their whining finally got to the point that God said, "You want meat? Get ready! You're going to get meat. You're getting so much meat that it's going to make you sick!" God recognized that the whining was a sound that came from a deep problem. The Israelites were rejecting God, and it was evidenced by their ingratitude.

I read this story, think about this passage, am appalled at the Israelites, and then get concerned. I can look in the mirror and see that I am ungrateful for many, many things I have received from God. I am guilty of challenging him at times with my whining and complaining, "I want this and I want that . . ."

The moral from today's passage is that we'd best not reject God through our ingratitude. We'd best be careful as we ask him for things, making sure we ask from a thankful heart. As the Israelites learned, "Be careful what you ask for; you might get it!"

Lord, thank you for so much in this life. Forgive me when I whine and complain. You are gracious beyond measure, and I often fail to rest in your blessings as I should—with a grateful heart and with thanks in my prayers. In your name, amen.

SEPTEMBER 9

And the LORD said to Moses, "Is the LORD's hand shortened? Now you shall see whether my word will come true for you or not."... And a young man ran and told Moses, "Eldad and Medad are prophesying in the camp." And Joshua the son of Nun, the assistant of Moses from his youth, said, "My lord Moses, stop them." But Moses said to him, "Are you jealous for my sake? Would that all the LORD's people were prophets, that the LORD would put his Spirit on them!" (Num. 11:23, 27–29)

A decade or so ago, *Psychology Today* published an article entitled "Jealousy Is a Killer." The author spoke of many problems arising from jealousy. It ends relationships. It brings out destructive behavior. It reduces our ability to function at a high level. It can even lead to crime and violence. Human jealousy, as we use the word today, is closely related to anger, agitation, and worry. (We should not confuse our term *jealousy* with the biblical idea of God as a jealous God. The Hebrew idea is much different.) Human jealousy is not only not productive; it is destructive.

Moses was a model of one who was *not* jealous, even when most would have found jealousy justified. He had lived his adult life seeking to stay out of the limelight. When God forced him into a leadership role he really didn't want, he went, but he went reluctantly. This was a responsibility that was wearing Moses out, physically and emotionally. He was never fully comfortable in the role, often finding himself in the middle between God and the people.

In the midst of God working among the people as Moses had heard and declared, a lad came running up to Moses, reporting that two other fellows were also speaking for God in the camp. This news upset Joshua. Joshua had been Moses' assistant for a long time, and Joshua was none too happy. He counseled Moses to stop those people immediately.

Many people would have felt a jealous response. God was what made Moses special. Without God's voice, Moses was just an old shepherd way past his prime. It was God who made Moses unique, who gave Moses his identity. This could make even the most righteous man jealous.

But not Moses. Moses wasn't worried about God speaking through others. This was never about Moses. This was about God. God had a message and Moses was the reluctant prophet. If God's message could come out through others, Moses was at peace. Moses just wanted God's voice heard.

I wish I were as good at prioritizing God's plans and words. I wish I were as good at putting myself far distant from things that don't really matter. I have work to do!

Lord, forgive me often making things about me instead of you. In your name, amen.

SEPTEMBER 10

The LORD spoke to Moses, saying, "Send men to spy out the land of Canaan, which I am giving to the people of Israel. From each tribe of their fathers you shall send a man, every one a chief among them." So Moses sent . . . Shammua the son of Zaccur . . . Shaphat the son of Hori . . . Caleb the son of Jephunneh . . . Igal the son of Joseph . . . Hoshea the son of Nun . . . Palti the son of Raphu . . . Gaddiel the son of Sodi . . . Gaddi the son of Susi . . . Ammiel the son of Gemalli . . . Sethur the son of Michael . . . Nahbi the son of Vophsi . . . Geuel the son of Machi. . . . And Moses called Hoshea the son of Nun Joshua. (Num. 13:1-16)

Have you ever met a Shammua? How about a Jephunneh or Palti? I haven't. Have you ever met a Caleb or Joshua? I have! Several of the names in today's passage have passed into obscurity and history. Several have become significant and are still routinely used over three thousand years later.

Why is this so? For some of the names, we might suspect it is the concern over a child ever learning to spell it ("Jephunneh"?), but "Igal" and others are easily spelled. We might think it is because some sound better than others, but I'm not sure "Caleb" sounds that much better than "Sethur."

These names aren't simply labels; they stand for the deeds known behind the names. Some people do things that get associated with their names, and further generations don't want to saddle their children with the associations. Hence, after World War II, most Germans didn't name their sons Adolf, even though it was a very popular name prior to and during the war. Some names carry a stench that lasts beyond a few generations, even as deep as thousands of years. Few people still today, at least among those familiar with the biblical stories, will name their daughters Jezebel.

The twelve people listed above were chosen to go into the Promised Land to discover its blessings, to spy out the inhabitants and their defenses, and to report back to Moses and the military leaders. Ten of the twelve came back scared of what they saw. Even though God Almighty had promised to deliver the land, their cowardice trumped their faith. Joshua and Caleb let faith rule their decisions.

Ten names got lost in history. Two names lived on. I'm not sure life will find any of us famous in this life or later, but people are always watching. Do we want to be known for fear and cowardice or faith and confidence?

Lord, grow me in faith. I don't want to be defined by my cowardice and fear. I want to be strong in my confidence in you. I want "In God We Trust" to be more than a slogan. I want to live it daily. In your name, amen.

SEPTEMBER 11

Moses sent them to spy out the land of Canaan and said to them, "Go up into the Negeb and go up into the hill country, and see what the land is, and whether the people who dwell in it are strong or weak, whether they are few or many, and whether the land that they dwell in is good or bad, and whether the cities that they dwell in are camps or strongholds, and whether the land is rich or poor, and whether there are trees in it or not. Be of good courage and bring some of the fruit of the land." . . . At the end of forty days they returned from spying out the land. And they came to Moses and Aaron and to all the congregation of the people of Israel . . . Caleb quieted the people before Moses and said, "Let us go up at once and occupy it, for we are well able to overcome it." Then the men who had gone up with him said, "We are not able to go up against the people, for they are stronger than we are." (Num. 13:17–31)

Some people are natural-born leaders. Others have to work to develop leadership traits. But in our interconnected world, everyone, regardless of her or his natural skill level, is a leader to some degree or another. People will watch you and look for you to give insight and wisdom into how to live.

In practical terms, "leadership" means living in such a way that you are a source for others' inspiration. You show them what should or can be done. You give them ideas. You give them encouragement to do one thing or another. You might be bold about it, or you might not even realize it is happening, but you will affect the actions of others.

Today's passage explores the actions of clear leaders within the Israelite community. These are people who were selected to do a job—spy out the land—by Moses and others. These were leaders. When they came back, they showed a huge lack of faith in God. Their fear was like a contagious flu that was quickly transmitted throughout the community. They tainted the faith of others, and they were directly responsible for a devastating lack of trust in God.

Leadership carries a responsibility. How we lead affects others. We need to be conscious that our lives are often under a magnifying glass. When we live with a demonstrable faith, others will be inspired. When we live cowering from fear, others will be fearful. Life isn't a solo show where our actions affect only ourselves.

This raises an important question of self-examination. What kind leaders are we? When people watch us, listen to us, or examine us, what do they see? How will we affect them? I need to think about this and be a lot more careful.

Lord, may my life reflect a vibrant and confident faith in you. May I inspire others to trust you deeply. In your name, amen.

SEPTEMBER 12

Then all the congregation raised a loud cry, and the people wept that night. And all the people of Israel grumbled against Moses and Aaron. The whole congregation said to them, "Would that we had died in the land of Egypt! Or would that we had died in this wilderness! Why is the LORD bringing us into this land, to fall by the sword? Our wives and our little ones will become a prey. Would it not be better for us to go back to Egypt?" And they said to one another, "Let us choose a leader and go back to Egypt." (Num. 14:1–4)

It happens to all of us. Some days are easy and good, but other days are harsh and tough. How we react to the days that are tough defines us and our faith. Those days are thermometer moments spiritually. They allow us to determine our spiritual health. We can tell if we are running a fever or not.

Today's passage records the reactions of the faithless people to the news that the spies believed the inhabitants of the Promised Land were too powerful for Israel to overcome. This was difficult news that challenged the people. These were people that were faithful when the days were good. When God supplied them manna in the wilderness and protection from Pharaoh's army, these people were happy and rejoicing. But once they were faced with news that incited fear, their faith vanished. Their thermometer showed them spiritually sick.

The right reaction to the time of difficulty would have been to fall on their knees before God, imploring his intervention and declaring their trust in him. Instead, they were ready for mutiny. They were ready to dispose of Moses and his God and get another leader who could take them back to Egypt, the land where they had been abused as slaves.

This story unfolds in our lives. There are times when life is very difficult. The Psalms demonstrate that it is OK to question God when times get rough, but it should be done respectfully. It should be done in faith. We need to be careful that we don't join our questioning with a decision to go our own way.

Thermometers don't dictate our temperature; they tell us what is already true. In this sense, it wasn't the moment of crisis that turned the Israelites faithless. The moment of crisis demonstrated their faithlessness. We should live carefully so when the crisis sits before us, we don't flee. Instead we confront it in faith, entrusting ourselves to the Lord.

Lord, I tend to worry about things that should not concern me, at least not as much as they do. Please forgive my moments of doubt and help me to learn to walk humbly and with trust in you and your name. Amen.

SEPTEMBER 13

"The land, which we passed through to spy it out, is an exceedingly good land. If the LORD delights in us, he will bring us into this land and give it to us, a land that flows with milk and honey. Only do not rebel against the LORD. And do not fear the people of the land, for they are bread for us. Their protection is removed from them, and the LORD is with us; do not fear them." (Num. 14:7-9)

Have you ever talked with someone who almost seems like he or she is from another planet? You may speak the same language, but the conversation seems like two ships passing in the night. I am hesitant to impute human emotions to God, and he certainly doesn't have human limitations, but otherwise, it would not be surprising to me if God didn't feel similarly at times.

Moses and the Israelite leaders sent twelve handpicked men into the land of Canaan to spy on the land prior to military conquest. God had told the people that this land would be amazing, a land flowing with milk and honey. The spies went into the land. They appraised the cities and fields. They looked at the crops (and stole some as an example). They carefully studied the men they would have to fight. Then the spies returned, with ten of the twelve quivering with fear. They scared all of Israel with reports of, "The people are giants!" "The cities are protected!" "Yes, the crops are massive and abundant, but we don't stand a chance in a military campaign!"

I wonder what the people were thinking beforehand. Of course the land was occupied by strong people! God was giving them great land! Did they actually think that there would be fantastic land with fantastic crops under the oversight of weak people who would be easily overrun? The mindset of the people must have been incredibly naïve, or more likely, the people hadn't really thought the situation through.

The Israelites were never going to win the land through military conquest. They couldn't even leave Egypt without God's strong intervention. This was choice land, guarded and owned by really strong people. If it had been controlled by weak people, someone strong would have already overrun it, and then the strong people would have remained. It is only logical. The key is that Canaan was "the Promised Land." God promised the land and God would deliver it. As the two faithful spies reported in today's passage, it was a great land, and it would be delivered to Israel by a great God.

I think I have a tendency to see the world through human eyes. I need better vision. I want my thoughts to align with God and not be a ship passing in the night.

Lord, give me your vision to see the world, to see myself, and to see you as I should. Then influence me to live faithfully in your might. In your name, amen.

SEPTEMBER 14

And the LORD said to Moses, "How long will this people despise me? And how long will they not believe in me, in spite of all the signs that I have done among them?" (Num. 14:11)

I meet a lot of people who do not believe in God. I am somewhat amazed. Some tell me they don't believe in God because they believe in evolution. When I inform them that respectable Bible-believing people believe in God and evolution, they are stunned. I then say, "So aside from evolution, why don't you believe in God?" There are many reasons given, but generally they boil down to three: (1) they've had a bad personal experience that they believe a good God would not have allowed, (2) they have some emotional or visceral reason that precludes their belief, or (3) they just haven't thought much about it.

Today's passage probably doesn't change anyone's mind, but it should. God placed into his conversation the recognition that many don't believe in him because they "despise" God. This attitude is akin to emotional reactions that come from bad personal experiences or some other visceral reaction. God then pointed to the positive. He noted this was in spite of all God had done among them.

Consider the implication of God's statement in today's passage to the modern mind-set of disbelief. Someone might not believe God because the person has endured atrocious abuse. "How could a good God allow that?" the person thinks. Often unspoken is the next layer of thought: "Even if there is a God, I wouldn't want to believe in him if he allowed that." This isn't an intelligent unbelief. It is an emotional unbelief. It is like that of the Israelites in today's passage.

God asks the question, Why do the people ignore all God has done? Yes, there are horrible things that happen to everyone, some worse than others. There is no doubt about that, and none of that should be minimized. It should be a cause for mourning and even anger. But there is more to the story. There are marvelous things that happen to everyone also. If God (or the absence of God) is going to get the blame for the bad, why doesn't he get credit for the good? Why do we believe the good is self-earned, or simple luck, but the bad is evidence there is no God (or emotional justification for denying him)?

This is the key to the passage today. There is a God, whether we believe in him or not. There are bad things that happen, but he is in the business of redemption. He promises to take the bad and bring good out of it somehow. There is also much good that happens, and we should be giving credit to him for that. Let us not refuse a belief in God without carefully considering life. Belief should not be driven by emotions or feelings.

Lord, give me eyes to see you, a heart to believe in you, and a mind to understand you. In your name, amen.

SEPTEMBER 15

"None of those who despised me shall see it. But my servant Caleb, because he has a different spirit and has followed me fully, I will bring into the land into which he went, and his descendants shall possess it." (Num. 14:23-24)

When I read the Bible, I often find myself injecting my own life into the circumstances of biblical characters. I ask myself, "What would I do in that situation?" Some of the characters become heroes. They are the people I'd like to be, doing things I'd like to do. Some of them aren't so much heroes as they are characters I'd rather not be! I learn from positive influences (be like them) and negative influences (don't be like them).

Caleb is a positive influence. He was one of the twelve spies sent by Moses into Canaan to uncover important information about the land and its people prior to the Israelite invasion. The land was terrific, but the people were terrifying. The spies returned to give their report, and the consensus opinion was that the Israelites didn't stand a chance. The cities were too fortified, the inhabitants were too strong, and the Israelites were too scared.

While the majority (ten of the twelve) gave this fearful report, Caleb had the faith to see the situation differently. He also had the fortitude to stand up and be heard, advocating what he believed, even though it ran against the majority opinion. This was an amazing display for the young man, and it brought good results for him.

Everyone is faced with lifetime decisions that call for a full evaluation of the situation, the parties involved, and the possible results. Scripture teaches us that we are to be thoughtful about such things, as we see from Moses sending out spies in the first place. We are to prayerfully consider the situation, something else Moses did as he sought out God's plan for the people. Then, when we understand what God wants us to do, we are to act out of faith, trusting in God to take care of the consequences.

The people did the first two things. They went out as spies to assess the situation thoughtfully. They also had Moses talk to the Lord about it, seeking God's counsel in prayer. Where the people failed was step three. They didn't follow through in trust that God was up to what God promised. The people let fear trump faith.

Caleb wasn't like the rest. He and only one other (Joshua) stood up against all the other spies and urged the people to faithfully trust and follow God. After the events unfolded, God announced that all of the unfaithful spies would not enter the Promised Land. Neither would those who followed the unfaithful spies and refused to enter. Caleb and Joshua, however, would be blessed to enter the land before they died. I want to be like Caleb.

Lord, give me wisdom, faith, and strength to follow you. In your name, amen.

SEPTEMBER 16

When Moses told these words to all the people of Israel, the people mourned greatly. (Num. 14:39)

Society is not short of people offering answers to life. In most any city, for ten bucks you can get your fortune read. You can read a horoscope for free on the Internet or in a paper. You can find people giving advice in self-help books. Social media has opened up a wealth of places for advice. There are professional counselors, semiprofessional counselors, and counselors who are rank amateurs! Of course, many of our friends and even acquaintances are often quick to give us advice with our problems.

A question that arises from the background behind today's text is "Who are you going to listen to?" The background: Moses sent twelve spies to discover the strengths and weaknesses of Canaan before Israel invaded. Ten spies came back selling the people a line of fear. Two spies returned selling a line of faith and confidence in God. Most all of the people listened to the fearmongers, not the faithful, and Israel balked about going into the Promised Land.

God was immediate in pronouncing his judgment. The people who were frightened and embraced the naysayers were doomed to wander in the wilderness for forty years, never setting foot in the Promised Land. Today's passage is found after the people had heard this judgment. The people "mourned greatly," and then some of the less bright ones decided that if God was punishing the unfaithful, they would invade Canaan on their own. Moses pointed out that this idea was foolish and their efforts would meet doom under the rubric of "too little too late." But the people went out to battle the next morning anyway. The Israelites were slaughtered.

These people had a problem listening. They failed to listen to God about the initial invasion—strike one. When the spies returned, the people listened to the ten fearful folks rather than the faithful ones—strike two. Then, when the people decided to invade and Moses told them an invasion at that point was doomed to failure, they went anyway—strike three. The third strike was the final one.

I need to be careful about the people to whom I listen. Even the sturdiest of wills can be swayed by advice from others. I want to make sure I am listening to people who are well grounded in their faith and whose lives show that they are making wise, godly choices. I may not always follow the advice, for I still have to make the decision myself, but I know the advice stems from a faithful heart, and that makes a difference.

Lord, give me good counselors, and help me to be a good counselor to those in need. In your name, amen.

SEPTEMBER 17

And they rose up before Moses, with a number of the people of Israel, 250 chiefs of the congregation, chosen from the assembly, well-known men. They assembled themselves together against Moses and against Aaron and said to them, "You have gone too far! For all in the congregation are holy, every one of them, and the LORD is among them. Why then do you exalt yourselves above the assembly of the LORD?" (Num. 16:2–3)

Webster's dictionary defines *disease* as "a condition of the living animal . . . or of one of its parts that impairs normal functioning and is typically manifested by distinguishing signs and symptoms." A contagious disease is one that is transmittable from one person to another. We generally think of diseases as medical conditions such as the flu or a cold. Today's passage is rooted in a different contagious disease, one more insidious than the flu. This disease is envy.

If we use Webster's definition of *envy* as "a resentful awareness of an advantage enjoyed by another joined with a desire to possess the same advantage," then we have a classic case in the storyline behind today's passage. The disease of envy began with Korah, a man from the Kohath family line and the tribe of Levi along with several others, including Dathan and Abiram from the tribe of Reuben. These men, who camped next to each other in the camps as laid out during Israel's wilderness wanderings, were envious of the special roles God gave Moses and Aaron. The envy was clear: a resentful awareness of a role that they desired to have.

This resentment spread like the contagious disease it was, and soon, 250 chiefs among the Israelites were turned to the same envy. The large group gathered and came to Moses and Aaron in the presence of the larger congregation, challenging their leadership. The mutinous mass had a very "fair" sounding message. "Why do you have special roles of holiness that set you apart from the rest of the congregation? Everyone should be regarded as holy."

This was not a humble concern. It came out of hearts of envy. These were people who didn't understand or didn't regard God's role in things. They saw the entire organization of Israel as a concoction of Moses and Aaron. They didn't like it, and they wanted it to be different. They believed they had the necessary skill set, and they were demanding that they be given the equal chance to complete the tasks. This didn't turn out well for them. They soon saw the power of God. They suffered, and so did the others who caught the disease.

Unlike the flu or a cold, envy is a disease of choice. We have a role in becoming envious and choosing how to act when we feel envy. We need to be cured and not spread it around!

Lord, please take any envy from my heart. May I embrace you. In your name, amen.

SEPTEMBER 18

And Moses sent to call Dathan and Abiram the sons of Eliab, and they said, "We will not come up. Is it a small thing that you have brought us up out of a land flowing with milk and honey, to kill us in the wilderness, that you must also make yourself a prince over us? Moreover, you have not brought us into a land flowing with milk and honey, nor given us inheritance of fields and vineyards. Will you put out the eyes of these men? We will not come up." (Num. 16:12–14)

Making my living in the courtroom, I am constantly at odds with the opposing parties, their lawyers, and sometimes even with judges. Most of the time, the confrontations are respectful. We disagree. We both think we are right and the other wrong. But we are able to disagree and present the evidence and law without treating one another like contemptible sewer rats.

Occasionally, circumstances and behavior rise to a point where decorum suffers. At some point respect is lost, and while formality may dictate a threshold level of civility, disrespect still shows around the edges. Today's passage goes far beyond what we normally see, and the shock to the reader is the realization that the real object of scorn and disrespect isn't Moses. It is God.

Dathan, Abiram, and others decided that they were unhappy with the roles God gave them in Israel's society and government. They started a rebellion against Moses and Aaron. Moses called Dathan and Abiram to discuss the mutiny, and the men refused to even come talk to Moses. When summoned, they responded that Moses was a failure as a leader, he hadn't delivered on taking them to a land of milk and honey, he had failed to deliver on giving them homesteads and farms, and he was likely leading them to their deaths in the wilderness. They made it plain that they wouldn't even deign to give Moses an audience.

SPOILER ALERT: Dathan and Abiram get killed in a most demonstrative way. Regrettably, they failed to come to Moses in a constructive way, explain what they believed to be real concerns, and try to learn or come to a constructive resolution. Instead they fostered their envy, spread discontent among the masses, treated Moses and Aaron contemptuously, and brought ruin upon themselves, their families, and their followers.

I read this and am appalled at the open rebellion against God and his leaders. But whenever I get appalled at something, alarm bells sound in my head because I might be blind to how close I get to a similar behavior. Now I haven't fostered open rebellion against God to my knowledge, but I do know that my actions can speak volumes about how I see God. And those actions aren't always good. I want to do better!

Lord, forgive my rebellious heart. Lead me in obedience. In your name, amen.

SEPTEMBER 19

They assembled themselves together against Moses and against Aaron and said . . . "You have gone too far!" . . . When Moses heard it . . . he said to Korah . . . "You have gone too far, sons of Levi!" . . . "Hear now, you sons of Levi: is it too small a thing for you that the God of Israel has separated you from the congregation of Israel, to bring you near to himself?" . . . Dathan and Abiram the sons of Eliab said to Moses, ". . . Is it a small thing that you have brought us up out of a land flowing with milk and honey, to kill us in the wilderness, that you must also make yourself a prince over us? Moreover, you have not brought us into a land flowing with milk and honey . . . Will you put out the eyes of these men?" (Num. 16:3–14)

Have you ever met someone who twists everything you say? Maybe it's because I practice courtroom law, but I have come across my fair share. These are people who can take a positive comment and turn it into something sinister. They purposely misconstrue statements to serve their own purposes. It is not only frustrating but also damaging. In trial, I spend 20 percent of my time trying to clarify such efforts to confuse and mislead.

Today's passage shows this going on over three thousand years ago. This twisting of words was not motivated by winning a lawsuit; it stemmed from rebellious hearts. Korah, Dathan, and Abiram instigated a rebellion against Moses and Aaron. The dialogue shows their twisted thinking. The defiant Israelites began accusing Moses and Aaron of having "gone too far." They had it wrong. Moses pointed out that the rebels were the ones who had "gone too far." They needed to repent. Ostensibly the rebellion was over the malcontents being given lesser responsibilities than they wanted. They were envious of Moses and Aaron's status in the community. Moses explained that they had important jobs, saying, "Is it too small a thing that . . . ?" and then listing what God gave them to do. Continuing in their defiance, Dathan and Abiram twisted Moses' words and responded to him, "Is it too small a thing that . . . ?" citing where they believed Moses had failed. The twisting of ideas and words continued as they pointed out that Moses failed to live up to his promise to bring them to a land of milk and honey. (Never mind that it was the people's lack of faith that precluded entrance into the Promised Land.) Instead they claimed Moses *pulled* them from a land of milk and honey. Then the rebellious men added, "Will you put out the eyes of these men?" That was an idiomatic expression akin to "Are you going to pull the wool over their eyes?" They insinuated Moses was deceiving the masses.

When one rebels against God, it affects the way one thinks, especially about him. The rebellious may think themselves sharp and cute, but they aren't. The twisted mind of the rebellious leads to death. Each of the above rebellious characters is destroyed by the time the story ends. I don't want to be rebellious!

Lord, please give me a clear, obedient mind for you and your will. In your name, amen.

SEPTEMBER 20

Then Moses rose and went to Dathan and Abiram, and the elders of Israel followed him. And he spoke to the congregation, saying, "Depart, please, from the tents of these wicked men, and touch nothing of theirs, lest you be swept away with all their sins." So they got away from the dwelling of Korah, Dathan, and Abiram. And Dathan and Abiram came out and stood at the door of their tents, together with their wives, their sons, and their little ones. And Moses said, "Hereby you shall know that the LORD has sent me to do all these works, and that it has not been of my own accord." (Num. 16:25–28)

Some people live at a distance from God. They don't spend time getting to know him, and then in their ignorance, they believe they have a good grasp of reality, including whether there is a God and what that God must be or think. This ignorance about God comes from superficially reading the Bible. For the Christian, it also means ignoring the depth of insight we get into God by studying the life of Jesus, God's Son.

We see this ignorance and its effect in today's passage. Dathan, Abiram, and Korah have instigated a rebellion against Moses and Aaron, seeking the positions of leadership held by those two. What the rebellious didn't grasp was that God called Moses and Aaron into their roles. This was not two alpha males trying to lord positions over the rest of the community. This was a work of God. Moses had called them to counsel on the issue, and they refused. Moses had tried talking sense to them, and they twisted his words against him. Finally, with open sedition and no chance of change, Moses declared judgment on them. Moses instructed the rest of the community to separate from the rebellious, in clear anticipation that something drastic was about to happen. Dathan and Abiram, still brazenly defiant, came out of their tents and stood there facing Moses. This was itself an inherent taunt. It was them saying, "What are you going to do about it, old man?" (Moses was well past eighty years old.)

Moses did nothing to them, but God did. Once Moses declared God's judgment, God caused the ground to open up and swallow every indication that the rebellious had even been there. They, their families, their supporters, their tents and possessions—all were swallowed up in the ground. It is sad to me, in the same way I find sadness even in the judgment on horrible people in recent history. Hitler was as bad a human as we can think of. As judgment came on him, countless children and others were hurt in the process. I don't blame the liberating armies for this; I blame Hitler. I don't blame God; I blame Hitler. Could God have intervened and bent the laws of nature to protect the children during judgment? It doesn't generally work that way. Dathan and Abiram, or Hitler for that matter, could have sent the children out of harm's way, but they chose not to. We are left seeing that those clueless of God have no fear of God.

Lord, may I see you, understand you, fear you, and love you. In your name, amen.

SEPTEMBER 21

And the LORD *spoke to Moses, saying, "Say to the congregation, Get away from the dwelling of Korah, Dathan, and Abiram."* . . . *So they got away from the dwelling of Korah, Dathan, and Abiram. And Dathan and Abiram came out and stood at the door of their tents, together with their wives, their sons, and their little ones.* (Num. 16:23–27)

When we set ourselves against God, even if we don't realize it, we are setting ourselves up as God. This might not make sense without some explanation. Many people today will declare that God isn't real. They know better, or so they think. These people believe that their three-and-a-half-pound brains, clumps of gray cells about the size of one's fist, have considered and thought through the universe and reality and fairly concluded that there is no God, at least in the sense that God has claimed to have revealed himself through the Bible. God is gone, and their minds reign supreme. They are the highest and greatest thing. In a sense, even though unaware, they have set themselves up as God the Supreme.

Today's passage explains this through carefully written Hebrew. We may not notice it reading the passage in English, however. The key to understanding this is in a Hebrew word, *mishkan.* This word in its singular form is used over one hundred times in the Torah, always referring to the tabernacle, the "dwelling" of God among his people. It is occasionally used in the plural form, and then it is referring to the dwellings of people (e.g., "How lovely are your tents, O Jacob, your encampments [plural of *mishkan*], O Israel!" [Num. 24:5]). In today's passage, *twice* the dwellings of the rebellious Korah, Dathan, and Abiram are referred to with *mishkan* in the singular. The Torah is telling us that these people stood present in front of their own tabernacles as their own gods, even as Moses stood before *the* tabernacle as the representative of *the* God.

The rebellious got it all wrong. They were called to serve God. God had assigned Korah's clan the important tasks guarding the ark of the covenant and other holy articles (Num. 3:29–31). Instead, they wanted jobs they thought more prestigious, and they rebelled against Moses, Aaron, and God. They set themselves against God and stood outside their homes defiantly. The Torah makes it clear in Hebrew; they had made their own homes their god and temple, serving as they saw fit. But they had the wrong god and the wrong temple.

This is the way of many. If we set ourselves against God, we set ourselves up as God. Yet we aren't God. We never have been and we never will be. Rather than thinking we have it all figured out, it is much smarter to pull some humility up around our brains and set ourselves to learning more about who God really is. This will change our lives for the better. Wrong god = bad result. Right God = good result!

Lord, may I learn of you better and more fully. May I never set myself up as God, but may I seek the one true God instead. In your name, not mine! Amen!

SEPTEMBER 22

Then the LORD spoke to Moses, saying, "Tell Eleazar the son of Aaron the priest to take up the censers out of the blaze. Then scatter the fire far and wide, for they have become holy. As for the censers of these men who have sinned at the cost of their lives, let them be made into hammered plates as a covering for the altar, for they offered them before the LORD, and they became holy. Thus they shall be a sign to the people of Israel." (Num. 16:36–39)

Do you ever play the "what if?" game? What if I had chosen a different college? What if I had chosen a different job? What if . . . ? The possibilities are endless. Some of these "what ifs" also concern sin and errors. "What if I had never . . . ?"

Sin is not a good thing. It never has been and it never will be. Sin has bad repercussions. It always has had and always will have. Still, we must always remember that even in the midst of sin's harsh damage, God is able to rescue something serviceable for him and his kingdom. Today's passage illustrates this truth.

Korah, Dathan, and Abiram stirred up a community rebellion against Moses. Included among the rebellious were 250 leaders from various clans of Israel. The core of the rebellion was the issue of who got to do what tasks in service to God and the Israelites. The rebels didn't like the tasks being assigned to Aaron. Moses called them all to a showdown. They were told to come to the tabernacle the next morning, bringing their fire trays ("censers") and incense to burn to the Lord. Aaron would do the same. Moses told them all that God would show whom he had chosen.

The next morning the 250 came with incense in the fire trays. God devoured the 250 men that challenged Moses, Aaron, and God, leaving the fire trays rattling on the ground. After God finished dealing with the rest of the mutineers, he told Moses to have Aaron's son Eleazar take the trays of the sinful 250 and hammer them into a covering for the altar, "for they have become holy."

God used the remnants of the sinful rebellion to remind future Israelites of God's holiness, purity, and purpose for people. Everyone who looked onto the altar could see and learn of God. The scars of these burned vessels would indicate the sin and need for forgiveness from the holy God.

The sin in this story was not good or pretty. It was disastrous. But God still used the events to build up his kingdom and purpose for those with observant eyes and listening ears.

Father, I repent of my sins and pray for your forgiveness. I also ask you to redeem my sins and wrestle some good usage from them. In your name, amen.

SEPTEMBER 23

And the people of Israel said to Moses, "Behold, we perish, we are undone, we are all undone. Everyone who comes near, who comes near to the tabernacle of the LORD, shall die. Are we all to perish?" (Num. 17:12–13)

It is a good thing God has mercy, for his judgment is absolute. God's judgment presents a real predicament set up in the Torah. The beginning is, appropriately, in the book of beginnings. In Genesis, God created humans for a relationship. He placed them in a utopian garden called Eden, and God would walk in the garden and talk to Adam and Eve. God gave them great liberty and responsibility, making them custodians and caretakers of everything around them. God put only one restriction on them. The boundary was that they not eat of one particular tree. To do so would be rebellion by the couple. Rebellion against God brings one punishment—death. The people were warned.

Warning didn't do much good, however, because at some point, the people chose rebellion. They ate of the fruit. God could have destroyed them then and there, but instead God promised a way of redemption. God would satisfy his judgment another way. God's righteousness would be met by one born of woman. The relationship between God and people could be restored through this coming savior.

The predicament was set out in Genesis, and the theme of needed redemption from judgment is found over and over in the Torah and the Bible as a whole. In today's passage the people of Israel are worried about how they can survive God's judgment after God cleansed the camp of the rebels Korah, Dathan, Abiram, and others. They gave a threefold cry of despair: (1) we perish, (2) we are undone, and (3) we are all undone. Three was a symbol of the divine, and the judgment was indeed God's divine judgment. The three also corresponds to the actual number of judgments God executed. As the ancient Jewish explanation given two thousand years ago noted, "Behold some of us were killed by the sword" (Targum Onkelos 14:45), "some were swallowed up by the earth" (16:32), "while others died in the plague" (17:14).

What shall we do with the judgment of God? The Christian understanding is that in the sacrificial death of Jesus, there was a full atonement for the sins of humanity that met the full judgment of God. This allows a restored relationship between God and people. This is what made Jesus the Messiah, the meaning of the Greek word for "Christ."

Without Jesus, I am left atoning for my own sins or seeking a God that doesn't really punish sin. I don't find either of those options reasonable. Hence my belief system. I know God is a God of mercy, but he also executes full divine justice.

Lord, I fall at your feet seeking your forgiveness for my sin. I want to be in a relationship with you. Thank you for your mercy. In your name, amen.

SEPTEMBER 24

Now the Lord spoke to Moses and to Aaron, saying, "This is the statute of the law that the Lord has commanded: Tell the people of Israel to bring you a red heifer without defect, in which there is no blemish, and on which a yoke has never come." (Num. 19:1-2)

I can almost guarantee that no one reading this book is without someone else who holds authority over her or him. It may be in a job setting or at home. Perhaps it is in a church, synagogue, or organization. If nothing else, there are laws that play an authoritative role over us. We may not like it. We may rebel against it. It may run contrary to our nature, but it is reality. In this life, there are always rules that will apply to us, always an authority over us. Even the President of the United States has limitations.

Israel was going to have to make a service decision. Was Israel going to serve God or serve someone/something else? Were the Israelites going to serve their own complacency? Were they going to serve those in rebellion against God? Were they going to serve their common sense? Were they going to serve the pressure of friends? Were they going to serve their appetite? How about money? Or popularity? Maybe they would serve power. We all serve somebody or something.

In today's passage God sets out instructions for Israel dealing with issues of being unclean. Whether from coming into contact with dead people or objects around dead people, God set up a process for making one clean.

One might ask, "Why would God make someone unclean for touching a dead person? Why set out long rituals to make someone clean after becoming unclean?" God didn't provide an explanation. He just gave the Israelites instructions, and they got to choose whom they would serve.

If they had chosen to serve God, they would have minimized exposure to diseases and germs, though they would have had no idea. It would be millennia before anyone would know what a germ was. If they had chosen to serve God, their theology would have been better informed. They would have understood the close tie between sin and death. Death itself is "unclean," a synonym for something being ungodly. In other words, they would have realized that death was never God's goal for humanity, but death was the result of sin. It was a curse; it was never the highest and greatest good. They would have understood that sin and death breed sin and death. Consider that the price to be paid for someone being unclean was the sacrificial death of a beast. This is a cycle. One becomes unclean because of being in contact with a dead person, which is a result of sin, and that results in another death. Perhaps most importantly, they would have been expectant of some final sacrifice that was sufficient to clean all sin and uncleanness.

Lord, may I do a better job serving you, living under your blessings in your name. Amen.

SEPTEMBER 25

Now there was no water for the congregation. And they assembled themselves together against Moses and against Aaron. And the people quarreled with Moses and said, "Would that we had perished when our brothers perished before the LORD!" (Num. 20:2–3)

One of my dad's favorite movies was the musical *The Music Man*. He loved each song, but his particular favorite was "Ya Got Trouble." Dad would frequently break out into the song whenever trouble might arise in life. "Friend, either you're closing your eyes to a situation you do not wish to acknowledge or you are not aware of the caliber of disaster indicated . . . Ya got trouble, folks, right here in River City. Trouble with a capital 'T' and that rhymes with 'P' and that stands for pool!"

How do you respond to trouble? Most don't simply sing about it like Dad (though in fairness to him, that was not all he did!). Do you ever play the blame game, blaming the problem on someone else? A lot of people are quick to point their finger everywhere but at themselves. That was the approach of Israel. Even before we delve into what happened during this crisis of the Israelites (which we do in the next several devotions), we need to pause and look at what Israel was doing here.

Israel was nearing completion of a forty-year wandering in the wilderness. They were not in the wilderness because of anything Moses did or failed to do. Similarly, they shouldn't have been blaming God for the wilderness wanderings. The reason Israel was stuck in the wilderness for that length of time was because of the unbelief and betrayal of their parents and the generation that had a chance to invade the Promised Land as God instructed.

As the people endured the wilderness experience, they hit a point where their water supplies were depleted. They had trouble, with a capital T. Rather than admit the true source of the problem, they quarreled with Moses and Aaron. This is no way to deal with trouble.

As I was typing this, I interrupted the devotional writing to deal with an emergency at work. Trouble has arisen needing ASAP correction. The emergency is arguably my fault. I got to put this devotional to firsthand use in (1) admitting my error and (2) rather than casting blame, trying to figure out the best way to deal with the troublesome situation while also trying to ensure the problem doesn't arise again. That is the proper way to deal with capital-T Trouble!

Lord, I do make a lot of errors that lead to trouble. Please help me see the error of my ways, correct my mistakes, and walk in your wisdom and forgiveness. In your name, amen.

SEPTEMBER 26

The LORD spoke to Moses, saying, "Take the staff, and assemble the congregation, you and Aaron your brother, and tell the rock before their eyes to yield its water. So you shall bring water out of the rock for them and give drink to the congregation and their cattle." And Moses took the staff from before the LORD, as he commanded him. Then Moses and Aaron gathered the assembly together before the rock, and he said to them, "Hear now, you rebels: shall we bring water for you out of this rock?" And Moses lifted up his hand and struck the rock with his staff twice, and water came out abundantly, and the congregation drank, and their livestock. And the LORD said to Moses and Aaron, "Because you did not believe in me, to uphold me as holy in the eyes of the people of Israel, therefore you shall not bring this assembly into the land that I have given them." (Num. 20:7–12)

Ugh. Every time I read today's story, I get a bad feeling in my gut. This story is a sad event in the life of a marvelous man of God. Moses was getting quite old, and the Israelites were placing at his feet responsibility for their plight—lots of people, lots of livestock, lots of wilderness, and no water!

Moses did right in taking the matter to the Lord, but from there, Moses began failing miserably. God gave Moses clear instructions. Moses was to speak to the rock and God would see that the rock brought forth water. Moses didn't comply. Instead of speaking to the rock, Moses struck the rock twice with his staff. What makes matter worse, instead of speaking to the rock, Moses spoke to the Israelites, and his speech was one that made Moses and Aaron the center of the miracle, not God. Moses proclaimed, "Shall *we* bring water for you out of this rock?"

Moses, as marvelous and holy a man as Moses, stumbled in sin and became the god who was bringing out water. God still supplied the water. The people didn't perish. But God made it clear to Moses, Aaron, and the people that it was God who did it, not Moses and Aaron. God expressed this point and told Moses that neither Moses nor Aaron would be allowed to accompany Israel into the Promised Land. It would be plain to all of Israel that God was in charge, even of Moses. One God was over all Israel, not Moses and God.

Today's passage causes me deep reflection. Even Moses stumbled before the Lord in pride, and I am not remotely close to the holiness of Moses! I know I need to examine my life and objectively seek to follow God more closely. I need to make this life and what I do a testimony to him and not me. I need people to know that God is God, and I am honored to be his servant.

Lord, forgive me for my many times of pride and arrogance. Forgive me for failing to make my life always point to you. May I serve you better. In your name, amen.

SEPTEMBER 27

And the people of Israel, the whole congregation, came into the wilderness of Zin in the first month, and the people stayed in Kadesh. And Miriam died there and was buried there. . . . And the LORD said to Moses and Aaron at Mount Hor, on the border of the land of Edom, "Let Aaron be gathered to his people, for he shall not enter the land that I have given to the people of Israel, because you rebelled against my command at the waters of Meribah. Take Aaron and Eleazar his son and bring them up to Mount Hor. And strip Aaron of his garments and put them on Eleazar his son. And Aaron shall be gathered to his people and shall die there." Moses did as the LORD commanded. And they went up Mount Hor in the sight of all the congregation. And Moses stripped Aaron of his garments and put them on Eleazar his son. And Aaron died there on the top of the mountain. Then Moses and Eleazar came down from the mountain. (Num. 20:1, 23–28)

The Pink Floyd song "Time" begins with the sounds of ticking clocks and alarms. The lyrics begin, "Ticking away the moments that make up a dull day / You fritter and waste the hours in an offhand way . . . You are young and life is long and there is time to kill today / And then one day you find ten years have got behind you . . . And you run and you run to catch up with the sun but it's sinking / Shorter of breath and one day closer to death." David Gilmour and Richard Wright do a masterful job of describing the path so many take. Time moves on, whether we are conscious of it or not.

In today's passage, we read about Moses' two siblings dying. Miriam, his sister who saw him drawn out of the Nile by Pharaoh's daughter a lifetime earlier, dies and is buried in the wilderness. Then Aaron, Israel's first high priest, the first to wear the garments, the first to intervene with the Day of Atonement sacrifices, the only one to enter the Holy of Holies on behalf of the people, dies.

Death awaits us all, and while we may not consider that too much in our youth, it should cause us to think in two directions. First, how are we going to spend our time on earth? Are we careful and deliberate, making the most of our opportunities to love and serve the Lord? Do we spend our moments building up our families and those we love? Do we invest and build in the world to make it a better place?

Second, do we give regard to what happens when we die? Do we have a relationship with the one who exists beyond the grave? Have we found how his mercy coexists with his justice?

Time moves on. Live wisely today. Prepare to meet your maker. Prepare to leave earth.

Lord, make me aware of time. Let my life be lived wisely each day and in preparation for eternity in death with you. In your name, amen.

SEPTEMBER 28

From Mount Hor they set out by the way to the Red Sea, to go around the land of Edom. And the people became impatient on the way. And the people spoke against God and against Moses, "Why have you brought us up out of Egypt to die in the wilderness? For there is no food and no water, and we loathe this worthless food." Then the LORD sent fiery serpents among the people, and they bit the people, so that many people of Israel died. (Num. 21:4–6)

I have a very close friend, so close that we don't need to say "please" and "thank you" because we know each other's hearts. Yet without fail, any time I give my friend a gift, he responds with a written thank-you note. It is *totally unnecessary* and heaven knows I am not good at doing it in return, but my friend is a thank-you note king.

Notes aren't always indicative of a thankful heart, and it isn't the note that's important. But an attitude of gratitude makes a difference. It makes a difference in the heart of the one who receives the appreciation. But it also affects the one who is appreciative. When we are appreciative, we are getting outside ourselves. We are practicing a thankfulness that is an important trait of godliness.

The opposite of appreciation is self-indulgent importance. It reflects an attitude of deserving. It makes us think we are something more than we really are. It shows an arrogance and pride that are repugnant to God and most everyone we meet.

One of the ways we see the lack of appreciation is in a level of complaining and whining. Today's passage illustrates this. The Israelites have received from the Lord many more benefits than they would ever deserve. God gave them life—truly. He brought them out of slavery, gave them a special dispensation of law and understanding, related to them as with no other people, gave them prophets to guide them, gave them food in the wilderness, protected them from antagonistic nations, offered to give them a Promised Land (and kept the promise to their children when the parents were unfaithful), and secured their well-being for forty years. Then the people ran out of water. This had happened before, and God had supplied them water. But this time, the people started whining, complaining, and finding fault with God for not treating them better. The people who should have been appreciative were anything but.

I don't want to be that way. I know there are hard days and difficulties in life. But as they come, I don't want to whine and complain. I don't want to challenge or question God. I want to be thankful for the mercies I have received, for the days that were sunshine, and for the knowledge that he will rescue me.

Lord, forgive my complaining. Teach me to trust you better. Thank you for the many blessings in my life. You have been amazing to me. In your name, amen.

SEPTEMBER 29

And the people came to Moses and said, "We have sinned, for we have spoken against the LORD and against you. Pray to the LORD, that he take away the serpents from us." So Moses prayed for the people. And the LORD said to Moses, "Make a fiery serpent and set it on a pole, and everyone who is bitten, when he sees it, shall live." So Moses made a bronze serpent and set it on a pole. And if a serpent bit anyone, he would look at the bronze serpent and live. (Num. 21:7–9)

Today's passage holds fascination for a lot of different types of people. To the archaeologist, it is fascinating as the first biblical reference to bronze (other than in a Genesis genealogy). The Exodus occurred during the Late Bronze Age (c. 1550–1200 BC), and archaeology has discovered a major bronze mine in the nearby region of the Timna Valley.

For Jewish believers, the story is fascinating as a reminder of the judgment of God and the mercy of God that reaches to his repentant people. The story also unfolds Moses' role as an intermediary with God who would intercede on behalf of the people.

For Christian believers, the story reverberates with Old Testament imagery and symbolism adopted by Jesus. The serpent is first found in the Torah in the book of Genesis. It was a serpent that tempted Eve and brought sin to Adam and Eve. God judged that serpent and promised that from the seed of woman, one would come who would trample upon the serpent, also known as the deceiver. Moses was one who was like the Messiah, but he wasn't the promised one. As Moses himself said, speaking about the time after the Israelites came into the Promised Land, "The LORD your God will raise up for you a prophet like me from among you, from your brothers—it is to him you shall listen" (Deut. 18:15).

Christians believe that Jesus was and is God's promised Messiah who would trample on the serpent and set aright what was fallen. How he would do it is foreshadowed by this serpent scene in Numbers. Jesus explained to his followers that "as Moses lifted up the serpent in the wilderness, so must the Son of Man be lifted up, that whoever believes in him may have eternal life. For God so loved the world, that he gave his only Son, that whoever believes in him should not perish but have eternal life." (John 3:14–16) Jesus taught that he would be lifted up (an image of the crucifixion) and be the object that people would look to for healing from sin, rescuing the people from the serpent's destructive work.

Today's passage has a lot to unpack. It is one I plan to go back to over and over.

Lord, teach me the truths in your word. Help me to see and understand what you have secured for our study. Thank you for your healing and mercy. In your name, amen.

SEPTEMBER 30

For Heshbon was the city of Sihon the king of the Amorites, who had fought against the former king of Moab and taken all his land out of his hand, as far as the Arnon. . . . "So we overthrew them; Heshbon, as far as Dibon, perished; and we laid waste as far as Nophah; fire spread as far as Medeba." Thus Israel lived in the land of the Amorites. (Num. 21:26, 30–31)

A lot of people wonder about God as written about and described in parts of the Old Testament. For some, God seems vindictive and hostile. Some extreme cynics have even termed God genocidal and homicidal. One of the examples is the Old Testament saga of God destroying the Amorites and giving their lands to Israel. These questions are important ones, and the character of God is worthy of our deep consideration and prayerful reflection. In the process, we should also emphasize the importance of contextual study, looking at both historical context and context within Scripture.

The story of the Amorites is a good example. The Amorites were a specific group of people, but the name was also used to refer in general to the inhabitants of Palestine. The group was subject to a prophetic word given to Abraham in Genesis 15. God told Abraham that his descendants would be held in a foreign land until they returned to Canaan. This would happen once "the iniquity of the Amorites was complete" (Gen. 15:16). This indicates that the Israelite conquest of Canaan was not timed simply from when God thought judgment needed to fall on Egypt's pharaoh. The timing was also tied to the status of the people Israel would conquer and displace. The actions of Israel, and God, were also actions of judgment wrought upon a people who had reached a point of no moral return.

We never have enough information to fill in all the data for these points. The world has about 57.258 million square miles of land. Israel at its peak was maybe one one-hundredth of a million square miles. We try to understand biblical times by studying the archaeology of a miniscule microdot of land, four thousand years ago, with few to no active records of who those people were and what they did. This leaves us interjecting our own twenty-first-century ideas of our land and culture. That is a big mistake.

We may not have all the answers about God, but the Bible makes it clear that God does nothing out of an arbitrary hatred. God despises sin, and he works to bring redemption to all who would seek his face. But most don't seek his face, and many are downright evil. God will not let evil conquer, but he will eventually bring all evil to the end of death.

Lord, I do not always understand you and your ways, but I pray you will give me wisdom and faith to follow you. Enlighten me as you lead me, in your name, amen.

OCTOBER 1

Then the people of Israel set out and camped in the plains of Moab beyond the Jordan at Jericho. And Balak the son of Zippor saw all that Israel had done to the Amorites. And Moab was in great dread of the people, because they were many. Moab was overcome with fear of the people of Israel. . . . So Balak the son of Zippor, who was king of Moab at that time, sent messengers to Balaam . . . saying, "Behold, a people has come out of Egypt. They cover the face of the earth, and they are dwelling opposite me. Come now, curse this people for me, since they are too mighty for me. Perhaps I shall be able to defeat them and drive them from the land, for I know that he whom you bless is blessed, and he whom you curse is cursed." (Num. 22:1–6)

Today's passage begins a story that takes up three chapters in the Torah. The story has important lessons explored over the next several days. Today the lesson is drawn from an unspoken yet powerful message in the storyline.

Israel had almost made it through its wilderness exile. The people were near the border of Moab, and the Moabites were scared. Balak, king of the Moabites, sent for a well-known seer named Balaam. Balak wanted Balaam to come and curse the Israelites in hopes that Balak would then be able to destroy them in battle. Balaam consulted with God. God told him that the Israelites were to be left alone. They were under God's protection. Balaam refused to help, and the delegation returned to King Balak delivering the news. Balak thought Balaam was negotiating, so the king sent a greater delegation to up the offer and get Balaam's aid. This time God told Balaam he could go with the delegation, but that he had better not say anything except what God told him to say.

Balaam arrived, and the king took him to a hilltop where Balaam could see a portion of the Israelites encamped on the horizon. Balaam didn't curse Israel; he blessed them instead. King Balak was none too happy. The king took Balaam to another location to see more of the Israelites, requesting that Balaam curse this grouping. To the king's dismay, again Balaam blessed Israel; he wouldn't curse them. Exasperated, the king said, "If you're not going to curse them, fine. But don't bless them!" Then the king took Balaam to a third location, perhaps thinking things might finally work. But once again Balaam blessed the people of Israel. The king had a final confrontation with Balaam, and Balaam returned home. End of narrative.

The powerful unspoken message in the narrative is simple: the entire storyline occurs with Israel none the wiser. Israel never knows that the king has sought their destruction through a sorcerer. But God protects Israel anyway. This is our lives. We can see many blessings of God, but how often is God taking care of us and protecting us in ways we never see? We have a lot to be thankful for that we don't even realize!

Lord, thank you for your protection and provision in ways unseen. In your name, amen.

OCTOBER 2

Balaam rose in the morning and saddled his donkey and went with the princes of Moab. But God's anger was kindled because he went, and the angel of the LORD took his stand in the way as his adversary. Now he was riding on the donkey . . . And the donkey saw the angel of the LORD standing in the road, with a drawn sword in his hand. And the donkey turned aside out of the road and went into the field. And Balaam struck the donkey, to turn her into the road. Then the angel of the LORD stood in a narrow path between the vineyards, with a wall on either side. And when the donkey saw the angel of the LORD, she pushed against the wall and pressed Balaam's foot against the wall. . . . Then the angel of the LORD went ahead and stood in a narrow place, where there was no way to turn either to the right or to the left. When the donkey saw the angel of the LORD, she lay down under Balaam. And Balaam's anger was kindled, and he struck the donkey with his staff. . . . Then the LORD opened the eyes of Balaam, and he saw the angel of the LORD standing in the way, with his drawn sword in his hand. And he bowed down and fell on his face. And the angel of the LORD said to him, "Why have you struck your donkey these three times? Behold, I have come out to oppose you because your way is perverse before me. The donkey saw me and turned aside before me these three times. If she had not turned aside from me, surely just now I would have killed you and let her live." Then Balaam said to the angel of the LORD, "I have sinned, for I did not know that you stood in the road against me." (Num. 22:21–34)

The Balaam story is loaded with irony. One of the most important ironic elements is found in today's passage. Balaam the Seer is going Moab in response to the Moabite king's request that Balaam come curse Israel. Balaam consulted God, who warned him that he'd better not say anything about Israel other than what God told him to say.

Somehow in the midst of the drama, Balaam started thinking he was going to be able to complete his mission and make a good bit along the way. God sent a messenger to interrupt that thought! The encounter with the messenger is the ironic element with a powerful message to the reader: everyone can see the angel in to road *except* Balaam *the Seer!* The donkey sees the angel. The reader sees the angel. It is Balaam the Seer who is blinded. The story isn't specific on what was going through Balaam's mind, but it isn't hard to read. Balaam stood to make a lot of money in this process. The king asked Balaam to go, and God said, "No!" The king then offered more money, and Balaam went back to God for a second opinion! God said, "OK, you can go, but you'd better not say anything except what I tell you!" Balaam then left, perhaps thinking through all the money he would make. God had a lesson to teach the seer. Enter the angel with sword drawn and the unfolding story in today's passage.

How often does sin blind us to God and his message?

Lord, may I look past my desires and see you and your will. In your name, amen.

OCTOBER 3

And Balaam took up his discourse and said, "From Aram Balak has brought me, the king of Moab from the eastern mountains: 'Come, curse Jacob for me, and come, denounce Israel!' How can I curse whom God has not cursed? How can I denounce whom the LORD has not denounced?" (Num. 23:7–8)

When I was a young lawyer, my mentor and boss gave me a court hearing to handle. I don't remember what the motion was that I was supposed to argue to the court, but I remember calling my mentor from a payphone (pre-cell phone era!) before the hearing began. He asked me if I was prepared, and I told him I was. I also told him that I expected we would lose. He asked why. I explained that the law was against us, and I didn't see being able to persuade the judge otherwise. After a moment of silence, Ernest said to me, "Stand up and tell the judge, 'Your honor, we are not contesting this motion.'" I verified that I had heard him right, and he told me, "Yes. Here is the rule: we don't lose. If we have a losing position, we either put the hearing off or we give in before it starts. Losing is not an option."

Balak, king of the Moabites, did not have the same mentor! "Balak" sounds like the Hebrew word for one who "swallows up" or "destroys" (*bala'*). That is a good name to have for your king if you're worried about foreign invaders and marauding tribes. You want the destroyer on your side, not the other. But with Israel, Balak could not live up to his name. He knew he was going to have trouble destroying Israel in a head-to-head fight. So the king sent for a sorcerer known for his ability to bless and curse to great effect. Balak offered a huge sum to get the sorcerer to curse Israel. God told the sorcerer, and the sorcerer told the king, that God would not allow a curse on Israel. Instead Balaam was ordered to bless Israel.

Balak wasn't just picking a fight against Israel; he was picking a fight against God. That is a fight no one can win. Ernest would have told Balak to save his money and figure out a way to make peace with God.

How about you and me? Where do we land on relating to God and the world? Do we consider what God's plans are before we launch into our own? Do we consider how God wants someone treated before we treat him or her based on how we feel? Do we consider God's direction before we walk in the path we choose?

Balak didn't choose his fights wisely. He fought against God and never really realized it. I want to be wiser. I have read his story and I know better!

Lord, please give me wisdom to see the world as you do. May I see your path and follow it, whatever the personal cost. In your name, amen.

OCTOBER 4

And Balak said to him, "Please come with me to another place, from which you may see them. You shall see only a fraction of them and shall not see them all. Then curse them for me from there." (Num. 23:13)

I was trying a case in deep cajun Louisiana, for a man who developed cancer from using a certain drug, and the jury returned a rather large verdict. Some days later, I had a chance to visit with the jury foreperson. I asked him how the jury had determined the amount it gave. The gentleman explained that he had urged the jury to give a higher amount. One of the jurors was an elderly lady, who'd said to him, "Whoo-weee . . . that's a lot of money! I don't think I could give that much money." The foreperson asked her, "Well, how much could you give?" She answered with a much lower number, causing him to throw his truck keys on the table, protesting, "That's not much more to this company than buying a new truck." She pondered this, agreed, and then said, "Wha-chu got in mind to do?" He replied, "I got a plan B!" He then suggested a middle ground, to which she and the other jurors immediately all agreed.

Sometimes Plan B works, but not always. Where God is concerned, we shouldn't think we can get to an end he is set against just by devising a Plan B. King Balak learned that the hard way.

Balak, king of Moab, was trying to destroy God's people, the Israelites. Knowing that his army was overmatched, Balak thought he could get a sorcerer to conjure up a spell of cursing against the Israelites that might overcome the odds. Balaam didn't want to come because, as he explained to the king's emissaries, God was supporting Israel, not opposing them. The king upped the ante and offered Balaam more money to bring the curses. Balaam came to the king, but he warned that he would only curse if God allowed it. Balak sacrificed, Balaam sought God, and the decision came. Balaam stood on a hilltop and *blessed* Israel. He wouldn't curse them. With Plan B failing, King Balak went to Plan C! He thought he could convince Balaam to end-run God by finding another group of Israelites to curse. When Plan C crashed into failure as Balaam again blessed the Israelites, King Balak went to Plan D! A third time Balaam was coaxed into trying to curse Israel, this time with the king explaining, "If you won't curse them, at least don't bless them!" Plan D nosedived too. Israel was blessed a third time.

What foolery to think we can trick God. It isn't going to happen. Now, like King Balak, we probably fool ourselves into thinking we just need a new approach. Maybe God won't pay attention if we pretend he isn't there! Maybe God isn't that real anyway. Or maybe he has better things to do than monitor our corner of Earth. Such reasoning is futile nonsense. God is GOD. He is. Period. We won't trick him. We won't catch him unaware. We have no Plan B, C, D, or even Z that will work to thwart God.

Lord, forgive my efforts to force something contrary to your will. In your name, amen.

OCTOBER 5

And Balak's anger was kindled against Balaam, and he struck his hands together. And Balak said to Balaam, "I called you to curse my enemies, and behold, you have blessed them these three times. Therefore now flee to your own place. I said, 'I will certainly honor you,' but the LORD has held you back from honor." And Balaam said to Balak, "Did I not tell your messengers whom you sent to me, 'If Balak should give me his house full of silver and gold, I would not be able to go beyond the word of the LORD, to do either good or bad of my own will. What the LORD speaks, that will I speak'?" (Num. 24:12–13)

The power of money is great. It is found over and over in the Bible, in history, and even in songs of the rock-and-roll era.

In March 1964, the Beatles released their number-one hit "Can't Buy Me Love." The lyrics are well known over half a century later: "I don't care too much for money / Money can't buy me love / Can't buy me love, everybody tells me so / Can't buy me love, no, no, no, no." In interviews, McCartney would explain that the song is about the truth that material possessions are all well and good, but they don't buy what he really looks for in life.

In 1979, Neil Diamond hit the top twenty in the charts with "Forever in Blue Jeans." His lyric was similar to McCartney's: "Money talks / But it don't sing and dance / And it don't walk / And as long as I can have you / Here with me, I'd much rather be / Forever in blue jeans."

Money does some wonderful things. It also can be very destructive. But one thing money can't do is buy the Lord! In today's passage, Balak, king of Moab, tried to get a curse on Israel by offering to pay Balaam, a man with the reputation of being a curse-master. Balaam checked with God, who told him not to curse Israel. When Balaam refused, his refusal was taken by the king as negotiation. After all, why wouldn't someone do the king's bidding as long as the money was enough?

God doesn't need your money or mine. God doesn't need your sacrifices or mine. God doesn't need your praise or mine . . . your worship or mine . . . your attention or mine . . . your love or friendship or mine. God has everything he needs. God loves us because it is his nature, not because of what he gets out of it. God desires a relationship with us because he made us, and it is the best good for us. God isn't lonely without us. We don't buy his affections or his curses. Money can't buy me love . . . or curses.

Lord, give me insight into the truth of who you are and what is really important in life. Let me serve you in truth and not some manipulative maneuver. In your name, amen.

OCTOBER 6

And Balak said to Balaam, "What have you done to me? I took you to curse my enemies, and behold, you have done nothing but bless them." And he answered and said, "Must I not take care to speak what the LORD puts in my mouth?" (Num. 23:11–12)

As a young boy, I played a good bit of professional chess. I would go to tournaments on weekends and play against all sorts of folks, generally several decades older than me and occasionally sixty or seventy years older. I enjoyed the game for a number of reasons, not the least of which was the solo nature of what I was about. I moved the pieces where I decided they should be moved, based on my strategy and my vision of possible responses. Of course, when I lost, it was always my fault.

Some may think life is like a chess game, but it isn't. Life is not a personal decision where we win or lose based on our moves. There is something beyond us in play. God is not a piece we move around our chessboard. He is outside our game, even though we may not want to admit it.

Balak, king of Moab, learned this the hard way. Balak was worried about Israel's army and set about getting some help. The king sent for Balaam, a sorcerer famous for accurate curses and blessings. In the king's mind, and in the mind-sets of most in that time and culture, the gods were subject to manipulation by supernaturally informed people who bore the titles of sorcerers or seers. Sorcerers supposedly knew the magical spells or incantations that could bend the gods to the sorcerer's will. That's what Balaam was being hired to do. Balaam was supposed to use his knowledge of magic to force God's hand into doing what Balak wanted to happen.

But Balak learned the hard way that God is not a chess piece that we can move about the board where we want to deliver on our strategy in life. People who think they can control God are people who are deluded. I cringe when I hear someone in the name of God declare, "If you do ABC, then God will do XYZ." We do not need to be in the business of declaring God bound to do one thing or another. Of course, we can properly be confident that God will hold to his word, but that is different.

Life can be funny. We can tend to think of God as our personal concierge who will get us dinner reservations if we ask and are willing to tip him. Or God is our bellman who will bring our luggage up when we tell him our room number and tip him. God is no such thing. God is the chess master, not the chess piece. God will tell us what to do to execute his plans, not vice versa. We need to move where God instructs us. We need to carry his luggage where he tells us. He is God and not to be manipulated.

Lord, I repent of taking you for granted. Put me to work where you will, in your name. Amen.

OCTOBER 7

While Israel lived in Shittim, the people began to whore with the daughters of Moab. These invited the people to the sacrifices of their gods, and the people ate and bowed down to their gods. So Israel yoked himself to Baal of Peor. And the anger of the LORD was kindled against Israel. (Num. 25:1–3)

Is *idiot* too harsh a word to use in a devotional book? If not, I want to apply it to Israel, and in fairness, I have to apply it to myself too!

Today's passage makes the most sense if we consider how it is placed in the Torah. For the three chapters before this one, Balak, the king of Moab, had been trying to render the Israelites vulnerable for fear that Israel would conquer Moab. Balak had sent for a seer named Balaam, famous for pronouncing curses that come true. Balak's goal was to lessen the number of fighters for Israel so that a battle would be more favorable for Moab.

Balaam refused to curse the Israelites, and he blessed them instead. This happened not once, but three times. King Balak offered a large sum of money if only Balaam would curse Israel, but God kept intervening protecting his people.

Then, in an absurd turnaround, as Balak's efforts failed, the Israelites managed to winnow down their fighting force on their own. What money and sorcery could not accomplish, Israel inflicted on itself through sin. A number of Israelite men couldn't say no to the women of Moab. They philandered with them, and they didn't stop with sexual infidelity. These Israelites then started sacrificing to the Moabite idols, eating the nonkosher food, and worshipping the idols as their gods.

After the Israelites basically violated about half of the Ten Commandments and countless other laws given to the people, God's just anger burned, and Israel's sin accomplished what no stranger or enemy of Israel could. God punished those involved.

How on earth could the Israelites be so stupid? God told them what to do and how to do it. God explained that if they would follow his commandments, he would protect them. It would be as if God were an umbrella to block out the harsh rain that can fall in life. But God warned them also. If they failed to walk with God, the umbrella of protection would be removed, and they would reap the whirlwind that follows sin. It happened.

I get a little nervous over this one. I know how tempting the moment can be. For most people, it won't be the whores of Moab or the altar of Baal. It will be the easy lie, the greed, the envy, the materialism, the gluttony, or the lure of power or popularity. We can bend the knee to many different gods if we are not diligent.

Lord, give us insight into our choices, wisdom, and discernment. In your name, amen.

OCTOBER 8

And the LORD said to Moses, "Phinehas the son of Eleazar, son of Aaron the priest, has turned back my wrath from the people of Israel, in that he was jealous with my jealousy among them, so that I did not consume the people of Israel in my jealousy. Therefore say, 'Behold, I give to him my covenant of peace, and it shall be to him and to his descendants after him the covenant of a perpetual priesthood, because he was jealous for his God and made atonement for the people of Israel.'" (Num. 25:10–13)

Almost every American law school requires the applicant to submit test scores from the LSAT (Law School Aptitude Test). This test supposedly measures whether someone is likely to do well in law school. One of the sections is a logic section. In it, people are tested on how well they recognize logical associations and patterns. The ability to recognize patterns has long been used also as a tool in IQ tests. A simple example is asking what comes next in the sequence: 1, 3, 5, 7 . . .

A careful reading of the Torah sets up an association between two important concepts: atonement and peace. Both are present in today's passage.

The passage comes in the context of Israel about to enter the Promised Land. That means for decades, the Israelites had been taught the importance of holiness, that God alone should be worshipped, that sexual relations were between spouses, and that blessings would flow from obedience, while disobedience would bring punishment. In spite of this, with the Israelites on the cusp of the Promised Land, many of them were enticed by the Moabite women and began defiling themselves with the women, worshipping Moabite gods, sacrificing to these gods, and eating the sacrificial meals. God's punishment was immediate, and a plague broke out. The Israelite priest Phinehas took umbrage over the defiance and disregard of God, and he brought judgment on several of the defilers. God stopped the plague.

In announcing the cessation of judgment, God confirmed the link between atonement and peace. The sins of the Israelites were atoned for—that is, a price of death was paid for those sins—and as a result, God entered into a covenant of peace through the atonement.

This link between atonement and peace is important to Christians. We see in this a foreshadowing as well as a pattern. Humanity's sin is a death-deserving problem, and Jesus died the death that others should have. This is an atoning sacrifice that brings peace. As Messiah, Jesus brings peace between people and God. Without atonement, there can be no real peace between disobedient, sinful people and the holy and righteous God.

Lord, I confess that I am not a righteous person on my own merit. My best deeds are like dirty clothes compared to you. Please give me atonement. In your name, amen.

OCTOBER 9

The LORD said to Moses and to Eleazar the son of Aaron, the priest, "Take a census of all the congregation of the people of Israel, from twenty years old and upward, by their fathers' houses, all in Israel who are able to go to war." . . . But among these there was not one of those listed by Moses and Aaron the priest, who had listed the people of Israel in the wilderness of Sinai. For the LORD had said of them, "They shall die in the wilderness." Not one of them was left, except Caleb the son of Jephunneh and Joshua the son of Nun. (Num. 26:1–2, 64–65)

Reliability is a huge thing for me. I depend on a lot of people in my trial work. Trial work is often complicated, and many aspects of the job involve critical deadlines and exacting paperwork. Having to rely on people is both a blessing and a curse. The job is easier when your coworkers meet or exceed expectations. I have learned the hard way that when you rely on people who are unreliable, the job can quickly go off the rails.

God is 100 percent reliable. He never changes. He is the same yesterday, today, and tomorrow. We can have confidence that he will keep his word. His character is one of a loving God. He is also a just God. We do not need to worry that tomorrow God might change his mind and decide he only likes blonds or brunettes, or some other type of person. We needn't fear that God might change and become a hateful and spiteful God, looking to devour humanity in favor of bears or squids or something else.

God's reliability is both a blessing and a curse. The blessing comes from the confidence we can place in him. We needn't fear that he will fail to keep his word or covenant. He can be trusted fully. The curse comes from the same character trait of reliability. When God declares something, it will come to pass.

We see it in today's passage. Almost forty years before the events set out above, Israel was prepared to go into the Promised Land. God had Israel take a census to set out the fighting forces. The spies sent into Canaan returned to Israel's camp and gave a frightful report. The people were afraid they would not be able to defeat the Canaanites. Fear trumped Israel's faith, and as a result, God informed the Israelites that those of fighting age would not be allowed to enter the Promised Land. The people would wander in the wilderness for forty years while that generation died out—all but Caleb and Joshua, who had believed that God would ensure his people's victory.

Forty years later, another census was taken. All the old fighting force had died, save Caleb and Joshua. God was reliable and true to his word. He still is.

Lord, I praise you as a marvelous God, fully reliable and dependable. I trust in you and rest in your loving care. In your name, amen.

OCTOBER 10

The LORD said to Moses, "Go up into this mountain of Abarim and see the land that I have given to the people of Israel. When you have seen it, you also shall be gathered to your people, as your brother Aaron was, because you rebelled against my word in the wilderness of Zin when the congregation quarreled, failing to uphold me as holy at the waters before their eyes." . . . Moses spoke to the LORD, saying, "Let the LORD, the God of the spirits of all flesh, appoint a man over the congregation who shall go out before them and come in before them, who shall lead them out and bring them in, that the congregation of the LORD may not be as sheep that have no shepherd." (Num. 27:12–17)

Oh, how I wish life had a rewind button! If it did, I would have likely worn it out by now. There is much I want to rewind because of mistakes and errors I've made. If I could rewind life, I could fix them! I would also hit the button for replaying joyous moments. Becky and I often replay moments from the younger days of our five children, but we have to do it with words and memories. We would love an actual rewind button.

I suspect Moses might have wanted a rewind button for the sin he committed when the Israelites had run out of water a second time. Moses had asked God what should be done, and God told Moses to talk to the rock and God would produce water. Instead, Moses struck the rock, taking credit for the water that issued forth. As a consequence of the sin, God told Moses that he would not be allowed to enter the Promised Land.

Some time later, the time for Israel to enter Canaan was about to arrive. God reminded Moses of the consequences of the sin and that Moses would not be allowed to enter. But God did tell Moses that God had picked out a spot where Moses would be able to see the people and the Promised Land. The spot is Mount Nebo in modern Jordan. I have stood on the hilly prominence, and you command a great view of the Rift Valley, the Jordan River, and the Jericho oasis on the far side of the river. There Moses spent his last days.

Before Moses died, however, he finished his course in this life. Moses secured the anointing of a successor. He knew the people needed a shepherd who would listen to God faithfully and who would obey the word of the Lord.

Some sin can't be backed away from. Sometimes in our sin, we turn a corner. The consequences are real and lasting. But that doesn't mean that God is finished. It doesn't mean that God doesn't have a plan. He does. God will still extend mercy, even if there is no rewind button to be pushed. As believers, we need to do as best we can. We accept that the consequences are real, but we still do the best we can in acceptance.

Lord, I regret my sins in this life. I pray that you will forgive me and show me your road that is left for me to follow. Give me strength and wisdom to walk that road as best I can. In your name, amen.

OCTOBER 11

Then drew near the daughters of Zelophehad the son of Hepher, son of Gilead, son of Machir, son of Manasseh, from the clans of Manasseh the son of Joseph. . . . And they stood before Moses and before Eleazar the priest and before the chiefs and all the congregation, at the entrance of the tent of meeting, saying, "Our father died in the wilderness. He was not among the company of those who gathered themselves together against the LORD in the company of Korah, but died for his own sin. And he had no sons. Why should the name of our father be taken away from his clan because he had no son? Give to us a possession among our father's brothers." Moses brought their case before the LORD. And the LORD said to Moses, "The daughters of Zelophehad are right. You shall give them possession of an inheritance among their father's brothers and transfer the inheritance of their father to them. And you shall speak to the people of Israel, saying, 'If a man dies and has no son, then you shall transfer his inheritance to his daughter.'" (Num. 27:1-11)

I love this passage. Three reasons come to mind. First, I love the fact that over three thousand years ago, when culture and society insisted it was a man's world, God made it clear the women were not to be ignored in the legal system. God said women had a right to property when the neighbors thought women were property. It wasn't the absolute equality under the law that we are still seeking today in many places, but it was an unheard-of step forward.

This movement forward in the rights of women leads naturally into a second reason I love this passage. It reminds me of the time I was moderating a discussion between two U.S. Supreme Court justices—Justice Antonin Scalia and Justice Stephen Breyer. They were discussing constitutional interpretation. Justice Scalia was a strict constructionist, meaning he followed the U.S. Constitution to the letter. Justice Breyer believed the Constitution set a trajectory, and several hundred years later, interpretation should flow with the trajectory and read the constitution within the context of today's societal changes. In a sense, one can see in Israel a development of the law beyond how it was originally written. The law first given to Moses gave property inheritance through the male line. In today's passage, an unusual set of circumstances left no male heir, and the law was given a fresh set of principles to allow the daughters property rights. This leads to my third reason to love the passage.

The daughters and Moses didn't change the law by rebelling against God. They laid their concerns down before him, ready to accept his will. God honored their attitude as well as what was right to do. This teaches me the importance of attitude in seeking God's will in my life. Putting all this together, I am left knowing that as I learn God's will, as I seek to apply it to new circumstances, my attitude is important.

Lord, give me insight into your will and how I can best apply it. In your name, amen.

OCTOBER 12

So the LORD said to Moses, "Take Joshua the son of Nun, a man in whom is the Spirit, and lay your hand on him. Make him stand before Eleazar the priest and all the congregation, and you shall commission him in their sight. You shall invest him with some of your authority, that all the congregation of the people of Israel may obey." (Num. 27:18-20)

I live in a country that prides itself on independence. The United States was founded on a declaration of independence. Americans have fought for the freedoms inherent in independence. I grew up in Texas, a state where independence is considered a virtue that many in Texas history died to secure. In the midst of all this independence sits a biblical concept addressed in today's passage: the role of authority.

Moses was about to leave the Israelites and go off by himself to die. For over four decades, Moses had been God's authority to the Israelites. Moses was a prophet, proclaiming the word of the Lord; a judge, administering God's justice and laws; a priest, intervening with God as necessary on Israel's behalf; and an everyday leader, telling Israel when to go and where to go. As the time for Moses' departure drew nigh, God set out a new authority for the Israelites. Joshua the son of Nun had God's Spirit within him, and he was to receive some of Moses' authority to lead the people.

In spite of all our ideas of independence, there are institutions of authority in our lives. Children have parents. Workers have bosses. Synagogues and churches have leaders. We have courts, police, and political powers. To some degree, each of these exercises a measure of authority over people. These institutions of authority are important because they remind and teach all of the independence-valuing people of the role of submitting to authority.

Submission to authority is important because it is ultimately what we are called to do with God. God is the ultimate authority, and everyone is called to be in submission to his will and plans. When we rebel against God, that is where the trouble starts.

I think independence is a good thing, but within certain bounds. There need to be structures in place where we honor authorities, if for no other reason than to learn how to do so. We learn that we are not really fully independent. Then we are able to not only rely on God but also honor him as God. We can live under his authority, knowing we are to do his will.

Lord, it is not always easy to live under authority. It stirs up a rebellious streak in us. Help us with a submissive spirit to live under your authority and follow your plans for our lives. In your name, amen.

OCTOBER 13

"'On the Sabbath day, two male lambs a year old without blemish, and two tenths of an ephah of fine flour for a grain offering, mixed with oil, and its drink offering . . . At the beginnings of your months, you shall offer a burnt offering to the LORD: two bulls from the herd, one ram, seven male lambs a year old without blemish . . . On the fourteenth day of the first month is the LORD's Passover, and on the fifteenth day of this month is a feast. Seven days shall unleavened bread be eaten . . . On the day of the firstfruits, when you offer a grain offering of new grain to the LORD at your Feast of Weeks, you shall have a holy convocation . . . On the first day of the seventh month you shall have a holy convocation. You shall not do any ordinary work. It is a day for you to blow the trumpets . . . On the tenth day of this seventh month you shall have a holy convocation and afflict yourselves . . . On the fifteenth day of the seventh month you shall have a holy convocation. You shall not do any ordinary work, and you shall keep a feast to the LORD seven days.'"
(Num. 28:9, 11, 16-17, 26; 29:1, 7, 12)

These two chapters in Numbers set out the various feasts and times of worship for Israel. These designated times of holiness to God included the seventh day of each week (the Sabbath), the first day of each month (based on the moon's cycle of twenty-eight days), the Passover, the Feast of Weeks, the Day of Atonement, and the Feast of Tabernacles.

These festivals were to order Israel's life. Each festival stood for something significant, serving to educate the Israelites, help them remember the role God played in their lives, help them see what God had promised for the future, and give them insight into living.

Israel was called to be a worshipping community, understanding who God is, and honoring him as God with praise and adoration. Israel was to be a holy nation, living as a united people set apart by God, as indicated through its holy days. Israel was to be a pure nation, honoring only God and no other. Each of these celebrations was for God, the one who made promises to Abraham, who led the Israelites out of Egypt, who secured their exodus for forty years, and who promised to lead them victoriously into Canaan. This is the God who promised a messiah who would bring peace to the people of all ethnic groups, ending the hostility between sinners and a just God.

Today we are no less called to be a worshipping community. Worship is not entertainment for the worshippers. It is a holy time of praise and adoration of God. It is a time that sets apart those who know God from those who don't. It is a call to holiness and sacrifice to God. It is not only an individual expression, but one of community. I need this time to grow before God and be transformed in his presence. It helps me be a better me as I remember and grow in understanding my God.

Lord, teach me to worship you better. Help me to see the importance of worship. In your name, amen.

OCTOBER 14

"'These you shall offer to the LORD at your appointed feasts, in addition to your vow offerings and your freewill offerings, for your burnt offerings, and for your grain offerings, and for your drink offerings, and for your peace offerings.'" (Num. 29:39)

The psalmist rightfully sings out, "The earth is the Lord's and everything that's in it, the world and those who dwell therein" (Ps. 24:1). Think about that for a minute. God made the world. God is the reason there is life. It is futile to think that God needs us, needs what we give him, or needs what we withhold. God doesn't get hungry. God isn't needy. God isn't lonely. God doesn't lack for anything. God is complete, holy, and fully God.

So what do we make of today's passage? What do the instructions about sacrifices, offerings for vows, free will offerings, and so on inform us about, when we know they are not needed by God? These sacrifices inform us about *our* needs.

We are the ones that need to recognize the presence and reality of God. We need to recognize that everything is God's, and what we have is given to us as stewards. We are caretakers of his blessings. Do you have a good mind? You didn't earn it; God gave it to you. Were you born into a good country? You didn't choose it; God gave it to you. Have you had success in business? Maybe you worked hard to get the success, but you need to realize that God blessed you with the open doors, the opportunities, and the wherewithal to get where you are. Do you have a good family? You may have worked for your family life, but don't be deluded into thinking you got it independently of God.

Every good thing we have comes from God. We need to handle those things accordingly. That begins with giving back to him. In sacrifices and freewill offerings, we give to God, acknowledging that what we have is his. Then, the things that we keep possession of are his, but he entrusts us to put them to work for him.

We try to determine where God would have us use our time, resources, talents, and gifts, and then we use them there. This is the right way to live. It is living as servants of God Most High. It is living under the lordship of God Almighty. It is living as a testament to something greater than our own desires.

This realization isn't a onetime thing. The earth is the Lord's, and I will bear witness to it by how I live!

Lord, I praise you as the Great God and confess that I often am short-sighted about my responsibilities as your steward. Forgive me and guide me in your name, amen.

OCTOBER 15

"If a man vows a vow to the Lord, *or swears an oath to bind himself by a pledge, he shall not break his word. He shall do according to all that proceeds out of his mouth."* (Num. 30:2)

I was taking the sworn testimony of the president of a large company to play in front of a jury. The case centered on the company agreeing to sell oil fields to my client and then backing out of the agreement the day before closing. The company claimed it was backing out because of environmental problems. The truth was the company had reevaluated the fields as part of the closing, and they determined the fields were worth over three times the selling price.

In the deposition I asked the president if he'd been taught growing up that your word is your bond, that you do what you say, that a deal is a deal, or any such principle. He said, "No! Why?" I said I was asking because his company had backed out of an agreement and I was trying to figure out if he had a few bad apples in the company or if it was rotten all the way to the core. He replied, "You listen to me! If my people can make more money for my company by backing out of an agreement, then they are instructed to back out of the agreement. Their job is to make money, not live up to their deals."

That president and his company didn't live by today's Torah passage. God instructed Moses, and Moses told the Israelites, that they were expected to keep their word. If someone made a promise, he was to keep his promise. Guarantees are guarantees. If you make a commitment, you keep it. Integrity is a statement of our character.

Most people can be expected to keep their word when it works to their advantage. The real challenge is keeping one's word when it is to one's detriment to do so or when no one will know otherwise. For example, when someone tells you something in confidence and you agree not to tell others, do you live up to that agreement, or do you tell others with the preface, "Don't tell anyone, but . . . ?"

These statements about our character are also statements about our faith. If God has instructed us to be honest and faithful to our word, do we believe that God pays attention? Do we understand that God is watching? Do we really think that he cares? I want to examine my life. I want to be more careful about the commitments I make. I want people to be able to trust me to keep my word. My words need to have the power of conviction and commitment. It is part of maturing in holiness.

By the way, the jury in that case I wrote about above gave a lot of money to my client. People expect integrity and honesty.

Lord, help grow my character. May I be a man of my word. In your name, amen.

OCTOBER 16

The Lord spoke to Moses, saying, "Avenge the people of Israel on the Midianites. Afterward you shall be gathered to your people." (Num. 31:1-2)

We have been blessed in life to raise five marvelous children, watching them grow into amazing adults. When they were infants, our rules were different than when they got older. The toddlers were not allowed to play around swimming pools. We wouldn't let our six-year-olds drive a car. As they aged, the rules changed. Each of our children was driving with a permit at fifteen and had a license at sixteen.

Not only did the rules change as our children grew, but so did the explanations. When they were young, we weren't able to explore the full reasons behind why they must behave a certain way. But as they aged, they had the sufficient knowledge and experiences to understand fuller explanations.

God's revelation to his people has also progressed as they have matured and developed. The revelation of God has always been limited by the vocabulary, experience, and culture of those receiving the revelation. I can't tell a two-year-old about certain nuances of God's love that I can explore with an adult. When we read passages of antiquity, where God reveals himself and his instructions to a primitive people in an entirely different culture, and three millennia later, when we look at it in light of our culture and understanding, we see that the revelation of God has progressed.

A lot of people are troubled by Torah passages concerning rules for concubines, the treatment of slaves, the punishment of an eye for an eye rather than mercy, obscure dietary laws, and so on. Many reasons exist that explain and inform our understanding of these ancient laws, but within them all, we must consider that God has progressively revealed himself and his will to humanity.

In today's passage, God sent Moses to do an act of revenge. The Midianites had seduced the Israelites into sexual immorality and idolatry; God showed the Israelites that they needed to remove temptation. God also had unfinished business for Moses. God had another opportunity to teach another generation of Israel that sin is a serious matter, that judgment follows rebellion.

When I read troublesome passages in the Old Testament that seem a world away from our reality today, I remember that they are a world away! I need to find the ideas and principles present and read them in the framework of God's progressive revelation. As a Christian, such passages show the importance of seeing in Jesus God's fuller revelation of who he is and how we should live.

Lord, give me wisdom and help me mature in understanding you. In your name, amen.

OCTOBER 17

Moses spoke to the people, saying, "Arm men from among you for the war, that they may go against Midian to execute the LORD's vengeance on Midian. You shall send a thousand from each of the tribes of Israel to the war." So there were provided, out of the thousands of Israel, a thousand from each tribe, twelve thousand armed for war. And Moses sent them to the war, a thousand from each tribe, together with Phinehas the son of Eleazar the priest, with the vessels of the sanctuary and the trumpets for the alarm in his hand. (Num. 31:3–6)

The moral to today's passage: don't go to war unless the Lord tells you to, and then don't go without the Lord!

The Midianites had been bent on destroying Israel. They had tried cursing them, seducing them, and converting them, all to no avail. They had hurt Israel, but they hadn't done any irreparable damage. Israel was getting ready to strike back. God gave Israel the instructions about when to fight back and how to do it. Israel went forth and defeated the Midianites.

Most of us don't head out to physical war, although many courageous people serve in the military. But that doesn't mean we don't engage in battles. We need to know that our battles should never be solo affairs. Whatever war we wage, whether in a military uniform or in civilian clothes, the principle should be the same. We need to be sure we engage as God would have it.

In true military wars over the centuries, the doctrine of "just war" has evolved. The medieval scholastic Thomas Aquinas framed three criteria for a "just war," arguing they were inherent in understanding the biblical God and natural philosophy. To be just, (1) the war must be waged by a proper authority, (2) the war must be for a good purpose (not simply self-gain), and (3) peace must be a core motive even in the violence. The Bible would add that while those criteria make a war just, the war should not be fought without God's support and presence.

If we consider the wars of everyday life, the criteria might change slightly, but the central thesis remains. Fight for something worth fighting for, and do so with the proper authority. Most importantly, in the midst of all fighting, look for peace.

I don't like to fight, but it is my life in the courtroom. I always want to take on just cases, and I want to do so seeking a peaceful resolution. In my personal life, I wage my just wars with sin—those I have no hope of winning without God on my side. War is like life. We need to see where God wants us engaged and then engage with his strength.

Lord, give me peace in life. Where war is required, go with me. In your name, amen.

OCTOBER 18

They warred against Midian, as the LORD commanded Moses, and killed every male.
(Num. 31:7)

Our culture is replete with sayings that communicate important principles of life. "We need to focus on the big picture." "See the forest, not just the trees." "Play football for all four quarters; the score only matters at the end." "Life is a moving picture, not a snapshot." "It's not who wins the battle; it's who wins the war."

All of these sayings express the need to understand that the moment is not what matters most. It is what is lasting that counts. Only a fool or immature person knowingly trades long-term joy for temporary pleasure.

Israel was set to enter Canaan, the land God had promised to Abraham, Isaac, Jacob, and generations of Israelites. But the Midianites stood in the way. The Midianites had tried to take Israel out piece by piece and had successfully hurt the people. The king of Moab had tried magic and sorcery to no avail, but moral depravity was the tool that worked well.

Still, God had promised to get Israel into Canaan, and skirmishes would not rule the day. Not even immorality was going to eclipse God's promise to Abraham and others. God was faithful and remembered his covenant. God instructed Israel to assemble a fighting force, and God sent that force into battle. Israel won—not simply a battle but the war. Midian was defeated.

I have struggles and battles in my walk. We all do. I do well to remember this story. I am not trying to go kill a set of people physically barring me from possessing the joys and promises God has given me. But I still face obstacles. Some are external and others are of my own making.

As I face these struggles in life, I do well to remember several things. First, I may stumble. I may fail at times. It may be my own fault. But our faithful God is working on the bigger picture. He knows my frailties all too well. But he is stronger than those set against me. He is able to overcome and bring me to a place higher than I stand today. I need his forgiveness and mercy, but he has assured me of those as well.

God is a fearsome warrior God. He is able to conquer the enemies of his will. He is able to bring holiness into my life. I need to look to him and walk in his strength and forgiveness.

Lord, please forgive my sins, show your mercy, and strengthen me for battle in your name, amen.

OCTOBER 19

"We will take up arms, ready to go before the people of Israel, until we have brought them to their place. And our little ones shall live in the fortified cities because of the inhabitants of the land. We will not return to our homes until each of the people of Israel has gained his inheritance. For we will not inherit with them on the other side of the Jordan and beyond, because our inheritance has come to us on this side of the Jordan to the east." So Moses said to them, "If you will do this, if you will take up arms to go before the LORD for the war . . ." The people of Reuben said to Moses, ". . . your servants will pass over, every man who is armed for war, before the LORD to battle, as my lord orders." (Num. 32:17, 20, 27)

Do you ever examine your motivations in life? Do you have a true heart-to-heart with *yourself* where you prayerfully think through what drives you in life? It is rarely simple.

Some people in the world are driven by a need to survive. If you are drowning in the ocean, your sole thought is likely for air. Many are driven by a need for love. We may not have been loved in formative years and would do most anything to feel loved as we age. Some are driven by power. They make choices and live in ways to increase their power and control over others. Some live for affirmation. Some live for pleasure. Some live for money. Some don't have any purpose or motivation, and they live day to day adrift on the sea in meaninglessness.

Today's passage speaks to motivation. Israel was preparing to march into the Promised Land, going to war against the inhabitants to take what God had promised them. Once the Israelites were successful, the land was going to be divided among the tribes. Two of the tribes, however, liked the land where Israel was encamped. They asked for that land as their inheritance. This request prompted a concern that those two tribes were trying to get out of fighting for the land that the rest would occupy. The two tribes then offered to go fight with the rest of Israel and, when the fighting was completed, return to the land they wanted.

Within that dialogue, something interesting happened related to the issue of motivation. The fighters in the two tribes offered to take up arms and "go before Israel." In other words, they would fight for their fellow Israelites. Moses replied that they were to take up arms to "go before the Lord." In other words, they weren't fighting for their fellow Israelites. Their motivation was to follow God! The fighters got the message. They answered Moses that they would be armed for war and go "before the Lord."

That should be our real motivation. We need to do what we do, whatever we do, for the Lord!

Lord, help me purify my motives in life. May I follow you. In your name, amen.

OCTOBER 20

"Every armed man of you will pass over the Jordan before the LORD, until he has driven out his enemies from before him." (Num. 32:21)

How hot does your credit meter run? I am not asking about how much you owe on credit cards! I mean, when something good happens, how quickly do you take credit for it? People love affirmation, and so when we accomplish something, it feels good for people to compliment us, congratulate us, and give us high fives for what we've done. All of that is magnified when we feel like we deserve it. But somewhere in here, warning bells should sound.

In today's passage, the Israelites are getting ready to invade Canaan. They would sharpen their weapons, devise their strategies, and fight with their army, but the Lord was the one who would drive out their enemies. No one should fear what they face if they face it with God. But just as importantly, no one should forget that God was there once the victory arrives.

Anytime we accomplish something of note, we need to remember the role God played in our result. If I win a courtroom battle, I am a puffed-up balloon if I think it was through my skill, my drive, or my hard work, or even that of my staff. Hopefully I won because God saw to a just result. God gave me the skill. God gave me the strength to work hard. God gave me a great supporting cast. God gave a fair court. God moved the heart of the judge and jury to find justice. God is the key. My credit meter needs to turn into a praise meter. God gets the glory and praise, and I am honored to humbly serve him and his cause.

So, I don't want to be puffed up, proud, or arrogant in victory. Puffed-up balloons had better be careful because we live in a world of sharp needles. The proud get brought down low. It is a fact. Write it down. It is God's cosmic karma. The humble get lifted up, but the proud stumble.

God drives out the enemies; I don't. He uses me. This whole matter, like most others in this devotional book and the Torah (and the whole Bible), boils down to something fairly simple: it is all about God and his will. Not you. Not me. Not anyone or anything else. If we fail to grasp that, we live in a charade. We live in a fictional world no different than we find on the fantasy/science fiction shelves at the local bookstore. Reality is all about God.

Lord, I confess I often lose sight of you, and I ask for your forgiveness. I have robbed you of the praise for the great things you do. I thank you for your love and care, in spite of my lousy focus! In your name, amen.

OCTOBER 21

"If you will not do so, behold, you have sinned against the LORD, and be sure your sin will find you out." (Num. 32:23)

Passages like today's scare me to death. Sin does find you out. Ugh.

This passage reminds me of an obscure song by Randy Stonehill entitled "Under the Rug." His melody and lyrics are both haunting as he sings of his hidden sin: "I have a secret I can't tell / And I've learned to conceal it well / Ah but this disturbing smell / Keeps coming from the carpet . . . Bury your sins and they won't survive / I told myself till the big surprise / Down in the dirt is where they thrive / Like little poison toadstools / Under the rug . . . I hear the ticking of my telltale heart / Like a bomb set to blow my world apart / I wish that guilt would make us smart / But I'm sweeping all this garbage . . . Under the rug."

Sin is not friendly. It is sticky and nasty. It gets all over you. It is the tar baby from Uncle Remus' stories about Brother Fox and Brother Rabbit (or "Bre'r Fox" and "Bre'r Rabbit," as he pronounces them). In an effort to trap Bre'r Rabbit, Bre'r Fox makes a baby out of tar and sets it by the side of the road where Bre'r Rabbit would come hopping by. Bre'r Rabbit sees the tar baby and starts talking. When the baby doesn't reply, Bre'r Rabbit gets angry and wallops the tar baby, getting his hand stuck in the cheek. Unable to get his hand out, Bre'r Rabbit strikes the other cheek, getting his second hand stuck. Then his kicks get both feet stuck.

This is the way of sin. It grabs hold of us and won't let go. We tend to get deeper and deeper into it as it breeds destruction. We try to hide sin, but it bears fruit, even if no one sees it or finds out about it. Sin has a burden.

What can we do about this? God says that sin is really an offense against him. God made us to be pure and holy, and he calls us to purity and holiness. When we walk in rebellion, when we sin, we are really offending God. We are putting ourselves against him. We have true moral guilt because we are truly morally guilty. We must make our sin right before God, and that is the biblical concept of atonement.

God teaches us to first admit our sin. We must confess and own up to it for it to be handled. Admitting our sin, we need to seek his forgiveness. In the Torah, God set up the principle of sacrificing an innocent beast to atone for the sins of the guilty. The Christian understands that this foreshadowed the true sacrifice of Jesus the Messiah as an innocent who paid the price of our sins. As we confess and repent, getting the atonement of God, we have release from sin. It may still bear bad fruit we carry, but moral guilt is gone. Thank you, God! No more sweeping under the rug!

Lord, I confess myself a sinner. Please forgive me for your name's sake. Amen.

OCTOBER 22

On the day after the Passover, the people of Israel went out triumphantly in the sight of all the Egyptians, while the Egyptians were burying all their firstborn, whom the LORD had struck down among them. On their gods also the LORD executed judgments. (Num. 33:3–4)

"Coping tools" are the mechanisms that we develop to handle life's disturbances and concerns. The concept gives meaning to "comfort food." It causes rampant spending. It can drive people to drink or gamble. It can push personal pleasure as an escape. It might mean withdrawal from other people. Some have harsh coping tools, expressing anger in frustration or lashing out physically. In a subconscious way, these coping tools become the gods of rescue and refuge for people when trouble arises.

Egypt had its own set of gods developed to help cope with life. The ancients had gods to explain the world: one of the Nile, one of the sky, one of the Sun, and so on. They also had gods that more directly affected and oversaw life. One of the main gods for the Egyptians was Pharaoh. Pharaoh was responsible for ensuring the other gods supplied food, protection and safety, and basic everyday needs. As part of his employ, Pharaoh had priests who daily executed service to the gods (over one hundred that we know of) who ensured that life would go forward, especially when times were tough.

When Moses came forward on God's behalf to demand the liberation of the Israelites, Pharaoh would have nothing to do with it. The Israelites were Pharaoh's and Egypt's slave workforce. The Israelites were tools for the gods to use to build, repair, and sustain Egypt. The Egyptians' gods would not give up their tools so readily. God's act of redemption, freeing the Israelites from the Egyptian overlords, involved defeating the Egyptian gods. The Lord not only defeated them, but he also executed judgment on them. Each of the plagues was judgment over an Egyptian god. The final plague took the next pharaoh's life (the firstborn of the reigning pharaoh). With Pharaoh being a god, this was the execution of one of Egypt's primary deities.

God explained to Israel that there is only one God. Israel was to worship none but the one true God. The Torah and Bible use an expression: God is a "jealous" God. He is. He will not allow his people to follow other gods that aren't even real. He knows the shallow superficiality of any claimed god, and he executes judgment on them all.

Comfort food? Out-of-control spending? Drunkenness? Gambling? Personal pleasure? Anger? Any of the gods we might turn to for sustaining us in life are shallow and of no real use. God will execute judgment on them as well. In life's troubles and difficulties, we need to turn to the one true God.

Lord, forgive me for chasing other gods in place of you. In your name, amen.

OCTOBER 23

And the LORD spoke to Moses in the plains of Moab by the Jordan at Jericho, saying, "Speak to the people of Israel and say to them, 'When you pass over the Jordan into the land of Canaan, then you shall drive out all the inhabitants of the land from before you and destroy all their figured stones and destroy all their metal images and demolish all their high places. . . . But if you do not drive out the inhabitants of the land from before you, then those of them whom you let remain shall be as barbs in your eyes and thorns in your sides, and they shall trouble you in the land where you dwell.'" (Num. 33:50–52, 55)

Israel was set to invade the Promised Land. Canaan was riddled with people who worshipped idols. These idols were human attempts to explain life in a nonscientific age. The Baal who rode the skies in storms was the primitive explanation of thunder. The idols were supposedly giving sustenance and protection. The fertility goddess explained why crops succeeded or failed. The gods had to be worshipped, appeased, and even fed to ensure their good disposition. If a god required a child sacrifice to help a community survive, the child would be slain. If a god required a particular gift, the gift would be supplied. Different gods had different needs, and it was a regular task to appease and satisfy this group of gods.

The Israelites were coming into this land. They were to drive out the idolaters and destroy the idols. The Canaanites might flee before the coming Israelites, especially as the Israelites' reputation spread, but the danger of idols left behind was still significant. Israel had a propensity to worship idols, and any idol left was going to be trouble. God knew that if any Canaanites remained, and if the Canaanite idols remained, that Israel would pay the price. The idols and idolaters would be "as barbs in your eyes and thorns in your sides."

If we correctly define idolatry as putting anything before God or in the place of God, then we will find lots of idols in our lives. We need to go on an idol hunt, seeking to destroy our idols before they destroy us!

How do we do this practically? We should note it is a community effort. We can't always recognize the sin and idols we set in our lives. If we are close to those with godly insight, we can likely do a bit better at identifying the idols. Once we identify the idols, we need to go about breaking them. This can involve praying about the idols, confessing to God that we have let something else take his place in our hearts or lives. We can also seek to replace the idol with God. We should put God where he belongs in our lives, and then everything else moves to a more proper place. I should go to God for life's challenges. God gives the answers to my questions. No more idols for me!

Lord, I let things, actions, and feelings take the position in my life that you should hold. Forgive me and help me destroy these idols. In your name, amen.

OCTOBER 24

"'You shall take possession of the land and settle in it, for I have given the land to you to possess it.'" (Num. 33:53)

Have you ever met a Nathaniel? Nathaniel is a composite of two Hebrew words, *natan*, or "gift," and *el*, or "God." Nathaniel is a gift of God. You might not be named Nathaniel, but that doesn't mean that God hasn't given or won't give you gifts.

In today's passage, we read about the Israelites about to head into Canaan, the land that God gave them to possess. The land was God's gift, a gift promised to Abraham, Isaac, Jacob, and their innumerable offspring. Israel's job was to possess the land.

This is not the first or only gift God gives. In the Torah God gave many gifts to his people, including the gift of life. If we limit our study to only those times when the actual word "gift" (*natan*) is used, we find God giving great things, including food (Gen. 9:3), insight (Gen. 41:16), favor before others (Exod. 3:21), guidance (Exod. 13.21), law and instruction for living (Exod. 21:12), rest (Exod. 33:14), rain (Lev. 26:4), peace (Lev. 26.6), and victory (Deut. 20:4).

These were gifts that God gave to his people, but they were also gifts that the people were expected to possess. In other words, we need to take what God gives us. Often, however, these gifts were tied to certain actions. These actions were what Israel needed to do to gain the gifts. For example, God gave the Israelites the Promised Land, but Israel was going to have to take possession.

Sometimes in the Torah, we read that certain actions will cause God to give gifts we'd rather not have. God says if we don't follow his will, he will give us diseases and afflictions. This is akin to a wake-up call! If Israel failed to worship and follow God, God would give them "a trembling heart and failing eyes and a languishing soul" (Deut. 28:65).

These passages all make sense if we see that God is involved in our lives. He made us as beings that can and should relate to him. He set us in a world with morality that operates with cause and effect. We need to understand that and walk in his blessings and gifts. Failing to do so will result in affliction, trials, and tribulation. God will not let us cavalierly ignore him and his will.

As I walk with God, I want to be sure I am attentive to his gifts, thankful for his gifts, and careful to use his gifts as he would have me do. I'm not a Nathaniel, but I am still a receiver of God's gifts!

Lord, forgive me for taking so many of your gifts for granted. Thank you for all you do for me and my loved ones. May I grow in appreciation as I walk and pray in your name, amen.

OCTOBER 25

The LORD spoke to Moses, saying, "These are the names of the men who shall divide the land to you for inheritance: Eleazar the priest and Joshua the son of Nun. You shall take one chief from every tribe to divide the land for inheritance." (Num. 34:16–18)

Throw away the puppet strings! God's not looking for puppets who are at his beck and call as he pulls the strings. God isn't micromanaging every minute point of our existence. The God who made our brains expects us to use them. The God who wired us with a moral compass expects us to live morally. The God who gave us an ability to make choices charges us to make them based on what is right and true, but he leaves it to us to do so. This is an affirmation of humanity and life.

In today's passage, God is laying out how the Israelites will divide the Promised Land after they capture it. The Israelites were easily divided into twelve tribes, descended from the twelve sons of Jacob. At God's command, Moses had conducted a census, and the people knew how many were in each of the twelve tribes. God told Moses, once the land was conquered, to select Eleazar, the high priest; Joshua, the leader who would take the place of Moses; and one leader from each of the twelve tribes. This commission would determine how to divide the land. God instructed that the land was to be divided fairly, with larger tracts going to larger groups.

God could have done the dividing himself. God could have specified which tribes would get which land, and the people would have marched to that tune. But God didn't. God had the people select. God set up a procedure to ensure that every tribe had a voice in the selection process, and God ordered that the division be fair and equitable. But beyond that, God told them to figure it out!

I like this passage a lot. It helps inform me how to live. I wish at times I were a puppet and that God would give me explicit instructions so I would know precisely what to do, where to go, and how to choose. But God rarely works that way. Instead, God sets out principles I am expected to learn and use. God teaches me priorities I am to model in my life. God instructs me in goals I am to strive to achieve. God promises to help me accomplish what I am set to do, as long as I am seeking to do it to his glory and seeking his blessings in my efforts. The writer of Proverbs expressed it this way: "Trust in the LORD with all your heart, and do not lean on your own understanding. In all your ways acknowledge him, and he will make straight your paths" (Prov. 3:5-6).

As I live and acknowledge God, as I prayerfully seek to follow his principles and priorities, and as his goals are my goals, he sets me free to think, to make decisions, and to act with the assurance that he will make my paths straight. This charts my course today!

Lord, give me insight, direction, and strength to live under your will in your name, amen.

OCTOBER 26

"But if he pushed him suddenly without enmity, or hurled anything on him without lying in wait or used a stone that could cause death, and without seeing him dropped it on him, so that he died, though he was not his enemy and did not seek his harm, then the congregation shall judge between the manslayer and the avenger of blood, in accordance with these rules." (Num. 35:22–24)

Most of us who have become lawyers had three years of law school. While in school, most students take at least one course in criminal law. Today's passage is a law student's passage, and the lawyer in me cannot pass over it without a devotion.

In criminal law, there are different crimes associated with one person killing another. There is first-degree murder, which generally entails a premeditated murder where the killer plans the murder or lies in wait for the victim. Second-degree murder is generally where the murder is intentional and there is malice, but the murder wasn't planned ahead. Third-degree murder can vary state by state but generally is killing without a prior intent, where the circumstances would so inflame a reasonable person that he or she might commit such a crime. There is another kind of killing called involuntary manslaughter. A classic example of this is the unintentional killing that might arise from a reckless use of some tool, like driving while intoxicated.

These different crimes have different punishment schemes. This wasn't some great invention by legal scholars in the Western tradition; they come from the legal code found in the Torah. The United States legal system is modeled after that of England. England modeled its criminal code after laws informed, in large part, by the Bible.

In the Torah, in today's passage, there was accorded a difference in the crime of killing another based on whether or not one intended to do so. If one intended to kill another, then the murder was punishable by death. If instead the killing was done by another who had no intent and the crime was an accident or committed in a moment of passion, then the killer was not subjected to the death penalty but was "imprisoned" after a fashion in one of the cities of refuge. If this killer left the city of refuge, then one could avenge the death of the victim and kill the killer. Whether the vengeance was proper would be for the "jury" or "congregation" to decide.

Aside from my lawyerly interest in where we derive much of our legal code, this passage informs me of how much God cares about the heart. Our intent is important to him. Jesus would point to the intent over a thousand years later when he instructed his followers not only to avoid adultery but also to avoid lust. Not only should we not kill, but we shouldn't hate. I need to work on my motives and heart, not simply my actions.

Lord, help me purify my life and my heart, living to your glory. In your name, amen.

OCTOBER 27

*"You shall not defile the land in which you live, in the midst of which I dwell, for I the
LORD dwell in the midst of the people of Israel."* (Num. 35:34)

My wife is the queen of entertainment. Whether it's throwing a party
for nine thousand people (something she has truly done multiple times) or
having a few people over for dinner, my wife is the consummate party giver.
One of the reasons Becky is so great at this is her sensitivity toward who
people are and how they will respond to certain things. If you are a vegan
and my wife knows it, you can be sure you will find great vegan fare. When
we have had Orthodox Jews for dinner, she has always made sure every
item of food is kosher. It isn't something hard for my wife. It is her nature.

Not everyone is as sensitive to social matters as my wife. Some, like
me, have to work at it, but most everyone I know, if she or he is aware of
someone with a particular habit or viewpoint, will behave in a way that
doesn't purposely rub someone's nose in it.

Some view God as a visitor in their lives. It is as if we have our own
lives, and God is allowed to knock on the door and occasionally come in for
a visit. When he does, we try to treat him with respect, as we would any
visitor. We clean up our language, modify the subjects we talk about, treat
others kindly in front of God, change the television when a show comes
on that might offend the Almighty, and so on. Today's passage, however,
indicates that such a view is askew.

Today's passage is unfolding Israel's preparation for going into the
Promised Land. God makes it clear in the passage that the land should not
be considered Israel's with God as a visitor. In truth, God owns the land.
God dwells there. Israel is coming in as the guest, not vice versa. The Israelites shouldn't take it that they are the owners who occasionally throw a
party and will be careful when God is on the invitation list to follow God's
proclivities about food, entertainment, behavior, and so on. It is the other
way around, but with a further twist. Being present in the land, God told
the Israelites that they could take possession with certain rules, much as
a homeowner might rent out a home but not allow the renter to tear down
walls and rebuild the home to the renter's delight.

We have an important lesson to learn from this. This world is God's,
not ours. He is pleased to have us live in it, but we are expected to live in
accordance with his instructions. This world doesn't revolve around you,
me, or anyone else. God is at the center of everything, and the lives of the
faithful should reflect that.

*Lord, forgive me for treating you as a visitor. May I conduct myself properly in your
home. In your name, amen.*

OCTOBER 28

These are the commandments and the rules that the LORD commanded through Moses to the people of Israel in the plains of Moab by the Jordan at Jericho. (Num. 36:13)

I have an incredible piece of exercise equipment. It is a Peloton stationary bike. One of the great things about it is that world-class instructors/ trainers give classes that you can use live, as the class unfolds, or download later to use at your convenience. Peloton features a number of super instructors, but one of my favorite instructors teaches a concept that I really don't like. She tells those riding that some things fall into our comfort zone (riding at a slower pace with harder resistance, for example), while other things are more difficult and less "fun" (like the contrary riding at a fast pace at a lower resistance). This instructor says we should make it a point to do the rides with things we don't like. Here is her reasoning: we like what we are good at doing and dislike what we aren't so good at doing. She says we need to practice what we *aren't good at doing*, so we improve in those areas of weakness.

Today's passage rubs some people the wrong way. It falls into the category of things they don't like, perhaps because they aren't good at them. The passage is the overarching theme of a section where God lays out commandments for the Israelites. Some people are rule followers and see commandments as a blessing. They set out clear rules to be followed. But some people have a rebellious streak, and the idea of anyone telling them what they must do makes them want to do the exact opposite. This is true even when it is God giving the instruction.

I think that we need to take a moment and consider both groups of people in light of what God says. For those that follow rules well, we should note a warning that God is concerned not simply with the letter of the law but with the spirit too. We can't just follow the rules; we need to have the proper heart to go with that obedience.

For the rebellious group, it is worth emphasizing that God is God. God is able to tell us what we are expected to do and what we are expected to be. We need to consult him, listen to him, and obey him. While God's rules may run counter to our natures, that likely indicates that our natures need some taming and modification.

It's like an exercise bike. If you aren't good at something, you need to practice it until you get good at it. I want to be obedient to God, and I have a goal of learning about him through the Bible so I can best understand his nature and traits for me to follow.

May God help me!

Lord, I need your help to be obedient, not just in the nitty-gritty of every day but in the heart behind my actions. Help me, please, in your name, amen.

OCTOBER 29

"See, I have set the land before you. Go in and take possession of the land that the Lord *swore to your fathers, to Abraham, to Isaac, and to Jacob, to give to them and to their offspring after them."* (Deut. 1:8)

I am a Christian. By that I mean that I believe that Jesus (Yeshua is his Hebrew name) was and is the Jewish Messiah (*Christ* is the Anglicized Greek word for Messiah). I believe that Jesus was God made flesh and that as a human he died on my behalf. I was slated to die as the just punishment for my rebellion and sins against God, but instead I have trusted God that he will let the death of Jesus be the atoning price that justice requires for my sin.

My parents were both Christians. So were my grandparents. I didn't know any of my great-grandparents save Grandmother Davis, my maternal grandmother's mother. She was a Christian.

This is my history. It is a part of my personality and who I am. I am not new to the faith like many of my close friends.

Christianity is a historical faith. It has been around for almost two thousand years, since the earliest disciples believed and trusted that Yeshua, as they knew him, was Messiah. Even the earliest Christians, however, were in a historical faith. They were Jews. It wasn't for at least a decade that there were many non-Jews among the Christians.

Judaism is also a historical faith. It always has been. Even when the Israelites were going into the Promised Land over a thousand years before Yeshua, the faith was tied to history. God told the Hebrews to take possession of the land he promised to Abraham, Isaac, and Jacob. These were historical figures. This was a historical faith.

The idea of Yeshua as Messiah is based on this historical faith. He was of the seed of Abraham, Isaac, and Jacob and is seen to be the offspring that God promised would bring blessing to the larger non-Israelite world. His atoning sacrifice was not simply for the Jews of his day. It was for all people.

This amazing historical drama that brought the Messiah goes back to the earliest recordings we have of God interacting with people. It is the ancient history of the Ancient of Days. Yet it is still here now. May God open our eyes to the historicity of faith.

Lord, thank you for your hand in history. Let me see it clearly. In your name, amen.

OCTOBER 30

*"May the L*ORD*, the God of your fathers, make you a thousand times as many as you are and bless you, as he has promised you!"* (Deut. 1:11)

What do you give the person who has everything? Another pair of socks? Gift cards to restaurants? What do you give a person when you need or want to give a gift but have no real money to spend? Do you knit her or him a pair of socks? My suggestion: pray a blessing from God for the person. Write it out and give it to her or him.

Blessings go back to the most ancient times. God instructed his people to seek blessings for each other. It is an appropriate prayer to offer. I suggest you pick out a person or two and let this devotion give you ideas of blessings you can pray over that person.

- May God give you the spirit of wisdom and of revelation in the knowledge of him, and may he enlighten the eyes of your heart, that you may know what is the hope to which he has called you and what are the riches of his glorious inheritance in the saints.
- May you be rooted and grounded in love, with the strength to comprehend the breadth and length and height and depth of God's love.
- May the Lord answer you in the day of trouble! May the name of the God of Jacob protect you! May he send you help from the sanctuary and give you support from Zion! May he grant you your heart's desire and fulfill all your plans! May we shout for joy over your salvation.
- May you be filled with the knowledge of his will in all spiritual wisdom and understanding, so as to walk in a manner worthy of the Lord, fully pleasing to him, bearing fruit in every good work, and increasing in the knowledge of God; may you be strengthened with all power, according to his glorious might, for all endurance and patience with joy.
- May God grow his fruit of love, joy, peace, patience, kindness, goodness, faithfulness, gentleness, and self-control in your life.
- May your eyes be open to see the wondrous things he has done for you, bringing you close to his heart in wisdom and understanding.

In lieu of the normal closing prayer at the end of this devotion, pray these things over the people God puts on your heart. As today's passage inspires us, may we seek God's blessings for each other!

OCTOBER 31

And I charged your judges at that time, "Hear the cases between your brothers, and judge righteously between a man and his brother or the alien who is with him. You shall not be partial in judgment. You shall hear the small and the great alike. You shall not be intimidated by anyone, for the judgment is God's." (Deut. 1:16–17)

Yes, these verses are the mantra of a trial lawyer. They express the goal of fair courts everywhere. The idea that justice trumps power, money, connections, sympathy, pity, position, and so on is rare, even though it is the goal of a just society.

That the Bible should trumpet fairness in the courts denotes two significant things. First, it shows that this must be deliberately pursued. It is not the natural course of things in society. The natural course is that those in the know, those who are tight with the right people, those who have the resources to buy the best lawyers and legal preparation team win. I practice law in the United States, and with thirty-five years in courts around the country, I have seen cases where the justice is as pure as one could hope. I have also seen cases where the question is who knows the judge, who has the power to buy the biggest and meanest lawyers, and who has the appellate courts under lock and key. It makes one sick to see, and it is something we should all be working to change.

This leads to the second significant point to be derived from this passage. God is a just God. We treasure justice because humans are made in God's image, and we are hardwired to respect and see justice as a virtue. Even those who don't believe in God are hardwired for justice. One of the major complaints cynics make about God is the idea that "I could never believe or follow a God who allows such unfair things to happen." Usually these people cite examples of a child getting an incurable disease or the like.

This is a tragic example of matters that shake us to our cores *because it doesn't seem just.* Humans believe justice is a higher and greater good, even though they aren't very good at embracing it when they are personally involved in the court.

The Bible explains this reality well. In the Torah we read that God made all people in his image. People are hardwired to believe in things like justice. Yet humans have fallen from God, rebelling against his purity. As a result, in spite of how we are made, we have a strong tendency toward sin and selfishness. This perfectly sets out why we can treasure justice yet still look for our advantage in court.

This informs me as a lawyer. It gives me purpose and a goal. It also informs me as a person. I need to push for fairness to everyone, regardless of status or money. I need to seek the higher God I know as a child of God.

Lord, give me wisdom to see justice and energy to pursue it. In your name, amen.

NOVEMBER 1

"This day I will begin to put the dread and fear of you on the peoples who are under the whole heaven, who shall hear the report of you and shall tremble and be in anguish because of you." (Deut. 2:25)

I learned early in the practice of law that talk is cheap. The lawyers I faced who were constantly trying to scare me, telling me how good they were, how many trials they had won, how much experience they had—these were not the lawyers to fear. Their words betrayed the truth. They were really just trying to win with fear. The lawyers I learned to fear and respect were the ones who let their work do the talking. These were the ones who didn't tout their victories but just went about their work. They didn't need to impress me. They were that good!

The invading Israelites did not have to boast about who they were, how many swords they carried, or the military genius behind their commander. The Israelites had God as their ruler. God told them where to go and whom to fight. God was behind their victories, and God couldn't be stopped.

This is why the nations feared Israel. God was at work. Whether they realized it or not, what the nations before Israel feared was the Lord. This was a legitimate fear. No one in heaven or on earth can stand against the Lord. If the Lord is on your side, you win. If the Lord is set against you, you lose.

We have to consider this as we live. Every day we get to choose whether we fight for God or against him. Some people don't think of God each day, but they are still making a choice, even if by default. Some people don't believe God exists, but he does, and they are still making a choice. Some people purposely choose against God. People who contend against God should tremble unless they are fools.

I want to deliberately seek God's face today. I want to know what he has turned his hand to do and pursue it with him. I will prayerfully seek his will, and I will look for ways to do it with him. I want to treat people with his love and mercy. I want to stand up for what is right. I want my words to be seasoned with grace. I want to flee self-centeredness and make my actions about serving others. I want to be an encourager. I want to show patience and self-control.

As I do these things, I can be assured that I am walking with my God. The fear of the Lord is real.

Lord, give me the wisdom and insight to follow you today. May your plans be my plans. May your goals be my goals. In your name, amen.

NOVEMBER 2

"Sihon came out against us, he and all his people, to battle at Jahaz. And the LORD *our God gave him over to us, and we defeated him and his sons and all his people."* (Deut. 2:32–33)

There is military conflict in our world. Some who read this may be soldiers involved in that battleground. There is also a spiritual battle that rages around the world. It is a spiritual and moral battle not limited by national borders. It rages in our communities, our cities and states, and our countries. But it also rages in our jobs, our families, and even our own minds.

How do we fight these wars? Both the physical and the spiritual wars need to be fought with the Lord as our weapon. God must be on our side. When God joins us in battle, we stand ready for any enemy.

As I look at those in military conflict, I want to make sure that the war is just. That means that the war needs to be waged to protect people, to increase security, and to stop thugs from aggression. I want to pray for our military that they will be fighting with a heart to seek peace. That they will have the emotional fortitude to do what they do each day. That they will know God and will be strengthened in knowing they are about a just cause. I also want to work within the political system to make sure our military forces have the best arms and supplies to minimize the loss of life and to make the conflict as short and efficient as possible.

When I consider spiritual conflict, I have a slightly different approach, but it is based on the same idea: make sure that God is engaged in the struggle, knowing that victory comes from him. If I am looking at others (or myself) in spiritual conflict, I will pray for them (or me). I will pray that God will give them good motives and a pure heart. That they will have the resources to deal with the conflict. That they will know the Lord and his guiding hand. That they will seek to conquer the forces arrayed against them, trusting in God's strength to do so. That God's peace will guard their hearts and minds while they seek to win the battle. That God's Spirit will empower them, giving them wisdom, conviction, and strength to overcome the struggle.

As a Christian, I will also pray that they have the peace and spiritual success that comes from knowing the saving work of Jesus. That Jesus has already conquered sin and even the grave gives me great courage to know that I can conquer as well in his name and with his strength. In a real sense, he has already won the battles that count! The weapons of the spiritual war are not carnal weapons. But the battle must be won!

Lord, be with those fighting wars, military and spiritual. Be their vision, their confidence and strength, and their guide. In your name, amen.

NOVEMBER 3

"Og the king of Bashan came out against us, he and all his people, to battle at Edrei. But the LORD said to me, 'Do not fear him, for I have given him and all his people and his land into your hand.'" (Deut. 3:1–2)

When I was a young boy, I had a recurrent bad dream. I will tell it here, but you must promise not to laugh. This was when I was *young*, and hence I must be cut some slack!

In my dream, on a dark night, our family was eating dinner around the dining table. We heard a loud fire engine siren. I got up and ran to the door, opening it to see what was going on. The men on the fire truck had a machine gun, and as everyone on the block opened the door to see the truck behind the siren, the men gunned them down. I was petrified.

Now my dream took that form once, but the second time I had it, it got worse! The second time as I was dreaming it, I was aware of the earlier dream. So the second time, I was at the dinner table thinking, "Gee, this is like the time when the fire engines came and machine-gunned everyone who opened their doors." Just as I was thinking that in my dream, I heard the sound of a fire engine siren! Now, even though I was dreaming, I thought, "Don't go open the door. You know how this plays out! That fire engine has machine gun–toting bad guys." Still, unable to stop myself, I went and opened the door in my dream only to see the fire engine loaded with men firing machine guns! I was terrified.

Those fears were not rational. They were the dream world of an eight-year-old boy who watched too many machine gun movies! Fears come from rational and irrational places. There really are a lot of legitimate things to fear in this world, starting with our own bad choices! As a very successful friend of mine has repeatedly told me, "We are all only seven bad choices from living under a bridge." We know the fear called a "health scare." We can fear loss of loved ones, loss of jobs, loss of financial security, and many other things.

Fear is a disease that can infect our lives and cause us to miss out on opportunities. Fear can drive us to do things we wouldn't otherwise do and maybe shouldn't do. Fear can paralyze us and make us powerless when we shouldn't be.

But there is an antidote to fear. The antidote is God. If God is for us, who can be against us? If we are fighting God's battles, whom should we fear? If God is the Lord of our lives and he is in control, why would we ever be afraid of what lies before us?

Lord, you told the Israelites long ago not to fear the battles where you engage. Please engage in my life. Let me fight your battles with no fear. In your name, amen.

NOVEMBER 4

"I commanded Joshua at that time, 'Your eyes have seen all that the LORD your God has done to these two kings. So will the LORD do to all the kingdoms into which you are crossing. You shall not fear them, for it is the LORD your God who fights for you.'" (Deut. 3:21-22)

Yesterday's devotion spoke to the truth that with God on our side, we need not fear, come what may. Today's passage continues with the idea of fear, but with an added twist. Those with eyes that see God do not live in fear.

Joshua was getting some last instructions from Moses as Moses handed over the leadership reins. Moses was going to be dead soon, and God had selected Joshua to be the new leader for the Israelites, taking them into the Promised Land. Joshua wasn't the king. God was Israel's king. But Joshua was a military general, the voice of God to the people, a civil leader, and much more. This was new to Joshua. Moses had filled that role with help from Aaron, who was already dead.

I think it would be natural for Joshua to be tentative and afraid. What if God didn't talk to Joshua as he did Moses? What if God didn't help Joshua feed the starving people, give water to the thirsty, or judge the mutineers? The "what ifs" must have been knocking on the door of Joshua's mind all day and through the night.

Moses knew this was likely true, and he spoke some solid wisdom to Joshua. Moses told Joshua to consider the two battles the Israelites had just won. Those were won because God was fighting for Israel. The real battle was the Lord's, not Moses', not Joshua's, not even the Israelites'. Joshua needed to see that, and then Joshua would need have no fear. "For it is the Lord your God who fights for you."

This is the balm I need today. I want to take the time and see what God has done in my life. I can remember the battles he has won. I was there when he rescued me and delivered me. I was there when he raised me up against all odds.

I have seen what God has done, and eyes that see God need not fear. God is my present help. He is my light in darkness. He is the rock in shifting sand. He is my stability in a shaking world. He is my security in times of trouble. He is my resource in times of want. He is my wisdom when I face important decisions. He is my comfort in times of pain.

The Lord is my God. He does fight for me. I need not fear.

Lord, even writing (and reading) this, I must confess my fears. You have done great things, but often our faith weakens. Please take my fears and be my stronghold in times of trouble. May I rest faithfully in you. In your name, amen.

NOVEMBER 5

"You shall not add to the word that I command you, nor take from it, that you may keep the commandments of the LORD your God that I command you." (Deut. 4:2)

If you have read many of the devotions in this book, you have likely found a number of typographical errors. I tend to make typos frequently. If you have not spotted any, then either your brain reads past them the way that mine does or the editors and friends who have helped me proof-read this have done a remarkable job.

Generally, typos are simply a nuisance and distraction. Occasionally, however, they lead to a different meaning. There is a book entitled *Eats, Shoots, and Leaves*. If the comma is before *and* in the title, then it means someone eats, then shoots, and then departs (leaves). This might be seen in a Western film. If there is no comma, however, it might be referring to a panda bear at a zoo that eats (bamboo) shoots and leaves (plural of leaf). Grammarians and careful readers like this book because they believe it shows a comma can save a life.

The Israelites, through Moses, were entrusted with the oracles of God. They were assigned the responsibility of knowing them and transmitting them faithfully. They did so with great care.

Before the advent of copy machines, or even carbon paper, Scripture was propagated by scribes copying each manuscript carefully letter by letter. Of course, errors crept in through the copying process, but those errors are generally easy to identify (for example, misspellings). When one compares the Dead Sea Scroll Scripture copies found in the mid-twentieth century to the medieval handwritten manuscripts still extant today, it is amazing to see the accuracy of the Jewish scribes in over a thousand years of copying manuscripts.

The Hebrew scholars were so careful because they understood today's passage. Each word that God gave in his Scriptures was a holy word that God chose. These words were not to be removed or added to by anyone transmitting the Scriptures. Jewish scholars have been faithful to the charge of God for thousands of years, and we reap the benefits today. When we read the Scriptures, we can be confident that we are getting the content intended. We can parse the sentences, dwell on certain words, and meditate with confidence.

After all the work that people have gone through for thousands of years, what a pity it is that so many believers spend so little time in the Scripture. Every word is important, and yet we often have trouble spending five minutes a day to figure out why. I want to seize my opportunities to study God's word.

Lord, thank you for the blessing of your word. May I dwell in it in your name, amen.

NOVEMBER 6

"See, I have taught you statutes and rules, as the LORD my God commanded me, that you should do them in the land that you are entering to take possession of it. Keep them and do them, for that will be your wisdom and your understanding in the sight of the peoples, who, when they hear all these statutes, will say, 'Surely this great nation is a wise and understanding people.'" (Deut. 4:5–6)

People are watching you! Your coworkers are watching to see if you do what you say. Your children are watching to see if you practice what you preach. Your enemies are watching to see if you walk the walk or simply talk the talk. People are watching you for consistency and authenticity. Are you what you claim to be? Do you preach God with your mouth but worship money with your life? Do you really believe in God, or are you simply going through the motions?

Today's passage spoke to the Israelites in Moses' day, but it also speaks to all of us in a broader sense today. Israel was strategically placed for people to watch how the Israelites behaved and what they believed. Israel could and would influence the nations.

Israel was a unique land geographically. It formed a bridge between the great civilizations that grew up around the great rivers in the Middle East. To the north were the civilizations of Mesopotamia (literally, "between the rivers"), an area including Assyria and other empires that arose between the Tigris and Euphrates Rivers. To the south was Egypt, a civilization thriving around the Nile River. If you wanted to venture from one to the other, you went through the land God was providing to Israel. Israel served as a bridge on trade routes, war expeditions, and more. It was the fertile ground that God called to be a beacon.

Israel was told, "Live right before God, and you will shine and be blessed." Israel could have become mighty by living right before God. Instead, Israel traded faith for idolatry and unbelief. The opportunities were squandered, and Israel continued to exist only by the grace of God.

Each of us is uniquely placed in this world. People who watch and connect with me will not be precisely the same as the people who watch and connect with you. We have a divine responsibility to show people who we are and who God is. Our lives should be consistent with the words we speak. Our walk should mirror our talk. Our children should be able to model their lives off ours. This is God's blessing and instruction. The alternative is not pretty.

Lord, help me to do a better job showing people my faith and trust in you by how I walk. Forgive me where I fall short, and lead me in your path. In your name, amen.

NOVEMBER 7

"Only take care, and keep your soul diligently, lest you forget the things that your eyes have seen, and lest they depart from your heart all the days of your life. Make them known to your children and your children's children." (Deut. 4:9)

As a child, I was fascinated by my inability to keep water in my hands. I would cup my hands together really tight. I would inspect them to see that there were no spaces between the fingers. I would then scoop up water, but try as I might, I could never get the water to stay in my hands long. It would dribble out through the unseen cracks.

I have found a way around water dribbling through my hands. I use a cup. Unfortunately, I haven't figured out a way to keep knowledge and experience fresh in my brain. I don't have a ready cup for that. Instead, I must make a deliberate effort to remember.

Today's passage gives a warning to the Israelites and to us who study it. It warns us that we must be diligent and careful to "keep our soul." The Hebrew for *keep* also means to "watch" or "guard," to "preserve." We need to be on our guard and be watchful. These are ideas that require deliberateness. If we aren't deliberate in remembering and nurturing the work of God in our lives, we will decide one day that our experiences with God are quaint memories from our immature days, when we were naïve, and before we aged into wisdom.

Such couldn't be further from the truth. In the story from my childhood, water was in my hands, but it slipped through the cracks. It disappeared with only a damp reminder, not because it wasn't real but because I couldn't keep it.

God tells us to never forget his hand in our lives. We need to write it down. We need to mark it in our conscious minds, and most importantly, we need to tell others about it. "Tell your children," God told Moses. This wasn't simply so the children would know. It was also so Moses would remember. When we tell others about God's work in our lives, it keeps his work recent and vibrant. It is a way that we secure the memory and don't forget what our eyes have seen.

Before leaving today's passage, I have an action step to take. I am going to recount to myself, in good detail, acts of God in my life. Where he has rescued me from deep waters. Where he has lifted my soul. Where he has secured his work in my life. As a Christian, I am especially mindful of where he forgave my sin.

We all have a lot for which to be thankful.

Lord, thank you for this life, with all the blessings, large and small. Help me to remember them and to tell others readily about the amazing God. In your name, amen.

NOVEMBER 8

*"Then the L*ORD *spoke to you out of the midst of the fire. You heard the sound of words, but saw no form; there was only a voice. And he declared to you his covenant, which he commanded you to perform, that is, the Ten Commandments, and he wrote them on two tablets of stone."* (Deut. 4:12–13)

I think most every person, at some time or another, wishes to have some visual sighting of God. I know as a child that I wondered why God didn't make a visible appearance to each person, thereby ensuring their faith. Of course, as I grew, I understood that a visible appearance doesn't ensure faith. By definition, faith is something you don't see. I also learned that should God make an appearance, what I "saw" would not be God. God is not a physical being in the sense of our universe. God isn't a part of our universe; he created it. In spite of our inability to see God with our eyes, we are called to follow him.

Moses had the call to follow God, even as he had a physical experience of God in the form of a voice emanating from a bush that was burning but wasn't consumed. Moses saw a manifestation of God's greatness in the form of the burning bush, but he didn't see God. Moses heard God speak from that bush, and he was expected to follow God based on what he heard, not a vision of the Almighty.

Later on, Israel had the commandments of God that Moses had brought down from his mountain experience with God. The Ten Commandments were manifestations of God's presence and work, but they weren't God. Israel could see the words that God had given them, but Israel didn't see God.

I understand the desire to see God. I would also like to see loads of things that my human eyes, even aided with modern equipment, will never see. Some things aren't visible to the human eye. Science teaches that black holes are stars so condensed that their gravitational pull allows nothing visible to escape. We see evidence of this from measurements and scientific deductions, but no one is visibly seeing the star that forms the black hole. Nevertheless, it is there. I can't see the love that I have for my wife, yet I know I love her. I would quickly lay down my life to save hers. Yet love is not a visible reality. It is a reality we know based on the evidence we see.

I love my faith in God. I've written books and articles on it. It isn't something I embrace simply to feel good, to give inspiration, or to have a good social group. My faith is based on my best deductions that make sense of the evidence I see. This evidence includes the humanness of humans, why we are the way we are, why we think the way we think, and why we are hardwired for justice and fairness, for objective morality, and for love. The God who revealed himself through Scripture gives the best understanding I have of life.

Lord, thank you for revealing yourself in your works and love. In your name, amen.

NOVEMBER 9

"Therefore watch yourselves very carefully . . . And beware lest you raise your eyes to heaven, and when you see the sun and the moon and the stars, all the host of heaven, you be drawn away and bow down to them and serve them, things that the LORD your God has allotted to all the peoples under the whole heaven." (Deut. 4:15–19)

When I was young, we sang a song in church that I loved both for its melody and for the way it drew my attention to God. Titled "O Worship the King All Glorious Above" and written by the British lawyer Sir Robert Grant in 1833, the words began, "O worship the King all-glorious above, / O gratefully sing his power and his love: / our shield and defender, the Ancient of Days, / pavilioned in splendor and girded with praise." It was and is one of my favorite worship songs.

Praise and worship properly come before God. At their cores, praise and worship are acknowledgments of the worthiness or value of that receiving the worship. God is the ultimate value; God is of infinite worth. God should naturally be the recipient of our praise in song, prayer, and life overall.

In today's passage, Moses is giving an admonition to the people to worship God the Creator and never get beguiled into worshipping the creation of God. This admonition was important to Israel, surrounded as it was by idolatrous people. But it is no less important to us today.

Most people today don't worship the sun, moon, and stars as personal gods. Most people don't have idols in their homes that they bow down to and believe to be inanimate representations of personal beings. But that doesn't mean that we don't look at the creation and begin to give it the wonder, awe, and praise that are properly due God. Many people get "academic" about the physical world in ways where they are so enamored with it, they believe the world is all there is. A friend of mine calls himself a "physicalist." He believes that the only things that are real are material/matter. If it isn't made up of matter, it isn't real.

This friend, obviously, does not believe in God. His mind has trumped the divine. His perception of the universe seems to him to be the real truth in life. He worships what he sees and thinks, believing it to be of ultimate value and worth. This friend took his eyes off God.

As Moses warned, we need to watch ourselves very carefully. We need to be certain that we are living with God, embracing him, and seeking his help at each of life's turns.

Lord, may I carefully live in relationship with you, seeking your will daily and dedicating myself to your mission. May my life praise you as well as the words of my mouth. In your name, amen.

NOVEMBER 10

"Hear, O Israel: The LORD our God, the LORD is one. You shall love the LORD your God with all your heart and with all your soul and with all your might." (Deut. 6:4–9)

Today's passage will be familiar to many. It is said daily by Jews who practice the *Keri'at Shema'* (or the "saying of the *Shema*"). *Shema* is the first word in the passage read in Hebrew. In English it is translated most often "hear" or "listen." Christians recognize the importance of this passage too, not only because Jesus said it was the most important or central law of the Torah but also because it forms the foundation of the Christian understanding of the Trinity (the idea that God is one, even though he is three persons within that unity, with the Spirit of God and Jesus being the other two persons).

If we consider the book of Deuteronomy a collection of Moses' speeches to the Israelites, then the *Shema* is found at the beginning of Moses' second discourse. Early in this sermon, Moses has repeated the Ten Commandments (Deut. 5:6–18). The *Shema* is often seen as part of a sermon on the first commandment, "I am the LORD your God, who brought you out of the land of Egypt, out of the house of slavery. You shall have no other gods before me."

The unity of God—the fact that God is one, not multiple—is what forms the foundation of monotheism (literally, "a belief there is only one God"). Israel's neighbors believed that God would not be so grand. Save for a limited experiment in Egypt under Pharaoh Akhenaten, who became a quasi-monotheist, Israel's neighbors were replete with gods.

This foundational uniqueness of Israel was based on revelation, not logic. Logic would drive many to monotheism later, especially as the Greeks began to explore the idea of what a god was and whether there could be a situation of competition between multiple gods or there must be a singular god. For Israel, God wasn't something people figured out. He was never the invention of human thought. Humanity wasn't smart enough and didn't have the resources to figure out who God was in any clear sense. It took God revealing himself to us for us to begin to understand him. Even then, our understanding is primitive at best. How dare we think our three-and-a-half pounds of gray cells we call a brain can greatly understand the one who created the depths of this vast universe with all that is in it!

The *Shema* will be used for tomorrow's devotion as well. For today, we pause to acknowledge the greatness of the God who revealed himself to us.

Lord, you are great and greatly to be praised. For all you've done on a vast scale, and for the individual way you make yourself known to us, we praise you and thank you in your name, amen.

NOVEMBER 11

"Hear, O Israel: The LORD our God, the LORD is one. You shall love the LORD your God with all your heart and with all your soul and with all your might. And these words that I command you today shall be on your heart. You shall teach them diligently to your children, and shall talk of them when you sit in your house, and when you walk by the way, and when you lie down, and when you rise. You shall bind them as a sign on your hand, and they shall be as frontlets between your eyes. You shall write them on the doorposts of your house and on your gates." (Deut. 6:4–9)

The Lanier household believes that our children must know certain things before they are allowed to be considered "grown up" and leave home. If high schools and colleges have "prerequisites" for graduation, these things are Lanier household graduation prerequisites. One is debate. All five of our children were not allowed to conclude their high school educations without having taken debate. A second is important aspects of music history, especially the classics. That isn't Beethoven and Bach; that's Springsteen and Dylan.

Of all the things we can and should teach our children, however, none rise to the importance of who God is. This is the import of today's passage and devotion. Look carefully at Moses' instruction to Israel. He didn't simply say, "Teach your children there is a God." He told the people of Israel to teach their children about who God is. This is Moses' commentary on the first commandment, which begins, "I am the LORD your God, who brought you out of the land of Egypt, out of the house of slavery. You shall have no other gods before me" (Deut. 5:6). This is "LORD" God. The large and small capital letters in our translations come from Moses using God's name, the Hebrew letters equivalent to English *YHVH* (often typed *Yahweh*, adding vowel sounds and using the German *W* for the Hebrew *V*). This is the name God gave Moses from the burning bush so Israel would know who he was.

We must teach our children who God is, and that is best done by telling them what he has done and how we honor him today. Much of what people learn is by observation, especially children. Children are constantly watching their parents, imitating and becoming what they see. So Moses instructed the Israelites to model their understanding and faith in who God is by talking of it constantly, by putting it in their homes inside and out, by wearing it physically and figuratively, and by making it the cornerstone of how they saw the world and how they walked through life.

It should be no different for us today. The centrality of who God is should shape the way we see life, the way we live, and the way we talk, and it should be the foundation of what we model and teach our children.

Lord, may I better see you, understand you, and share you. In your name, amen.

NOVEMBER 12

"And because you listen to these rules and keep and do them, the LORD your God will keep with you the covenant and the steadfast love that he swore to your fathers. He will love you, bless you, and multiply you." (Deut. 7:12–13)

Always remember your dependence on God, even when you prosper in this world.

Success is a strange thing. It can go to our heads. It can also lead to independence and self-sufficiency. When we are in need, when we desperately need help to cover bills, to rescue a loved one, to handle a crisis at work or school, to resolve a betrayal, to deal with a health crisis, to mend a broken relationship, or to heal some other difficulty or trauma, we turn to God. We need God. The problems scare us and exceed our abilities to handle our problems alone. Faith is a strong refuge in those times. God becomes very dear to us. We are more careful in walking in God's will and less quick to offend him!

But when we achieve worldly success, when we prosper economically, when we have abundance in money, health, love, and more, we sometimes lose our mooring. We begin to think, at least subconsciously, that we really need no one. We think we have life under control. We think that we can make it on our own.

We may not say this out loud. Heavens, we may not even say it to ourselves, but we live it. Our prayer lives become more hollow or rare. Our pursuit of a holy lifestyle becomes less intense. Our priorities subtly shift. Our humility drops as our self-confidence rises. We might not think it can happen to us, but the heart is deceitful above all things.

Today's passage is in the flow of a long sermon by Moses where he challenged the Israelites to follow God, confident that God will bless them. But Moses had a concern, and he speaks of it bluntly. Moses knew as success came to the Israelites, so would the likelihood that they would forget their reliance on God. They might forget it was God who gave them the victory.

History shows that not all Israelites heeded Moses' instructions. Over time, the directive faded into oblivion. The people became self-reliant. They traded worship of the Lord God who brought them into the land in favor of the gods of the land that were defeated. It didn't go well with Israel after that.

I need to remember to rely on God—24/7, every month, every year, for the rest of my life. God is my rock; why should I stand on anything or anyone else?

Lord, thank you for the life you have given me—the talents, gifts, opportunities, and responsibilities. May I rely on you 100 percent, giving you all the glory for anything good. In your name, amen.

NOVEMBER 13

*"You shall not be in dread of them, for the L*ORD *your God is in your midst, a great and awesome God."* (Deut. 7:21)

Have you *ever* been in dread of someone or something? I am a trial lawyer. I make my living trying cases before juries and judges. In every case, there is a fateful moment when the jury, judge, or panel of judges announces the decision of who won and who lost. I dread those decisions. In other areas of my life, I have found dread as well. If *dread* denotes fear and trembling (which the Hebrew word does), then we have all found times when we dread.

There is an answer to what you dread. The answer lies in this truth: our God is an awesome God. We need not fear anyone or anything other than him! If we are walking with him in love, we can be assured that he knows our paths and that he protects us. That doesn't mean we will never suffer. It doesn't mean that no harm will befall us. It doesn't mean that we will never be sick, lonely, depressed, sad, frustrated, or even angry. But it does mean that when we are those things, he will be with us and will show us the way.

So we needn't fear. We needn't dread today or tomorrow. Others should not instill dread in us. The times shouldn't scare us. Foreign events shouldn't cause us to tremble. We don't need to lose sleep if the stock market crashes. We need to draw close to our God and let him walk alongside us, giving us strength and direction.

As we walk with God in faith, we will find that the worst the world throws at us isn't so much that it overpowers us. When we worry about today, we know God is there, and we can have peace. When we toss and turn in our beds, concerned about tomorrow, we know God has tomorrow well in hand, and we can go to sleep. When we are sick, we have assurance that the Great Physician has matters under control, and whether we recover or pass on to life after death, we can trust God with our bodies. If we are lonely, God is ready to talk in prayer. If we are depressed, we can take heart that God will give us joy in life. If we are mourning, we can know his comfort in the midst of grief. If we are frustrated or angry, we can pause and draw on his strength to assess things apart from anger and walk in patience and love, even when the situation is difficult.

I know fear and dread, but I also know the one who drives out fear. I have nothing to dread. It is a shadow that is dispelled as I live in the light of the Lord. This is where I need to stand today and every day. It is the difference between being a one-man or one-woman show and being in fellowship with the Almighty.

Lord, thank you for your love, strength, presence, and engagement in my life. Help me to better trust you, love you, and live in your care. In your name, amen.

NOVEMBER 14

"The LORD your God will clear away these nations before you little by little. You may not make an end of them at once, lest the wild beasts grow too numerous for you." (Deut. 7:22)

God's timing isn't ours, and that's a good thing!

Many of us live our lives around clocks. We have watches, our phones are timepieces, our computers keep up with our calendars—where we need to be when—and we make and keep appointments based on time. Many of us also live our lives around speed. We get fast food. Roads always post speed limits but rarely display speed minimums. We try hard to pick the shortest lines.

Put these together, and it's no surprise that we like quick solutions to our problems. No one wants difficulty to linger. We don't like it when our problems stick around without resolution. The idea of waiting for answers, when we don't know what to do or how to do it, becomes a heavy weight of dread and concern.

We have faith that God is real, and we know that God can help us, but even there, we get impatient. I want God to help me, and I want his help *now!* But if I've learned anything about God in this life, I have learned that his timing is not mine.

In today's passage, God is explaining how the Israelites are going to conquer Canaan through God's strength. Of course, God could do it in one fell swoop. God could have put great fear in all the inhabitants of the land and had them leave it in a mass caravan. God could have sent plagues to wipe all the people out. God could have inspired marauding tribes to vacate the land of inhabitants before returning to their homelands, leaving Canaan ready for Israel. But God did none of those things.

God explained to Israel that he would be clearing out the people little by little. It was a process. It would take time. God had set it to happen by God's calendar, and that calendar ran based on God's insights, not those of any human. To help the Israelites understand the importance of what God was doing, Moses explained that if God rid the land of inhabitants all at once, then the wild animals would take over, destroying vineyards and farms, ruining villages, and causing mayhem.

In other words, God's timing is based on what is best for God's people. It may not be the timing we would choose, but it is the timing we need. When we are faced with problems and we seek God's help, we shouldn't be dismayed that his help comes in his timing rather than our own. That is a good thing. We just need to trust him.

Lord, thank you for hearing my prayers and helping me in my need. Please help me to be patient and to be strong in faith, knowing your timing is best. In your name, amen.

NOVEMBER 15

"You shall remember the whole way that the LORD your God has led you these forty years in the wilderness, that he might humble you, testing you to know what was in your heart, whether you would keep his commandments or not. And he humbled you and let you hunger and fed you with manna, which you did not know, nor did your fathers know, that he might make you know that man does not live by bread alone, but man lives by every word that comes from the mouth of the LORD." (Deut. 8:1-3)

For forty years, the Lord had the Israelites in the wilderness. They wandered those forty years because they had faltered in their faith, not believing that God was able to conquer Canaan through them and on their behalf. During the time in the wilderness, God worked to prove their hearts and faith. Those who were malcontents, who tried to mutiny against God and take the Israelites further away from faith, God dealt with justly. Those who were trying to follow God were affirmed by God.

When the people were hungry and their food supply fell short, God provided them manna. (*Manna* was a word made up by the Israelites. It comes from the Hebrew *m—*, meaning "what." In a real sense, *manna* in Hebrew was in modern English basically "whatchamacallit.") The manna fell from heaven. It gave the Hebrews food beyond their bread. The Israelites could learn from it that God's words and deeds provided sustenance and life beyond that found in Israel's traveling pantries.

Over a thousand years later, a Jewish carpenter was beginning a ministry as a rabbi, teaching those who would follow him. This carpenter went into the wilderness, not for forty years like the Israelites but for forty days instead. During this time, he was tempted to confirm his faith or expose his lack of faith. One of the temptations was for this carpenter—Jesus—to use miraculous powers to turn rocks into bread. Jesus replied to the tempter, "It is written that man does not live by bread alone, but by every word that comes from the mouth of the Lord." Jesus quoted from today's passage in the Torah.

As a Christian, I pay special notice to what Jesus said. But whether or not one believes that Jesus was and is God's Messiah, sent to deliver the faithful from the price and bondage of sin, there is still a lesson here. We should never forget, especially when our faith is being tested, that we are to follow God and rely on him. It is more important than what we eat. It is more important than what we do. It is more important than our own self-sufficiency. Following God's words and living faithfully with him are the most important things that should dictate all our actions.

Lord, I know weakness, and many times I have failed to live faithfully. But I also know the forgiveness you have justly provided me, and I am deeply grateful. Teach me to live faithfully by each word that comes from your mouth. In your name, amen.

NOVEMBER 16

"Know then in your heart that, as a man disciplines his son, the Lord your God disciplines you. So you shall keep the commandments of the Lord your God by walking in his ways and by fearing him." (Deut. 8:5–6)

Have you ever seen an espaliered apple tree? They can be shaped to look like football goalposts or almost anything else. It is done by cutting and pruning certain locations and tying the branches to supports in other locations, with the effect of a specifically shaped tree bearing fruit. Perhaps you're more familiar with a potter throwing a pot. The clay is prepared by kneading and shaping. Then it is typically put on wheel, where hands mold and form the pot. Frequently, the potter will need to use tools that cut off parts of the clay, but the result is a pot that meets specifications.

Whether espaliering trees or shaping a pot, the basic approach is the same. You cut, shape, mold, and form the end result. Consider the similarities to parenting a child. The goal of a parent is to form in a child the faith, traits, and character that will allow the child to grow into maturity, achieving her or his potential in this life. That isn't done without significant parenting work. We need to mold our children, teach our children, and even discipline our children. Through discipline, a child learns discipline. Discipline can reinforce good and right by teaching the negatives of evil and wrong. Discipline can be light (like making a child apologize or putting a child in time-out), or discipline can be more severe. As parents, our goal was always to use the least severe discipline to achieve the lesson that needed learning.

At various places in Scripture, God uses each of my illustrations above in allegorizing his actions in our lives. Scripture speaks of God shaping us as one shapes a tree. It speaks of him molding us as a potter molds clay. In today's passage, it speaks of God disciplining us as a parent disciplines a child.

Most children don't like discipline. I've never seen a child rejoice over losing cell phone privileges or being grounded. But discipline is important. An undisciplined child generally grows up with some very difficult and negative habits that need addressing. Similarly, we aren't often fond of the discipline that God dispenses. We are like the child who thinks the parent shouldn't enforce rules or seek to modify behavior. Yet every good parent does, and God does as well. This is how he shapes us. This is how we learn and mature. God loves us enough not to leave us immature and lacking in his graces. He will teach us, whether we like it or not!

Thank you, Lord, for your discipline. Thank you for caring enough to teach me and mold me. Help me to learn quickly from your discipline so I can better walk in your ways. In your name, amen.

NOVEMBER 17

"Beware lest you say in your heart, 'My power and the might of my hand have gotten me this wealth.' You shall remember the LORD your God, for it is he who gives you power to get wealth, that he may confirm his covenant that he swore to your fathers, as it is this day." (Deut. 8:17–18)

One Saturday afternoon, when I was a young man in my final year of law school, I remember being at a college football game. It seemed like I was going to get a good job after law school, so the road ahead looked bright. I bumped into my preacher, Ken Dye. We visited during the game, and he was encouraging about what lay before me. Toward the end of our conversation, he put his hand out on my arm, and he said with a mixture of concern and joy, "When you get out there and start your big legal career, don't start thinking you're something on a stick!" I had never heard that before, nor have I since.

In the language of my childhood, he meant the same thing my mom or dad would when they spoke about people getting "too big for their britches." I shouldn't start thinking of myself as something greater than I was.

This is a common concern! It seems a bit of human nature that when we find a measure of success, we believe we earned it. The success goes to our heads. We think we are the reason for the success. Pride and arrogance can set up shop quickly.

God warns Israel about this and, in so doing, gives a warning to us all. God knew that Israel was going to successfully conquer Canaan and become a prosperous nation. It was going to be done not because of military genius or the force of Israel. It would happen because God would see to it. God was the reason. Israel wouldn't see it unfold like a movie. Israel would have a role. But Israel's role was simply to follow the lead of God. The Israelites needn't trust in chariots, horses, or any weapon. They needed to trust only in God, and that trust would produce obedience to his orders, which would then produce success.

The proper response of Israel would not be to think that Israel accomplished the great feats. Israel should give the credit and glory to God. God was the author of the plan. God empowered the Israelites. God instilled fear in their enemies. It was always about God.

Human nature needs some instructions. We don't naturally do right; we need to learn it. This passage teaches us an important lesson. We do what we do in the care of God. Then, when success comes, we give God the praise. We don't take credit that belongs to him. We should never think we are something on a stick.

Lord, you have done wondrous things in our lives. May we praise you and give you all the glory. In your name, amen.

NOVEMBER 18

"And now, Israel, what does the LORD your God require of you, but to fear the LORD your God, to walk in all his ways, to love him, to serve the LORD your God with all your heart and with all your soul, and to keep the commandments and statutes of the LORD, which I am commanding you today for your good?" (Deut. 10:12–13)

Verses like this stun me. The idea that God would put into plain English (actually, plain Hebrew that gets translated in English!) such direct talk causes me to sit up and take notice.

What does the Lord your God *require* of you? The answer to this question is huge. It is monumental. It is what I want to know. It is what I want to do. It is how I want to live. This is insight into the mind of the Almighty. This moves to the front of my "What is important to do today?" line. This slows me down in my reading so I can study each word. This isn't "What does God want?" or "What does God prefer?" It's not even "What does God think is a good thing?" Today's passage asks what God *requires*!

Here it is with numbers: First, God requires we fear him. Now that may not sound loving or nice, but it is both! To fear God is to know God. God is something far beyond our cozy pictures of him. He is all powerful, all knowledgeable, unchanging, with a character that we describe as "perfection." He is perfect and pure light. This is fearsome because I have darkness that can't exist in pure light. That truth should stir up fear. God requires us to live in truth and reality, not some fictional world of our making.

Second, God requires that we walk in his ways. I am to follow his light. I am to be pure as he is. I won't be successful, try as I might, so I am going to need his mercy, even in the midst of his justice. This means he will need to justly fix my impurities. As a Christian, I believe he has done this through the sacrifice of Jesus on my behalf. Jesus paid the penalty I owe.

This leads me to my third point: God requires we love him. I love God *because* he first loved me, and he gave of himself to purify and justify me ("justly declare me OK"). This "requirement" critically comes before my last point: God requires I serve him with my heart and soul, keeping his commandments. I am not obedient to God simply because he will turn me into a crisp if I'm not. Giving God my best comes out of my love for him. As I have learned of God, as I have seen his actions on my behalf, as I have seen his faithfulness even when mine lags, I have experienced his love. That love has stirred in me a responsive love. That love has taught me how to love. That love motivates me to live for him.

Lord, may I fear you, give you my best, find your forgiveness, honor you, love you, and serve you. In your name, amen.

NOVEMBER 19

"See, I am setting before you today a blessing and a curse: the blessing, if you obey the commandments of the LORD your God, which I command you today, and the curse, if you do not obey the commandments of the LORD your God, but turn aside from the way that I am commanding you today, to go after other gods that you have not known." (Deut. 11:26–28)

There's a price to be paid for every choice we make.

We have all sorts of expressions that state this truth: "If you want to dance, you've got to pay the band!" "Don't do the crime if you can't do the time." "What goes around comes around." "Karma!" "You reap what you sow." These are just a few of the sayings we hear that recognize our actions have consequences.

The scientific age has given us tools to better comprehend and express this truth. We speak of "cause and effect," recognizing that in physics, every action has an equal and opposite reaction. Biblically we learn that God made this world a cause-and-effect world not only in physics but also in ethics and morality.

Good moral choices bear good fruit. Poor moral choices bear poor fruit. Think of some rather obvious examples. You can get drunk, drive a car, and as a result, have a wreck with disastrous consequences. Many a young life has been ruined by poor choices made before grasping the truth of today's devotion. Hopefully, as we mature, we realize the importance of moral cause and effect.

But I believe there are more subtle levels, where we deceive ourselves into thinking that we can beat the moral cause-and-effect law. There are days when we think we can fudge the truth or choose to be selfish and moments when gossip doesn't seem so destructive. There are times when we dwell on sinful thoughts (envy, lust, greed, etc.) and think that the consequences may not really follow, or if they do, they won't be too severe.

When we think we can defy the moral laws, we need a cold splash of water to our face. The results may not always be seen immediately, and the results may be inward where they are never seen, but the results are real. What we do makes a difference in the world. What we say makes a difference in the world. What we think makes a difference in the world. And those things also make a difference in who we are.

I want to make wise decisions. I want the positive effects from good decisions.

Lord, I am aware of my many shortcomings and how poor my own efforts can be in doing right. Please forgive me and strengthen me for your name's sake. Amen.

NOVEMBER 20

"You shall surely destroy all the places where the nations whom you shall dispossess served their gods, on the high mountains and on the hills and under every green tree. You shall tear down their altars and dash in pieces their pillars and burn their Asherim with fire. You shall chop down the carved images of their gods and destroy their name out of that place." (Deut. 12:2–3)

"Cancer!" That is a word no one ever wants to hear the doctor say. It is associated with painful treatment and often death. Skin cancer, liver cancer, lung cancer, breast cancer, and so on—it is hard to think of any area of the body that can't be stricken with cancer.

At this point in my life, I have never had to battle cancer personally, but my loved ones have. I have also dealt with more lawsuits involving cancer than I can count. Cancer cells are nasty little things. Most cells in the human body produce other cells and then die. This allows the body to live for longer than a cell lives. We are constantly turning over our cells, some places faster than others. But some cells are abnormal. They don't die. They breed and produce other cells that have the same abnormality, and pretty soon these reproducing and undying cells become a cancerous tumor.

Treatment for cancer varies. Doctors use surgery to cut the cancer out. Doctors use chemical poisons or radiation to kill the cells that won't die on their own. Doctors know that they need to try and rid the body of every cancer cell, or the ones that are left will just start the process all over again. Doctors try to get the cancerous cells before they spread to other parts of the body and begin to grow tumors in different organs. Cancer is a nasty business.

God taught the Israelites that idolatry is a nasty cancer. It is destructive and invasive, and the solution isn't to tolerate it but to destroy it. Like cancer cells, idolatry must be terminated. Today's passage contains God's instructions to Israel to find any cancerous idolatry and destroy it by any means possible. Destroy the places of idolatrous worship. Tear down altars to idols. Burn them. Chop the idols up into unrecognizable bits. Leave even a shred of idolatry, and it will come back to power, spreading its cancer around.

We need to heed this. We need to find anything that we put in the place of God and see it as the idol it is. When we see our idols, we don't need to play with them, flirt with them, dabble with them, or leave them nearby. We need to seek them out and destroy them. We need our lives under the subjection and worship of God and God alone. Nothing should have the value and place that belongs exclusively to God.

Lord, help me see the idols in my life. Help me utterly destroy them to worship you alone. In your name, amen.

NOVEMBER 21

"There you shall eat before the LORD your God, and you shall rejoice, you and your households, in all that you undertake, in which the LORD your God has blessed you." (Deut. 12:7)

John Piper has popularized the phrase "Christian hedonism." When I first heard it, I was intrigued. I knew of hedonism from the Greek word *hēdonē*, which denotes "pleasure" or "delight." I had also read classical philosophy, so I knew of the ancient Greek hedonistic approach to life that said one should live for whatever is the greatest or most pleasurable. But to pair the term *hedonism* with Christianity was something brand new. It didn't quite fit within the other uses I knew.

Piper uses this phrase to emphasize the importance of the biblical teaching that the highest and greatest calling of humanity is to find the ultimate pleasure that comes from an intimate relationship with God. This isn't an exclusively Christian concept, although the awareness of Jesus' role as Messiah certainly propels one to a deep joy. This is a biblical concept found first in the Torah.

Today's passage is one of many that talk about the importance of joy in the Lord. The people of God aren't to be always sour faced, walking around miserable, worried that someone may be experiencing joy and delight in life. The faithful are called to be one with God. This brings a deeper and everlasting joy that shines radiantly from the faces and lives of God's people.

Because I walk with God, and because I have been declared righteous by the Eternal Judge through the righteousness I have in the Messiah, I am overjoyed at the prospects of today. Don't get me wrong; some very tragic things might happen today. Someone I love might be stricken with disease or tragedy. People will die today. People will cry today. Each day can bring a heartache of anguish, but I am still overjoyed. God is with me today. He gives me strength, love, forgiveness, and more. Those aren't idle concepts; they are profound truths. In this I can rejoice, even when the world is falling apart! Let the foundations shake; I have an intimate relationship with one who is sturdier than any earthly foundation.

Today's passage reflects God's instructions to the people to eat before God, to rejoice before God, to celebrate his love and protection. This was to be an important part of Israel's worship and life. They were to rejoice before the Lord.

Rejoice in the Lord! Always! Let us say it again: REJOICE! We have a reason to do so.

Lord, thank you for your love, your attention, your affection, your mercy, your comfort, your care, and your concern. I rejoice in you, my God. In your name, amen.

NOVEMBER 22

"Be careful to obey all these words that I command you, that it may go well with you and with your children after you forever, when you do what is good and right in the sight of the LORD your God." (Deut. 12:28)

Having children changes the way you see the world. When our first child was born (we have five), I remember holding him fresh from the womb, seconds after delivery, praying over him. My thought at that time was new to me. I thought, "If I do nothing with my life other than bring this child up right before the Lord, I will have the most incredible life possible. I will have done something magnificently important."

Rearing children is not always easy. There are classes in it, but they are the clear-cut classes that teach you rearing children the way math class taught us multiplication tables. There are books on it, but they tend to be kind of like classes. Every child is different, and there aren't one-two-three rules that get you across the parenting finish line victoriously.

While the rule books aren't absolute, I did learn one extremely important rule. Children watch what their parents do, and they model the behavior they see. You want your children to cuss? Cuss around your children. You want your children to be short-tempered? Be short-tempered around your children. You want your children to love God, love God around your children! You want your children to value material things? Value material things around your children. You want your children to understand service? Model acts of service around your children.

Children are not going to do what we say unless it aligns with what we do. They will almost always do as we do, in spite of our wishes to the contrary.

Today's passage conveys that truth through the warning to parents to follow God's instructions. Moses explained that as the parents did right and good in the sight of God, then their children would be blessed and would have better lives. The negative is implied. If the parents do evil in the eyes of God, the children would bear those consequences as well.

Some reading this devotional may not have children yet or ever. The principle and devotion still apply, however, because it's not just children but people who are watching you and me. People will see what we do more than hear what we say. The best sermons are lived, not preached. What you do makes a difference in the lives of others. We can inspire them to greatness before God, or we confirm in them an aimlessness in life. This is our challenge today. People are watching!

Lord, may I model for others your love and the truths you teach. In your name, amen.

NOVEMBER 23

"Take care that you be not ensnared to follow them, after they have been destroyed before you, and that you do not inquire about their gods, saying, 'How did these nations serve their gods?—that I also may do the same.' You shall not worship the LORD your God in that way." (Deut. 12:30–31)

Imagine the world on its axis, as we see with most globes. The world is slightly tilted, but it revolves around a line that stretches from the North Pole to the South Pole, referencing an imaginary pole that cuts right through the heart of the earth.

Science teaches us that the earth is molten rock at its core. We need to remember this because we tend to live as if we are to be found in the center of the earth. The human condition is one that tends to place us at the center of things. We might not say it, might not think it, but we often operate on some level as if the world revolves around each of us. Yet it doesn't. It never has, and it never will. We are passengers on this big dirt clod rotating around a fireball in an obscure corner of the Milky Way galaxy.

The world, the solar system, the galaxy, and the whole universe really revolve around God. We must always remember that. This truth lies behind today's passage.

The Israelites were not alone in the area of Palestine. There were many other people who were instilled with an innate desire to find God, and they tried to find him in many different ways, just as people do today. God had done something special to Israel, however, and it was something God did to benefit the entire world. As God had said to Abraham centuries earlier, he would bless the world through the offspring of Abraham. One way that was coming true was by God revealing himself in truth through the Israelites. God did so on Sinai. He did so through prophets. He did so through Scripture, and as a Christian, I believe he did so through the Messiah.

Because God was revealing himself beyond what humans could conjure up simply trying to uncover the truth behind the drive for God, people needed to follow God as God revealed himself. It is simple. When we see God clearly, we need to follow and worship the clearer vision.

I may like what I like. I may want what I want. I may desire my ideas of God and my worship of him. But it isn't about me. It never was and never will be. The world doesn't revolve around me, regardless of what I think. Where and how God revealed himself trumps any of my desires, wishes, and ideas. Today is about God, not me.

Lord, may I worship you for who you are, not who I want you to be. In your name, amen.

NOVEMBER 24

"For there will never cease to be poor in the land. Therefore I command you, 'You shall open wide your hand to your brother, to the needy and to the poor, in your land.'" (Deut. 15:11)

"Needs" and "wants": two related yet distinct concepts. Some things in this life I need: food, oxygen, clean water, sleep, and so on. Some things in this life I want: a comfortable house and car, a family vacation, time for a good book, dessert, and so on. How do we balance those two concepts? That is a tough question of daily life.

People tussle with the idea of how we decide what is right to spend on our different levels of want versus how we help those who are missing a certain level of need. In high school, I enjoyed the driving sound of Dan Fogelberg's song "Loose Ends." In it, he brought this problem into focus, saying, "Surrounding myself with possessions / I surely have more than I need / I don't know if this is justice, hard earned, / Or simply a matter of greed." Good question, Dan!

With this problem in mind, consider today's passage. God instructs the Israelites that there will always be poor people in the land. Recognizing this, one can have two reactions. First, one can say, "Well, since there are always poor, there is nothing I can do about it. I might as well live my life for my family and loved ones," and then leave it there. Or one can say, "I need to help the poor, even if I can't solve poverty." Then one has to figure out how and how much to help the poor.

This issue came before Jesus when he was discussing the law with a Jewish scholar. Jesus had told the scholar the commandment to love our neighbors was important. Agreeing, the scholar asked Jesus, "Who is my neighbor?" In reply, Jesus told the story of the Good Samaritan. The moral to Jesus' story is that in life we will come across those in need. When we do, they become our neighbor, and we are to help them.

Sometimes this help means giving people a meal. Other times it means teaching them how to work for a meal. It might mean giving them education and opportunity. It might mean helping them off drugs or giving them mental health care to stabilize their ability to fend for themselves. It could even mean tough love where we don't condone laziness but make people work for their livelihood. Whichever it is, we are to thoughtfully figure out how to help those in need.

God works through his people. God wants to help the helpless, and when we do it in his name, it is God doing it. This also means *we don't do it to earn praise from others!* I want to have open eyes to see where I can help the poor and helpless.

Lord, open my eyes and heart to help those in need in your name. Amen.

NOVEMBER 25

"You shall rejoice before the LORD your God, you and your son and your daughter, your male servant and your female servant, the Levite who is within your towns, the sojourner, the fatherless, and the widow who are among you." (Deut. 16:11)

Some people go to church; some don't. Some people go to synagogue; some don't. Some people watch sermons on television or the Internet. Some people read books about God and faith. Some people listen to podcasts on faith. Some people are careful to pray each day. Some people do the above in various combinations. I believe each has a place in our lives, but behind them all is a fundamental truth we should grasp. Our failure to grasp this truth will stunt our growth and maturity in life.

The fundamental truth is the importance of praise and worship. To those with an "achievement mentality," praise and worship may seem superfluous if not nonsensical. Some wonder what it means and why we should do it. It is important for us to understand the answers to both questions, just as it is important we do it.

Praise and worship are simple things. They mean to mentally and physically spend time according value to God. Mentally we do so by thinking about his merit, worth, value, qualities that we rightly esteem and aspire to, character that challenges us, love that teaches us, justice that meets with mercy, and more. We think about these aspects of God, and then we physically give him honor and glory for who he is. This can be by praying, singing, giving back to him, listening to others extol his virtues, reading his word (Scripture), and other acts, but praise and worship join our bodies with our minds in demonstration of our true conviction that God is worthy of our devotion.

Understanding what praise and worship are is important. So is understanding *why* we do them. We worship God because he is worthy. In other words, it is the right thing to do. When we ascribe him praise, it takes our eyes off of other things in this world that try to demand our devotion, whether money, power, pleasure, social status, material goods, or anything else. Worshipping God and mentally acknowledging his greatness also takes our eyes away from ourselves. We better see ourselves for who we are. We move aside pride and embrace humility. We recognize our shortcomings. We find in him the answer to our problems. Praise and worship sets us in the truth that God is God and we aren't. We come into his presence to worship and adore him, and it transforms us when we do.

God taught Israel to praise and worship. This isn't because God needs the attention. It is because we need to be his devoted people in order to become who we are supposed to be in this life. I will seek to praise God!

Lord, you are loving, kind, just, all knowing, all seeing, all sufficient, and worthy of all my devotion, praise, and dedication. I honor and praise you as my king. Amen.

NOVEMBER 26

"You shall not pervert justice. You shall not show partiality, and you shall not accept a bribe, for a bribe blinds the eyes of the wise and subverts the cause of the righteous. Justice, and only justice, you shall follow." (Deut. 16:19–20)

Think about today, if you're reading this in the morning. If you're reading in the evening, think about tomorrow. With how many people will you or did you interact? Some days it may be few. Other days it may be many. Are most of them friends and family, or do you find yourself interacting with strangers? Whichever it is, God speaks often in his word about the importance of how we treat others.

Today's passage is about treating each other fairly. Fair treatment is an important part of the biblical concept of justice. Justice exists in the court system, we hope, but that isn't the only place. Justice starts outside of court.

I make a living through the court system, and I am intimately familiar with judicial justice. I have seen fair play and I have seen partiality. I even handled one case where jurors admitted afterward to accepting bribes from the other side. Bribery and partiality in courts are not godly. That is clear. But the court system only comes into play when something *unjust* has happened outside of court. It is the disputing of whether injustice happened outside of court that makes the system important.

Today's concern is not about the court system but what happens beforehand. How are we going to treat each other outside of court? When we agree to do a job, do we do it as agreed? That is part of treating others justly. One of my daughters recently had a school project that was done with a partner. When you are in that situation, do you do your part of the job? You will be trusted by others to deal justly with their property; will you deal with that property as a good steward, or will you do it to your own advantage?

A lot of my business comes about because people cheat each other; people cut corners; people hide important information, putting others at risk; and more. These acts are generally to make money. When I asked one president of a company why his company failed to honor its agreement with my client, his response was, "My people are instructed by me to break any deal they can if it will make our company more money." That is injustice *outside* the courtroom. It isn't "business." It is an offense to God.

God cares about how we conduct our business. He cares about how we treat each other. He cares about justice in court. God wants people to be godly in all areas of life. I am going to be careful in my treatment of others.

Lord, help me to see how to live more justly toward others. In your name, amen.

NOVEMBER 27

"When you come to the land that the L*ORD* *your God is giving you, and you possess it and dwell in it and then say, 'I will set a king over me, like all the nations that are around me,' you may indeed set a king over you whom the* L*ORD* *your God will choose. One from among your brothers you shall set as king over you. You may not put a foreigner over you, who is not your brother. Only he must not acquire many horses for himself or cause the people to return to Egypt in order to acquire many horses, since the* L*ORD* *has said to you, 'You shall never return that way again.' And he shall not acquire many wives for himself, lest his heart turn away, nor shall he acquire for himself excessive silver and gold." (*Deut. 17:14–17)*

Twenty-first-century America is a material world. Our economy is built on business, buying and selling, and consumption. We are taught when we are young that we can achieve anything we want. If our efforts are great enough, the sky is the limit to what we can have or do.

I knew a fellow in high school whose goal in life was a Corvette. He worked hard to get it. He sacrificed grades by working during time he should have been studying so he could buy and drive that car. There are people who live wanting more and more, and the acquisition of material things drives their every waking hour. They can be stingy because of the drive to accumulate. They can overlook the poor and needy because they are intent on getting more. That is not how God would have us be.

At the time of the Torah, Israel didn't have an earthly king. God was Israel's king. But in his foreknowledge, God knew that Israel would soon enough change its form of government and choose a king. Therefore, God set out instructions for what that kingship should look like. Israel's king was not expected to be treated with an exceptional luxury. The king was to lead the people in exhibiting moderation in lifestyle. The king in that culture could have as many wives as he chose, and records show that some kings had harems in the thousands, but not the king of Israel. Some kings could have horses far in excess of what would be useful, but not the king of Israel. Some kings would work to conquer and pillage lands and institute onerous tax burdens to increase their holdings of gold and silver, but the king of Israel was not to be so inclined. The king of Israel was to be moderate in tastes and acquisitions.

I doubt any king is going to read this, but the lesson from today's passage is for ordinary folks too. We are all looked at by someone else. None of us escapes observation. Everyone is to live with moderation in mind, not accumulation. It isn't "Who dies with the most toys wins." It is "Whoever uses his or her resources for the Lord wins." For some, that is a lot; for others, a little. But it is for him, not us.

Lord, help me to live with you as my goal, not possessions. In your name, amen.

NOVEMBER 28

"And when he sits on the throne of his kingdom, he shall write for himself in a book a copy of this law, approved by the Levitical priests. And it shall be with him, and he shall read in it all the days of his life, that he may learn to fear the LORD his God by keeping all the words of this law and these statutes, and doing them, that his heart may not be lifted up above his brothers, and that he may not turn aside from the commandment, either to the right hand or to the left, so that he may continue long in his kingdom, he and his children, in Israel." (Deut. 17:18–20)

In the 1200s in England, King John ruled with an iron fist. Using a doctrine called *vis et voluntas* ("force and will"), John believed himself above the law. In Latin parlance, the phrase often used was *rex lex*, meaning "the king is the law." The idea was that the king set the law for everyone else, but the law was whatever the king determined. The king himself was over the law. An ironic part of this was that the king used religion as the justification for his actions. The argument was that God had appointed him king; therefore, as king he had the authority of God, including the ability to make law whatever he chose.

The king was not too well informed about Scripture. As Moses explained, once Israel moved to a monarchy, the kings were going to be required to write their own copy of God's law, the Torah. The kings were to write it, learn it, study it, live it, and teach it. The king wasn't above the law. The law was above the king. It wasn't *rex lex* (the king is the law) it was *lex rex*! (The law is the king!)

The people began making changes soon. In 1215, King John was forced to negotiate with rebellious barons upset over his policies. The rebels would stop their fighting only if the king signed a great charter of rights. This charter is called by the Latin for "great charter"—the Magna Carta. The king was not deemed over the law. The king was deemed and agreed to be subject to the law.

Society is based on the idea that people will all submit to a common scheme of rules. There are criminal rules and civil rules, but these are all based on the idea that there is a God behind law. This God is just and cares about the treatment each person affords the other. So he instituted a legal system for ancient Israel. The king was subject to it, and so were all others.

Many of ancient Israel's laws are laws that go beyond the nation of Israel. Many of them are common laws that reflect the character of God and would apply to any people in any time. It is never right to murder, for example. As we study the law in these devotions, we need to remember that no one is above the law. The law is given, among other reasons, to make sure we treat each other in godly ways, whether we are king or subject.

Lord, please help me treat others with love and justice. In your name, amen.

NOVEMBER 29

"When you come into the land that the LORD your God is giving you, you shall not learn to follow the abominable practices of those nations." (Deut. 18:9)

A classmate of my wife and me in our high school speech and debate program was an articulate young lady named Malena. One year, Malena wrote an oration with which she had a good bit of success. The oration began talking about a contagious illness that had infected our high school. It wasn't just at our school in Lubbock, but it was actually a nationwide epidemic. This disease was not getting much press attention, and oftentimes the consequences were mild. But sometimes the consequences were severe, even killing some students. After building up the tension, Malena finally told the listeners the name of the disease: "peer pressure."

I suspect the power of peer pressure is greater at certain ages, perhaps peaking in high school and college, but we always tend to be like those we hang around, especially if we look up to them or find them appealing. It is a human trait that is hard to escape.

Today's passage shows this concern on a grand scale. Israel was going to invade Canaan, and there would be plenty of Canaanites left around. The Canaanites had worshipped false gods, and they didn't have a revelation of the Lord God. Moses and God were rightly concerned that Israel would succumb to worshipping the gods of its neighbors rather than leading the neighbors into an understanding and worship of the true God. History proved the concern well placed. The Bible and archaeology confirm that for most of its history, Israel was an idolatrous people. The Israelites spent more time pursuing and worshipping the false gods of the regional people than they did the God who rescued them from Egypt and gave them a clear revelation in the wilderness.

God's people are to be moral leaders, not moral followers. God takes time to teach us so that we can teach others. Jesus explained to his followers that they were to be like a city set up on a hill, whose light can't be hidden at night. God's people are to shine into the darkness of the world, not be part of the darkness.

In daily living, how we treat others, our honesty and integrity, our hard work and motivation, our kindness and love, and more should be our stock in trade. They are traits that we should hold on to in the midst of a world that might teach the opposite—do what you must, but get away with what you can, for example.

I don't want peer pressure to sicken my efforts to be godly. I want to be a moral leader who others will follow. Let peer pressure work for good, not evil!

Lord, please help me walk in the light of your word, showing and encouraging others to do the same. In your name, amen.

NOVEMBER 30

*"The L*ORD *your God will raise up for you a prophet like me from among you, from your brothers—it is to him you shall listen."* (Deut. 18:15)

Moses was a great leader for the Israelites. He was God's tool to rescue them from slavery. God delivered his law through Moses. Moses held an intimacy with God that was unmatched by any other. Moses was God's prophet, speaking on God's behalf. Moses interceded with God when the people's sins were about to bring great retribution. Moses also declared God's judgment on the unfaithful. Moses was a great leader, but like other great leaders, he died and left Israel to the care of others.

Before Moses died, however, he offered one of his greatest prophecies. Moses assured the people that God was going to raise up another prophet like Moses. This prophet would arise out of Israel, and the people were to be on the lookout.

The idea in the Hebrew passage certainly gives instructions that would be important for any prophet who arose after Moses—for indeed, Israel had many—and God expected Israel to listen to each one. But this promise of Moses is one that had many eyeing it as a promise of the coming messiah. "Messiah" itself means "anointed"; anointing is something that happened to prophets, priests, and kings in ancient Israel. The prophet that was to come was not found in Israel, even by the time the finishing touches were put on the Torah after the death of Moses. Deuteronomy 34:10 says that no prophet had arisen in Israel to that point in time that was like Moses, one who knew the Lord face to face.

As Christians, we see this prophecy of Moses finding its final fulfillment in Jesus, the Messiah who was anointed as prophet, priest, and king. Jesus was the one who rescued God's people from slavery—not from the slavery of Egypt but from the slavery to sin and death. Jesus delivered God's law beyond that given to Moses. Moses instructed ancient Israel in a legal code that said "an eye for an eye." Jesus instructed his people in a personal moral code that said, "If someone slaps you on one cheek, turn the other rather than striking back." Jesus was the full and final intercession for people with God. He merited God's forgiveness on our behalf by bearing our punishment for sin (dying) when he himself was sinless, and thus the punishment was unjust for him. It was just only if it was for the sins of others. Jesus was a great leader, but upon his death, he didn't fade into history. He was resurrected and lives everlastingly, offering that same resurrection to his followers.

Moses was never God's final word. If we read about him without expecting another, we miss out on what God had planned.

Lord, open our eyes to see and our ears to hear the wonders of your love and plan. In your name, amen.

DECEMBER 1

"You shall not move your neighbor's landmark, which the men of old have set, in the inheritance that you will hold in the land that the Lord *your God is giving you to possess."* (Deut. 19:14)

I knew a young lad who would go to the movie theater and buy his ticket and snacks but not buy a drink. Instead, he would grab a drink cup out of the trash and take it back for a free refill. Aside from the obvious gross-factor of pulling a cup out of the trash, something a lad this age can be excused for doing, the practice struck me as something more significant than germs. The honesty issue bothered me.

This young man was wrongly portraying the cup as his and using that misrepresentation to get a drink that he had not bought. The wildest part to me what that the fellow was a devout young man who didn't seem the least bit fazed by what he was doing.

Today's passage speaks to everyone, not just landowners. The idea behind the passage stems from the practices of antiquity, before we had metes and bounds, with surveyor equipment and GPS precision that could mark out territory. If you and I wanted to divide a field, we would put markers out to define where one person's property started and another's ended. The rule set out in the command is that no one is to move those markers. In other words, no one is to change a boundary; if my field goes up to Rock A, some dark night I shouldn't be moving Rock A fifty feet away to increase the size of my field.

In the law, whether Israel's law of old or the law today, certain principles are often set out, but the law can't give every situation where that principle will come into play. It is up to the judges and legal system to sort that out. This fact is relevant here because today's passage is setting up a principle that isn't limited to property lines.

The principle is simple. Don't cheat, even in the dead of night, even if you don't get caught. And if you have cheated another, fix it! This applies to property lines and cinema soda cups. It applies to giving the good honest day's work for which you are paid an honest day's wage as well as the obligation to fairly pay workers. It applies to returning excess change given to you at the grocery store as well as paying what you owe on your taxes.

Integrity is a narrow highway, but it is the road the godly are called to travel. May our honesty in dealing with others be our hallmark, even if no one but God knows.

Lord, help me to be convicted to living honestly. Help me see where I fail and work to correct those mistakes. In your name, amen.

DECEMBER 2

"When you go out to war against your enemies, and see horses and chariots and an army larger than your own, you shall not be afraid of them, for the LORD your God is with you, who brought you up out of the land of Egypt . . . 'Hear, O Israel, today you are drawing near for battle against your enemies: let not your heart faint. Do not fear or panic or be in dread of them, for the LORD your God is he who goes with you to fight for you against your enemies, to give you the victory.'" (Deut. 20:1–4)

Read today's passage carefully.

Over five hundred years after it was written, a shepherd boy named David was sent by his father to check on his brothers serving in King Saul's army. Saul was Israel's first king, and he was battling the Philistines. The parties had drawn up battle lines in the valley of Elah. Among the Philistines was a giant named Goliath. Each day, the giant Goliath would come out from the Philistine line and challenge the Israelite army and king. Goliath would say, "Why should a lot of people die in battle? I am one man. Israel should choose one man and let him come out and fight. If I win, Israel will be our slaves. If this fellow can beat me, we will be Israel's slaves. This can get us where we are headed with minimal bloodshed."

Israel was petrified. No one wanted to fight the giant until David arrived—then the scene changed. David was talking to his brothers when Goliath ventured out into the no-man's land between the armies. He made his now-familiar challenge, and David was dumbfounded. Importantly, David was not scared. David's response was predicated on how dumb David thought Goliath was.

David said to the soldiers around his brothers, "Who is this uncircumcised Philistine that he should taunt the armies of God? I'll go fight him!" From David's perspective, there should have been a line of people eager to fight Goliath. David understood that with God behind them, the Israelites could do anything. This wasn't a giant versus a small person. This was God versus a human of any size, and no human is competition for God.

David spoke with the king. Rejecting unfitting, unfamiliar armor in favor of the sling and stones he'd known from the fields, David selected some smooth stones from the brook, and the rest is history.

This was God's victory, not just David's. It was God at work as today's passage teaches. Read today's passage once more. Understand it. Now let's go slay some giants!

Lord, I see giants in my life everywhere. Some I face are outside me. Some are inside me. Please slay the giants in your name. Amen.

DECEMBER 3

"You shall not see your brother's ox or his sheep going astray and ignore them. You shall take them back to your brother." (Deut. 22:1)

For decades, State Farm has advertised with a catchy jingle that sticks in your head. I remember it as a kid, and I still hear it. It triggers in my mind with passages like today's. The jingle is, "And like a good neighbor, State Farm is there . . ." I can't speak to State Farm as an insurer, but I can speak to being a good neighbor, and I am not alone. In the Torah, God instructs us to be good neighbors.

At the time of Moses and afterward, Israel was predominantly an agrarian culture. It had livestock to supply meat, milk products (yoghurt, etc.), clothing, and labor. Once Israel settled in Canaan, they had farms and vineyards. They dug wells and harvested crops, but the livestock was still important. Oxen could pull a field plow or a cart or turn a grindstone. Even for the tradesfolk who settled in towns and cities, livestock maintained its importance. It was used in sacrifices and could be bartered, and many homes kept a sheep, goat, or even ox on the first floor of the house. (People generally lived on the second story and rooftop.)

If someone's ox or sheep got loose, that could be a huge loss for the owning family and a big boon to the finder's family. In a day without modern branding, wandering livestock was also something that could easily be taken.

God instructed Israel about handling the wandering livestock, a problem that must have been common. God didn't say, "Don't steal it." Nor did he say, "Leave it alone so it can find its way back home." God said, "If you see it, get involved! Be active! Do what needs to be done to take care of the animal and get it to its rightful owner."

This is good neighboring to the tenth degree. This is treating someone else the way we would like to be treated. This is going the extra mile in a way that makes a real difference. This is a principle that goes beyond an ox or sheep, and it is one I want to follow.

Where I see a way to help a neighbor, I need to step up. It might be finding a stray dog or cat, but it might be something more. Someone sick may need a meal. Someone may need a ride somewhere. I may know a lonely neighbor who needs a visit. There may be some chore I can help a neighbor complete. The possibilities are endless, and being a "good neighbor" is important. I am going to work on this.

Lord, give me insight to see where I can be a better neighbor. Let me show concern, love, and kindness in your name, amen.

DECEMBER 4

"When you are encamped against your enemies, then you shall keep yourself from every evil thing." (Deut. 23:9)

Passages like today's strike me as a bit odd. I need to chew on them a while to make sense of the instruction. On its face, today's passage seems to make perfect sense, but for me it doesn't. The instruction says to "keep yourself from every evil thing" when "you are encamped against your enemies." Well, while it makes sense on the surface, I think, "But aren't we *always* supposed to keep ourselves from every evil thing? Does this passage imply that when we aren't encamped against the enemy, it's OK to flirt with evil things?"

My answer to the question that might be raised through the seemingly weird wording comes from chewing on it and also from experience. Let me explain. First, we should always avoid every evil thing. That is a given from Scripture, and the Torah confirms it in multiple places. But there is something more.

There are times when we face big decisions. We wage war against physical and spiritual enemies. We try to discover God's will in times of importance, wanting to make sure we step where we should. These are times when we need to be extra deliberate and careful to focus on godliness. Holiness is always important, but in those moments where our senses are heightened to danger, worry, concern, and fear, we need to carefully weed out of our lives any possible ungodliness. We need to refrain from feeding our minds the disease and pollution of the world's ideas, seeking only to learn and hear from God.

There was one particular time in my life that stands out as a clear example of what I think this passage is teaching. I was faced with making a huge decision with monumental implications for me, my family, my job, and my friends. Every area of my life would be affected by the decision I was going to make. It was critical for me to get the decision right. I prayed about it, but I didn't stop there. I began journaling the prayers as well as my thoughts about the decision. I decided to take a thirty-day "influence fast." For thirty days, I sought to eliminate any ungodly influence from my life. I didn't watch television. I refrained from listening to secular music. I limited my reading outside of the Bible and devotional/study material to what was vital for work. I sought to focus as best as I could on hearing God.

God came through. My decision was the right one. It wasn't easy, but there was peace knowing I had sought God and could be confident he had answered. Today's passage teaches us that we should always avoid evil, but especially as we listen to and seek the Lord, we should be diligent in what we feed our soul.

Lord, help me devote myself to you. Teach and guide me in your name, amen.

DECEMBER 5

"Because the LORD your God walks in the midst of your camp, to deliver you and to give up your enemies before you, therefore your camp must be holy." (Deut. 23:14)

When we were young, Mom always kept a fairly clean house. I can remember she would have us make our beds and keep our rooms tidy. We would have evenings where my older sister and I would be responsible for cleaning the kitchen. When folks dropped in, I am sure they would have seen the house as well kept.

But occasionally a significant visit would be set. We were living in upstate New York, and my mom's parents lived in West Texas. But once a year, my grandparents would journey up from Texas to New York, and before that trip, Mom took cleaning to a whole new level. I had never thought about the need to make sure baseboards had no dust. Nor did I dream you cleaned *behind* the toilet! The idea of removing a light fixture to clean it was foreign to me, as was sweeping under the sofa.

Mom went to all this extra trouble because she wanted to show her mother that she took housekeeping seriously. Mom wanted Grandmother to know that she had been well taught. Mom put her best foot forward, and all of us kids helped get it done! My grandmother loved us and would have been happy regardless of whether the floor behind the toilet was spotless. But that didn't minimize the importance to Mom.

Today's passage draws on the same idea but with a different emphasis. The Israelites were to keep their camp spiritually clean. This meant that the camp was to follow the instructions God gave about purity. This was to teach Israel a lesson.

The Israelites were to learn from this that God walked in their midst. God does not inhabit impurity, and so the Israelites had to keep their camp pure. It was a statement about God and his character, and the Israelites' purity would show their understanding.

We don't worry about God coming into our homes or yards. We understand that God desires to be in our lives. God wants to be an intimate part of who I am and what I do. Thus, the Torah passage gives me important instructions. I am to seek purity so that God will walk with me in purity. I can analogize it to light and darkness. God is light, and so I am to keep my life "light" to walk with him. What fellowship would God as light have with darkness? The two don't occupy the same space.

God walks in holiness. I want to walk with him, so I need to walk in holiness too.

Lord, purify me in your love, and bring me into a holy walk with you. For your name's sake, amen.

DECEMBER 6

"If you make a vow to the LORD your God, you shall not delay fulfilling it, for the LORD your God will surely require it of you, and you will be guilty of sin. But if you refrain from vowing, you will not be guilty of sin. You shall be careful to do what has passed your lips, for you have voluntarily vowed to the LORD your God what you have promised with your mouth." (Deut. 23:21-23)

Occasionally, I hear people say, "I swear to God. . . ." When they do, I always cringe a bit. Usually these folks are just using an expression to express earnestness, a bit like saying "I'm serious" or "Honestly." It seems to me that people have many options for expressing their sincerity beside swearing to God.

Perhaps it is the trial lawyer in me that makes me carefully listen to words. I do tend to understand them literally, even when they are not meant to be taken so. I have always viewed words with power. They express our innermost thoughts and tend to reflect our attitudes. While people may consider the eyes to be the windows of the soul, I find words often better convey what lies beneath one's surface appearance.

Passages like today's make me even more careful with language. Swearing to God is not to be taken lightly. There really is a God. He takes invoking his name and character seriously, and so should we. Yet often some people say they "swear to God" as if it means nothing more than a verbal underlining. It is the equivalent of using a boldface font in what they are saying. It means emphasis.

I would be more careful about my speech. God's name is not to be invoked simply as underlining for our sentences. The real God is present, is listening, and should be treated with the dignity of the greatest being possible.

Our words aren't just mumblings of formed soundwaves that we send out through our windpipes. God used words to create the world. Words communicate our thoughts and hearts. Words reflect what we value and esteem. Words form ideas and inspire others to achieve. Words have power. We should speak carefully.

Even beyond the words, however, making a vow to God speaks to integrity. Vows should reflect careful thought. They come from decisions of the will. To speak a vow rashly is foolish. To fail to keep a vow demonstrates an integrity lapse. It also shows a disregard and disrespect for the person to whom that vow is made. In this case, that means a disrespect and disregard of God. Heaven forbid!

Next time I hear someone say, "I swear to God," I might reply, "Be careful with that!"

Lord, forgive my rash vows. Teach me to respect you better. In your name, amen.

DECEMBER 7

"When a man is newly married, he shall not go out with the army or be liable for any other public duty. He shall be free at home one year to be happy with his wife whom he has taken." (Deut. 24:5)

When I was a law student, I made the moot court team. This was a team that our school put into interschool competitions where we mock-argued cases to mock appellate courts. Our moot court coach was an adjunct professor named Don Hunt.

At our first meeting, the newly selected team sat down with Coach Hunt, and he gave us important preliminary instructions. Almost forty years later, I still remember him saying, "Our moot court work is time consuming. I expect you to put your faith and family first in your life, then your schoolwork. Beyond that, I want every minute of your time."

Coach was right on with the scriptural mandate to put your faith and family first. God's instructions would be the same. Family is important to God, and it always has been. God was the one who said about Adam, "It is not good that the man should be alone" (Gen. 2:18). Ideally, husband and wife become "one flesh," with their hearts tied together, and from this union come children. God set up family. Of course, not everyone is in a marriage or has children, but friends can be closer than a brother (Prov. 18:24), and most everyone knows someone who is "family" even if not related by blood.

Today's passage is another example of God's emphasis on family. Israel was about to invade the land possessed by Abraham generations earlier. Israel needed an army for the invasion. This would not be the only time Israel would need an army, and God set up the principle that every man should serve in the army, if he was at the right age. But there were exceptions. One was based on the priorities of family. If a man was newly married, rather than head out for military campaigns, that husband was to stay home for a year so that both he and his wife could enjoy each other and bond their marriage in ways that require time together.

I like the priorities that Coach Hunt gave us. I preach them to the lawyers who work for me. I regularly speak to law students and give commencement addresses. I give some variation of the same speech to them. If we put our family first, that is not the family trumping faith. It is faith that teaches us to put family first. When we do that, we needn't worry that the world will fall apart. God instructs us to take care of our families, and we can be confident that as we do so, God's will can be done. One of my bosses told me when I was a young lawyer that I would never be an A-plus lawyer unless I put my job over my family. He didn't know what God could do, and I'd rather have my family than be an A-plus lawyer anyway!

Lord, show me how to put my family first in this world, to your glory! Amen.

DECEMBER 8

"You shall not oppress a hired worker who is poor and needy, whether he is one of your brothers or one of the sojourners who are in your land within your towns. You shall give him his wages on the same day, before the sun sets (for he is poor and counts on it), lest he cry against you to the LORD, and you be guilty of sin." (Deut. 24:14–15)

When I was young, before the days of GPS and handheld navigation aids, we were taught how to use a compass. The amazing instrument has a magnetized needle that points toward the North Pole. You could hold the compass, turn it so that the "N" on the dial aligned with the direction the needle pointed, and voila, you knew north, south, east, and west.

The children of God are to have a moral compass. We are to orient and turn our lives so that we align with the needle that points in the direction God gives. We get insights into where God's needle points from passages like today's.

Moses received the law for people and culture before time clocks, before federal wage laws, before checking accounts, before banks, and before deductions for insurance, social security, and so on. There were wealthy landowners, wealthy merchants, and wealthy traders, but there were also a lot of people who were poor and who lived hand to mouth. There were many who would find places where they could work for a day, or longer. The day's work would be for an agreed-upon wage. God wanted the poor and needy to get their wages paid the day they did the work.

God explained his reason. Poor people live hand to mouth, and they rely on getting the money. God wants to ensure that the poor and needy are taken care of. Their well-being is part of God's moral compass, and he instructed his followers to that end.

I read passages like today's and I want to be sure I don't cut short those who might do work for me. But many people don't have others who work for them. Does this passage not apply to them? It absolutely does. The passage should be seen as a moral compass. It points to the importance of providing for and caring about those who need help. It instructs everyone, employer and nonemployer, to be attentive to the needs of others and make choices that help them. This applies to everyone.

I want to be better at seeing those in need. The passage ends with the point that abusing the needs of others is sin before God! This is not just a moral compass; it is a serious matter.

Lord, help me see those in need, see how to help them, and then help them immediately. In your name, amen.

DECEMBER 9

"You shall not have in your bag two kinds of weights, a large and a small. You shall not have in your house two kinds of measures, a large and a small. A full and fair weight you shall have, a full and fair measure you shall have, that your days may be long in the land that the LORD your God is giving you. For all who do such things, all who act dishonestly, are an abomination to the LORD your God." (Deut. 25:13–16)

Before I opened my own law firm, I worked for a large firm that billed its clients on an hourly basis. If you did an hour's work, you put down on time sheets the one hour, the client file to be billed, and what you did in that hour. If you only worked for fifteen minutes on the file, you put in a quarter of an hour. At the time, that was the smallest time increment you had. So, we were instructed that if you worked on a matter for ten minutes—say handling a phone call—you would still bill one quarter of an hour (fifteen minutes) for that ten-minute call. I hated that.

Today's passage was a constant reminder to me that God expects honesty in our transactions with others. This isn't simply a duty owed to each other; it is a responsibility before God. In ancient days, many transactions were conducted based on weight. The obvious examples might be how much metal (gold, silver, bronze, etc.) is being bought or sold. A less obvious example is the price of bread, which in many societies was based on weight, not type. In those ancient transactions, the scales were often as simple as a bar holding two plates suspended from string tied to the bar. The scales looked like those we see Lady Justice holding up in pictures or in a sculpture. The merchant would have a set of weights he would use on one plate to measure how much the material in the second plate weighed. The concern of today's passage is that merchants should not have two sets of weights. The concern in today's measurements could be said, "Don't have a one-ounce weight that really weighs a fifteen-sixteenths of an ounce." It was a common way to cheat.

God wants his people to have integrity. He wants his people to be honest. Whether in transactions in the market place, in relationships at home, or in a larger social context or any other place of interaction, the children of God should have unquestionable integrity. In legal ethics, one of the core instructions lawyers are to follow is to "avoid even the appearance of impropriety." While not all lawyers necessarily follow this stricture, it is a godly admonition. As followers of God, we are to avoid even a hint of dishonesty or poor ethics. Our weights should be real.

I don't bill my lawyer time by the hour any more. I haven't in almost 30 years. I suggested once to a billing partner that what we were doing might be wrong. He told me that the clients knew and approved the process. I still didn't like it.

Lord, help me to be honest and above reproach in dealing with others. In your name, amen.

DECEMBER 10

"A wandering Aramean was my father. And he went down into Egypt and sojourned there . . . And the Egyptians treated us harshly and humiliated us and laid on us hard labor. Then we cried to the LORD, *the God of our fathers, and the* LORD *heard our voice and saw our affliction, our toil, and our oppression. And the* LORD *brought us out of Egypt . . . And he brought us into this place and gave us this land, a land flowing with milk and honey."* (Deut. 26:5–9)

In almost six decades of living, I have learned a few things about life. One of the realities of this life is the ups and downs we experience. Some periods of our lives are easy. Our health is good, our relationships are sound, our economics are in the black, and we smile, enjoying most days. But there are also dark times in life. These are times when life is hard. Maybe our health fails, or our relationships fall. We may be struggling to make ends meet, worried about how we will make it financially. These are days of difficulty.

Today's passage recognizes both aspects of life, and it gives good instructions for us to follow. As Moses was coming to the end of a long four-decade journey taking Israel out of Egypt and managing the wilderness while an entire generation died off, he gave some instructions to Israel. The instructions were based on what had happened. The Israelites were the descendants of Jacob, also called "Israel." He lived for a long time in Aramaea (Gen. 29–31) before going to Egypt with his sons and family. Over time, as the Israelites grew more populous and the government of Egypt changed, the treatment of the Hebrews became abusive. The Israelites were enslaved by Pharaoh and subjected to harsh labor.

While in the dark times of harshness and humiliation, the Israelites cried out to the Lord. They saw no way out and, at the end of their rope, sought divine intervention. History showed that the Israelites didn't know God too well, but that didn't stop them from seeking divine intervention, and it didn't stop God from hearing their prayers and answering them.

God heard their voice and came to their rescue. The relief wasn't immediate, but it was sure. The road wasn't easy, but it led to the Promised Land, a good and productive land that would thrive under the Israelites. Israel was called to give praise to God and recognize his deliverance in worship.

I like this. In good days, it reminds me that these days are here by the grace of God. My job in these days is to love him, show him honor, and give him the glory. But when the days are bad, I needn't give up. My job is to call on God, crying out to him for rescue. I need to seek his presence and all that comes with that—his wisdom, his power, his guidance, his love, his mercy, and more. Then, as God rescues me, something that may not be immediate, I return to days of praise for his deliverance.

Lord, please be my rescuer and deliverer. I need you. In your name, amen.

DECEMBER 11

"And behold, now I bring the first of the fruit of the ground, which you, O LORD, have given me.' And you shall set it down before the LORD your God and worship before the LORD your God. And you shall rejoice in all the good that the LORD your God has given to you and to your house." (Deut. 26:10-11)

If you're reading this devotional book, one of several things is likely true. You might be a Christian reading to enhance your walk with God. You might be Jewish, seeking to do it for similar reasons. Or perhaps you are Jewish and curious about what a Christian lawyer might have to say about your Torah. You might be neither Christian nor Jew; maybe you happened upon the book or are reading it just to see what it might say.

Regardless of who you are, today's passage contains some bold instructions for you and me. Moses was giving the Israelites some instructions about how they were to honor God once they settled into the Promised Land. He instructed them to take the first part of their first harvest and offer it to God as a sacrifice of gratitude. The sacrifice was to be part of their worship to God.

Worship is an interesting word. The Hebrew word used here denotes the idea of bowing down to the ground, being subservient, and showing honor and deference. It is what a subject might do before a king. The point is a bodily acknowledgment that God is worthy of our attention. God is not simply our buddy. God isn't an intellectual concept. God isn't something so far and mysterious that he has no reality to us. God is a real being. He is an awesome and marvelous being that is beyond us. We don't walk up to him and shake his hand; we bow before him.

Worship extends beyond bowing. We are also to rejoice in all the good God has given to us and our houses. This acknowledges that God isn't simply there but active. He is involved. He is the source of all the good things we have. We shouldn't take credit for the good in our lives. We don't need to give ultimate credit to our parents, friends, associates, jobs, or luck. We see that God is the source, and we rejoice, verbally acknowledging with praise the God who provides and cares.

This is a true calling for everyone. Whether one knows God or not, he is worthy of this praise. If we don't realize it, then we don't know him. If we are in that situation, we need to get to know him! We can change that. God is knowable and desires to be known. If we do know him, then we need to worship him and rejoice before him. We need to be vocal people who give credit, glory, and honor to the God who has made us and given us every good thing. Amen!

Lord, give us a fuller vision of you. We lift you up in praise and adoration as an amazing God. We thank you for the great things in our lives. We worship in your name, amen.

DECEMBER 12

"When you have finished paying all the tithe of your produce in the third year, which is the year of tithing, giving it to the Levite, the sojourner, the fatherless, and the widow, so that they may eat within your towns and be filled, then you shall say before the LORD your God, 'I have removed the sacred portion out of my house, and moreover, I have given it to the Levite, the sojourner, the fatherless, and the widow, according to all your commandments that you have commanded me. I have not transgressed any of your commandments, nor have I forgotten them.'" (Deut. 26:12-14)

One of the things I hate to do is ask people for money. I would rather take a beating than be a fundraiser. I am not good at it, and I don't want to be good at it. It makes me break out in a rash. It is a pity, because there are some really good things worthy of our money. One of my friends, Uncle Ken, is really good at fundraising. I asked him once how he does it. He said, "I only raise money for good and worthy projects. It makes me happy to help people give their money to something that is worthy." Wow. I am not good at that, but I do know something that is worthy! It's found in today's passage.

What could be worthier of your money than one of God's projects? If God has something that God wants you and me to fund, that surely is worthy of our parting with some of our resources. We may think that this is a plea for funding our churches and synagogues, but it is something more than that.

Look carefully at today's passage. God instructed Israel to pay a "tithe." *Tithe* comes from the Hebrew word for "ten." A tithe is a "tenth" of whatever we are speaking of—whether income, a crop, or some other thing. God told the Israelites that when they gave their tithe to the Levite, sojourner, fatherless, and widow, they were giving it as God instructed. The Levites were in charge of the sacrifices and worship of Israel. These were the ancient equivalent of our churches and synagogues of today. The sojourners were newcomers to Israel. They were often temporary dwellers, with no real property rights. Today we can roughly equate them to immigrants. The fatherless and widows were those in society who had no providers. They didn't have property and had no easy way to make money.

Consider God's projects and what he would have us do with our tithes to him. God cares about seeing that our worship and those who work in our churches and synagogues are paid for their work. God's projects also reflect his deep desire to take care of the outcasts, the poor, the disadvantaged, and the impoverished who cannot care for themselves. This is a worthy endeavor that we too often leave to the government, but God's instructions were for his followers to do this. Here is something worth our money!

Lord, give me eyes to see those in need that I can help. Then give me the resources and will to help them in your name. Amen.

DECEMBER 13

"'Look down from your holy habitation, from heaven, and bless your people Israel and the ground that you have given us, as you swore to our fathers, a land flowing with milk and honey.'" (Deut. 26:15)

Most people, at some time or another, hold a job. For many it means waking up in the morning, getting ready, and heading off to work. Some may work from home. One person may work by taking care of his or her home while another earns the money needed to sustain the household. Almost all of us were at one time students going to school to prepare us to be useful citizens and adults, working or doing what we can to live in some measure of comfort and happiness.

But today's passage tells us there is more to this life than just preparing for work and working. If we aren't careful, we become rats in a cage, going over to the wheel and running hard, just to get off, eat, rest, and get back on the wheel, running again. This isn't what life is about.

Moses told the Israelites that they needed to pray to God for their lives. They should ask God to look down from heaven and bless his people and what they were doing. Work shouldn't be a treadmill that goes nowhere. Work should be done under God's divine care, with the direction that God gives. We needn't work for the comforts of life; we should pray for God to bless the work of our hands with the things that matter to him. He may give us comforts, and if he does, we need to be mindful to give him back the first shares from those blessings. We need to share the comforts and blessings with others.

But whether we get what we want or just what we need, we should always be seeking those things from God's hands. We ask him for his blessings, and we give him glory for providing them.

Looking at life as a strictly human endeavor may seem OK, as long as we are busy enough not to notice it is meaningless at its core. But somewhere along the way, most will wonder why they are on life's treadmill. There is purpose, however—a purpose that goes far beyond surviving. The purpose is an eternal plan by a divine God who can use each of us to further his kingdom and bring light to a dark world, comfort to bereaved and hurting people, deliverance to those in bondage, promise to those defeated, life to those who are barren, and more. God will use us in that plan, and then our blessed life isn't a rat's wheel, getting the job done. It is a journey led by one who infuses us with joy in the process.

What a God!

Lord, please bless us and our houses. Give us purpose and use us. In your name, amen.

DECEMBER 14

"You have declared today that the LORD *is your God, and that you will walk in his ways, and keep his statutes and his commandments and his rules, and will obey his voice. And the* LORD *has declared today that you are a people for his treasured possession, as he has promised you, and that you are to keep all his commandments."* (Deut. 26:17–18)

Before my wife, Becky, and I dated, we were friends. We would occasionally see each other in a variety of settings and have a good laugh or visit. Over time, the friendship developed into a romance, and we started dating each other. After a time of this, I convinced her we ought to get married! What a day! We have been married since, and our relationship has grown, intertwining our hearts to a point where I'm not always sure where mine stops and hers starts. She knows me like a book, and I know her, if not like a book, at least like a short story!

Relationships grow and take various forms. It is no less true for our relationship with God. Many people have a relationship with God that is based on occasional visits. We bump into him here or there and maybe even seek him out when we have a God-sized problem. But the intimacy isn't too great. The opportunity with God is greater than one of mere acquaintance or the occasional visit. God seeks an intimate relationship with each of us.

Today's passage uses language of intimacy. It is similar to language used in ancient wedding vows. It comes in the context of the Israelites having declared themselves to belong exclusively to God. They declared themselves, in essence, to be his bride. This meant more than an occasional visit. This meant that God would be their Lord and they would walk in his ways. In reciprocal fashion, God also declared himself the spouse of Israel. He pledged himself to treasure the Israelites, promising to care for and protect them.

God's desire to have a relationship is amazing to me. I know all my faults and warts, and I don't understand why a perfect God with zero faults and warts would desire intimacy with me. I am also aware of the problem from a justice perspective. How can a pure, unchanging God be intimate with an impure, unholy me?

The key to both God desiring me and God justly walking with me is found in the love of God. God desires me, having made me in love and having made me capable of returning that love. God doesn't love me because I am worthy. He loves me because that's the kind of God he is. The justice side of the equation is solved in my Christian faith, by God sacrificing a perfect Son to atone or pay the price for my shortcomings. In Jesus, I have God's perfection imparted to me. What an amazing, loving God!

Lord, thank you for your love. May I find a deeper walk with you. In your name, amen.

DECEMBER 15

"On the day you cross over the Jordan to the land that the LORD your God is giving you, you shall set up large stones and plaster them with plaster. And you shall write on them all the words of this law, when you cross over to enter the land that the LORD your God is giving you." (Deut. 27:2–3)

I was only a junior in high school when my English teacher, the great Mrs. Kingston, declared that everyone, EVERYONE, needed to participate in the graduation ceremony. Each person needed to don cap and gown, hear his or her name called, walk across the stage, shake the hand giving out the diploma, and finish the ceremony. One student asked Mrs. Kingston if the graduation ceremony was required. "Don't we get the diploma anyway? What difference does it make if we attend the ceremony?" Mrs. Kingston replied that it made a big difference. It was a marker in life. It would be something we would look back on, but it would also be something our parents would see. They would realize that we were moving on to a new stage. A corner was being turned. We were "growing up."

We need markers in our lives. We need visible reminders of where we have been, what we have done, who we are, and who we hope to be. It helps us and teaches those around us. God knew this well and has always given his people ceremonies, rites, and other markers to serve as reminders as well as teaching tools.

Today's passage is a marvelous example. Moses told the Israelites that the very day they entered with their first few steps into the Promised Land, crossing the Jordan River, they were to stop and erect a pillar of stones. After plastering the stones, God wanted them to write on the stones the Torah he had given them. This was a marking of what the Israelites had been through, the commitments they had made, and the promises and warnings of God. This marker would serve that generation and the generations to come. They would know who God was and what difference that truth made.

We still need markers in our lives. For the Christian, baptism is such a marker: a signifying moment of commitment to God and association with his death, burial, and resurrection. For Jews and Christians, the Pesach (Passover) and Lord's Supper (Eucharist), respectively, serve as reminders that God redeems his people from bondage. The Pesach reminds Israel of God's deliverance from Egyptian slavery. The Lord's Supper serves as a reminder that Jesus willingly gave his life to deliver God's people from the bondage of sin.

I want to be mindful of markers. I don't want to lose track of what God has done and is doing in my life.

Lord, thank you for your constant love. May I never forget or fail to tell others. In your name, amen.

DECEMBER 16

Then Moses and the Levitical priests said to all Israel, "Keep silence and hear, O Israel: this day you have become the people of the LORD your God. You shall therefore obey the voice of the LORD your God, keeping his commandments and his statutes, which I command you today." (Deut. 27:9–10)

Some people very dear to me are always fun to call on the phone. They can talk and talk and talk. It can amuse me and brings me great joy. Occasionally, however, a time comes when talking needs to cease and someone needs to listen. I have seen times of frustration when something critical has happened and one person blithely drones on and on without giving anyone a chance to break the important news. Have you ever heard someone say, "Shut up and listen!"? If so, then you know about such times.

"Shut up" has an element of rudeness to it, so today's passage shouldn't use that in its translation of the Hebrew, but take away the rudeness, and you have the words of Moses to Israel. "BE QUIET AND LISTEN!" Moses exclaimed. Moses had something very important to say. The Israelites needed to put down their cell phones and focus!

Once Israel made the real commitment to follow God, it was a BIG DEAL. This was not some one-day commitment. It wasn't something done during a harsh or dark time to be forgotten once the day got brighter. It was a lifetime decision. The people of Israel committed themselves to God as their Lord. That was a game changer. It carried responsibility. They were committing to following his instructions. God's lordship wasn't simply a title; it was a role. He was their Lord. What he said was law. He was to be followed moment by moment.

It is no different for us today. When we give our lives to God, when we claim him as Lord and make a lifetime decision to follow him, he is no longer simply our teacher. He isn't just our coach, encouraging us to follow his game plan. He isn't merely a counselor giving us advice that we may take or not, depending upon how we feel. He is Lord. He is king. He is ruler. He reigns in our lives, and we are his people.

This means we trust him and follow him. It also means he will take care of us and be our protection. Difficulties can still arise. We can suffer unfair tragedies and we will have periods of pain in life. But we have a compassionate God who will give us direction and walk with us through those days and difficulties. This is the walk of faith. We give ourselves to God without regard to how others will feel about it. We give our lives and commit to following him as he says. It is a big decision, not made lightly, but it gives life meaning and purpose and brings the greatest joy.

Lord, I give myself to you. Please show me how to best follow you in faith. In your name, amen.

DECEMBER 17

"Therefore keep the words of this covenant and do them, that you may prosper in all that you do." (Deut. 29:9)

Have you ever seen the cartoon drawings of God as some old man with a beard, occasionally seen rocking in a chair? Many people have a view of God as some fellow who sat up in heaven, wagging his finger over certain behaviors and deciding that those behaviors would be off-limits. They would be "sins." As David Letterman popularly said of some things, "[They're] more fun than humans should be allowed!"

God's instructions were never an arbitrary set of guidelines where he just happened to isolate certain things as sins. Right and wrong were never determined by God rolling the dice or by the mood God was in on a certain day. Scripture teaches that the instructions of God are a reflection of his character as well as directions for people to follow for the *best possible life*. In other words, God's instructions are for our good. They make a positive difference in our lives.

Today's passage gives the core understanding of this principle. God, through Moses, explains that keeping God's commandments will lead to a prosperous life. Some may wish to debate whether some of the commands of the Torah apply so easily to life today. I believe that many of them were written for the nascent nation of Israel to give the society a legal structure for success. But many are apparent as everlasting moral code. The Ten Commandments, for example, aren't simply for a successful nation. They teach life lessons that can lead one to a happy, prosperous life—and disobeying them can send one down a destructive path.

I am frequently asked by younger students about the secrets to a successful life. Generally they mean "success" in the eyes of the world, with all that generally implies, like making a good living, having a measure of fame, and so on. I always try to emphasize that success is altogether different. Success begins with being at peace with God, filled with his joy and finding fulfillment in his plans. Success includes having a family filled with love and respect. Those things can't be bought with money, and they are much more valuable. Within that framework, the prosperous and successful life is not hard to find. It is found in trusting and obeying God.

It may sound simplistic, and to some degree it is. Yet it is the challenge of each day. The temptation is always to trust our ourselves rather than God. We think we know better. We think our ideas are better. We are easily deceived! We are the Dufflepuds in *The Voyage of the Dawn Treader* by C. S. Lewis (read it and see what I mean!).

Lord, give me the discipline and understanding to trust you first and foremost and then to live in obedience to your words. In your name, amen.

DECEMBER 18

"You are standing today, all of you, before the Lord your God: the heads of your tribes, your elders, and your officers, all the men of Israel, your little ones, your wives, and the sojourner who is in your camp, from the one who chops your wood to the one who draws your water, so that you may enter into the sworn covenant of the Lord your God, which the Lord your God is making with you today." (Deut. 29:10–12)

Back in the early 1970s, a series of television commercials came out for Skin Bracer, a men's aftershave. In the ads, the aftershave was poured onto the hands and then slapped onto the freshly shaven face. The man receiving the slap would then pause and say, "Thanks! I needed that!" Today's passage is one that slaps me on the face and leaves me saying, "Thanks! I needed that!"

Moses spoke to all the people of Israel as they were getting ready to enter the Promised Land. What became a forty year long venture was drawing to a close. Moses then told them all, "You are standing before the Lord your God." No one was to miss what Moses was saying. Everyone, all of them, stood before God. This included the people who weren't paying attention. This included the people who were distracted. This included the people who were not convicted about God. This included the people who were apathetic. This included the troublemakers. This included the faithless. It was men and women, young and old, servants and those they served, the educated and the uneducated—everyone stood before God. Everyone had a decision to make.

I like the way Bob Dylan put it into words in "You Gotta Serve Somebody" three millennia later:

> You may be an ambassador to England or France / You may like to gamble, you might like to dance / You may be the heavyweight champion of the world / You may be a socialite with a long string of pearls . . . You might be a rock 'n' roll addict prancing on the stage / You might have drugs at your command, women in a cage / You may be a businessman or some high-degree thief / They may call you Doctor or they may call you Chief . . . You may be a state trooper, you might be a young Turk / You may be the head of some big TV network / You may be rich or poor, you may be blind or lame / You may be living in another country under another name . . . You may be a construction worker working on a home / You may be living in a mansion or you might live in a dome / You might own guns and you might even own tanks / You might be somebody's landlord, you might even own banks . . . You may be a preacher with your spiritual pride / You may be a city councilman taking bribes on the side / You may be workin' in a barbershop, you may know how to cut hair / You may be somebody's mistress, may be somebody's heir / But you're gonna have to serve somebody, yes indeed / You're gonna have to serve somebody / Well, it may be the devil or it may be the Lord / But you're gonna have to serve somebody.

The same is true for you and me. We stand before the Lord. Today we get to choose whom we will serve.

Lord, I choose you. I want to serve you. Show me the way. In your name, amen.

DECEMBER 19

"Beware lest there be among you a root bearing poisonous and bitter fruit, one who, when he hears the words of this sworn covenant, blesses himself in his heart, saying, 'I shall be safe, though I walk in the stubbornness of my heart.' This will lead to the sweeping away of moist and dry alike." (Deut. 29:18–19)

In the process of selecting verses for this devotional study book, I looked for a variety of things. Often I passed over some passages that would make for a good devotion simply because I didn't have enough room. Sometimes the passages shouted for a devotion. Today's passage is one I kept setting aside and then coming back to. Two things in the passage keep resonating in my head, and I had to write on them.

First, Moses uses powerful imagery in speaking of a "root bearing poisonous and bitter fruit." We can readily identify much of the fruit that we see, be it good or bad. Good fruit is marvelous to be around. Fruit like love, joy, peace, patience, kindness, gentleness, and self-control are potent. They build up those around them. They encourage others, sustain others, comfort others, empower others, and inspire others.

Not so with bad fruit. Impurity, sensuality, enmity, strife, jealousy, fits of anger, rivalries, dissensions, division, envy, and similar fruits are destructive. They tear down rather than build up. They alienate instead of unite. They are damaging and hurtful.

These fruits don't magically appear. In Moses' analogy, they come from roots. We need to be deliberate and careful to kill them at the root. We need to seek fellowship and intimacy with God and his Spirit, finding his sustaining life to nourish and establish our root in his character. This will bring good fruit, not bitter and poisonous fruit.

The second part of today's passage that calls out to me is Moses speaking of a "man who blesses himself in his heart." Over and over in the Torah we have read of the calling for God to bless each person. The priests and others offer prayers of blessing, seeking God's touch on our lives, with all the benefits that come from that touch. What person can bless him- or herself? One who is arrogant, proud, and deceived. Such a person ignores God, thinking him- or herself sufficient without God or maybe even above such an idea as God. Such a person is destined for failure. There is no good fruit that comes from a self-blessing. The good fruit comes from the blessing of God.

So I write on this passage because I need this passage. I need to be reminded that I want God's blessing so I can walk with God's fruit in my life. I don't want what I can conjure up on my own.

Lord, please bless my life with good fruit to use for your service. In your name, amen.

DECEMBER 20

"The secret things belong to the LORD *our God, but the things that are revealed belong to us and to our children forever, that we may do all the words of this law."* (Deut. 29:29)

To better understand today's passage, we should consider two concepts about God found in the words *truly* and *fully.* We can know God "truly," but we will never know God "fully."

The Bible teaches that God is not simply some supersized human being. We should never fall into the trap of thinking of God as human but bigger, human but stronger, or human but smarter. God isn't a human in any shape, form, or level.

God is an altogether different being. He isn't a part of the natural world, but he exists beyond the realm of the natural world. As humans, we are limited to our experiences in the natural world, and we have it as our frame of reference. Since God is outside that natural order of things, it makes sense that God cannot be truly known by humans. However, that is not right.

God can be known truly *because God has chosen to reveal himself to humanity.* That is the point of the Torah. God revealed himself progressively through experiences with Abraham and his offspring. Then, once Moses entered the scene, God's revelation progressed noticeably. God revealed himself though a name. He revealed his interest in Israel. He revealed his power over Pharaoh. He revealed his justice on Sinai. He revealed his exclusivity through the wilderness. God can be truly known because God has truly revealed himself.

But we should never assume that because we can know God truly, we can know him fully. That is an altogether different word and concept. God hasn't revealed himself fully to humanity. Indeed, no human brain could fully comprehend God.

God is far beyond our ability to even imagine. His substance isn't of this world, and we can't fathom it. The best we can do is realize that God is "spirit." His thoughts are beyond our thoughts. His character is one we admire, emulate, and recognize, but that doesn't mean we can fully fathom it.

Today's passage makes it clear. God has secrets that no one will know or understand. He is interested in us, he loves us, and he reveals himself to us. But he is much more than we think he is.

This should cause all of us to stop in wonder, to praise and glorify the Almighty One who is beyond all we can think or conceive and yet reveals himself to us in love.

Lord, show me more of who you are. To your glory and praise. In your name, amen.

DECEMBER 21

"And when all these things come upon you, the blessing and the curse, which I have set before you, and you call them to mind among all the nations where the LORD your God has driven you, and return to the LORD your God, you and your children, and obey his voice in all that I command you today, with all your heart and with all your soul, then the LORD your God will restore your fortunes and have mercy on you, and he will gather you again from all the peoples where the LORD your God has scattered you." (Deut. 30:1-3)

Sometimes I have disappointed those I love. It leaves me feeling kicked in the gut. The idea that we are not all we can be, when we should be—it is a miserable fact of life. There are times when I haven't been the kind of parent I should be. Ugh. There are times when I haven't been the husband I wish I were. Ugh. There are times when I haven't been the kind of friend I would like to be. Ugh. There are times when I haven't been the leader I should be. Ugh. Disappointing others can leave one feeling wretched.

I know I haven't been as faithful to God as I should be. Without a doubt, I have sinned, erred, fallen short, missed the mark, and blundered before my Lord. Sometimes I have done this through mishap. But I have also done it fully aware and with malice.

What a wretched man I have been at times—arrogant, prideful, self-absorbed, and more. It makes me cringe to walk through these things in my memory. I would like to forget them. I suspect I am not alone. I suspect any honest reader can relate to what I am saying. This is why passages like today's mean so much to me.

God is a forgiving God. God isn't blind to what we do, nor is he dismissive. God is just, and he recognizes in a real sense that sin is wrong. Sin should be eliminated and so should the sinner. But God doesn't obliterate all sinners. God stands ready to forgive. Even when the wrong is atrocious and intentional.

The Christian understanding, which is rooted deep in the Torah, is that the just God who desires to forgive must find a just way to give that forgiveness. The justice comes from the death or extermination of someone pure in place of the deserving sinner. The pure one bears the punishment of the sinner, and to the sinner is transferred the righteousness of the pure one. In court terminology, I am guilty, but someone else pays my penalty, so I am forgiven and go free.

God taught the Israelites that their sin would reach points where it brought destruction and judgment on them. Yet even then, when they repented and returned to God, God would have mercy on them. The God who exists outside of time knew of his divine act where he would justify the sinners, meriting forgiveness on their behalf. I need God's mercy.

Lord, please forgive me of my many sins. Grant me mercy for your name's sake. Amen.

DECEMBER 22

"And the LORD your God will circumcise your heart and the heart of your offspring, so that you will love the LORD your God with all your heart and with all your soul, that you may live." (Deut. 30:6)

Moses used some interesting metaphors when explaining the life of the Israelites. One of them is found in today's passage: circumcision of the heart.

Circumcision was a rite performed on Israelite males. If a male wasn't circumcised in infancy, it was done later in life. It was an important procedure that marked the Hebrews as a special people for God. While circumcision technically was a cutting of the foreskin of the male child, God and Moses used it to illustrate something altogether different.

Earlier, in Deuteronomy 10:16, Moses told the Israelites to "circumcise the foreskin of your hearts, and be no longer stubborn." That preceded today's passage where Moses explains that "God" will "circumcise your heart" to the end that the people will "love" God with their hearts and souls.

These two verses go hand in hand. They illustrate a concept that is seen from a human and divine perspective. From the human perspective, we can easily fall into a trap of being stubborn before God. This might happen because we are upset over something God "let happen" to us in our lives. It might be because of a painful experience we've had. Or maybe it stems from a seemingly unanswered prayer. When we have times of stubbornness, we should recognize that it is a heart problem. It is one that requires us to cut away the stubbornness and find tenderness toward God.

The second verse, today's passage, is closely related. As today's passage speaks of God circumcising our hearts, it does so toward a similar end. It doesn't say it removes a stubborn heart, but it does say that it brings one into a greater love for God. When we cut away the negatives in our hearts, when we eliminate that which doesn't warm to God, we are able to grow in our love. We excel in seeking him, understanding him, honoring him, and worshipping him. It is no longer ritual; it is an act of love.

I want this in my life. I don't want to be cold to God out of a stubbornness born from hard-heartedness. I want to be tender to God. I want to love him with all my heart and soul. I want to care about him and seek to please him. I want his agenda to be my agenda. I want to share his priorities. I want to show his love to the world.

Lord, please soften my heart. Teach me to love you more truly and more fully. Help me to circumcise my heart and run from stubbornness. In your name, amen.

DECEMBER 23

"For this commandment that I command you today is not too hard for you, neither is it far off. It is not in heaven, that you should say, 'Who will ascend to heaven for us and bring it to us, that we may hear it and do it?' Neither is it beyond the sea, that you should say, 'Who will go over the sea for us and bring it to us, that we may hear it and do it?' But the word is very near you. It is in your mouth and in your heart, so that you can do it." (Deut. 30:11–13)

Our precious granddaughter is just a few months shy of her second birthday as I write this. We spent some good time today playing hide and seek. For Ebba, hide and seek involves her placing a napkin over her head while I call out her name, supposedly unable to find her. She then rips the napkin off and giggles with glee as she shows me where she is. In her mind, if she can't see me, I can't see her. We can play this for a long time before she bores of it.

God doesn't play hide and seek. He is even easier to find than Ebba. His will is not hard to find. God makes it plain for those who diligently look with a heart and mind to find it.

Today's passage speaks to the nearness of God and his word. God's commands are not hard to find, requiring a great Odyssean feat to find them and retrieve them. We needn't go up to heaven and haul the word of God to earth. We don't have to find seaworthy ships to sail far and wide to get the commands of God to our shores.

God wants to be found. He wants his instructions found. God wants a relationship with each of us, and he has granted us ready access to him through his teachings.

All that is incumbent upon us is to seek what God has made readily available. We are to hear and read the word of God and then do what it says. If it were a taxing problem to get to God's words, maybe more people would rise to the challenge, and do what needs to be done to find and uncover God's word. Maybe then the adventure and rarity would challenge people to seek it out.

But God's word isn't that way. The challenge isn't to find it. It is to do what it says. The word is readily available, and that is one reason behind these Torah devotions. But God's word extends beyond the Torah. In the Hebrew Bible, the Christian "Old Testament," there are other prophetic books and writings. Christians also find God's word expressed in Jesus and the writings inspired by God's Spirit, known as the New Testament.

May we seek the word of God and seek it in its fullness. But just as importantly, as we find it, may we follow it!

Lord, show me your instructions, and help me to follow them. In your name, amen.

DECEMBER 24

"See, I have set before you today life and good, death and evil. If you obey the command-
ments of the LORD your God that I command you today, by loving the LORD your God,
by walking in his ways, and by keeping his commandments and his statutes and his rules,
then you shall live and multiply, and the LORD your God will bless you in the land that you
are entering to take possession of it. But if your heart turns away, and you will not hear,
but are drawn away to worship other gods and serve them, I declare to you today, that you
shall surely perish." (Deut. 30:15–18)

Have you ever eaten at a buffet? Most everyone has. Large buffets have
a wide selection of foods that you can put on your plate. Often, they begin
with a variety of salads and then have vegetables and side dishes, breads,
meats, and main dishes, followed by desserts. The beauty about buffets is
that you get to choose what you want. You want liver and onions? Go for it!
Me? You will never see liver and onions on my plate at the buffet. I would
rather not eat than eat liver and onions. I can't handle the flavor, smell, or
texture.

God explained that life is like a buffet in the sense that you make
choices. You choose what goes on your plate, and you choose how you live
your life. The strong thrust of today's verse is that those choices have consequences. You have to eat what you put on your plate!

If we choose to trust in God and we follow his instructions in life, the
road before us is one of blessing. If we thumb our noses at God and his
instructions, the road before us is one of ruin.

That our choices have results is in large part *why God gave us the instruc-*
tions! We live in a cause-and-effect world. If I stick my finger in fire, I am
going to burn it. Fire will burn my flesh. This isn't God's fault. It is the way
the world has been made.

Similarly, when we sin, we bring ruin on our lives. That is the way the
world is. This is why God has told us what sin is and that we should avoid
it. God knows the negative consequences for us. He knows the sin will burn
us as certainly as fire burns flesh.

Of course, often we seduce ourselves into thinking we know better.
We convince ourselves that the outcome of sin is sweet, that the negatives
won't be there this time, or that we can actually make life rougher by being
honest, pure, and so forth. This is a deception that stems from a lack of
faith. We aren't trusting in the truth God has given us. Then when things
go haywire, we sometimes even blame God. "Why did he let this happen?"
Yet in truth, he is the one who warned us ahead of time. I want to do better
at trusting him and obeying him.

Lord, open my eyes to see and my ears to hear you. In your name, amen.

DECEMBER 25

"Be strong and courageous. Do not fear or be in dread of them, for it is the Lord your God who goes with you. He will not leave you or forsake you." (Deut. 31:6)

This past week, I was with a friend whose father died early in the morning. With tears in his eyes, my friend explained that his father was ninety-two, and the death was expected, yet it still hurt. My father died fourteen years ago, but in some ways, it seems like yesterday. We discussed the empty void we experienced. When Dad was alive, I knew he would be there for me. I knew he (and Mom) would take a bullet for me, no questions asked. Once Dad was gone, there was a vacuum, a realization that the buffer between me and the world was gone. That shield I could run and hide behind, even as a man in my midforties, no longer existed. It is part of the alone feeling that follows the death of a parent.

Here is where faith steps in and where passages like today's become so meaningful. Moses is reaching the end of his life. For over forty years, Moses was the fixture for the Israelites. Moses stood between them and their slavery as God's visible tool to win their release from Pharaoh. Moses stood between Israel and Pharaoh after the release, when Pharaoh unleashed his army and sought to destroy the fledgling nation that had embarrassed him and cost him the life of his firstborn. Moses sought the Lord and got water for the thirsty Israelites in the wilderness. When they were running out of food, Moses cried out to God and saw to their manna coming from heaven. When the people sinned, Moses stood in the gap to stop the all-consuming judgment of God from executing death on the sinners. Moses had been their buffer and intermediary with God. God gave Israel the law through Moses. God spoke to Israel through Moses. God appeared to Israel through Moses. Moses served as a judge and leader for the people.

All of this, and Moses was about to die. The people were on the verge of their biggest military challenge. Lives hung in the balance. They would survive and thrive or die. This was the time when the great Moses was needed more than ever. Yet Moses would not be there. The great Moses—buffer, leader, intimate of God—was staying back to die.

Before leaving the people, Moses had some last key advice and instructions for them. Notably he told the people what we read in today's passage. They were to be strong, not dreading what was coming. They were to have courage, not fear. This wasn't because they were a great nation. It wasn't because Moses had selected another to take his place. It wasn't because things had changed and Moses was going with them after all. It was for one reason and one reason alone: the Lord God was going with them, and he wouldn't leave or forsake them. He was reliable. He was the buffer. He was the success behind Moses. He would be there for them. My earthly father is gone, but my heavenly Father still sits on the throne, and he envelops me in his love. Thank you, God.

Lord, thank you for your love and presence in my life. In your name, amen.

*"It is the L*ORD *who goes before you. He will be with you; he will not leave you or forsake you. Do not fear or be dismayed."* (Deut. 31:8)

What do you face in your life? Is life full of joy and roses? Does everything always look positive? Is there nothing in this world that seems precarious or dangerous? Do you live without any concern for today or tomorrow?

If you are like me, there are days that are smooth sailing, but sometimes life's weather is rough. Sometimes doom seems around the corner. Maybe it's a specific concern I have, or maybe it's a general dread, but there are times when life is scary.

Israel was in a place like that as it began its march on Canaan, the land God had promised for generations. The inhabitants of the land had scared off Israel's previous generation, and the ones about to invade had to have some level of concern as well. The concern was likely heightened by the realization that Moses would not be joining them on the invasion. He was staying behind to die on Mount Nebo.

Into the concern the Israelites must have been feeling, Moses gave them stout advice. He said, "Do not fear or be dismayed." *Fear* is a word we readily understand, but we may read right past *dismayed* if we are not careful. The two words go together frequently in the Hebrew, and we ought to consider why. "Dismayed" is our translation of a Hebrew word that is used for "shattered," as in "shattered pottery." First Samuel 2:10 speaks of God breaking his adversaries into pieces. The same word translated "dismayed" (*chatat*) is translated as "broken to pieces" or "shattered."

Fear can do that to us. Fear can not only paralyze us but break us down. It can shatter us. Fear can leave us in pieces as we struggle to function and are unable to achieve what we might have otherwise.

Importantly, Moses doesn't tell people not to fear because they are strong enough to win. The confidence doesn't come from some inner resource found in the people. The confidence doesn't come from knowing their neighbors join in the struggle. The confidence comes in the Lord "who goes before you." The Israelites were taught to *follow* the Lord, not launch out on their own hoping God would follow them. If we are following God, we needn't fear. We don't need to worry about being broken to pieces. God is blazing the trail. We are going where he leads. This is now about him and his decisions.

If God leads, and God is with me, what shall I fear?

Lord, please lead me in your way. Please be with me on the way. Replace my fears with faith. In your name, amen.

DECEMBER 27

"Give ear, O heavens, and I will speak, and let the earth hear the words of my mouth. For I will proclaim the name of the LORD; ascribe greatness to our God! The Rock, his work is perfect, for all his ways are justice. A God of faithfulness and without iniquity, just and upright is he." (Deut. 32:1–4)

Can we take a moment and comment on the greatness of God? As this Torah devotional winds down toward the Torah's last verses, it is a worthy and worthwhile thing to do. Review the greatness of the Lord as revealed in the Torah.

God existed in relationship beyond this natural order. God created this natural order out of nothingness. Then God spoke in that relationship, "Let us make man in our image," and he did so, making people in male and female forms. God loved his creation, and he placed the man and woman into a garden of paradise. The humans were made in God's image, but they weren't God! They still had boundaries. In the garden there was one tree off-limits. If they rebelled against God and ate from that tree, it would be sin, and sin brings death. The wily serpent played the pride card on the humans, and they ate, thinking it would make them like God. No rules would be left! They could do as they chose. Yet it didn't work that way. The people were set to die, and God spoke into their lives with a promise. From the offspring of woman would come one who would set things right. He would restore the life with God that the people had before sin. He would step on the deceiver's head and stop his work.

Over time, people got worse and worse, but God kept his promise. He found righteousness in Noah and saved Noah and his family from the world's corruption through a flood. Then as Noah's descendants took root, God called out Abram, sending him to Canaan with a promise that God would work through him to make a great nation and to bring an offspring who would redeem humanity from the curse of Eden. This promise of a Savior was passed from Abraham to Isaac and on to Jacob. Then came an apparent intervention into the promise. Israel was enslaved in Egypt. After a four-hundred-year absence from the land promised to Abraham, God brought forth the Israelites from Pharaoh's grip, through a forty-year wilderness wandering. God gave them the law, shaped them into a coherent people, weaned them from their idolatrous tendencies, informed their understanding of him, and promised them he would continue with them. He gave them Moses and promised that a coming prophet would arise again who, like Moses, would know God intimately, would intercede for the people, would give the law, and more. This was always God's promise. He was (and is) going to make right that which was lost in Eden. The Torah is a saga, and it is a love story. It is the love of God for his people.

"Give ear, oh heavens, and I will speak!" How great is our God!

Lord, you are great—too marvelous for words. I sing and pray in your name, amen.

DECEMBER 28

"You were unmindful of the Rock that bore you, and you forgot the God who gave you birth." (Deut. 32:18)

When our son was little, he loved magic tricks. He got books on magic, got magic supplies, and worked on learning how to do the tricks. Most any magic book you get will teach you the power of distraction. If someone is looking away from where the "magic" is happening, they will not notice the sleight of hand that becomes "magic."

Distraction is powerful. Distraction captures our attention and diverts it. That can be a good thing, as almost any parent can tell you. With children, sometimes you want to distract them to stop them from crying, to keep them out of trouble, or for a myriad of other reasons. But distraction can also be damaging. Some things should command our attention. Some things are so important we should seek them out and not get distracted on the way.

So it is with God. God should be our single focus. We should be seeking to find him and serve him in all we do. Our thoughts should be oriented around him. Our gratitude should flow to him. In times of trouble, we should look to his hand to help us. In times of peace, we should rest joyfully, knowing our God reigns.

But like a child, we are often easily distracted. We can forget God, being distracted and looking the other way. Life can do that. We can get so busy, we get distracted from God. We can fill our heads with knowledge that we don't integrate with God, and suddenly there is no room for God. We can find other loves that take the place of God in our hearts. Then we find ourselves in the position of today's passage.

Moses was foreseeing a time when Israel would be distracted from God. The days were coming when Israel would be consumed by other appetites. The hunger for God would be replaced. Israel would be busy elsewhere, and the attention given to God would evaporate. The Israelites would soon forget the God who brought them out of Egypt and sculpted them into a nation. Their unmindfulness of God, their distraction from him, would lead them into unbelief.

I want to know God today and not forget him tomorrow. I don't want to get distracted. I don't want to grow cold. I want to get into him deeper and deeper as each day goes by. I want to see him more clearly. I want my love for him to grow. I want to fan the embers of my godly desires into a consuming fire that molds me into a strong tool for his service.

This all begins with mindfulness. I refuse to get distracted!

Lord, please draw my focus onto you. Give me strength and wisdom as I learn and know you more fully. In your name, amen.

DECEMBER 29

"Take to heart all the words by which I am warning you today, that you may command them to your children, that they may be careful to do all the words of this law. For it is no empty word for you, but your very life, and by this word you shall live long in the land that you are going over the Jordan to possess." (Deut. 32:46–47)

The Dutch artist and designer Maurits Cornelis Escher (1898–1972) produced graphic artworks that are mesmerizing. Showing his adept skill at architecture, design, and mathematics, Escher produced pictures that are fascinating to observe at any angle. Many of his drawings are both coming and going, with no real starting place and no real end. They go on and on and on, almost like a mirror showing a mirror, showing a mirror, and so on.

In a sense, that is what God's instructions to Israel were to be. The Hebrews in the exodus had experienced God's divine power, love, redemption, and instruction firsthand. If they were a drawing, they would be complete unto themselves. But God told them they were not to be a single drawing. They were more like an Escher design. They were to take who they were and what had happened to them and teach it all to their children. God's commands were to be taught to their children. This was so that their children would have and do those commands as well. Of course, this means that the children would also be passing on the commands and stories to their children. That third generation of Israelites would then know they were to pass it obediently on to the fourth generation, and so on.

This is the way of God. God's words are to be living and breathing words of life. They go to each generation and bring life and vitality. Like an Escher drawing, they repeat over and over.

In this sense, today's passage affirms that God's words are not "empty." The Hebrew word for "empty" (*req*) means precisely that. Hollow or empty, devoid of content. That is not the word of God! God's words are full. They are pregnant with meaning. They give forth life. They give direction. They meet needs. They provide meaning. They impart wisdom. They are *worth* passing on to each generation.

Look up M. C. Escher designs on the Internet, and you will see the pattern I am talking about. Consider this pattern as the word of God—active and penetrating and worthy of teaching to the next generation. Don't let your children, or those children you have contact with, grow up without understanding and receiving the vital, life-giving words of God!

Lord, thank you for your words. Help me to live them and to share them to your glory. In your name, amen.

DECEMBER 30

This is the blessing with which Moses the man of God blessed the people of Israel before his death. . . . "The eternal God is your dwelling place, underneath [upon the earth beneath God] are the everlasting arms." (Deut. 33:1, 27)

"Objection: hearsay!" Those words come out in just about every trial. Every law student takes a course in evidence, where many classes are spent exploring the hearsay doctrine. The idea is that firsthand evidence subject to cross examination is the most reliable evidence, and so it's the evidence juries should hear. Hence I can testify about what I saw, but I can't generally testify about what someone else told me *they* saw. That is hearsay. The jury should only hear that from the actual witness who *saw* whatever is at issue. That is a witness that can be cross-examined and inspected for reliability.

There are exceptions to the hearsay rule. There are some statements that have inherent credibility and so can be repeated, even though the original person declaring them is not available to come to court. One of the standard exceptions is called a "dying declaration." The idea is that when people are dying, they are careful about their words. They don't readily lie on their death beds. Their words are selected with care, not haphazardly.

Today's passage has a dying declaration of Moses. The words of Moses are worthy of full attention. Moses knew these were his last words to Israel, a people he'd led for over forty years, a people for whom he'd given his life. Moses took the time to bless them, tribe by tribe. Moses then assured them that the "eternal God" was their dwelling place. This is an assurance for all time. It should still assure you and me. That is the beauty of "eternal." God isn't temporary. He doesn't change with the times. He isn't absent on vacation some days. He is and always will be. We can dwell with God all our days.

Moses then added that "underneath" are the everlasting arms. Moses understood God doesn't dwell on earth. Earth is not the center of existence. God is beyond the natural world, but here "underneath" God, his everlasting arms reach out to hold us. Like the eternal God, his arms are "everlasting." They do not tire or droop. They aren't weary of holding us or caring for us. God is a constant security and an integral part of our lives.

Life goes fast. Days can be long, but the years fly by. As this year draws to a close, we can be mindful that we are closer to our date with death than we've ever been. This dying declaration of Moses is worth our hearing and thinking about. It is touching to think that in his final blessing, Moses wanted the last words for his people to be ones that point to God. They weren't words about Moses, memories of the good times the people and Moses shared, or lamenting about what could have been. Moses pointed the people to God—a direction we should still be looking today.

Lord, be our dwelling place. Protect us in your arms. In your name, amen.

DECEMBER 31

And Joshua the son of Nun was full of the spirit of wisdom, for Moses had laid his hands on him. So the people of Israel obeyed him and did as the LORD *had commanded Moses. And there has not arisen a prophet since in Israel like Moses, whom the* LORD *knew face to face, none like him for all the signs and the wonders that the* LORD *sent him to do in the land of Egypt, to Pharaoh and to all his servants and to all his land, and for all the mighty power and all the great deeds of terror that Moses did in the sight of all Israel.* (Deut. 34:9–12)

These are the final words of the Torah, the Jewish books of instruction and law. Of Jews who read through the Torah annually, most will finish the year and begin again at the very start of Genesis (*Bereshit*), indicating the Torah cycle doesn't end. The Torah itself, however, not only emphasizes the importance of reading it over and over; it also points Israel and those who read the Torah forward. It points them to someone else.

Moses had explained several chapters earlier that God would raise up another prophet like him, one who knew God intimately. One who displayed works of God's miraculous power. One who was anointed and spoke on God's behalf to his people. One who could and would intercede with God's people.

The tagline added to close the Torah makes it clear that no such prophet had arisen yet. The prophesied one was still to come. Throughout the rest of the Old Testament Scriptures, the Jewish *Tenak*, we do not find a prophet like Moses in those ways. Many prophets spoke for God, but they didn't display miraculous power like Moses. Elijah was a prophet who God used to perform a few miracles, but again, he wasn't on the level of Moses, dispensing God's will for all his people.

As a Christian, I see the promised one in Yeshua (Jesus), the one born in Bethlehem who grew up to call God's people into a deeper walk of faith. He instructed them in the ways of God. He kept the commandments of the law faithfully. He was, we believe as Christians, God incarnate in ways that we can't fully understand. He was the purchase price for our sins. He was delivered up to die, though he had done nothing wrong and was the long promised Messiah.

For decades, the only "Christians" were Jews who were persuaded that Yeshua was Messiah. Over time, the Christian faith became heavily Gentile and eventually was even at odds with Judaism. That is a pity and was never God's ideal. Christians are grafted onto the tree of Judaism and share in the common roots of the patriarchs, the Torah, wisdom writings, and the prophets. In Yeshua, one finds answers.

Lord, as this year ends and another begins, open our eyes to see fuller truth of who you are and what you wish for us to do. In your name, amen.